D1459795

LORD ALFRED DOUGLAS

The Annotated Oscar Wilde
Secret Intelligence Agent
The Atom Bomb Spies
The Londonderrys
Solitary in the Ranks
Neville Chamberlain
British Air policy between the Wars 1918–1939
The Cleveland Street Scandal
Crime Has Its Heroes
Oscar Wilde: A Biography
The Trials of Oscar Wilde
Baldwin: The Unexpected Prime Minister
Stalin: The History of a Dictator
The Other Love
Their Good Names
Henry James At Home
Lord Reading
Norman Birkett
Oscar Wilde: The Aftermath
The Quiet Canadian
Sir Patrick Hastings
The Trial of Sir Roger Casement
The Strange Death of Lord Castlereagh
Carson
Mr and Mrs Beeton
Cases That Changed The Law
Mexican Empire
Judge Jeffreys
John Law
Princess Lieven
The Rise of Castlereagh

LORD ALFRED DOUGLAS AT OXFORD IN 1893
From a chalk and pastel drawing by Sir William Rothenstein
in the possession of Lord Walston

H. Montgomery Hyde

LORD ALFRED DOUGLAS

A Biography

Dodd, Mead & Company • New York

First published in the United States in 1985

Copyright © Harford Productions Ltd 1984

Published by Dodd, Mead & Company, Inc.
79 Madison Avenue, New York, N.Y. 10016
Manufactured in the United States of America

First Edition

Originally published in Great Britain by Methuen London Ltd, 1984

Library of Congress Cataloging in Publication Data

Hyde, H. Montgomery (Harford Montgomery), 1907–
Lord Alfred Douglas: a biography.

Bibliography: p.
Includes index.
1. Douglas, Alfred Bruce, Lord, 1870–1945—Biography.
2. Poets, English—20th century—Biography. I. Title.
PR6007.O86Z69 1985   821'.912 [B]   85-6733
ISBN 0-396-08693-4

For Teddy and Sheila
who both did so much for Bosie

It is rather a humorous stroke of Fate's irony
that the son of the Marquess of Queensberry
should be forced to expiate his sins by
suffering a succession of blows beneath the belt.

Bernard Shaw to Frank Harris 4 September 1916

Contents

List of Illustrations

Oscar and Constance Wilde
Photos: courtesy of the late Vyvyan Holland

Inscribed copy of Wilde's *Poems*
From the Robert H. Taylor Collection

Oscar Wilde and Alfred Douglas
Photo: William Andrews Clark Memorial Library UCLA

Babbacombe Cliff
Photo: courtesy of Babbacombe Cliff Hotel

Caricature of Max Beerbohm
Courtesy of late Eva Reichmann. From Lord Alfred Douglas Oscar Wilde and Myself *London 1914*

Wilde and Douglas at Oxford, summer 1893
Photo: William Andrews Clark Memorial Library UCLA

Robert Ross and Reginald Turner
Photo: courtesy of Giles Robertson

Alfred Douglas in Cairo, spring, 1894
Photo: From The Border Standard *Galashiels 15 December 1923*

Lord Queensberry in 1895
From Lord Alfred Douglas Oscar Wilde and Myself *London 1914*

Queensberry's notorious card
Photo: courtesy of the Public Record Office

Queensberry attacks his son Percy, May 1895
Photo: courtesy of The British Library

Alfred Douglas, November 1895
From Lord Alfred Douglas Poems *Paris 1896*

Title page of *Poems* Paris, 1896

André Gide
From André Gide Journals Vol 2 *London 1948*

Wilde and Douglas in Naples 1897
Photo: courtesy of William Andrews Clark Memorial Library UCLA

Hardi
Photo: From The Border Standard *Galashiels 15 December 1923*

Olive Custance
Photo: From Brocard Sewell Olive Custance *London 1975*

Acknowledgements

Initially I must express my profound gratitude to Lord Alfred Douglas's literary executor Mr Edward Colman for his permission to quote from Douglas's letters and other writings, published and unpublished, and to reproduce relevant pictures in his possession. I am also under a deep sense of obligation to Mrs Sheila Colman for facilitating my access to the important Douglas material in her and her husband's possession, as well as for the generous hospitality which she and Mr Colman have extended to me and my wife in the course of numerous visits and meetings, apart from the interest they have shown in this book during the prolonged period of its composition. My indebtedness to them is one which I can never adequately repay but can only acknowledge gratefully. Their information and help have been invaluable.

The largest collection of letters and other Douglas memorabilia is in the William Andrews Clark Memorial Library in the University of California in Los Angeles. I wish to thank the library staff for the courtesy and assistance I received while working in the library, particularly Mr John Bidwell, the staff member responsible for acquisitions. Other public sources to which I am similarly indebted are: in the USA, the Berg collection in the New York Public Library, the Grolier Club, New York, NY, the Humanities Research Centre in the University of Texas; also the following individuals, Mrs Mary Hyde, for access to her unrivalled Oscar Wilde collection in private hands, and Dr Robert Pepper of Palo Alto, and the authorities of Stanford University, California.

Those institutions in the United Kingdom I particularly wish to thank for the use of material in their custody are the Bodleian Library in Oxford, the Department of Manuscripts in the British Library in London, the County Record Offices of Durham, Hereford and Worcester, the Fitzwilliam Museum in Cambridge, the National Library of Scotland, and the libraries of Queen's University, Belfast, Reading University, and Westfield College, University of London.

I also wish to thank Mr Merlin Holland on behalf of the Oscar Wilde estate for permission to quote from *The Letters of Oscar Wilde* (1962), edited by Sir Rupert Hart-Davis. Likewise the Society of

Authors on behalf of the George Bernard Shaw estate for permission to make a number of quotations from Shaw's letters to Douglas and Frank Harris. Also Miss Eva Reichmann and Sir Rupert Hart-Davis for similar permission in respect of Sir Max Beerbohm's *Letters to Reggie Turner* (1964), edited by Sir Rupert Hart-Davis.

I am glad to acknowledge the help I have received in various ways from the following: Professor Richard Ellmann, Mrs Joan Evans, Mr Gavin Henderson, Miss Wendy Hinde, the Countess of Longford, Professor Kevin O'Brien, Mr Michael Parkin, Miss Mary Parsons, Mr and Mrs John Piper, Mr John Rubinstein, Mr Brian Roberts, Mr Donald Sinden, Mr George Sims, Mr Timothy d'Arch Smith, and Dr D.P. Waley. In addition to Lord Alfred Douglas himself whom I knew and with whom I corresponded, those no longer alive who kindly communicated their recollections of him to me include his nephews Francis Marquess of Queensberry and Lord Cecil Douglas, also Sir Max Beerbohm, Sir John Betjeman, Mr Percy Colson, Mr Rupert Croft-Cooke, Mr Hugh Kingsmill, Mr Hesketh Pearson and Mrs Muriel Sherard.

Besides Mr and Mrs Colman, those to whom I am indebted for illustrations are indicated in the list of illustrations, and I thank them accordingly.

Finally, my thanks are due to my wife for her patience and understanding throughout the preparation of this book.

H.M.H.

Tenterden
March, 1984

I

Family and Youth

1

In the originally unpublished part of *De Profundis*, the long letter to his young friend Lord Alfred Douglas, written from Reading prison in 1897, Oscar Wilde reminded Douglas of how he had once threatened to kill himself because Wilde had refused to see him, and that Wilde had treated the threat seriously on account of the Douglas family history of mental instability. 'You had often told me how many of your race there had been who had stained their hands in their own blood,' Wilde went on; 'your uncle certainly, your grandfather possibly, many others in the mad, bad line from which you come.'[1] This was true enough.

Alfred's uncle Jim, Lord James Douglas, was an eccentric manic-depressive and a heavy drinker, who cut his throat from ear to ear with a razor in his bedroom in the Euston station hotel. Alfred's grandfather, Archibald, the eighth Marquess of Queensberry, was found shot through the chest in the grounds of his Scottish estate, Kinmount, when he was supposed to have been shooting rabbits. Beside his body was a double-barrelled gun from which a single shot had been fired piercing his heart with deadly accuracy. There was no public inquest. It was stated at the time that his death at the age of forty was due to the accidental explosion of his gun while he was loading the second barrel. But he was an experienced sportsman and the manner in which the bullet had entered his body strongly pointed to suicide. In sporting circles his death was thought not to have been accidental but deliberately self-inflicted following large betting losses he had recently had on the turf.[2] There was also the case of Alfred's twenty-seven-year-old eldest brother, Viscount Drumlanrig, the heir to the Queensberry marquessate. He was likewise allegedly killed by the accidental explosion of his gun when he was out with a shooting house-party in Somerset. At least so the jury found at the coroner's inquest. However, there are grounds for believing that he took his own life in the shadow of a suppressed homosexual scandal in which he feared exposure. It was whispered at the time that the Liberal Prime Minister Lord Rosebery, whose private secretary Drumlanrig had been, was connected with this unfortunate affair.[3]

Not all Alfred Douglas's ancestors were mad or bad or both, although a few of them were. James, third Marquess of Queensberry, for instance, was reputedly, 'an idiot from birth' and never used his titles which included that of Drumlanrig. He was called the 'cannibal-istic idiot' from a terrible incident which occurred in 1707. He was kept in confinement in a cell at Holyrood Palace, but was left unguarded, while the servants went out to see the riots in Edinburgh during the debates on the Act of Union. He escaped from his cell and went into the kitchens where he saw a cookboy who was turning the spit and whom he seized and killed, spitting and roasting him before the fire.[4] He died in 1715, having been passed over in the entail of his father's estates, except for the Queensberry marquessate and other Scottish titles, in favour of his younger brother Charles, who became third Duke of Queensberry on his father the second Duke's death in 1711.[5]

The Drumlanrig title had originally been a barony conferred by King James I of Scotland in 1412 on Sir William Douglas, illegitimate son of the second Earl of Douglas, who was killed at the battle of Chevy Chase in 1388 while fighting the English. His descendant, the ninth baron, was created Earl of Queensberry, Viscount Drumlanrig, and Lord Douglas of Hawick and Tibbers, in the Scottish peerage, by King James the Sixth of Scotland and First of England, as a reward for having entertained that monarch at Drumlanrig Castle in 1617. Drumlanrig accordingly became the courtesy title used by the Queensberrys' eldest son and heir. But it acquired a sinister significance with the passing of the years. According to the late Francis Lord Queensberry, the eleventh marquess, in his book *Oscar Wilde and the Black Douglas*, the title Drumlanrig seemed to carry a curse since almost everyone who held it met with an untimely end. James, the 'cannibalistic idiot', died a lunatic, while Alfred's brother probably committed suicide, as we have already seen. Another holder of the title killed himself by the accidental discharge of his pistol whilst travelling with his wife and parents, the third Duke and Duchess, from England to Scotland in 1754, since he feared there were highway robbers on the road. A third was drowned when he tried to jump his horse over a wide river and both rider and animal fell into the water. Others, writes Lord Queensberry, 'drank themselves into early graves.'[6]

Incidentally, the so-called Black Douglas was Sir James Douglas, the close friend of King Robert de Bruce and a nephew of William first Earl of Douglas. Sir James Douglas fought the English as far south as Yorkshire and in 1327 came near to capturing the English king, Edward III, who had just begun his reign. The Black Douglas was celebrated for his feats of arms, and of the seventy battles in which he engaged he was the victor in fifty-seven. The king's heart, by his dying wish, was entrusted to Douglas to fulfil a vow Robert de Bruce had been unable to execute in person of visiting the holy sepulchre in Jerusalem. Douglas took the heart, embalmed in a silver casket, with him on one of the crusades against the Saracens but was killed while fighting the Moors in Spain *en route*. The casket with its contents was subsequently recovered and brought back to Scotland, where it was buried with Douglas's remains in Melrose Abbey. Since that date the Douglases, later the Queensberry Douglases, have borne a human heart in their coats of arms together with the appropriate motto 'Forward'. It is worth adding that in addition to Froissart's *Chronicles* the Black Douglas figures conspicuously in Sir Walter Scott's novels and stories, notably *Castle Dangerous* and *Tales of a Grandfather*. 'The name of this indefatigable Chief has become so formidable,' wrote Scott, 'that women used in the northern counties to still their forward children by threatening them with the *Black Douglas*. His reputation for pugnacity was subsequently reflected in many members of the Douglas family, particularly Alfred's great-grandfather Charles, the sixth marquess, a noted prize fighter, and his father, the ninth marquess, who is credited with having formulated the Queensberry rules which govern the sport of boxing.

There were four Queensberry dukedoms, which lasted from 1683 to 1810. The first Duke rebuilt Drumlanrig Castle in 1689 but only spent a single night there, preferring his nearby property Sanquhar. Also noteworthy was the second Duke, who acquired a second dukedom (Dover) for his services in promoting the Anglo-Scottish Act of Union in 1707. For this reason he was known as the 'Union Duke'. His son Charles, the third Duke, and his wife, Catherine Hyde, deserve mention for patronising the poet and dramatist John Gay and quarrelling with King George II for refusing to licence *Polly*, the dramatist's sequel to *The Beggar's Opera*. Kitty Queensberry was an eccentric woman of fashion, a great hostess, and the friend of Swift, Congreve and Pope as well as Gay, and she continued to dress as a young woman when she was over seventy. She died as the result of eating too many cherries. Finally there was the third Duke's cousin William who succeeded him as fourth Duke and was known as 'Old

Q.' He was a notorious lecher and gambler in the Regency period. His most celebrated wager was that he could deliver a letter fifty miles away within an hour. He won it by stitching the letter into a cricket ball and having the ball thrown from hand to hand by a picked team. His mistresses were innumerable and his sexual appetite insatiable while it lasted, so that he ended up in Thackeray's words 'a wrinkled, palsied, toothless old Don Juan.'[7] In 1798 he cut down the woods at Drumlanrig to provide a dowry for the ballet dancer Marchesa Fagnani's daughter Maria on her marriage to the Earl of Yarmouth, later sixth Marquess of Hertford, supposing (probably rightly) that he was her father. He never married, so that on his death the Queensberry dukedom and his other English titles devolved upon the Duke of Buccleuch together with Drumlanrig Castle, later inhabited by various members of the Buccleuch family including the present Princess Alice Duchess of Gloucester. The Scottish titles including the Marquessate of Queensberry and Viscounty of Drumlanrig passed to Old Q's cousin Sir Charles Douglas, who became the sixth marquess. It was his nephew Archibald, the eighth marquess, who was found dead beside his gun at Kinmount.[8]

Alfred had an aunt and another uncle besides Lord James (Jim) Douglas who deserve a brief notice. Uncle Jim Douglas's twin sister Florence, or Florrie as she was generally called, was an eccentric tomboy who defied all the conventions, riding astride like a man, cutting her hair short and insisting on being presented at Court without the customary lace and feathers, for which she was sharply rebuked by the Lord Chamberlain. She rode across Patagonia, careless of her appearance and 'roughing it', without a servant, the result being an account of her adventures which became a bestseller. She brought back a pet jaguar which intensely annoyed Queen Victoria when it escaped into Windsor Great Park and killed several of the royal deer, after which it was sent to a zoo. She married a spendthrift baronet, gambler and drinker Sir Alexander Beaumont Churchill Dixie, known as Beau or Sir ABCD, as he liked to call himself. At different times in her life she was a war correspondent in South Africa, a novelist, an opponent of blood sports, a supporter of Home Rule for Ireland and women's rights, and, like her eldest brother the marquess, an agnostic, although she had been baptised a Catholic and educated at a convent. If she was not mad, she was certainly at times bad.

Florrie's second brother Francis was neither mad nor bad, but he was decidedly unlucky, since he lost his life at the age of eighteen while climbing the Matterhorn. He was a member of the party led by Edward Whymper which was the first to reach the summit of this famous Swiss mountain in July 1865. In the course of their descent,

Douglas Hadow, the youngest member of the party and an inexperienced climber, lost his foothold and dragged Francis Douglas and one of the guides named Michel Croz, as well as another climber the Rev Charles Hudson, down with him. They were all supposed to be roped together, another guide, Peter Taugwalder, being positioned between Francis Douglas and Whymper. All would probably have gone well if the rope had held with Taugwalder's experience. But it suddenly snapped, sending Douglas and the other three to their deaths. Rumours spread afterwards that Taugwalder had deliberately cut the rope, but they were convincingly disproved by Whymper, who showed from photographs that the rope was frayed and of inferior quality and should not have been used.[9] The deaths, particularly that of Lord Francis Douglas, caused a sensation in the English press and mountaineering was generally condemned as dangerous. Even Queen Victoria proposed that it should be prohibited by law in the case of her subjects.

The bodies of Hadow, Hudson and the guide Croz were discovered at the bottom of the precipice over which they had fallen. But there was no trace of Francis Douglas, despite successive attempts to find his body. Forty years later, shortly before she died, Florrie was convinced that the Matterhorn glacier had shifted and would reveal Francis's refrigerated body. However, the Alpine experts persuaded her that this was unlikely since Francis had probably fallen into a crevasse and disappeared. At all events his body was never found.

In spite of the many blots on the Douglas family escutcheon, exemplified by gambling, drinking and lechery, Lord Alfred Douglas was immensely proud of his aristocratic ancestry on both his father's and his mother's side. 'Thus,' he wrote in his *Autobiography* 'when my father married my mother, the direct descendant in the male line of Douglas killed at Chevy Chase married a descendant of the Percy who was taken prisoner by the Douglases at the same historic battle. Consequently I combine in my own veins the blood of the two greatest houses in Scotland and England ... and I must ask my readers to remember this when judging my actions and my methods of looking at life.'[10]

2

Alfred's father, John Sholto, the ninth Queensberry marquess, was born at Kinmount, the family's principal estate, a few miles north of Annan on the high road to Dumfries, in July 1844.[11] He was only fourteen when his father, the ill-fated Archibald, was killed, as already related, and he came into a fortune estimated at £78,000, although it was largely tied up, and properties amounting to some 30,000 acres with an annual rent roll of £20,000. The Kinmount mansion house was a large grey stone building constructed about 1815 to replace an earlier wooden one which had been destroyed by fire. Set against a background of Scotch firs and magnificent copper beeches, it was a large, impressive house, with its porticos and pillars, commanding a view to distant Solway Firth. But John's mother Caroline, who had eloped with his father to Gretna where she was married over the anvil in the famous forge and liked to be known as 'the Gretna Green Marchioness' was English, the daughter of a Buckinghamshire MP. As time went on she cared less and less for Kinmount and her gambling husband and more and more for Harleyford, her father's house in Buckingham, and her English friends. In 1861, she and her eleven-year-old son Archie, John's younger brother, were received into the Roman Catholic Church much to the annoyance of her Presbyterian mother-in-law Sarah, a Douglas cousin, who was still alive and who tried to seize Archie and the twins, Jim and Florrie. But Caroline outwitted her and escaped to France with her three children and their nurse. Archie was later to become a Catholic priest, ordained by Cardinal Manning.

Of the eighth marquess's six children – four sons and two daughters – John Sholto, his eldest son and heir, was most like his father, whose trim build, broad shoulders and ruddy complexion he shared, as well as his love of horses, gambling, women and fighting. When his father died, he was at a naval training school at Portsmouth with a view to entering the royal navy which he did in 1859 and in which he spent five years. Such naval discipline as he was subject to seems to have had little effect upon his reckless combative character, since his escapades as a midshipman were largely overlooked because he was a marquess. He and his fellow midshipmen once beat up a group of Portuguese while their ship was in Madeira, for which they spent several hours in prison and were fined for their misbehaviour. To their surprise their commanding officer congratulated them when Queensberry and his companions went aboard, regretting only that they had not 'marked' their opponents more than they did. On returning to England in 1864, Queensberry resigned his commission and went up to Magdalene College, Cambridge. Why he did this is unclear. He may have been attracted by the sporting facilities provided by the university, particularly hunting and boxing, at both of which he was already proficient, although he was always contemptuous of formal education. He left at the end of his second year without a degree, which he later declared he had never known 'to be worth two pence to anybody.'[12] He was due to come of age in July 1865 and great preparations were made for the event at Kinmount, where a mass of guests had been invited and many of them actually arrived. But everyone and everybody had to be put off when the news was received of Lord Francis Douglas's death on the Matterhorn.

Like his mother, Queensberry was devastated by Francis's death and he hurried off to Zermatt in the hope of finding his body. He spent a night on the slopes of the Matterhorn in the course of his search and would no doubt have been frozen to death if the local guides had not rescued him. 'I have not been able to find a trace of darling Francy's body,' he wrote home a week later. 'I am convinced it is useless to search further, and that his dear body is resting beyond the power of mortal man to reach him.' He was right. Some years later he gave expression to his feelings in a blank verse poem *The Spirit of the Matterhorn*, in which he was probably helped by his sister Florrie since, apart from this effort, with its pantheist – if not agnostic – inspiration, he never showed any interest in poetry, or philosophy for that matter.

He was comforted in his grief by a pretty sweet-natured and sympathetic girl of his own age called Sibyl Montgomery, to whom he became engaged and eventually married. Sibyl's father Alfred was a Commissioner of Inland Revenue and her mother, born Fanny Charlotte Wyndham, was a daughter of George Wyndham, whose father, the first Lord Leconfield of Petworth, was the illegitimate son of the third Earl of Egremont. Alfred's father, Sir Henry Conygham Montgomery MP, had been created a baronet in 1808 for his services with the East India Company; he came from County Donegal in the north of Ireland and claimed descent from the noble Scots family of Montgomerie, Earls of Eglinton, whose Montgomerie forbears had allegedly come over from Normandy to Britain with William the Conqueror. However, that may be, the Donegal Montgomerys had long been settled in that county, certainly since the middle of the seventeenth century, and they belonged to the Irish 'Ascendancy' Establishment.[13] But Queensberry's children, including Alfred, kept very quiet about this for some reason, although Sibyl's mother was half-Irish. Like their father they preferred to pose as Scots with a dash of English blood. Indeed they were much prouder of their English connection through Sibyl who could also trace her ancestry to Joceline Percy, the eleventh and last Earl of Northumberland, whose father Sir Henry Percy, known as Hotspur, eldest son of the first Earl, had been taken prisoner by the Scots at the battle of Chevy Chase, when the second Earl of Douglas was killed.

Queensberry disliked his suave and socially popular father-in-law, the Inland Revenue Commissioner, whom he suspected – probably not without good reason – of being homosexual, in spite of his having had three children, a son and two daughters, of whom Sibyl's elder sister Edith married the sixth Duke of Beaufort's grandson the Rt Hon George Finch MP of Burley-on-the-Hill, Oakham, in Rutlandshire, the county which he represented as a Conservative in the House of Commons. Alfred Montgomery had begun his career as private secretary to the Marquess of Wellesley, the Duke of Wellington's elder brother, to whom he bore such a striking physical resemblance that gossiping tongues declared that he was the Marquess's son by his mother Lady Montgomery. Wellesley is known to have been very attracted to Lady Montgomery whom he probably first met when he was Governor-General of India and she was there with her husband Sir Henry. Alfred Douglas, who was called after his maternal grandfather, did not believe the story, 'though it would be interesting if it were true', he once remarked, 'and would make me the great-grand-nephew of the Waterloo Duke.' In 1832, when Wellesley became Lord-Lieutenant of Ireland for a second term, he took young Ally, as Alfred Montgomery was called, with him to Dublin and for the remaining ten years of his life is said to have positively doted upon him. When Wellesley died, he left Ally his portrait and other souvenirs including his regalia as a Knight of the Garter, which strictly speaking he should have returned to the sovereign.[14]

Although he must have received a good salary as head of the Inland Revenue Board, Alfred Montgomery constantly pleaded poverty. 'Having little or no income of my own,' he used to say, 'I live by collecting other people's.'[15] He also fell out with his wife Fanny when she became a Catholic convert, like Sibyl's mother-in-law Caroline Queensberry, her conversion being due to Cardinal Manning, whom she had known since girlhood. Ally and Fanny were really temperamentally unsuited to each other, since, while he was sociable and gregarious, being a particular friend of the Prince of Wales, she was retiring and serious-minded. Her conversion to the Catholic religion served as a convenient excuse for him to force her to leave home and go abroad, to which she had no objection, having money of her own from the Wyndhams. She eventually settled in Naples were she died, leaving her money to be equally divided between her daughters Edith and Sibyl.[16]

Nevertheless the Montgomerys did not do badly with their two daughters, considering that the younger was to marry a marquess and the elder a Duke's grandson and one of the landed gentry, a Privy Councillor and a Member of Parliament. The Queensberry wedding was arranged for 22 February 1866 at St George's Church, Hanover Square. There were to be ten bridesmaids including Florrie and her younger sister, Gertrude, while the groomsman or 'best man' was to be one of the bridegroom's naval friends. The ceremony was to be followed by a grand wedding breakfast at Alfred Montgomery's house in Chesterfield Street, and a mass of invitations were sent out to the wedding guests, who included two duchesses and the bride's grand-father Lord Leconfield. Unfortunately a few days before the intended ceremony, one of Sibyl's uncles, Colonel George Wyndham, died and the wedding had to be postponed. When it did eventually take place, on 26 February, it was something of an anticlimax, particularly since some of the more distinguished original guests cried off.

However Queensberry was deeply in love with his beautiful bride, with 'her delicate features and creamy complexion, pretty turquoise-blue eyes and her lovely little mouth, small as a rose bud and quite as bewitching.' So Gertrude described her sister-in-law, but she was the only member of the family who approved of the match without reservations. The bridegroom's other sister Florrie had her doubts. 'He thought he loved because he saw a beautiful face,' she wrote afterwards. 'He loved – or rather thought he did. Was that not enough?' Florrie, for one, thought not, and time was to prove her right.[17]

3

After a brief honeymoon in a borrowed house in Essex, Queensberry took his bride to Kinmount. They got off the train at Annan instead of the dreary local station (Cummertrees) and drove the remaining eight miles by carriage so that Sibyl could approach her future home in as pleasant a manner as possible, although it was a cold March day, there were few leaves on the trees, and the grey stone mansion house looked depressing. At first, after they had settled in, all went well, even if Sibyl missed the warm winters in the south of France to which she had been accustomed. Still, she liked being a marchioness and addressed by the servants as 'My lady', while her husband was very much the local squire and known as 'the wild young marquess', from his dare-dashing and rollicking ways. 'Q', as he was also called, joined the Dumfriesshire Volunteers in which he was immediately promoted to the rank of Lieutenant-Colonel, and he continued to go out with the Dumfriesshire Hunt, of which he rapidly became Master. Later the same year he paid a short visit to America with the Duke of Manchester and other sporting cronies who included an old Cam-bridge friend, John Graham Chambers, who was interested in boxing. At this period prize fighting was much more respectable in America than in England, where it was illegal, and the ring was widely supported on the other side of the Atlantic. Queensberry shared his friend's interest and while visiting a saloon near the ranch in California where they were staying, squared up to a pugnacious cowboy who had insulted him, knocking him out in a matter of minutes. 'The onlookers were very much impressed,' remarked the Duke of Manchester who also witnessed the fight, 'but Queensberry treated the incident as too trivial to trouble about.'[18]

Earlier the same year Chambers had founded the Amateur Athletic Club at Beaufort House in Walham Green, with the object of promoting a variety of sports and improving the conditions under which they were conducted. Indeed it was largely to study boxing that the American trip took place. The result was that a set of rules were drawn up initially by Chambers but supervised by Queensberry in such matters as weights. To encourage competitors Queensberry presented three silver challenge cups, and the first contest under the new rules took place at Beaufort House in July 1867. It was not exactly a success since only fifty spectators turned up to watch the bouts. Professional boxers, who depended upon their 'purses', scorned the new code, and it was not until a quarter of a century later that the Queensberry rules, as they had come to be called, were generally adopted. By this time Chambers was dead, but, to do Queensberry justice, he was always ready to admit that the chief credit for the rules belonged to Chambers.

The Queensberrys' first child, a son, was born at Kinmount within twelve months of their marriage, in February 1867. They called him Francis in memory of his dead uncle. He also inherited the ill-omened courtesy title of Drumlanrig. A few months later, in June, Sibyl's mother, Fanny Montgomery, paid the family a visit, and she immediately perceived that all was not well at Kinmount. Her daughter and son-in-law, it seemed, were drifting apart. She by no means altogether blamed Queensberry, whom she regarded as suffering from the overwhelming weight of his high rank with nothing useful to do in the public sphere. ('I am grieved to see a young man kept idle against his will.') Fanny no doubt realised that there were faults on both sides. What Queensberry needed was a sports-loving wife, who would join him in the hunting field and act as hostess to his horsey friends. Instead Sibyl's main interests were poetry, music and art, while housekeeping at Kinmount frankly bored her. There were occasions when Queensberry returned home at midday after a morning's cubbing to find his wife still in bed, reading a novel and not having ordered lunch although guests were expected.

Fanny was friendly with the Conservative leader and Prime

Minister Benjamin Disraeli, and after she had left Kinmount she wrote reminding him that Queensberry's father had been promised an English peerage by Sir Robert Peel under the title of Baron Solway. However, the eighth marquess had possessed his Scottish titles for such a relatively short period that there was no time for Peel's promise to be carried out. She now hoped that Disraeli would be able to implement it, since as a Scottish peer Queensberry was ineligible to sit in the House of Commons, unlike an Irish peer, and on account of his extreme youth it was unlikely that he would be elected one of the sixteen Scottish Representative peers who had seats in the Upper House. Unfortunately the Tories were defeated shortly afterwards in the General Election so that Disraeli could do nothing.[19]

The birth of the Queensberrys' second son Percy, Lord Douglas of Hawick and Tibbers, in October 1868, did not improve the relations between husband and wife. If anything they drifted further apart, Queensberry spending more and more time in the hunting field and leaving Sibyl to her own devices. He also began to hunt in the English shires, often staying with his wife's uncle George Finch in Rutland and going out with the Cottesmore and the Quorn. He liked the sport in the Midland shires so much that he looked round for the possibility of having an English pack of his own. In 1869 he heard that the Mastership of the Worcestershire hounds was available and he agreed to take it on. The result was that he moved his stables from Kinmount to Worcester and rented a house called Ham Hill about three miles south of the county capital outside the old village of Powick, famous as the birthplace and residence in the eighteenth century of the physician John Wall, whose experiments resulted in the first manufacture of Worcester china. It was at Ham Hill, originally known as Ham Hill Cottage, that his and his wife's third son Alfred was born on 22 October 1870.

The registration of births at this date was voluntary and did not become compulsory until several years later. Queensberry did not trouble to register his third son's birth, although he inserted a brief notice of the event in *The Times*. In spite of her husband's growing anti-religious feelings, the boy's mother insisted that he should be baptised. This ceremony took place in the Powick parish church on 27 November 1870 and was performed by the vicar, the Rev Cecil Hughes. The child was called Alfred Bruce; Alfred after Lady Queensberry's father and Bruce after Queensberry's friend and contemporary in the Royal Navy, Lord Robert Bruce, who was also the boy's godfather. As a christening present Bruce gave the baby, for whom he had stood sponsor, a beautiful inscribed silver bowl, which its recipient was to cherish throughout his life.[20] His godmother was his mother's first cousin and life-long friend Mabel Montgomery, daughter of Alfred Montgomery's elder brother Admiral Sir Alexander Montgomery, Bart, of The Hall, County Donegal.

BAPTISMS solemnized in the Parish of *Powick* in the County of *Worcester* in the Year 18*70*						
When Baptized.	Child's Christian Name.	Parents' Name. Christian.	Surname.	Abode.	Quality, Trade, or Profession.	By whom the Ceremony was performed.
1870 Nov. 27 No. 365	Alfred Bruce	John Sholto Douglas & Sibyl	Queensberry	Powick	Marquis	Cecil Hughes Vicar

4

Alfred Douglas cannot have remembered much about Ham Hill, since his father, who does not appear to have been liked by the members of the Worcestershire Hunt, resigned the Mastership after little more than two years and returned to Kinmount where he again became Master of the Dumfriesshire Hounds. 'I am afraid it would be as impossible to say that he was a good father as to say he was a good husband,' his third son was later to recall. 'He did nothing for us boys. When he saw us he was generally good-natured and kindly, but he never lifted a finger to teach, admonish or influence us in any direction.' It was one of his third son's greatest grievances against him that he never even taught him to ride, his equestrian instruction being left to coachmen and grooms. But when Alfred, or Bosie as he was known in the family, was six years old, his father did give him a pony called The Rat which he had bought at Tattersalls' for £60. ('It was a rattling good pony, and jumped like a stag.') Although he was rather nervous on a horse, Alfred rode a lot on the pony, with which, like his father, he went out with the Cottesmore and the Quorn from his uncle George Finch's place in Rutland. He also rode at Kinmount with his elder brother Percy, their favourite objective being the village of Ecclefechan, about five miles distant, where Thomas Carlyle was born and where there was a shop which dealt among other things in wooden swords, which the boys bought and to which the Kinmount estate carpenter added shields on which he painted the Douglas heart, which is a prominent feature of the Queensberry coat of arms. Fights ensued among the boys, in one of which Percy narrowly missed putting out Drumlanrig's eye.[21]

Although two other Douglas children were born in Kinmount, Sholto in 1872 and Edith in 1874, their births made no difference to the relations between their parents which continued to deteriorate. Sybil saw less and less of her husband and concentrated her affections on her children, particularly the third who became her favourite. Bosie, the pet name by which he was known not only by his mother and brothers and sister but also by his friends, was a contraction of Boysie, which his mother at first used to call him. 'The happiest days of my childhood were passed at Kinmount,' Bosie afterwards recalled. But they were all too short, since Queensberry decided to close the place in 1880, when Bosie was ten, and they never returned. They went to London where Queensberry, who was already living in rooms in James Street, Buckingham Gate, at first installed them in a rented house in Cromwell Road, from which they later moved to 18 Cadogan Place. Meanwhile Bosie was sent to Lambrook, a preparatory school near Windsor, which specially catered for sprigs of nobility and even royalty, since two of Queen Victoria's grandsons, Prince Victor and Prince Albert of Schleswig-Holstein, were also there and the old Queen used to come over from Windsor to see them and watch the cricket. Drumlanrig was at Lambrook too, in his last term, before going to Harrow to which his father agreed very reluctantly as he wished him to go to a Scottish school, although Queensberry had never been to one himself and had virtually severed all his connections with Scotland, since he was preparing to sell practically all his Scottish property.

1881, the year after Queensberry left Kinmount with his wife and family and closed the place, was an unfortunate one for the marquess. His leaving his wife and children in rented houses, while he himself took rooms elsewhere, soon became known and attracted unfavourable comment. For the past six years he had been a Scottish Representative Peer, although he made very little impression in the House of Lords. Like his fellow peers he was expected to swear the oath of allegiance to the sovereign at the beginning of each new parliamentary session. But in 1881 he suddenly and unexpectedly refused to do so, saying the oath was 'Christian tomfoolery'. The freethinker Charles Bradlaugh, MP for Northampton, had recently been unseated since he claimed the right to 'affirm' instead of taking the oath on the bible. However, his constituents re-elected him in the following year and he was again unseated, this time being expelled by force from Westminster. At the same time Queensberry was described by the *Annual Register* to be 'a supporter of Bradlaugh' which was quite true. But it made him immensely unpopular with the Establishment and the middle classes, who could not forgive his 'insult to the Queen', even if it had been perpetrated by the acknowledged author of the Queensberry rules of boxing. 'I believe Mr Bradlaugh to be an honest and sincere man, whose highest hope is the welfare of mankind,' he remarked at this time. 'He has my warmest sympathy.... I glory in the great battle which he is successfully fighting.... I hope myself some day to be foremost in the van, and where the battle is thickest, fighting to the death against all ignorance and superstition, where Mr Bradlaugh now so nobly stands, for the freeing of mankind.' His chance came in the following year when he attended a performance of the Poet Laureate Tennyson's unsuccessful play *The Promise of May*, in which the part of an agnostic and the villain of the piece was portrayed by an actor named Hermann Vezin. Queensberry interrupted the performance, throwing a bouquet of vegetables at the cast and when the curtain fell he tried to make a speech, but was removed by the ushers as he was speaking. Afterwards he explained his actions in a letter to the *Daily Telegraph*. 'I am a Secularist and a Freethinker,' he wrote, 'and as President of the British Secular Union I protest at Mr Tennyson's abominable caricature of an individual whom, I presume, he would have us believe represents some body of people, which, thanks to the good of humanity, most certainly does not exist among Freethinkers.'[22]

After Bosie had been at Lambrook for about a year, which he liked, there was a 'row' there, probably a homosexual scandal, as a result of which most of the pupils left and the school practically closed down. Bosie was sent to another private school called Wixenford, which he did not like nearly as much as Lambrook, chiefly because of the bearded headmaster's sarcastic tongue. 'Mr Arnold's attacks on me were purely verbal,' Bosie wrote afterwards, 'but I suffered agonies from them, being very sensitive and also (alas that I must say it!) frightfully spoiled at home by my mother, and my mother could not, or did not, resist me. The consequence was, of course, that I suffered proportionately more at school.'

> What was lacking in my home was a father. My mother's spoiling would not have harmed me if my father had been a real father, and had ever taken half as much interest in his children as he did in his dogs and horses. As it was, I scarcely ever saw him.... All through my childhood and youth the shadow of my father lay over me, for though I loved him, and had indeed a quite absurd admiration for his supposed heroic qualities, I could not be blind to his infamous treatment of my mother, even long before she was driven to divorce him which took place when I was sixteen.[23]

The summer holidays were spent at a house called The Hut, three miles from Bracknell in Berkshire, which Bosie's mother had leased from Lord Downshire. According to Bosie, 'The Hut was a picturesque, rambling ranch of a house, larger than its name might imply (at a pinch it would hold quite twenty-five people), which had been run up by Lord Downshire in the pinewoods as a temporary abode while his big place, Easthampstead, was being built.' Arthur (Artie) Downshire was about a year younger than Bosie and he had inherited his title and property as a minor, since his father, who built Easthampstead, had recently died, although his mother the Dowager Marchioness was still alive. They were Sibyl Queensberry's nearest neighbours, as well as being her landlords and warm friends both of her children and herself. 'Artie was an amiable though rather stolid boy, and he had a positive mania for driving farm-carts,' Bosie has recalled. 'His poor mother's desperate attempts to induce him to take his proper part in the elaborately organised cricket matches in the park at Easthampstead, at which my three brothers and myself were, of course, usually present, were continually being frustrated. When Artie's turn came to go in arrived he had generally disappeared, and was found later on seated on the shaft of a manure cart, admonishing the carthorse to "gee-up".'[24]

Queensberry only came to The Hut for a few nights in the year and then it was to cause trouble. One specific instance of this occurred during Ascot race week in 1886 when Sibyl had invited a party of her own and her children's friends for the racing. But her husband appeared at the last minute with his mistress and a band of their friends and summarily turned out his wife and his three sons and daughter who happened to be staying there. Poor Sibyl then had to take her family to London and send her guests telegrams putting them off. It is hardly surprising that in the following year Sibyl Queensberry should have divorced her husband on the ground of adultery and cruelty, the petition being uncontested and the case lasting a bare quarter of an hour.

When the time came for Bosie to leave Wixenford and go to a public school, he opted for Eton, largely because a close friend who had been at Wixenford was there, and also because his mother was in favour of it. However when it had been settled and all the arrangements made, Queensberry stepped in at the last moment and announced that he had entered Bosie for Winchester, saying that he would not have any of his sons turned into 'Belgravian loafers', such was his opinion of Etonians. 'My father was like that,' Bosie remarked afterwards. 'He knew nothing whatever about Eton, or any public school, having been on the *Britannia* and in the Navy himself; but his prejudices once

formed were as utterly insurmountable as they were unreasonable.'
This time, unlike his eldest son Drumlanrig and Harrow, Queensberry got his way and so Bosie became a Wykehamist.

Bosie was just under fourteen when he arrived at Winchester for the
Michaelmas term in 1884. 'Winchester was in a transitional stage at
that time,' he wrote of the school many years later. 'Just before I got
there it was still a very savage place.'

He was naturally very homesick at first. 'My own Darling,' he
wrote to his mother at the beginning of his second term. 'I have got
back all safe.... It is very wretched now.... I hope you feel quite
happy, my darling, but I wish you had someone with you....
Goodbye, my pretty. I always think of you, my darling, Your loving,
loving son, Bosie.'[25]

> I came in for the last year of the real savagery, which, really and
> truly, was very much like that of *Uncle Tom's Schooldays*. There was a
> boy in our House who might have been a model for Flashman. I
> remember thinking that my parents must be quite mad to send me
> to such an awful place. I don't like abusing my old school, for which
> I still have a great affection, but, truth to tell, it was a sink of
> iniquity.
>
> My first eighteen months there were pretty much of a nightmare.
> After that I got used to the conditions, adapted myself to the
> standard of morality (or rather immorality), and enjoyed the whole
> thing tremendously. I went up there a sensitive, dreamy child,
> passionately pure and devoted in my heart to every noble ideal. I
> had been brought up by my mother to love purity, truth and
> beauty.... I left Winchester neither better nor worse than my
> contemporaries – that is to say, a finished young blackguard, ripe
> for any kind of wickedness.[26]

He was also shocked by the irreverence shown by some of the senior
boys in matters of religion. For example, there was a picture of *The
Last Supper*, a reproduction of Leonardo da Vinci's famous mural in
Milan, hanging above the High Table in the dining room of his
House. A prefect, who was certainly the most powerful and influential
boy in the House, made a practice of hurling a piece of bread at this
picture every time he came in to tea, there being no master present,
his object being to hit the figure of Christ. 'I give this as a
comparatively mild instance of the attitude towards sacred things that
existed. By the time I was in my last year at Winchester I was neither
better nor worse than the other boys in my House. My moral sense
had been completely destroyed, and as to religion, it simply did not

exist in my day at Winchester. To say that it was treated as a joke would be a euphemism. It was treated with utter contempt, ridicule and blasphemy.'[27]

He was unable to take games as seriously as the average English boy takes them, being never any good at cricket and little better at football. But he was a good runner, and in 1887, when he was sixteen, he won the school steeplechase over a course of two-and-a-half miles across country. He also started a school magazine which was called *The Pentagram*, to which he contributed humorous verse. He was generally liked by his schoolfriends, particularly Lord Encombe, with whom he was later to share rooms at Oxford. He was already known familiarly as 'Bosie'. When he had been at the school for about a year, his elder brother Percy, then a midshipman in the Navy, was about to leave on his ship for a voyage to the Pacific and he sent him a telegram which contained the words, 'Good-bye darling Bosie.' The telegram was put in the 'hall' of his House, but he was not there when it arrived. However an inquisitive boy opened it and passed it round, so that when its recipient appeared he was greeted on all sides with cries of 'Hullo, darling Bosie!' From that day forth he was always called Bosie both by the boys in his House and his housemaster, as he was later to be at Oxford, and it stuck to him for the rest of his life.

According to Bosie the only boy with whom he went to bed during his time at Winchester was for a purpose quite other than homosexual. During one summer Bosie had been to Zermatt with a reading party which included Encombe and their housemaster; Zermatt may also have been chosen so that Bosie could see the Matterhorn and the scene of his uncle's death. While they were there both Bosie and Encombe contracted mumps, although they were not aware of it at the time. Bosie's developed as soon as he reached The Hut. At this time Artie Downshire's cousin, Lord Combermere's grandson Wellington Stapleton-Cotton, who was a particular friend of Bosie's, was staying at Easthampstead, and Bosie naturally wished to see him. But since Bosie had mumps Lady Downshire and Bosie's mother both forbad his visit. However, Bosie wrote his friend a note, covertly conveyed by Lady Queensberry's footman, asking him to come over early to The Hut before breakfast. Wellington duly did so and when Bosie pointed out that if his visitor could also contract mumps they might be able to spend the next three weeks together, suggesting that his friend should undress and get into bed with him, which Stapleton-Cotton did.[28] After half-an-hour together his friend got up and dressed and went back to Easthampstead. As things turned out Stapleton-Cotton failed to develop the slightest symptom of the complaint, while Encombe went back to Winchester, where he infected the whole House, who in turn passed it on to the rest of the school.

Not all the summer holidays were spent at The Hut. In August 1887 Sibyl Queensberry took Bosie to her uncle Percy Scawen Wyndham's and his wife Madeline's imposing new country house in Wiltshire called Clouds. The other guests included their daughter Mary Lady Elcho, later Countess of Wemyss, the Irish Secretary A.J. Balfour, the American novelist Henry James, and Percy Wyndham's first cousin Wilfrid Scawen Blunt, traveller, poet, Arab horse-breeder and lover of many women. Blunt noticed a little disapprovingly that throughout dinner one night Bosie played a noisy rhyming game with Pamela Wyndham, a younger sister of Mary Elcho. Lady Elcho, it may be noted in passing, was or was to become Balfour's mistress, while Pamela was to marry first Edward Tennant Lord Glenconner and secondly Lord Grey of Falloden.[29]

Bosie left Winchester at Christmas 1888, and early in the following year he was sent abroad for a few months with a tutor named Gerald Campbell, who was a nephew of Madeline Wyndham's (she was a daughter of Sir Guy Campbell Bart and a granddaughter of the famous Irish rebel Lord Edward Fitzgerald). The object of the exercise seems to have been that Bosie could learn French. It was while staying in a hotel in the south of France that Bosie had his first 'affair' with a woman. According to him, she was at least twelve years older than Bosie, the divorced wife of an earl, and a lady of 'celebrated beauty', who had run away with a lover but by this time they were separated. The affair proceeded along what Bosie called 'classic lines', except that there was no outraged husband. It culminated in a terrible moment one night when Gerald Campbell, who was the lady's cousin, knocked at the door of her bedroom and demanded in stern tones the restitution of his ravished ewe-lamb. The ewe-lamb, reduced to tears and dressed in one of the lady's much-beribboned nightgowns, rather like Cherubino in *The Marriage of Figaro*, was duly handed back to his tutor after a somewhat painful scene accompanied by loud barks from the lady's pet dog. She was afterwards attacked by Campbell and some other women for her wickedness in 'seducing an innocent boy'. At which Bosie protested loudly that after four years at Winchester he was no more an innocent boy than he was an angel out of heaven. 'I don't believe my protestations were taken seriously,' he admitted afterwards, 'and in any case I was of course separated for ever from my lovely lady and sent back to England in disgrace.'[30]

Meanwhile it had been arranged, apparently without any objection from his father, that Bosie should go up to Oxford and his name was entered at Magdalen College, where his friend Encombe was also to become an undergraduate. This college was a favourite with many

Wykehamists who received some preference, since its fifteenth century founder William of Wayneflete had been a pupil at the school and later bishop of Winchester.

5

Bosie went up to Magdalen at the beginning of the Michaelmas term, 1899, at the same time as his friend Encombe. He was allotted rooms in New Buildings, as they had continued to be called ever since their construction in the early eighteenth century. Although small, the rooms were pleasant, and the bedroom looked out on the college's celebrated deer park. In his second year Bosie moved to better and more modern rooms in St Swithin's, which really were new buildings, overlooking 'the High'. In his third and final year he moved out of college to rooms in 34 High Street, which he shared with Encombe.[31] The controversial journalist Frank Harris, who met Bosie for the first time a few years later, described him as 'still girlishly pretty.'[32] Admittedly he was exceptionally good-looking, but Harris's malicious description has a suggestion of effeminacy. In fact, there was nothing then or subsequently the least effeminate about either his appearance or his manners, of which contemporary photographs and the word of contemporary individuals afford ample testimony. On the other hand, his youthful appearance, which lasted into middle age, did prove a handicap, as when at the age of twenty-seven he was refused admission to the casino's gaming rooms in Monte Carlo as he looked well under the legal age (twenty-one) and he had to get his mother, with whom he was staying, to testify as to his real age. As George Bernard Shaw told him long afterwards, 'that flowerlike sort of beauty must have been a horrible handicap to you: it was probably Nature's reaction against the ultra-hickory type in your father.'[33]

During his first two years at Oxford, Bosie was much more of a 'hearty' than an 'aesthete', judging by his interest in running. In his first year he came second in the two-mile race in the Magdalen College sports and in his second year he won it. At the same time he entered for the three-mile race in the University Sports and he might well have won this race too and gained his half-blue, had it not been for an unfortunate happening. Just before the race he went to see his doctor about a slightly swollen vein behind his left knee. The doctor told him it was of no consequence but that to be on the safe side he would fix it up with a bandage. What the doctor did was to encase his knee in a stiff plaster with the result that Bosie's stride was shortened to such an extent that he had to drop out of the race after a couple of miles when he was fourth and about twenty-five yards behind the leader. This experience so upset and disappointed him that he gave up running altogether. He did not claim that he would have won the race without 'this wretched bandage' but about a week before the race he had had a trial three-mile run with a man who had got his half-blue and he had beaten him easily, so that if he had run to his true form he would have been 'there or thereabouts' at the finishing post. What particularly upset him was that he had told a few friends before the race that he was going to win.

Throughout his four years at Oxford he did little or no work in the way of reading for the BA degree or Greats. Indeed he failed in Responsions, colloquially known as 'Smalls', the first of the examinations which candidates for Greats are required to pass, being 'ploughed' in mathematics. He was consequently sent down for a term in his second year which he spent being coached by a 'most delightful parson' in Herefordshire called Lambert, who was also coaching Bosie's brother Sholto for the army. They both hired ponies and the vicar let them erect jumps in his fields. The Rev Lambert was also a fine musician with a splendid bass voice and formed quite a good choir in the village church which Bosie joined as an alto and attired in a surplice went there every Sunday, although by this time he had largely lost his belief in religion. However, when he returned to Oxford the following term and succeeded at his second attempt in passing 'Smalls', he had developed such a love of music that he rarely missed an evening service in Magdalen College chapel.[34]

If he endeared himself to his friends, he was far from popular with the college dons, who considered him lazy and unruly. Besides his trouble over Smalls, he was 'gated', that is not allowed out of college, for having gone to the Derby when he should have been attending tutorial lectures. With regard to these he had a frivolous card printed which he would send to his tutors. The card had gaps, which Bosie would fill in with his handwriting. As printed the card read:

> Lord Alfred Bruce Douglas presents his compliments to ... and regrets that he will be unable to ... in consequence of....

When completed the card would read something like this:

> Lord Alfred Bruce Douglas presents his compliments to Professor Smith and regrets that he will be unable to show up an essay on the Evolution of the Moral Idea in consequence of not having prepared one.

Bosie was also on occasion dangerously daring. During his first year, in the spring of 1890, there was a great frost when the Thames was completely frozen over and a coach-and-four was frequently driven along the river past the college barges. When the frost had lessened and the river was still jammed with ice Bosie conceived the idea of crossing the river by jumping from block to block of ice, and calling on the rest of his friends who were with him to follow. He got across safely, followed by the others. He then started to cross back again, jumping on to a large block of ice. To his horror, it dipped and pitched him into the swirling icy water, the block going right over his head. When he tried to come up, his head bumped against the ice, while his companions on the bank were splitting themselves with laughter. He was very nearly drowned when one of them named Reid realised that it was no laughing matter and waded into the river up to his waist and managed to pull Bosie out with some difficulty. Although he was clad only in a zephyr and running shorts, he was able to run back to his rooms and get warm without suffering any ill results from the experience.

At the end of his first summer vacation, before going up to Oxford for his second year, Bosie wrote his first serious poem. (His earlier efforts had been attempts at nonsense verse.) He was staying at The Hut with his mother at the time, and he called it *Autumn Days*. It was a wistful little lament for the year which was past, consisting of five stanzas of which the first three read:

> I have been through the woods today
>   And the leaves were falling,
> Summer had crept away,
>   And the birds were not calling.
>
> And the bracken was like yellow gold
>   That comes too late,
> When the year is sad and old,
>   And death is at the gate.
>
> Ah, mournful Autumn! Sad,
>   Slow death that comes at last,
> I am mad for yesterday, mad!
>   I am sick for a year that is past![35]

Bosie took *Autumn Days* back with him to Oxford and sent it to *The Oxford Magazine* which in due course published it. When the thirty-seven-year-old President of Magdalen, Mr (later Sir) Herbert Warren, who had helped to found the magazine and was also a contributor read it, he sent the poet a letter of congratulation. 'I thought it really passionate and really fine,' he wrote. 'I must confess I had no idea you could do anything so good.' Bosie remembered these words nine years later when his collected poems were published anonymously in London under the title *The City of the Soul*. The book included *Autumn Days* which the President no doubt recognised when Bosie sent him a presentation copy. This was after Bosie's name had been linked with Oscar Wilde's, whose verse Warren had also admired, besides supporting his candidature for membership of the Savile Club, although he was never elected. However, Warren immediately returned *The City of the Soul* to the author with a brief note, in which he remarked: 'I regret that I cannot accept this book from you.' This struck Bosie at the time as being 'rather a brutal and unnecessarily unkind thing to do,' and he remembered finding the President's letter about *Autumn Days* at the time and reading it again before tearing it up. 'The phrase I have quoted stuck in my memory,' Bosie wrote afterwards in his autobiography. 'I give this story as a typical example of the sort of thing I have had to put up with all my life as the result of my friendship with Oscar Wilde (who, by the way, was also an old friend of Sir Herbert Warren's and used to make a point of calling on him every time he came to see me at Oxford).'[36]

President Warren, whose long reign in Magdalen was to last for forty-three years, had achieved the reputation of an arch-snob and time-server. Certainly he had the knack of choosing the right men as members of the college, such as the Prince of Wales (later King Edward VIII) for which he was knighted, and His Imperial Highness Prince Chichibu of Japan. He had a similar knack of dropping the wrong ones when the time came, as it did with both Oscar and Bosie.[37]

II

The Fatal Friendship

1

In February 1890, Oscar Wilde paid a short visit to Oxford primarily to see Walter Pater, who was a don at Brasenose and who had praised Wilde's short stories in *The Happy Prince* on its recent publication. Wilde was a warm admirer of Pater, whose novel *Marius the Epicurean* particularly appealed to him as illustrating the highest ideal of the aesthetic life. Another friend and admirer of Pater was the poet Lionel Johnson, a homosexual, then an undergraduate at New College, whom Pater had apparently suggested that Wilde should meet. Wilde had also come up to see the performance of Robert Browning's play *Strafford*, which the OUDS was giving in the New Theatre with H.B. Irving in the name part. Johnson wrote to a friend at this time:

> On Saturday [15 February] at mid-day, lying half asleep in bed, reading [J.R.] Green [the historian] I was roused by a pathetic and unexpected note from Oscar: he plaintively besought me to get up and see him. Which I did: and found him as delightful as Green is not. He discoursed, with infinite flippancy, on everyone: lauded the *Dial* [a privately printed magazine run by Wilde's book designers Charles Ricketts and Charles Shannon]: laughed at Pater: and consumed all my cigarettes. I am in love with him. He was come to visit Pater; and to see *Strafford*.

On his return to London, Wilde wrote Johnson a note, apologising for not being able to see him again as he was kept at the theatre 'to see the realisation of some suggestions I had made,' and could not get away until just before his train started. 'I hope you will let me know when you are in town,' he added. 'I like your poetry – the little I have seen of it – so much, that I want to know the poet as well. It was very good of you getting up to see me. I was determined to meet you before I left Oxford.'[1]

This was Bosie's second term, but he did not meet Wilde during this visit. In fact he did not do so until eighteen months later. Meanwhile Bosie and Johnson had become great friends during what was Bosie's first year and Johnson's last at Oxford. They had both been to school at Winchester, but as Johnson was in College and Bosie was in a House, and Johnson was three years older, they had had little acquaintance there. The only occasion apparently on which they met, as Johnson used to remind Bosie 'with great gusto', was when Bosie was birched by the headmaster, and Johnson as Prefect of Hall had the duty of holding up his shirt tails.

'Lionel was a delightful fellow, though exceedingly eccentric,' Bosie later recalled, 'and alas! in his later years greatly addicted to potations, which his small and childlike frame could not withstand.'

> He had a mania for not going to bed, and if he could get anyone to sit up with him he would discourse in a most brilliant way till five o'clock in the morning. At other times of the day he was rather noticeably silent. He was a great scholar, and undoubtedly a great poet, but the austerity and profundity of his best work makes him one who is never likely to appeal to any but a very eclectic audience. It was one of the griefs of his later years that he introduced me to Wilde (though, of course, his doing so could not possibly have had any bearing on the events which followed).

On his own admission Lionel Johnson loved Wilde, and in 1892, when Bosie was still up at Oxford, he wrote a sonnet beginning, 'I hate you with a necessary hate.' This was meant for Wilde having, as Johnson believed, supplanted him by Bosie in his affections. Johnson denied to many people that Wilde was the subject of his sonnet when it was published, but he subsequently admitted to Bosie that it was intended for Wilde and that the 'friend' referred to in his sonnet was Bosie himself, whom he considered that Wilde was ruining.'[2]

Just after Bosie had come down from Oxford at the end of his second year, Johnson offered to introduce him to Wilde. Bosie, who had read some of Wilde's poems and was curious to meet him, accepted the offer. When he heard this, Wilde invited them to tea. Accordingly, one afternoon about the end of June or beginning of July 1891, Johnson called for Bosie in a hansom cab at his mother's house in Cadogan Place and they went on together to Wilde's house in Tite Street, where Wilde received them in his book-lined study on the ground floor facing the street and where tea was served. The room was decorated in red and yellow – yellow walls and scarlet enamel – and there was a cast of the Hermes of Praxitiles. There were also some pictures – Aubrey Beardsley's drawing of Mrs Patrick Campbell, a Simeon Solomon and a Monticelli – but most of the wall space was taken up with bookshelves and books, mostly Greek and Latin classics. The fireplace had a large oak mantelpiece.[3]

Frank Harris has given a highly coloured and misleading account of this meeting in his biography of Wilde, stating that Bosie hung upon his host's lips 'with his soul in his eyes' and 'before he had listened long Bosie declared his admiration passionately.' This was not so at all, according to Bosie. 'What really happened, of course, at that interview was just the ordinary exchange of courtesies. Wilde was very agreeable and talked a great deal. I was very much impressed, and before I left Wilde had asked me to lunch or dinner at his club, and I had accepted his invitation.' After tea Wilde brought his guests to the upstairs drawing-room where he introduced them both to his wife Constance. A few days later, at their second meeting, which was at Wilde's club, the Albemarle, Wilde gave Bosie a copy of the large paper limited edition of *The Picture of Dorian Gray* which had been published on 1 July and which he inscribed 'Alfred Douglas from his friend who wrote this book. July 91. Oscar.'[4] According to Bosie, on this occasion Wilde made homosexual advances to him, which Bosie resisted, as he was to do for the next six or nine months before finally giving in to him. Most of the long summer vacation Bosie spent with his mother and his grandfather Alfred Montgomery at Homburg, then a fashionable spa frequented by the Prince of Wales and his circle, who included Montgomery. There Bosie was presented to the Prince. Meanwhile, apart from a brief visit to the Lakes where he began work on his play *Lady Windermere's Fan*, Wilde stayed in London, as his letters show. They probably met once or twice after Bosie returned to England and before he went up to Oxford to begin his third year. During that term Oscar came up once or twice to Oxford where he stayed with Bosie in the rooms he was sharing with Encombe in the High Street.

Oscar took Bosie with him when he called on President Warren, whom Wilde astonished by remarking jocularly that he was thinking of presenting a statue of himself to the college, 'a colossal equestrian statue.' A little later, when their friendship became closer, Lady Queensberry had some doubts about its wisdom on account of the difference in their ages – Wilde was 37 and Bosie was 21. She wrote to the President and asked him if he considered Wilde was the sort of man who would be a good friend for her son. According to Bosie, the President, in reply, sent her a long letter in which he gave Wilde a very high character, praised his great gifts and achievements of scholarship and literature, and assured her that her son might consider himself lucky to have obtained the notice of such an eminent man. 'I mention this, not as anything to Mr Warren's detriment,' Bosie added, 'but simply to show the sort of reputation Wilde at that time enjoyed among the big-wigs of the University.'[5]

They met again during the Christmas vacation when both were in London. By this time Wilde was beginning to flatter his young friend, giving him presents, and making much of him in every way. He even wrote what purported to be a sonnet to him and gave it to him at dinner one night in a restaurant. In fact, the sonnet, which begins 'The sin was mine; I did not understand,' had appeared four years previously in *The Court and Society Review*, a periodical to which while it lasted Wilde was a frequent contributor. But Bosie was apparently unaware of this, since he reproduced it under the title *The New Remorse* in the undergraduate magazine *The Spirit Lamp* when he was editing it in 1892.[6]

Bosie expressed his feelings on the subject of his own behaviour and beliefs in relation to Wilde's in a memorable passage in his autobiography:

> Even before I met Wilde I had persuaded myself that 'sins of the flesh' were not wrong, and my opinion was of course vastly strengthened and confirmed by his brilliantly reasoned defence of them, which may be said to have been the gospel of his life. He went through life preaching the gospel which he puts into the mouth of Lord Henry Wotton in *Dorian Gray*. Wilde was, in fact, a most powerful and convincing heresiarch. He preached that it was the duty of every man to 'live his own life to the utmost', and to 'be always seeking new sensations', and to have what he called 'the courage' to commit 'what are called sins.' I am trying to be fair to Wilde and not to make him responsible for 'corrupting' me more than he did. All the same, I must say that it strikes me now that the difference between us was this: that I was at that time a frank and natural pagan, and that he was a man who believed in sin and yet deliberately committed it, thereby obtaining a doubly perverse pleasure. I was a boy and he was a *blasé* and very intellectual and brilliant man who had immense experience of life. Inevitably I assimilated his views to a great extent.[7]

Wilde's first successful play, *Lady Windermere's Fan*, opened at the St James's Theatre in London on 20 February 1892. The audience applauded the performance enthusiastically and Wilde responded to shouts of 'author' by coming on to the stage with a cigarette in his hand and making a short speech in which he congratulated the audience on the great success of *their* performance. After the show Constance Wilde went home, but the author took a group of young friends for supper at Willis's in King Street, St James's, then a favourite after-theatre resort. His guests included Bosie, who had shared the author's box and had come down specially from Oxford for the occasion. The date was a Saturday and the auditorium was filled with fashionable society theatregoers, since the habit of spending the weekend in the country, at least when Parliament was sitting, had not yet caught on. Wilde's party stayed at Willis's until the small hours of the following morning discussing the merits of the play.

While he was at Oxford, Bosie had become a lover of boys, even though he sometimes went with women as well. However his pederasty was to get him into trouble in the spring of 1892, since he was blackmailed at this time. The details are not on record, but Oscar was to remind him of them in his *De Profundis* letter.

> Our friendship really begins with your begging me in a most pathetic and charming letter to assist you in a position appalling to anyone, doubly so to a young man at Oxford: I do so, and ultimately through your using my name with [the solicitor] Sir George Lewis, I begin to lose his esteem and friendship, a friendship of fifteen years standing.[8]

Bosie's father learned of the matter, probably from Lewis, since he wrote afterwards to his other son Percy's wife: 'It is a horrible story, nothing to do with Oscar Wilde, and as it has been told me by a personal friend, an eminent lawyer who himself supplied the money, £100, to hush up the scandal, there can be no doubt of the truth of it.'[9] Queensberry was wrong in supposing that Oscar had nothing to do with it, although it was not in the sense that Queensberry evidently imagined. At all events, Bosie's letter, which would have related the story of his trouble, has not survived, so that we are none the wiser. Bosie probably destroyed it along with many others from Oscar which he was later to receive.

It was also probably at this time, during the Easter vacation, in 1892, that Bosie eventually gave in to Wilde and they had a brief homosexual relationship. Many years later Bosie wrote a circumstantial account of the precise nature of their relations for the benefit of Frank Harris:

> When I first met Wilde he started laying siege to me and I resisted him; not because at that time I had any moral objections to that sort of thing but simply because with a man older than myself it did not appeal to me. At school and Oxford I had been neither better nor worse than my contemporaries. What is euphemistically called 'the schoolboy nonsense' that goes on among boys at school and at college was perfectly familiar to me

and I had participated in it freely....

I admit that when I met Wilde first I was not any more innocent than other boys of my age (21). From the second time he saw me (when he gave me a copy of *Dorian Gray* which I took back with me to Oxford) he made 'overtures' to me. It was not till I had known him for at least six months, and after I had seen him over and over again and he had twice stayed with me in the rooms in High Street, Oxford, that I shared with my great friend the late Lord Encombe, that I gave in to him. I did with him and allowed him to do just what was done among boys at Winchester and Oxford. It is hateful to me now to speak or write of such things, but I must be explicit. Sodomy never took place between us, nor was it thought or dreamt of. Wilde treated me as an older boy treats a younger one at school, and he added what was new to me and was not (as far as I know) known or practised among my contemporaries: he 'sucked' me.

This happened the first time in his house at Tite Street after he had taken me out to dinner at the Savoy, a play (or music hall) and a supper at the Lyric Club. I was staying at my mother's house in Cadogan Place, but my mother was away and there was no one in the house but the servants. Wilde was alone in Tite Street. I was filled up with drinks by the time I got back to his house at about two o'clock in the morning. After about two hours discussion he induced me to stay the night in a spare bedroom and in the end he succeeded in doing what he wanted to do ever since the first moment he saw me.

Much as I was fascinated by Wilde and much as I really in the long run *adored* and was 'crazy' about him, I *never* liked this part of the business. It was dead against my sexual instincts which were all for youth and beauty and softness. After a time he tumbled to the fact that I didn't like it at all and only consented to it to oblige him, and he very soon 'cut it out' altogether.... Except in the case of Wilde I have never in my life had any immoral relations with a man older than myself. A little more than a year after Wilde's death I married: such perverted instincts as I had disappeared completely as soon as I lost contact with Wilde and his immediate *entourage*. If I had never met Wilde, they might or not have disappeared sooner ... I did not 'grow up' till I was over thirty, and my 'perverted' period was really a prolongation of my boyhood.

I always liked women and I went with a woman before I met Wilde and often afterwards even when I was at the height of my friendship with him. I say this with no feeling but one of regret. To me (as a Catholic since 1911) all forms of immorality are now anathema.[10]

When Bosie came down from Oxford at the end of his third year, in mid-summer 1892, he and Wilde stayed together at the Royal Palace Hotel in Kensington. 'Bosie has insisted on stopping here for sandwiches,' was how Wilde put it to his friend Robert Ross in a note written on the hotel's writing paper. 'He is quite like a narcissus – white and gold. . . . Bosie is so tired: he lies like a hyacinth on the sofa, and I worship him.'[11]

2

Wilde had recently met the great French actress Sarah Bernhardt at Henry Irving's, and she told him that she had heard he had written a play in French and would like him to read it to her. It was *Salome* and when Wilde did as she asked she immediately said she would like to play the title role. Consequently the play was put into production at the Palace Theatre in London and rehearsals began. After these had been going on for three weeks and the costumes and scenery were prepared, the Lord Chamberlain stepped in as official censor of plays and forbade its public performance on the ground that it introduced biblical characters, which at that time was not allowed. The 'divine Sarah' was naturally disappointed and also annoyed at having wasted time and money to no purpose. The author was furious and threatened to settle in France and take out letters of naturalisation. 'I will not consent to call myself a citizen of a country that shows such narrowness in its artistic judgment,' he remarked in a press interview. 'I am not English. I am Irish – which is quite another thing.'[12] Bernard Partridge drew an amusing cartoon of him as a French conscript, which appeared in *Punch*. Max Beerbohm, another cartoonist as well as a caricaturist, immediately seized on the point. 'I do not exactly know what course Oscar will take,' he wrote to his friend Reggie Turner: 'but inasmuch as French naturalisation entails a period of service in the French army, I fancy that his house in Tite Street will not be in the hands of an agent.'[13] Max was right. Oscar did not carry out his threat, but the Lord Chamberlain's action continued to rankle with him.

It was to take Wilde's mind off this trouble that Bosie invited Oscar to join him and his mother and grandfather Alfred Montgomery at Homburg for the annual summer season. Wilde accepted and the party arrived early in July 1892 at the spa, where they put up in fashionable lodgings in the Kaiser Frederick Promenade near the Curhaus and baths. 'Oscar is at Homburg under a regime,' Wilde's wife, Constance wrote to her brother, Otho Lloyd, 'getting up at 7.30, going to bed at 10.30, smoking hardly any cigarettes and being massaged, and of course drinking waters. I only wish I were there to see it.' This unaccustomed regime did not agree with Oscar, at least at first, since he wrote to the artist Will Rothenstein that he was 'very ill' as an excuse for not being able to write any more in a letter from which it is clear that he still felt sore over the banning of *Salome*.

> The licenser of plays is nominally the Lord Chamberlain, but really a commonplace official – in the present case a Mr Pigott, who panders to the vulgarity and hypocrisy of the English people, by licensing every low farce and vulgar melodrama. He even allows the stage to be used for the purpose of the caricaturing of the personalities of artists, and at the same moment when he prohibited *Salome*, he licensed a burlesque of *Lady Windermere's Fan* in which an actor dressed up like me and imitated my voice and manner!!!!'[14]

To Pierre Louÿs, the French writer who had helped in correcting *Salome*, Wilde complained that he was 'enormously bored' with Homburg, particularly since no less than five doctors had forbidden him to smoke. However he was compensated by having Bosie with him to talk if not make love to, and he also had the pleasure of meeting the Prince of Wales. But Bosie's grandfather Alfred Montgomery took a dislike to Wilde and they were to avoid each other in the future.

While Wilde went back to London at the end of July, Bosie and his mother and grandfather apparently went on to another watering place, in the Thuringian Forest, where there were thermal springs in the old town of Schmalkalden. Bosie wrote a poem called 'In Summer' while they were there.* The last stanza suggests the young poet's feelings of sexuality:

> And you came, my love, so stealthily
> That I saw you not
> Till I felt that your arms were hot
> Round my neck, and my lips were wet
> With your lips, I had forgot
> How sweet you were. And lo! the sun has set,
> And the pale moon came up silently.

In September 1892, Wilde took his wife and two small sons to a farmhouse which he had rented for the month at Felbrigg, a village two miles south of Cromer in Norfolk. Among those he invited to stay were Bosie, who had returned from Germany, and a neurotic youth named Edward Shelley. The latter worked in the office of Wilde's

---

*First published in *The Spirit Lamp*, 6 June 1893, the last issue to appear under Bosie's editorship.

publishers, Elkin Mathews and John Lane, and was later to give evidence against Wilde at his trials. Shelley refused the invitation apparently because his parents objected to his staying with Wilde, but Bosie came and spent ten days, playing golf with Oscar and amusing the two Wilde children, Cyril and Vyvyan, on the beach by helping them and their father to build sand-castles. Wilde was later to accuse Bosie of interfering with his work by making him waste his time unnecessarily, but he certainly did not do so on this occasion since it was when he was at Felbrigg that Wilde wrote the greater part of his play *A Woman of No Importance*, as was his wont calling his characters by local place names such as Lady Hunstanton and Lord Illingworth.

Constance had promised to spend a few days in that month with her relative, Lady Mount Temple, who lived at Babbacombe near Torquay. It was while Constance was there that Bosie was laid up with some complaint, possibly influenza or some kind of accident. When Oscar wrote and told her, she replied:

> Babbacombe,
> 18 September 1892
>
> Dearest Oscar,
> I am so sorry about Lord Alfred Douglas, and I wish I were at Cromer to look after him. If you think I could be any good, do telegraph for me, because I can easily get over to you. . . .
> I do hope you have been to Blickling, you must not miss seeing that, and give my love or whatever you think right to Lady Lothian. . . .
> Ever loving,
> Constance[15]

It is clear from this letter that Constance was still devoted to her husband and had no idea of his affair with Bosie or that he had also spent two nights in a London hotel with Edward Shelley. Shelley had also dined with the Wildes in Tite Street and Constance thought he was simply a young man in Wilde's publishers' office in whom her husband was taking an interest and was trying to help in his career. As for Bosie, initially he was always on the best of terms with her. 'I liked her and she liked me', he wrote in his autobiography. 'She told me, about a year after I first met her, that she liked me better than any of Oscar's other friends. She frequently came to my mother's house and was present at a dance which my mother gave during the first year of my acquaintance with her husband.' This was no doubt the 'coming out' dance for Bosie's sister Edith in the 1892 season.

Further on the subject of Constance Wilde, Bosie wrote:

> Honesty compels me to say that Oscar during the time I knew him
> was not very kind to his wife. He certainly had been (as he often
> told me) very much in love with her, and the marriage was purely a
> love match. At the time when I first met him he was still fond of
> her, but he was often impatient with her, and sometimes snubbed
> her, and he resented, and showed that he resented, the attitude of
> slight disapproval which she often adopted towards him. Towards
> the end of the time before the catastrophe (and they never met
> again after he came out of prison) the relations between them were
> distinctly strained. To try to make out that this had anything to do
> with me is simply dishonest and untruthful. Those who know the
> facts (and there are many now living who do know them) will, if
> they tell the truth, bear witness that I was never 'a bone of
> contention' between Oscar and his wife.\...[16]

In the following Michaelmas term at Oxford, the beginning of
Bosie's fourth year, Bosie was unwell, no doubt due to the Oxford
weather, and Oscar sent him a silver card-case. 'Dearest Bosie, I am
so glad you are better,' wrote Wilde in the first of his letters to Bosie
which has been preserved. 'I trust you like the little card-case. Oxford
is quite impossible in winter. I go to Paris next week – for ten days or
so. . . . I should awfully like to go away with you somewhere where it is
hot and coloured.' He added that he was 'terribly busy' in London
where the actor-manager, Beerbohm Tree, who had agreed to
produce Wilde's next play, *A Woman of No Importance*, and was then on
tour with his theatre company in Scotland, was 'running up to see me
on all occasions, also strange and troubling personalities walking in
painted pageants.'[17] This last phrase is obscure but has a hint of
blackmail about it, probably demands for money from Wilde's lower-
class homosexual associates.

It was in this term that Bosie began to edit *The Spirit Lamp*. This
was an undergraduate journal which Bosie took over from its founder
and first editor, Sandys Wason of Christ Church, who described it on
the cover as 'An Oxford Magazine without News.' Bosie changed the
design of the wrapper to include a drawing of Magdalen tower and, in
later issues, the description to 'An Aesthetic, Literary and Critical
Magazine.' Eight numbers in all appeared under Bosie's editorship
between November 1892 and June 1893, there being three contributions by Wilde, of which the first was his sonnet 'The New Remorse'.
Other contributors included Robert Ross ('How We Lost the Book of
Jasher') the author John Addington Symonds, a homosexual, ('To
Leander' and 'Beethoven Concerto in E Dur') and Beerbohm Tree's

half-brother Max Beerbohm, then an undergraduate at Merton, ('The Incomparable Beauty of Modern Dress'). It was during this term that Bosie failed again in an examination, this time apparently 'Mods', or Classical Moderations, for which he was rusticated for the following Lent term. He spent Christmas with his mother in Cadogan Place, staying on there alone after she had gone to Salisbury, where she had taken a house in the Cathedral Close, which he visited briefly during this period. Lionel Johnson was a guest in the Salisbury house at this time and it was in response to Lady Queensberry's request that he recommended an able young man named Campbell Dodgson to coach Bosie, particularly in logic, philosophy and history. Dodgson, who later became Keeper of Prints and Drawings in the British Museum, agreed to do this for a month as soon as Bosie had come down again from London.

The Wildes had now leased Lady Mount Temple's house Babbacombe Cliff and their two boys, Cyril and Vyvyan, were with them. In January 1893, Bosie sent Oscar a sonnet he had written in Salisbury entitled 'In Sarum Close' but which he posted from London.

> Tired of passion and the love that brings
> Satiety's unrest, and failing sands
> Of life, I thought to cool my burning hands
> In this calm twilight of gray Gothic things:
> But Love has laughed, and, spreading swifter wings
> Than my poor pinions, once again with bands
> Of silken strength my fainting heart commands,
> And once again he plays on passionate strings.
>
> But thou, my love, my flower, my jewel, set
> In a fair setting, help me, or I die,
> To bear Love's burden; for that load to share
> Is sweet and pleasant, but if lonely I
> Must love unlov'd, 'tis pain; shine we, my fair
> Two neighbour jewels in Love's coronet.

This evoked the following letter from Oscar to Bosie, which was to have unfortunate consequences for both of them:

Babbacombe Cliff
Babbacombe

My Own Boy,
Your sonnet is quite lovely, and it is a marvel that those red rose-leaf lips of yours should have been made no less for music of

song than for madness of kisses. Your slim gilt soul walks between passion and poetry. I know Hyacinthus, whom Apollo loved so madly, was you in Greek days.

Why are you alone in London, and when do you go to Salisbury? Do go there to cool your hands in the grey twilight of Gothic things, and come here whenever you like. It is a lovely place – it only lacks you; but go to Salisbury first.

Always, with undying love, yours

Oscar[18]

Bosie put the letter in his pocket, as he was in the habit of doing with other letters from Oscar, and he thought no more about it. However, he did go to Salisbury again to join Campbell Dodgson, who was waiting for him there with Lady Queensberry at the beginning of February. Bosie arrived in the evening, according to Dodgson, 'with a flutter of telegrams about him, and dishevelled locks, and plunged at once into editorial correspondence' about *The Spirit Lamp*, leaving his tutor to read Goethe and the *Westminster Gazette*. What happened then was described by Dodgson to Johnson:

The next day Bosie read Plato with zeal for one and a half hours. He then quietly informed me at lunch that we were going to Torquay that afternoon to stay with Oscar Wilde! I gasped amazed, but I am phlegmatic and have a strong constitution, so I bore the shock well, and resignedly spent the whole afternoon in repacking the portmanteau which I had just unpacked. Our departure was dramatic; Bosie was as usual in a whirl; he had no book, no money, no cigarettes and had omitted to send many telegrams of the first importance. Then, with a minimum of minutes in which to catch our train, we were required to overload a small pony chaise with a vast amount of trunks while I was charged with a fox terrier and a scarlet morocco dispatch-box, a gorgeous and beautiful gift from Oscar. After hurried farewells to the ladies, we started on a wild career, Bosie driving. I expected only to drag my shattered limbs to the Salisbury infirmary, but we arrived whole at the station.

Since Bosie had forgotten to warn Oscar that they were coming, 'a vast telegram' was despatched from Exeter. Finally they arrived at Babbacombe at nine o'clock in the evening and 'dined luxuriously' with their host, but without his wife who had gone off to stay with friends in Florence. 'This is a lovely house, full of surprises and curious rooms, with suggestions of Rossetti at every turn,' Dodgson wrote to Lionel Johnson.

Our life is lazy and luxurious; our moral principles are lax. We argue for hours in favour of different interpretations of Platonism. Oscar implores me, with outspread arms and tears in his eyes, to let my soul alone and cultivate my body for six weeks. Bosie is beautiful and fascinating, but quite wicked. He is enchanted with Plato's sketch of democratic man, and no arguments of mine will induce him to believe in any absolute standards of ethics or of anything else. We do no logic, no history, but play with pigeons and children and drive by the sea.

Oscar sits in the most artistic of all the rooms called 'Wonderland' and meditates on his next play. I think him perfectly delightful with the firmest conviction that his morals are detestable. He professes to have discovered that mine are as bad. His command of language is extraordinary, so at least it seems to me who am inarticulate, and worship Irishmen who are not. I am going back on Saturday. I shall probably leave all that remains of my religion and my morals behind me.[19]

'Bosie is very gilt-haired,' Wilde wrote at this time, 'and I have bound *Salome* in purple to suit him. That daughter of passion appeared on Thursday last and is now dancing for the head of the English public.'[20] The Lord Chamberlain could not, of course, prevent the play's publication in book form. Accordingly it was printed and published in Paris in February 1893; at the same time copies were imported into England for distribution by Wilde's English publishers, Elkin Mathews and John Lane. Later in the same year Bosie was to translate it into English. Incidentally the play was dedicated to Pierre Louÿs, who was to make a French verse translation of the extravagant letter which Wilde had written to Bosie from Babbacombe. Bosie was also to publish Louÿs's version in *The Spirit Lamp* of 4 May 1893, the penultimate issue of what the *Morning Post* later described as 'the best of Oxford's many momentary periodicals.'[21]

3

Towards the end of February 1893, a few days after the publication of *Salome*, Oscar and Bosie had a violent lovers' quarrel over some unknown but probably quite trivial matter, and Bosie left Babbacombe next morning in a huff. Four years later Oscar was to remind Bosie of his behaviour when he wrote to him from prison that 'so revolting had been the scene you had made the night before your departure', that he had determined never to speak to him again or to allow Bosie under any circumstances to be with him.

You wrote and telegraphed from Bristol to beg me to forgive and meet you. Your tutor, who had stayed behind, told me that he thought at times you were quite irresponsible for what you said and did, and that most, if not all, of the men at Magdalen were of the same opinion. I consented to meet you, and of course I forgave you. On the way up to town you begged me to take you to the Savoy. That was indeed a fatal visit to me.[22]

Oscar accordingly engaged a suite at the Savoy, consisting of two bedrooms and a sitting-room. There is some evidence that Oscar or Bosie or both entertained boys in these rooms. No doubt Oscar's excuse to his wife for staying at the Savoy was that it was necessary to be near the Haymarket Theatre, where Beerbohm Tree was casting his play *A Woman of No Importance* and preparing to rehearse it. After a week or so, Bosie left, apparently as the result of another quarrel, and returned for a short time to his mother's house in Salisbury. Evidently he wrote apologising to Oscar from there, as his letter produced the following reply:

> Savoy Hotel
> Victoria Embankment
> London
>
> Dearest of all Boys,
>   Your letter was delightful, red and yellow wine to me; but I am sad and out of sorts. Bosie, you must not make scenes with me. They kill me, they wreck the loveliness of life. I cannot see you, so Greek and gracious, distorted with passion. I cannot listen to your curved lips saying hideous things to me. I would sooner be blackmailed by every renter* in London than have you bitter, unjust, hating.
>   I must see you soon. You are the divine thing I want, the thing of grace and beauty: but I don't know how to do it. Shall I come to Salisbury?
>   My bill here is £49 for a week. I have also got a new sitting room over the Thames. Why are you not here, my dear, my wonderful boy? I fear I must leave – no money, no credit, and a heart of lead.
>
> Your own,
> Oscar[23]

---

*Current slang for homosexual blackmailer, perhaps one who thus obtained money for his own rent.

Unfortunately for himself, as it was to turn out, Oscar did not leave the Savoy immediately. Nor did he go to Salisbury, since Bosie, and possibly also his mother, had returned to Thuringia where they had been the previous year. Oscar stayed on for a while at the Savoy, since, as it was to emerge at his trial two years later, he took a youth named Charles Parker late one night to his rooms in the hotel. Meanwhile Bosie was in the Thuringian Forest where he wrote to John Addington Symonds, the elderly consumptive homosexual, who lived in Switzerland, and had promised to write an article on one of Beethoven's concertos for *The Spirit Lamp*. In his letter reminding Symonds of his promise, Bosie told his correspondent that he had been staying at the Savoy with Oscar. 'I daresay it is rather dreadful for you at Klein Schmalkalden,' Symonds replied on 30 March from Italy which he was visiting. 'But you'll shake down. You can't always be pampered at the Savoy. It was very pleasant for Oscar pampering you, I doubt not. I wish you would come and see how I can make you comfortable, and feed your soul on honey of sweet-bitter thoughts – in Italy – in Switzerland – it is all the same.'[24]

Bosie did not accept this invitation as he had promised Oscar to be back in London for the opening of *A Woman of No Importance*. The play was still being rehearsed when Bosie reached London. 'We have only just finished Act 2!!' Wilde scribbled in a hurried note sent round by hand to Bosie who was expecting to lunch with him. 'Order, of course, what you want. Lunch 1.30 tomorrow: at Albemarle. I do not rehearse tomorrow at all.'[25]

While the rehearsals were in progress, Beerbohm Tree received a disturbing communication about Oscar and Bosie, to which he immediately drew Oscar's attention. It came about in this way. Before coming down from Oxford when he had been rusticated, Bosie gave an old suit of clothes to an unemployed clerk called Wood, whom he had befriended at Oxford. In the pockets he had left several of Oscar's letters to him which he had unfortunately forgotten to remove. Wood, working in conjunction with two professional blackmailers named Allen and Clibborn, now attempted to use them as a means of extorting money from Wilde. Copies of the more seemingly compromising epistles were made by the blackmailers, and one such copy was sent to Tree. This was the letter beginning 'My Own Boy, your sonnet is quite lovely,' which Oscar had written from Babbacombe. Tree handed the copy to Wilde, remarking as he did so that its sentiments were liable to misconstruction. Wilde airily explained that it was really a 'prose poem' and that if put into verse it might easily be printed in such a respectable anthology as Palgrave's *Golden Treasury*. In fact, he added, it was shortly to be put into French verse by Pierre Louÿs.

A little later Wood succeeded in extorting £35 from Wilde in return for a bundle of his letters to Douglas, which he alleged had been stolen from him by Allen and which he had recovered with the aid of a detective. The money was good-humouredly handed over on the pretext of enabling Wood to start a new life in America. After Wood had left Wilde's house in Tite Street, Wilde discovered on examining the letters more closely that the original of the one sent to Tree was not among them.

In due course Allen turned up in Tite Street. 'I suppose you have come about my beautiful letter to Lord Alfred Douglas,' Wilde said to him. 'If you had not been so foolish as to send a copy of it to Mr Beerbohm Tree, I would gladly have paid you a very large sum of money for it, as I consider it to be a work of art.'

Replying that 'a very curious construction' could be put on this letter, Allen added that a man had offered him £60 for it. 'If you will take my advice, you will go to that man and sell my letter to him for £60,' Wilde rejoined. 'I myself have never received so large a sum for any prose work of that length: but I am glad to find there is someone in England who considers a letter of mine worth £60.' On Allen remarking that the man was out of town and Wilde assuring him that he was certain to come back, the blackmailer changed his tune and said he was in urgent need of money and had been looking for Wilde for some time. Wilde then told him that he could not guarantee his cab expenses, but that he would gladly give him half a sovereign, which he did. As Allen pocketed the money, Wilde remarked, 'The letter is a prose poem, it will shortly be published as a sonnet in a delightful magazine, and I will send you a copy of it.'

Allen thereupon departed. Five minutes later there was another ring at the doorbell. This time it was Clibborn, the other 'renter.' By this time Wilde was getting a little annoyed by these intrusions. 'I cannot bother any more about this matter,' he told him. Wilde was surprised when Clibborn produced the original letter from his pocket and said, 'Allen has asked me to give this back to you.' On Wilde asking him why, Clibborn answered, 'Well, Allen says you were kind to him, and there is no use trying to rent you as you always laugh at us.' On looking more closely at the letter and seeing that it had become badly soiled and creased, Wilde continued in his customary vein of banter, 'I think it quite unpardonable that better care was not taken of this original manuscript of mine.' At this Clibborn said he was sorry but pointed out that it had been in so many hands.

Wilde thereupon gave him half a sovereign for his pains, saying as he did so, 'I am afraid you are leading a wonderfully wicked life.'

'There is good and bad in every one of us,' said Clibborn.

'You are a born philosopher,' Wilde told him. And on this note they parted.[26]

Wilde put the letter away. But he was not aware that a copy had also come into Lord Queensberry's hands. And unfortunately for Wilde Queensberry did not view the matter in the same light as Beerbohm Tree.

Meanwhile the rehearsals of *A Woman of No Importance* had finished, and the play opened as planned at the Theatre Royal, Haymarket, on 19 April, with Tree in the principal part of the wicked Lord Illingworth. 'The first night was very brilliant in its audience,' wrote Max Beerbohm who was present, as was Bosie. 'Balfour and Chamberlain and all the politicians were there. When little Oscar came on to make his bow there was a slight mingling of hoots and hisses, though he looked very sweet in a new white waistcoat and a large bunch of little lilies in his coat. The notices were better than I expected: the piece is sure of a long, a very long run, despite all that the critics say in its favour.' In fact, the critiques with two exceptions were unfavourable. Nevertheless the play was to run for 118 nights in London, thirty-eight fewer than *Lady Windermere's Fan*. Max also went on the second night, as did the Prince of Wales. 'He had command of the Royal Box (is it not the irony of fate?) just after it had been allotted to Mrs Langtry,' Max added. 'I believe she suggested that they should share it but the Prince was adamant. After the play I supped with Oscar and Alfred Douglas (who is staying with him) and my brother at the Albemarle [Hotel].'[27]

The summer term began at Oxford in the following week, and Bosie went up for what was to be his last term, rejoining Encombe in their rooms in The High, where Oscar spent a few days with them. Bosie, Max told his friend Reggie Turner, was 'rather charming – a very pretty reflection of Oscar – and we get on rather nicely.' On one point, however, he was able to reassure Turner, who he thought might be jealous. 'You need not, by the way, be jealous of Alfred Douglas as he does not peculiarly fascinate me: he is for one thing obviously mad (like all his family I believe) and though he is pretty and clever and nice I never judge my friends from an Aesthetic, an Intellectual or an Ethical standpoint: I simply like them or dislike them. You are fortunate enough to have fallen into the former category....' A few days later he wrote to tell Turner that he had been to a dinner given by Denis Browne, a relative of the Marquess of Sligo, 'to meet the Divinity Oscar ' Bosie and his friend Encombe, who had previously had Wilde's old rooms on the Kitchen staircase in Magdalen, were there too; also the Earl of Kerry and Lord Basil Blackwood – ('quite a peers dinner: at any rate as regards aristocracy of intellect as represented by me and the Divinity.'[28]

While he was still in Italy, John Addington Symonds had been taken suddenly ill with pneumonia and he died in Rome in April. Thus the May issue of *The Spirit Lamp*, which contained his article on Beethoven's concerto, bore a tribute from the editor.

> It is not necessary here to make any detailed reference to his life and literary work. Suffice it to say that the world has lost in him a sweet poet, and a biographer, translator and essayist, as learned, as graceful, and as brilliant as the world has ever known. Only those who knew him can realize what a friend and what a man he was. A man of kindlier heart or a sweeter nature has never lived.
>
> It is only three weeks since, drawing a bow at a venture, I wrote to John Addington Symonds asking him for a contribution to the *Spirit Lamp*, a request which he complied with by sending the lines 'To Leander' (some of the best he ever wrote) which appeared in the February number of this magazine, and a letter of kind encouragement and interest which came like a sunbeam in mid-winter. From that time to this he has been as much to my life as the sun is to a flower, and to read again his last letter written three days before he died, and received on the very day of the announcement of his death in the papers, is like drinking the last drop of a great well which we had thought would spring for ever in a thirsty land, how thirsty who shall tell seeing how small a way I have walked in it? Alas! too he had not finished his work, there was more to do; there were chains he might have loosened, and burdens he might have lifted; chains on the limbs of lovers and burdens on the wings of poets. I can say no more. Words, words, words, – What are they? Only I see before me the bleak bare space in the way, and hear in the air the beating of the wings of the angel of Death.

Wilde had commissioned Will Rothenstein to do a drawing of Bosie, which the artist did. Entitled 'The Editor of *The Spirit Lamp* at Work,' it showed Bosie in profile, wearing flannels and lying back in an armchair. He now wrote to Rothenstein from Bosie's lodgings in The High, asking for the drawing to be put in a black-and-white frame with no margin or mounting, and enclosing a cheque:

> The lovely drawing is complete in itself. It is a great delight to me to have so exquisite a portrait of a friend done by a friend also, and I thank you very much for letting me have it.
>
> Enclosed is an absurdly coloured thing, which foolish bankers take in exchange and for which they give, in reckless moments, gold, both yellow and red.[29]

Another subject of Rothenstein's pencil at Oxford was an eccentric first year undergraduate named Trelawney Backhouse, a homosexual with a passion for jewels who ran up enormous debts and was at Merton, the same college as Max Beerbohm. According to Backhouse, in his unreliable memoirs written in his old age when he was living in China, he frequently dined with Max, Bosie and Oscar at this time and also recalled – with what truth it is impossible to say, since the evidence has not surprisingly disappeared – that 'Max Beerbohm produced a cartoon of Oscar and Bosie copulating, the expression on the former's face resembling the goat of Pompeii, while Douglas, the willing pathic, was deliciously satirised.'[30]

Bosie went down from Oxford for good at the end of the summer term in 1893, pleading illness as the reason why he could not take any further degree examinations. Oscar remarked that this was like Swinburne, who had determined to remain an undergraduate all his life. But both Bosie's parents in their separate ways, since by this time they were divorced, were very disappointed that he had left the university without a degree. Bosie himself admitted that he 'made a hash' of his last year at Oxford, 'even allowing that *The Spirit Lamp* was a meritorious effort on the whole, and that I did write a certain amount of good poetry.'[31] Some months later his father reproached him on one of his characteristically abusive letters: 'All the time you were wasting at Oxford I was put off with an assurance that you were eventually to go into the Civil Service or to the Foreign Office, and then I was put off with an assurance that you were going to the Bar. It appears to me that you intend to do nothing. I utterly decline, however, to just supply you with sufficient funds to enable you to loaf about.'[32] On the other hand, Sibyl Queensberry, who doted on her errant son in spite of his faults, had recently inherited a half share in her mother Fanny Montgomery's fortune, so that she was in a position to make up any deficiency on Queensberry's part.

4

During this summer of 1893 Oscar took a place called The Cottage at Goring-on-Thames from June to September.* Bosie was naturally invited to stay, and when he arrived bringing with him his Oxford servants – of whom one was a youth called Walter Grainger – Constance and her two boys, Cyril and Vyvyan, were there with her husband. But after a short while she took the children to Dinard, so that they could have a seaside holiday, leaving Oscar and Bosie

*Now known as the Ferry House and considerably enlarged, it afterwards belonged to the late Marshal of the Royal Air Force, Sir Arthur Harris, Bart.

behind, ostensibly working, Oscar on his next play *An Ideal Husband*
and correcting the proofs of his long poem *The Sphinx* and Bosie
working on *Salome*, which Oscar had given to him to translate into
English. But neither did very much work, spending much of their time
paddling about on the river in a canoe which Oscar described as
'curved like a flower' and 'finding that life in meadow and stream is
much more complex than is life in streets and Salons'.[33] In spite of
several rows they went up to London together for the last night of *A
Woman of No Importance* at the Haymarket on 16 August. With them
were Max Beerbohm, Robert Ross and the brilliant young artist
Aubrey Beardsley. 'The last of these had forgotten to put vine-leaves
in his hair,' wrote Max afterwards, 'but the other three wore rich
clusters – especially poor Robbie [who] is very much in debt, so he
tells me. I have just been reading *Salome* again: terribly corrupt but
there is much that is beautiful in it, much lovely writing: I almost
wonder Oscar doesn't dramatise it.'[34]

The local Vicar at Goring is said to have been rather shocked when
he called one afternoon at The Cottage, it being too hot to go on the
river, and found Oscar and Bosie lying on the lawn draped in bath
towels and drying off after they had turned the garden hose on each
other. 'I am delighted to see you,' Oscar said to the vicar, 'you have
come just in time to enjoy a perfectly Greek scene!' However,
according to Frank Harris, who states that Oscar told him about it
shortly afterwards, the scene was too much for the vicar, who 'got very
red, gave a gasp and fled from the place,' whereupon Oscar subsided
into a chair shrieking with laughter. Certainly the vicar was not
amused and no doubt spread tales of the scene he had witnessed,
which lost nothing in their telling.[35]

Less amusing were the same kind of rows between the two friends
as had occurred at Babbacombe and elsewhere, as Oscar was to
remind Bosie bitterly in *De Profundis*:

> Some of your Oxford friends came to stay from a Saturday to
> Monday. The morning of the day they went away you made a scene
> so dreadful, so distressing that I told you we must part. I remember
> quite well, as we stood on the level croquet-ground with the pretty
> lawn all round us, pointing out to you that we were spoiling each
> other's lives, that you were absolutely ruining mine and that I
> evidently was not making you really happy, and that an irrevocable
> parting, a complete separation was the one wise philosophic thing
> to do. You went sullenly after luncheon, leaving one of your most
> offensive letters behind with the butler to be handed to me after
> your departure. Before three days had elapsed you were telegraph-
> ing from London to beg to be forgiven and allowed to return. I had

engaged your own servants at your request. I was always terribly sorry for the hideous temper to which you were really a prey. I was fond of you. So I let you come back and forgave you. . . .

When after leaving Goring I went to Dinard for a fortnight you were extremely angry with me for not taking you with me, and, before my departure there, made some very unpleasant scenes on the subject at the Albemarle Hotel, and sent me some equally unpleasant telegrams to a country house I was staying at for a few days. I told you, I remember, that I thought it was your duty to be with your own people for a little, as you had passed the whole season away from them. But in reality, to be perfectly frank with you, I could not under any circumstances have let you be with me. We had been together for nearly twelve weeks. I required rest and freedom from the terrible strain of your companionship. It was necessary for me to be a little by myself. It was intellectually necessary.[36]

Oscar returned from Dinard to London by way of Jersey, where he went to see a performance of *A Woman of No Importance* by Tree's company. 'It was rather good and I had a great reception from a crowded house,' he wrote on 9 September from the Albemarle Hotel to Bosie, with whom he had again patched things up. 'I am off to Goring now, to try and settle up things. I don't know what to do about the place – whether to stay there or not – and the servants are a worry.'[37] In fact, the Goring establishment proved expensive as well as relatively unproductive from the literary standpoint. For this Bosie was largely responsible, since the expenses of The Cottage, including the rent for three months and the wages of Bosie's servants, amounted to £1,340, an enormous sum for those days, when food and drink and servants were relatively cheap.

While Oscar was at Dinard, Bosie went to stay with his uncle, George Finch, at Burley-on-the-Hill, and when there he wrote to the editor of *The Artist*, to whom he had been introduced by John Addington Symonds. Although *The Artist, or Journal of Home Culture*, to give it its full title, had no illustrations, it carried all the current art gossip, including that on literature, music and the theatre as well as the visual arts. Since 1888, it had been edited by a young solicitor, Charles Kains-Jackson, who gradually gave it a homosexual slant. 'I wonder what you thought about Kains-Jackson,' Symonds had written to Bosie after Kains-Jackson had accepted a poem by Bosie entitled 'Hyacinthus' which was definitely 'Uranian' in tone and appeared in the April issue. 'He rather took me aback when I first met him. But he is a very good fellow, I think and has a lot of enthusiasm. I wish all people who feel as deeply as he does, and had his courage and brains, could be also attractive by their manners and appearance. This would help very much.'[38]

On 31 August 1893, Bosie wrote to Kains-Jackson from Burley-on-the-Hill:

> I send you two sonnets to look at. The Oxford one I wrote some time ago. The second one I wrote about a week ago and I think you will agree that I have improved. I was so fascinated by the expression 'sugar lips' used of a boy in one of Burton's translations that I wrote a sonnet on purpose to bring it in. I haven't named it yet, I can't think of a good name. Something Eastern I think it ought to be. I have just finished translating Oscar Wilde's *Salome*. It is to be published in October.
>
> I shall be here for a few days more I think. I am bored to death and very unhappy and unloved! I am surrounded here by what is popularly known as 'a bevy of fair girls' which fills me with misery. I am also very seedy.[39]

The second sonnet read:

> I saw the white sails of the silver ships
> Bend to the bay's blue waters, ivory
> And bars of gold, a prince's treasury,
> The sailors brought, and odorous oil that drips
> From the full cask as the broad galleon dips
> And rises to the swell; and I saw thee
> In thy white tunic gowned from neck to knee,
> And knew the honey of thy sugar lips.
>
> Rarer than all the hoarded merchandise
> Heaped on the wharves, more precious than fine pearls,
> Than all the loot and pillage of the deep
> More enviable: oh! food to my starved eyes!
> (That gaze unmoved on wanton charms of girls)
> Fair as the lad on Latmian hills asleep.[40]

Ten days later, after he had heard from Kains-Jackson, Bosie wrote to him again:

> Thanks for your letter. I am glad you like the sonnets. Certainly put the one you like in the October *Artist*.... What I said about the 'Straw Hat' in my other sonnet was said quite deliberately. I was trying to get the *modern* sentiment in it. It was a bit of realism. Really I think a straw hat has all the feeling of a modern Oxford boy in it; it's my idea of a boy of that sort who should always have a straw hat on. And the 'green-haired daughter' is surely a quite correct and very old and long established idea, though I suppose properly speaking only sea-nymphs should have green hair.

With regard to Oscar I agree with you that to a certain extent he overdoes the 'jewelled style', but I think for all that he has a very dainty fancy, a great felicity of expression, a sense of the phrase, and an enormous dramatic instinct (I am not thinking of his plays, but of *Dorian Gray* and the *House of Pomegranates*). Of course his best things he has never written and I very much fear never will; some of his unwritten stories are astoundingly good, and convincing. Also I think the psychology in anything he writes will always bear the closest inspection which is a thing that can be said of very few people. Everything he writes grows out of an abstract psychological idea; whereas I think in most people that is reversed. I can't explain what I mean on paper. Only I think the general philistine attacks him quite enough without any assistance from the elect.

Perhaps nobody knows as I do what he has done for the 'new culture', the people he has pulled out of the fire and 'seen through' things not only with money, but by sticking to them when other people wouldn't speak to them. He is the most chivalrous friend in the world, he is the only man I know who would have the courage to put his arm on the shoulder of an ex-convict and walk down Piccadilly with him, and combine with that the wit and personality to carry it off so well that nobody would mind.[41]

Nothing further was heard of the Oxford sonnet and its text has not survived. But the other duly appeared in the October issue of *The Artist* under the title 'A Port in the Aegean'. But it was not to be published in England for more than forty years when it eventually came out in Bosie's collected *Sonnets* (1935), being then entitled 'In an Aegean Port'. Having by this time forsworn homosexuality, Bosie significantly rewrote the last three lines of this sonnet as follows:

> More enviable. Green pasture for young eyes,
> Visible dream of tender unripe girls
> Moon-rapt on Latmian hills, where are thy sheep?

Oscar had contracted with Elkin Mathews and John Lane for the publication of the English edition of *Salome* which Bosie had translated and sent to the publishers. 'I hope you will get proofs soon,' Oscar wrote to his friend in his letter of 9 September. But when Oscar saw the proofs, which arrived later the same month, there were further acrimonious scenes between the author and the translator when Oscar pointed out to Bosie what he called 'the schoolboy faults of your attempted translation of *Salome*,' as he later reminded him in the *De Profundis* letter when Bosie was living in France.

You must by this time be a fair enough French scholar to know that the translation was unworthy of you, as an ordinary Oxonian, as it was of the work it sought to render. You did not of course know it then, and in one of the violent letters you wrote to me on the point you said you were under 'no intellectual obligation to me of any kind.' I remember that when I read that statement, I felt that it was the one really true thing you had written to me in the whole course of our friendship....

And so I confess I saw in your letter, from which I have quoted, a very good opportunity of ending the fatal friendship that had sprung up between us, and ending it without bitterness, as I had indeed tried to do in that bright June morning at Goring, three months before. It was however represented to me – I am bound to say candidly by one of my own friends [Robert Ross] to whom you had gone in your difficulty – that you would be very much hurt, perhaps almost humiliated at having your work sent back to you like a schoolboy's exercise; that I was expecting far too much intellectually from you; and that, no matter what you wrote or did, you were absolutely and entirely devoted to me. I did not want to be the first to check or discourage you in your beginnings in literature: I knew quite well that no translation, unless one done by a poet, could render the colour and cadence of my work in any adequate measure: devotion seemed to be lightly thrown away: so I took the translation and you back.[42]

There were further complications over the publication due to the fact that John Lane had engaged Aubrey Beardsley to provide black-and-white illustrations and had objected to several on the ground that they were obscene. Oscar was drawn into the arguments both over Bosie's translation and Beardsley's pictures, as also was Kains-Jackson. 'Can you come and see me here tomorrow at 11,' Oscar wired Kains-Jackson from rooms he had taken in St James's Place. 'Wish to consult you professionally on *Salome* business', to which Bosie added in a telegram of his own that Lane was 'very bumptious'. Kains-Jackson came as requested, but the nature of his advice is not known. Probably it was to press for the retention of Beardsley's three questioned illustrations and also to support Bosie, with whom he had become friendly as a result of Bosie's contributions to *The Artist* and their sympathy with homosexuality as a mode of conduct. After Beardsley, at his own suggestion, had tried his hand at the translation and failed to satisfy the author even less than Bosie's effort had done, Oscar proceeded to revise Bosie's translation himself. Bosie thereupon protested that Wilde could do as he liked but that if his revisions amounted to much he would prefer not to have his name on the title page. In the event, as he subsequently admitted, he never regarded the final version as his translation.[43]

'I suppose you've heard all about the *Salome* row,' Beardsley wrote to Robert Ross at this time. 'I can tell you I had a warm time of it between Lane and Oscar and Co. For one week the number of telegraph and messenger boys who came to the door was simply scandalous. I really don't quite know how the matter really stands now. Anyhow Bosie's name is not to turn up on the title. The book will be out soon after Xmas. I have withdrawn three of the illustrations and supplied their places with three new ones (simply beautiful and quite irrelevant).'[44] In referring to the telegraph boys in this letter Beardsley was thinking of the Cleveland Street scandal in which a homosexual brothel in Cleveland Street in London was exposed as being frequented by telegraph boys from the General Post Office and patronised by members of the aristocracy including the Duke of Beaufort's son Lord Arthur Somerset, who was obliged to go abroad when a warrant for his arrest was issued.[45]

This trouble over *Salome* in November considerably upset Beardsley, who became quite ill, exacerbated by his tubercular condition, and he began to spit blood. Although he told Ross that he found letter-writing a terrible strain, he had sufficient strength to describe Oscar and Bosie as 'really very dreadful people.' Will Rothenstein also disapproved of Bosie's behaviour at this time and told a friend that Bosie had been 'going in for the wildest folly in London, and, I imagine, will shortly have to take a tour round the world, or something of the kind'.[46] In fact, Bosie did go to foreign parts as the result of a letter Oscar wrote to Lady Queensberry dated 8 November 1893.

> Bosie seems to me to be in a very bad state of health. He is sleepless, nervous, and rather hysterical. He seems to me quite altered.
>
> He is doing nothing in town. He translated my French play last August. Since then he has really done nothing intellectual. He seems to me to have lost, for the moment only I trust, his interest even in literature. He does absolutely nothing, and is quite astray in life, and may, unless you or Drumlanrig do something, come to grief of some kind. His life seems to me aimless, unhappy and absurd.
>
> All this is a great grief and disappointment to me, but he is very young, and terribly young in temperament. Why not try and make arrangements of some kind for him to go abroad for four or five months, to the Cromers in Egypt if that could be managed, where he would have new surroundings, proper friends, and a different atmosphere? I think that if he stays in London he will not come to any good, and may spoil his young life irretrievably, quite

irretrievably. Of course it will cost money no doubt, but here is the life of one of your sons – going quite astray, being quite ruined.

I like to think myself his greatest friend – he, at any rate makes me think so – so I write to you quite frankly to ask you to send him abroad to better surroundings. It would save him, I feel sure. At present his life seems to be tragic and pathetic in its foolish aimlessness.

You will not, I know, let him know anything *about my letter.* I can rely on you, I feel sure.[47]

Lady Queensberry took Oscar's advice and wrote to her friend Lady Cromer, whose husband was British Agent and Consul-General in Cairo with the rank of Minister Plenipotentiary. The result was that Bosie was invited to spend the winter with the Cromers in the Residency and to Oscar's immense relief left for Egypt at the beginning of December. 'My dearest Boy,' he wrote as Bosie was about to depart. 'Thanks for your letter. I am overwhelmed by the wings of vulture creditors, and out of sorts, but I am happy in the knowledge that we are friends again, and that our love has passed through the shadow and the night of estrangement and sorrow and come out rose-crowned as of old. Let us always be infinitely dear to each other, as indeed we have been always.... I think of you daily, and am always devotedly yours, Oscar.'[48]

But looking back four years later, Oscar was to remind his friend of his behaviour while Oscar was working, or trying to work, in the rooms he had taken at 10 and 11 St James's Place:

During the first week you kept away. We had, not unnaturally indeed differed on the question of the artistic value of your translation of *Salome*, so you contented yourself with sending me foolish letters on the subject. In that week I wrote and completed in every detail, as it was ultimately performed, the first act of *An Ideal Husband.* The second week you returned and my work practically had to be given up. I arrived at St James's Place every morning at 11.30, in order to have the opportunity of thinking and writing without the interruptions inseparable from my own household, quiet and peaceful as that household was. But the attempt was vain. At twelve o'clock you drove up, and stayed smoking cigarettes and chattering till 1.30 when I had to take you out to luncheon at the Café Royal or the Berkeley. Luncheon with its liqueurs lasted usually till 3.30. For an hour you retired to White's. At tea-time you appeared again, and stayed till it was time to dress for dinner. You dined with me either at the Savoy or at Tite Street. We did not separate as a rule till after midnight, as supper at Willis's had to wind up the entrancing day. That was my life for those three months, every single day, except during the four days when you went abroad. I then, of course, had to go over to Calais to fetch you back. For one of my nature and temperament it was a position at once grotesque and tragic.[49]

One of the last things Bosie did before leaving for Egypt was to write to Kains-Jackson on 29 November about a man called Burnand who had been charged with an assault on a boy and was awaiting trial. 'I am off to Cairo the day after tomorrow' he wrote. 'I want to ask you if you cannot do something for this poor man Burnand.... I saw a most piteous letter from him today which almost made me cry. Surely for the sake of the cause something can be done for this poor man who seems quite friendless and penniless. As far as I can make out, there is not a *bad* case against him, and if the thing was properly managed I feel sure he could get off. Do try and do something, my heart bleeds for the poor chap.' To this Bosie added: 'I am very unhappy about other things as well as this.'[50] His trouble with Oscar over *Salome* was undoubtedly one of them. It still rankled, although he and Oscar were eventually reconciled.

Bosie was in Egypt when the English version of *Salome* was published in February 1894 with a cover design and eleven pictures by Aubrey Beardsley. As agreed with the publishers, Bosie's name did not appear on the title page. However, the author's dedication read:

TO MY FRIEND
LORD ALFRED BRUCE DOUGLAS
THE TRANSLATOR OF
MY PLAY

'I am enjoying this place very much,' Bosie wrote to his mother on the Sunday after his arrival in Cairo. 'Yesterday I went over the bazaars, and today I am going to ride over to the pyramids with a chap called Rumbold who is one of the attachés, a very nice fellow.* All the attachés are very nice. Today is the Khedive's birthday, and there is a great display of flags. I went to the opera the first night I was here. It is a beautiful house, and looks very smart with all the people, and the singers are really rather good, though they perform indifferent music.'[51] During the winter season French or Italian opera companies performed and their repertoire was quite popular, particularly Verdi's *Aida* which had been composed at the Khedive's request in 1871 to celebrate the opening of the Suez canal. Bosie was a lover of classical

---

*Sir Horace Rumbold (1869–1941) had a distinguished career in the Foreign Service, ending as British Ambassador in Berlin from 1928 to 1933. Cairo was his first professional post.

music, particularly Bach, Mozart and Chopin, and he was quite a good pianist. He was also interested in horses and racing, and he gladly accepted Lord Cromer's invitation when Cromer asked him to accompany him to the races on the picturesque Gezireh island in the river near the Great Nile Bridge and almost within sight of the British Residency. Among the spectators on this occasion was the budding young novelist Robert Hichens, who took note of the top-hatted Lord Cromer driving past the stand in an open carriage with Bosie by his side, 'a young man, indeed almost a boy, fair, aristocratic, even poetic-looking', so Hichens thought. It was only when Hichens went up the Nile in one of Thomas Cook's river boats and disembarked in Luxor putting up at the Luxor Hotel, also owned by Cook's, where Bosie was staying, that he realised he was the young man he had seen with Lord Cromer at the races. They became friends, as Hichens also did with Reggie Turner and E. F. Benson, who were also 'wintering' in Egypt. Benson had just scored a success with his novel *Dodo* in which the heroine was supposed to be based on the brilliant young Margot Tennant, later Mrs Asquith. Hichens was trying to emulate Benson's example, which he was shortly to do, but at this time he was merely an unknown journalist. Together Bosie, Hichens, Benson and Turner went further up the Nile to Assouan, where they shot the first cataract and saw the other sights including Philae. It was while they were on board, according to Hichens, that Bosie wrote 'a very very fine sonnet'. This was 'The Sphinx' which Bosie dedicated to Turner, although Bosie's recollection is that it was written in the Residency in Cairo. The probability is that he brought it with him on the river trip and showed it to Turner who admired it so much that he secured the dedication. At all events it was a considerable improvement on some of Bosie's earlier poetic efforts, and was to be published two years later in the first edition of his collected poems in Paris.

'Alfred Douglas at that time was very good-looking in a blond poetic way,' Hichens later recalled, 'he was whimsical, capricious, exceedingly clever and amusing, and entirely unlike anything I had encountered before. The conversation at meals, especially between him and Benson, the one seeming to inspire and polish the wit of the other, was the most entertaining I had ever heard until then.'[52] According to Oscar, Bosie wrote to him by every post from Egypt, and Oscar ignored his communications until Bosie was on his way home in March 1894. ('I read them and tore them up. I had quite settled to have no more to do with you.') However, Bosie's letters to his mother at this time show his feelings towards Oscar and how he imagined Oscar felt about him. 'I am passionately fond of him and he of me,' he wrote.

There is nothing I would not do for him and if he dies before I do I shall not care to live any longer. Surely there is nothing but what is fine and beautiful in such a love as that of two people for one another....

There is no good saying any more, except that while I perhaps have no right to say that Oscar Wilde is a good man, neither you nor anyone else has the right to say that he is a bad man. A really bad man I might admire intellectually, but I could never love, and what is still more he could never love anyone faithfully, loyally, devotedly, unselfishly and purely as Oscar loves me.

Bosie's mother had got it into her head that Oscar's attitude towards him was the same as that of Lord Henry Wotton towards Dorian Gray in *The Picture of Dorian Gray*, although the novel had been written before Oscar met Bosie. 'If Mr Wilde had acted as I am convinced he has the part of a Lord Henry Wotton to you,' she wrote, 'I could never feel differently towards him than I do, as the murderer of your soul.' To which Bosie replied:

There is not *one single* point of resemblance between the two [Oscar and Lord Henry]. The whole thing exists in your own imagination, and to me who knows the truth it is hardly possible to conceive how you could have got yourself into such a state of mind.

The fact is that unless you can understand that Oscar is an Irishman through and through, you will never get an idea of what his real nature is. In many ways he is as simple and innocent as a child. He wouldn't hurt or wound any living creature, and your conception of him is a ridiculous and nonsensical unreality, which if you wish me to be frank I should say springs from a certain morbidity of mind, which really exists in you though you are quite far from suspecting it. The fact is that no person as Lord Henry Wotton ever existed. The whole book of *Dorian Gray* is a book of exaggerated types, it is all supernatural and unreal. Nobody wants to murder anyone else's soul. The whole idea and your whole attitude is really morbid and hysterical. You have created for yourself this imaginary tragedy that has no real existence at all. I verily believe that if Oscar had not written, and you had never read *Dorian Gray*, these ideas would never have occurred to you at all.

As for Lady Queensberry's euphemistic reference to Oscar's 'eccentricities and peculiar views of morality,' Bosie emphasised to his mother that he did not imbibe those ideas from Oscar and that Oscar did not put them into his head and encourage him. 'I had formed them in my own mind and I was quite certain of their truth *two years* before I had ever seen him or even heard of him.'

Now do try and get out of your head this absurd idea about the ruin of my soul and all that, and try and realise that both Oscar and myself are merely ordinary people who are very fond of one another and very anxious to live peacefully joyously and happily, and without scenes and tragedies and reproaches and all that sort of thing. I am so sick and tired of this sort of perpetual war that seems to go on whether I like it or not. Do let us for a change be a little more commonplace and a little less emotional. I am aware that in that respect I am as much to blame as anyone. I have in my blood the love of a scene and a tragedy, but I am convinced it is a mistake, and certainly in our family of all families somebody ought to make a determined stand against it. There is such a tendency to lift everything up on to the stilts of tragedy, we are such a theatrical family. Let us cease from this, and become a little bourgeois.[53]

Partly through the influence of Lord Cromer and partly through that of his grandfather Alfred Montgomery, Bosie was offered and accepted the post of honorary attaché at the British embassy in Constantinople. But instead of proceeding direct from Cairo to Constantinople, since he understood from Cromer that he was not expected before June, Bosie went back to England, stopping on the way first at Athens, where he spent a week with 'Dodo' Benson who had resumed his work on archaeology there. He went on to Paris, having previously written to Oscar asking him to meet him there. According to Oscar, he only consented to do so after Bosie's repeated entreaties, culminating in a telegram to Constance Wilde in which Bosie begged her to get Oscar to write to him. Again, according to Oscar, he at first refused, but eventually agreed to join Bosie in Paris, at the Hotel des Deux Mondes in the Avenue de l'Opéra, after a series of further telegrams from Bosie, including one eleven pages long addressed to Tite Street. Whether Oscar's version is correct is open to doubt or at least exaggerated, since Bosie was later to deny strongly in his autobiography that Oscar had 'determined to break away' from him and only came to meet him in Paris 'with reluctance.' At all events a tearful reunion apparently took place in circumstances in which Oscar was later to remind his friend: 'The unfeigned joy you evinced at seeing me, holding my hand whenever you could, as though you were a gentle and penitent child: your contrition so simple and sincere at the moment made me consent to renew our friendship.' According to Oscar, the eight days they spent in Paris cost him nearly £150 – Paillard's restaurant alone accounting for £85 – while Oscar not only paid Bosie's expenses but also those of the Italian servant Bosie had brought with him. 'At the rate at which you wished to live, Oscar afterwards pointed out to his friend, 'your entire income for a whole year, if you had taken your meals alone, and been especially economical in the cheaper form of pleasures, would hardly have lasted you for three weeks.'[54] Bosie had an allowance of £250 a year from his father, and he proposed to tell his father who was now beginning to object to Bosie's friendship with Oscar that he would rather give up the allowance than break off this controversial friendship. This he was eventually to do.

6

On his return to London at the beginning of March 1894, Bosie had an irresistible desire to go up to Oxford again which he did at the end of the Lent term. 'Many thanks for your sweet letter' Max Beerbohm wrote on 8 March to Reggie Turner who had also come back from Egypt: 'also for the nice things you say about me in your letter to Bosie, who, as I suppose you know, is up just now – very charming, always beautiful and seldom sober. He has taken his name off the Magdalen books, resenting their resentment at his presence in the University. Also Will Rothenstein is up and has done a lithograph of me for the Oxford Series [*Oxford Characters*]':

> A terrible *recontre* took place in my rooms. Enter upon Bosie, Will and me, John Lane, gentleman. Will, who has heard that John Lane, gentleman, has said various things against him, bowed very stiffly and relapsed Byronically into an arm chair, what time Bosie attacked the Publisher about the awful quarrels and so forth that have been. Imagine me! walking swiftly and suavely up and down the room talking about anything that came into my head while John Lane sat very red and uncomfortable on a high chair. Figure him moreover in very new dogskin gloves, a citron-coloured bowler and a very small covert-coat beneath which fell the tails of a braided black coat. Poor me. What a position.

'Dear Bosie is with us,' Max wrote again to Turner four days later:

> Is it you who have made him so amusing? Never in the summer did he make me laugh so much, but now he is nearly brilliant. Also is it you who have made him so abnormally, damnably, touchingly conceited about his poetry? Never was he so in the summer. The dons objected to his coming up, so he took his name off the books and wrote to Warren at the time saying that one day it would be Magdalen's proudest boast that she had for a time harboured him within her walls, her greatest shame that she had driven him forth – or something to that effect. I like his sonnet about the Sphinx.[55]

From Oxford Bosie went on to Tisbury, an attractive village in Wiltshire full of old buildings and a celebrated church, where his mother had taken Hatch House, having for some reason had to give up her house in nearby Salisbury. From here Bosie wrote to Kains-Jackson on 30 March, asking for those copies of *The Artist* where his poems had appeared. 'I am now collecting my poems with a view to publication and I find I have scarcely one MS in my possession so I have to rewrite everything from memory which is rather a trouble.' He thought of Dent or Methuen as a possible publisher and sought Kains-Jackson's advice on this. He also thanked him for his offer to propose him for membership of the Authors' Club, 'but as I am going to Constantinople this June for many months, it is hardly worth while at present.'[56] This disposes of the inference, no doubt mistakenly made by Bosie in his autobiography, that the reason why Sir Philip Currie, the British ambassador in Constantinople, was annoyed with him and in the event refused to accept him as an honorary attaché was because he had not gone direct to Turkey when he left Egypt. The intention always was that he should report for duty in June. However, in the meantime the ambassador had learned of his association with Oscar Wilde, of whom Currie disapproved, and this was the reason for his refusal.

Two days after Bosie had written to Kains-Jackson, he was back in London having a Sunday lunch with Oscar in the upstairs restaurant in the Café Royal. Queensberry was also there and saw them. According to Oscar, the 'Scarlet Marquess' as he called him, came up and shook hands with Oscar who invited him to join them, which he did. They chatted about Egypt and various other subjects on perfectly friendly terms, although Queensberry watched them both carefully. As Oscar was later to remind Bosie, Queensberry, having 'joined my table' and 'drank of my wine', then went back to Carter's Hotel in Albemarle Street, where he was staying, 'and that afternoon, through a letter addressed to you, began his first attack on me.'[57]

In his letter Queensberry began by reproaching his son for his unsatisfactory conduct at Oxford and went on to refuse to supply him with sufficient funds to enable him to 'loaf about'.

> Secondly I come to the more painful part of this letter – your intimacy with this man Wilde. It must either cease or I will disown you and stop all money supplies. I am not going to try and analyse this intimacy, and I make no charge; but to my mind to pose as a thing is as bad to be it. With my own eyes I saw you both in the most loathsome and disgusting relationship as expressed by your manner and expression. Never have I seen such a sight as in your horrible features. No wonder people are talking as they are.

Queensberry concluded this characteristic paternal epistle by stating that he had heard 'on good authority, but this may be false,' that Wilde's wife was petitioning 'to divorce him for sodomy and other crimes.' He wished to know whether this was true or did not Bosie know about it? 'If I thought the actual thing was true, and it became public property,' he concluded, 'I should be quite justified in shooting him at sight. These Christian English cowards and men, as they call themselves, want waking up.'[58] Queensberry, who signed this letter, 'Your disgusted so-called father', had forgotten, if he ever knew it, that Oscar Wilde was Irish. Nor was there any foundation in the statement that Constance Wilde was petitioning for divorce.

It was in reply to this letter that Bosie sent his father the famous facetious telegram which read: 'What a funny little man you are.' To which Queensberry retorted: 'You impertinent young jackanapes. I request that you will not send such messages to me by telegraph.'

By this time or very shortly afterwards Bosie learned that Sir Philip Currie did not wish to have him as an honorary attaché in the Constantinople embassy. This came as a great disappointment to his mother and also his grandfather Alfred Montgomery with whom he was consequently in disgrace. Sibyl Queensberry also probably wished to get Bosie away from Oscar and as she knew that her son had always been keen to see Florence she provided him with the necessary funds to go and stay there for a while.

On 9 April, Bosie wrote to Kains-Jackson from Wilde's rooms in St James's Place where he was probably staying:

> I am off to Hatch House, Tisbury, this afternoon and on Saturday [the 14th] I go to Florence. Is Lord Henry there? I wish you would write and tell me anything you know about Florence as I have never been there before and am going by myself. I mean of course anything you know with regard to the eternal quest for beauty to which I am bound?

Bosie added that he had sent his poems to Dent and also to Methuen, 'so that I can see which will do it better, that is if either of them is pure-minded enough not be afraid of them. I am afraid there is much virtue in that if.' He went on to say that he had seen a copy of the April issue of *The Artist* in which his poem 'Prince Charming' appeared immediately before what Bosie described as a 'brilliant and daring' article by the editor, 'The New Chivalry', extolling the virtues of male friendships. This was to result in Kains-Jackson's ceasing to be editor.

Incidentally, the Lord Henry mentioned in Bosie's letter was Lord

Henry Somerset, second son of the Duke of Beaufort and elder brother of Lord Arthur Somerset, who had been involved in the Cleveland Street scandal and had gone abroad to avoid arrest. Lord Henry, a former Conservative MP, Privy Councillor, and Controller of Queen Victoria's Household, was also homosexual, although married to a wealthy heiress by whom he had a child. Following a judicial separation, caused it is said by his love for a young man called Henry Smith, he was obliged to resign his public offices and also go abroad, where he settled first in Monaco before moving to Florence, then popular with British homosexual expatriates. Here Henry Somerset also achieved some reputation as a writer of popular songs, most of which in *Songs of Adieu*, which appeared in 1889, were inspired by his affection for young Smith. Bosie had already been in correspondence with Henry Somerset, since the latter had contributed a poem in Italian (*T'Amo*) to the penultimate issue of *The Spirit Lamp* (May 1893).

On 16 May 1894 Bosie again wrote to Kains-Jackson, who had been succeeded in his editorial chair by the twenty-one-year-old Lord Mountmorres, an Irish peer, who had been a contemporary of Bosie's at Oxford and was subsequently to become an Anglican priest. Bosie's letter was written from the Palazzo Ferroni, a well-known medieval building near the Ponte San Trinita and the Arno, and then used as a meeting place for the Italian Alpine Club and other organisations like the *Circolo Filologico*. No doubt Bosie enjoyed its facilities though Lord Henry Somerset.

> You promised to write to me before I left London, but I have not heard from you. Do tell me about *The Artist*. Henry Somerset lent me his copy. Why have you given it up? I am so sorry as I cannot say that I find it improved and I look in vain for any 'sympathetic' matter. Surely you have not deserted the cause and deprived us of our only organ of expression? I know of Mountmorres. He was at Oxford with me. I never heard that he was at all sympathetic, and I know he has recently married. Do write at once and tell me about it.
>
> I hope nothing unpleasant occurred in consequence of your charming outspoken 'New Chivalry.' I shall eagerly expect a letter from you, so please don't disappoint me. Also how are things going generally in London. I have had no news at all. I find Florence charming, but I have a slight home-sickness for Oxford now that the summer term is going on.

It must have been very shortly after this that Bosie did receive some news from London, in fact from Oscar, to whom he had sent a telegram. 'It was a joy to get it,' Oscar replied, 'But I miss you so much. The gay, gilt and gracious lad has gone away – and I hate everyone else: they are tedious. Also I am in the purple valleys of despair, and no gold coins are dropping down from heaven to gladden me.'

> How I envy you under Giotto's Tower, or sitting in the loggia looking at that green and gold god of Cellini's. You must write poems like apple blossom.
>   The *Yellow Book* has appeared. It is dull and loathsome, a great failure. I am so glad.[59]

In a second letter, written a few days later, Oscar modified his opinion of the *Yellow Book* to the extent of praising the article which Max Beerbohm had contributed on 'A Defence of Cosmetics.' Oscar described this as 'wonderful' and 'quite delightfully wrong and fascinating.' He added that he had had 'a frantic telegram from Edward Shelley, of all people! asking me to see him. When he came he was of course in trouble for money. As he betrayed me grossly I, of course, gave him money and was kind to him. I find that forgiving one's enemies is a most curious morbid pleasure; perhaps I should check it.'[60] Shelley's trouble was that he had lost his job with Elkin Mathews and John Lane because of his friendship with Wilde.

Oscar's impecuniousness at this time was largely due to the fact that he had had nothing produced in the theatre since *A Woman of No Importance*. However he was able to raise something from Mathews and Lane from the publication of the play in book form and also from his poem *The Sphinx* which both appeared in 1894. At all events he had enough money to make a visit to Paris and to go on from there to Florence, where he and Bosie took an apartment for a month. In fact, they only stayed there for about two weeks, but they both did some work, Oscar writing *A Florentine Tragedy* and Bosie writing what he later described as 'some of my own best poetry'. What caused them to cut short their visit together and return to London is unclear. It may have been due to the presence of André Gide who was also visiting Florence and to whom Oscar offered the apartment for the remainder of the month, an offer which Gide apparently refused, remarking that Wilde did not seem very pleased to see him as Wilde 'thought he was incognito.' Wilde may also have feared that Gide would spread the news that he and Bosie had been together again and that by returning to London he could forestall any further unpleasant behaviour on Queensberry's part. Another reason was that Oscar had an idea for a new play which he wished to discuss with George Alexander. This was *The Importance of Being Earnest*, destined to be Wilde's greatest theatrical success, although he was not to enjoy much of its fruits.

7

When Oscar and Bosie got back to London, which they did towards the end of June 1894, Oscar learned what Queensberry had been doing during their absence. 'Your father is on the rampage again – been to the Café Royal to enquire after us – with threats etc.,' he told Bosie. 'I think it would have been better for me to have had him bound over to keep the peace. But what a scandal! Still, it is intolerable to be dogged by a maniac.'[61]

A few days later on the 30 June, 'the Scarlet Marquess' presented himself at the Wilde's house in Chelsea without any previous warning. He was accompanied, as Wilde said afterwards, 'by a gentleman with whom I was not acquainted' – in fact a prize-fighter. The interview took place in the library on the ground floor.

'Sit down,' said the marquess, as Wilde walked over to the fireplace.

Wilde turned on him. 'I do not allow anyone to talk like that to me in my house or anywhere else.' He continued, 'I suppose you have come to apologise for the statement you made about my wife and myself in letters you wrote to your son. I should have the right any day I choose to prosecute you for writing such a letter.'

'The letter was privileged,' interrupted Queensberry, 'as it was written to my son.'

This time it was Wilde's turn to be angry. 'How dare you say such things to me about your son and me?'

Queensberry went on, seemingly unabashed. 'You were both kicked out of the Savoy Hotel at a moment's notice for your disgusting conduct.'

'That is a lie.'

'You have taken furnished rooms for him in Piccadilly.'

'Somebody has been telling you an absurd set of lies about your son and me. I have done nothing of the kind.'

'I hear you were thoroughly well blackmailed for a disgusting letter you wrote to my son.'

Again Wilde protested. 'The letter was a beautiful letter and I never write except for publication.'

Wilde thereupon changed his tone to one of the utmost seriousness. 'Lord Queensberry,' he asked his embarrassing caller, 'do you seriously accuse your son and me of improper conduct?'

Queensberry thought for a moment. 'I do not say you are it,' he said, 'but you look it, and you pose as it, which is just as bad. If I catch you and my son together in any public restaurant, I will thrash you.'

Although thus confronted with a bully and a bruiser, Wilde did not betray the slightest fear. 'I do not know what the Queensberry rules are,' he told his unwelcome guest, 'but the Oscar Wilde rule is to shoot at sight.'

With this, Wilde requested Queensberry to leave the house. Queensberry refused, whereupon Wilde threatened to call the police and have him put out.

'It's a disgusting scandal,' foamed the Marquess, as he made for the hallway.

'If it is so,' retorted Wilde, 'you are the author of the scandal and no one else.'

Then, following his visitors into the hall, he pointed out the marquess to the servant who was waiting there to show them out. 'This is the Marquess of Queensberry, the most infamous brute in London. You are never to allow him to enter my house again.'

It was now a fight to the finish, and no punches were to be pulled, to use a metaphor from the marquess's favourite sport. Queensberry had already stopped his son's allowance, and he now directed his venom towards the boy's mother, his own divorced wife, whom he accused of interfering in the quarrel. He wrote to her father, Alfred Montgomery, from Skindle's Hotel, Maidenhead:

> Your daughter is the person who is supporting my son to defy me. . . . She evidently wants to make out that I want to make out a case against my son. It is nothing of the kind. I have made out a case against Oscar Wilde and I have to his face accused him of it. If I was quite certain of the thing, I would shoot the fellow at sight, but I can only accuse him of posing. It now lies in the hands of the two whether they will further defy me. Your daughter appears now to be encouraging them, although she can hardly intend this. I don't believe Wilde will now dare defy me. He plainly showed the white feather the other day when I tackled him – damned cur and coward of the Rosebery type. As for this so-called son of mine, he is no son of mine, and I will have nothing to do with him. He may starve as far as I am concerned after his behaviour to me.
>
> His mother may support him, but she shan't do that here in London with this awful scandal going on. But your daughter's conduct is outrageous, and I am now fully convinced that the Rosebery–Gladstone–Royal insult that came to me through my other son [Drumlanrig], that she worked that – I thought it was you. I saw Drumlanrig here on the river which much upset me.[62]

The reference to Drumlanrig requires some explanation. It goes back to 1881 when his fellow peers refused to re-elect Queensberry one of the sixteen Scottish representative peers, because of his refusal to take the oath of allegiance to Queen Victoria on account of his agnostic opinions. Queensberry thought he should now have been made a British peer, since all his titles were Scottish. He wrote a letter of complaint in this sense to Mr Gladstone, then Prime Minister. Gladstone replied that he had always regarded the 'transaction' as 'one taking place within the precinct of the Conservative Party, and had not considered that the change of convictions on which you had (of course in my view most unhappily) been called upon to act, contributed a ground for your not being named by the Queen for a British Peerage.' This was true enough since Queensberry, whenever he had attended the House of Lords, invariably voted with the Conservatives, whose leader Disraeli could have recommended him. However the matter continued to rankle with Queensberry and it came up again over his eldest son and heir Francis, who was known by his courtesy title of Viscount Drumlanrig.

Drumlanrig had gone to Harrow and after leaving school had been commissioned in the Coldstream Guards. Unlike his father he was a Liberal and this fact commended him to Lord Rosebery when Rosebery was Foreign Secretary in the last Gladstone government. Drumlanrig, who was an amiable young man of twenty-four, resigned his commission in the Guards after Rosebery, who had taken a fancy to him, appointed him one of his private secretaries. He impressed his chief so favourably that Roseberry suggested that he should become a British peer so that he could hold the junior office of Lord-in-Waiting to the Queen which would enable him on occasion to represent the Government in the Upper House. At first Drumlanrig declined because he knew that his father would be annoyed if he had a seat in the Lords while Queensberry had not. Gladstone and Rosebery now proposed that Drumlanrig should consult his father which he did. Somewhat unexpectedly Queensberry said he would be delighted if his son received this honour. However, Drumlanrig, so as to be certain of his father's view, asked him to express his pleasure in writing. Queensberry did so and wrote to Gladstone accordingly. In the result in June 1893 Drumlanrig was created a British peer under the title of Baron Kelhead, although he continued to be styled Viscount Drumlanrig. However, within a month or so, Queensberry began sending insulting letters to Rosebery, Gladstone and the Queen, threatening to thrash Rosebery, whom he followed to Homburg. There he hung about Rosebery's hotel with a dog whip, waiting for the Foreign Secretary to appear. Fortunately, the Prince of

Wales, who was also in Homburg, intervened and persuaded Queensberry to desist. On the other hand, Queensberry refused to have anything further to do with his eldest son and never spoke to him again. Meanwhile Drumlanrig continued to hold his post of Lord-in-Waiting to the Queen, after Rosebery succeeded Gladstone as Prime Minister in March 1894.

Since Queensberry returned Bosie's letters to him unopened, Bosie was obliged to send his father a postcard. Although undated, it appears from the context to have been written early in July 1894:

> I write to inform you that I treat your absurd threats with absolute indifference. Ever since your exhibition at OW's house I have made a point of appearing with him at many public restaurants, such as the Berkeley, Willis's Rooms, the Café Royal, etc, and I shall continue to go to any of these places whenever I choose and with whom I choose. I am of age and my own master. You have disowned me at least a dozen times and have meanly deprived me of money. You have therefore no right over me either legal or moral.
>
> If OW was to prosecute you in the criminal courts for libel you would get seven years' penal servitude for your outrageous libels. Much as I detest you I am anxious to avoid this for the sake of the family; but if you try to assault me I shall defend myself with a loaded revolver which I always carry; and if I shoot you, or he shoots you we should be completely justified, as we should be acting in self-defence against a violent and dangerous rough, and I think if you were dead not many people would miss you.[63]

Wilde followed this up by instructing a firm of solicitors to write to Queensberry and demand an apology for the letters in which he had 'most foully and infamously libelled' Wilde and Douglas, particularly the letter of 1 April to Bosie quoted above. Wilde might have been expected to have gone to Lewis and Lewis, as he had been on friendly terms with that firm's senior partner Sir George Lewis, but as already related their relations had cooled somewhat through Douglas's conduct. At all events Wilde went to C.O. Humphreys, Son, and Kershaw, a respectable firm in the City which specialised in criminal cases. He chose this firm on Robert Ross's advice because they were Ross's solicitors. In the event he would have done better to have consulted George Lewis who had a reputation for settling awkward 'society' cases out of court.

Queensberry replied to Mr Charles Humphreys that he would certainly not tender any apology for letters he had written to his son. 'I have made no direct accusation against Mr Oscar Wilde,' he added, 'but desired to stop the association as far as my son is concerned.'

A few days later Queensberry went to see Humphreys and told him that he would inform the police about his son and his revolver, since Bosie had recently fired it from the roof of the Berkeley Hotel. But he held his hand on learning that Bosie had 'given up' his revolver. 'However, if this is to go on,' he wrote again to Humphreys on 1st July, 'and I am to be openly defied by Mr Oscar Wilde and my son by further scandals in public places, I shall have no other resort but to do as I have threatened and give information to Scotland Yard as to what has happened.'[64]

Oscar and Bosie met intermittently in London during July and the earlier part of August, when Bosie was not staying with his mother in Wiltshire. One night they dined with Reggie Turner at Kettner's, and on another day in August, they lunched with Max Beerbohm in 'the Royal Coffee House' as Max called the Café Royal. They were both 'very charming', Max told Turner of this occasion. 'Oscar was just in the mood I like him – very 1880 and withal brimful of intellectual theories and anecdotes of dear Lady Dorothy Nevill and other whores. Bosie came in a Homburg hat – dove-coloured – and wearing a *very* sweet present from you in his shirt-cuffs. . . . Oscar was all admiration and said that he supposed that "dear Reg's present to him was in some way delayed."'[65]

On 12 August, five days after the luncheon in the Café Royal, the police raided a house in Fitzroy Street in the Bloomsbury district of London and took a number of men into custody, including two in female dress, on suspicion of having committed homosexual acts. The men included Alfred Taylor, a transvestite homosexual, who had procured boys for Wilde and was later to stand beside him in the dock at the Old Bailey. A youth named Charles Parker, whom Taylor had introduced to Wilde, was also among those in the house. However, all the accused were either bound over or, like Taylor and Parker, discharged unconditionally, since nobody could be found to give evidence against them. 'Poor Alfred Taylor,' wrote Wilde at the time, 'It is a dreadful piece of bad luck and I wish to goodness I could do something for him, but, as I have had occasion to write to him many times lately, as I have no play going on this season I have no money at all, and indeed am at my wits' end trying to raise some for household expenses and such tedious things.'[66]

This episode which was reported in the newspapers caused Max Beerbohm to allude to it jocularly in one of his letters to Turner, transposing the scene and the two principal characters. 'Oscar has at length been arrested for certain kinds of crime,' Max wrote. 'He was taken in the Café Royal (lower room). Bosie escaped, being an excellent runner, but Oscar was less nimble.' Alas, Max's good-humoured witticism was to prove all too true.[67]

8

The furnished house which Oscar and Constance had taken for the summer holidays was in the Esplanade, Worthing; it was also small and had no writing room. Oscar told Bosie not to come as the children had 'a horrid ugly Swiss governess,' besides which children at meals were tedious. 'Also, you the gilt and graceful boy would be bored.' However, Bosie did come and stayed for about a week in a hotel, long enough to meet three boys, Percy, Stephen, and Alphonso Conway. Conway, whose acquaintance Oscar had made on the beach, sold newspapers and Oscar gave him a copy of *Treasure Island* and a straw hat with a pink ribbon on it. Percy who was also a visitor to Worthing seems to have been Bosie's favourite, but their relations, like Oscar's with the other two boys seem to have been quite 'innocent', since they played with the Wilde children. In spite of these distractions, Oscar was able to make some progress with his new play and also to get some money from George Alexander on the strength of it. Meanwhile Bosie had departed, probably to see his mother. However he wrote Oscar 'a sweet letter' and also sent him a 'delightful' telegram – 'delightful because I love you to think of me,' Oscar told him. Constance took the children back to London about the middle of September, presumably because they had to return to school. But Oscar stayed on for a few days in Worthing and wrote to Bosie suggesting they make a short trip together to Dieppe. ('I have a sort of longing for France, and with you, if you can manage to come.') Bosie countered by asking Wilde to take him to the luxury Grand Hotel in Brighton, much favoured by lovers for illicit weekends. Unfortunately Bosie was taken ill with influenza the night they arrived. When he had recovered, they moved into rooms where Oscar hoped to put the finishing touches to *The Importance of Being Earnest*, but he could do little since he caught the influenza from Bosie. The latter left him to go to London for a couple of days, leaving Oscar ill and miserable, for which he was bitterly reproached on his return. There were more scenes and they quarrelled again.[68]

Meanwhile a brilliant short novel called *The Green Carnation* had appeared anonymously and caused quite a sensation since it was a brilliant satire on the two friends, who appeared under the names of 'Esmé Amarinth' and 'Lord Reggie Hastings'. As a skit it was a daring publication since carnations artificially coloured green were worn at this time by homosexuals in Paris. The authorship was attributed to a variety of writers including Alfred Austin, Marie Corelli, and Ada Leverson, a witty contributor to *Punch* whom Wilde nicknamed 'The Sphinx'. Even Wilde himself was suspected of being the author, notably by the *Pall Mall Gazette*, a charge which he denied characteristically. 'I invented that magnificent flower,' he wrote to the editor. 'But with the middle-class and mediocre book that usurps its strangely beautiful name I have, I need hardly say, nothing whatsoever to do. The flower is a work of art. The book is not.' At the same time, having heard from Bosie about his meeting with Robert Hichens in Egypt, Oscar telegraphed Hichens that he had guessed he had written it, while Bosie also sent the author comic telegrams telling him that he had been 'discovered' and that he 'had better at once flee from the vengeance to come.' How they both guessed Hichens had written *The Green Carnation* Hichens has stated that he never knew.[69]

However, the secret of the book's authorship did not remain a secret for long. One night, possibly during the time Bosie had left Oscar in Brighton, Bosie called on Hichens and invited him to dinner at a restaurant. Hichens accepted and in the restaurant Bosie was recognised by several journalists, one of whom came over and asked Bosie if he knew who was the author. On Bosie saying that he did, he pointed at Hichens, who admitted that he was the individual responsible. The fact was quickly published in the press, and, in the second edition, which came out towards the end of the year, Hichens's name appeared on the title page. It was still a best-seller when Wilde was arrested in April 1895. Hichens then went to see the publisher, William Heinemann, and after talking it over with him they agreed that the book had better be withdrawn from circulation. 'It seemed to us both in very doubtful taste to continue selling such a "skit" on a famous man who had got into trouble,' Hichens wrote afterwards. 'And the sale of *The Green Carnation* was stopped.' It was not until more than half a century later after Oscar and Bosie were both dead that the author, in spite of repeated refusals on his part, eventually agreed to its re-publication in England, largely because it had been extensively 'pirated' in America where it was not in copyright.[70]

Oscar's chagrin at being neglected by Bosie during his illness turned to sympathy when he heard the appalling news of Drumlanrig's death on 18 October at a shooting party at Quantock in Somerset, supposedly due to the accidental explosion of a gun, just as his grandfather, the eighth Queensberry Marquess, had also been killed. Although a verdict of 'accidental death' was returned at the coroner's inquest, there were rumours that Drumlanrig had really taken his own life in the shadow of a suppressed homosexual scandal in which the Prime Minister Lord Rosebery was implicated. 'It is a great blow to Bosie; the first noble sorrow of his boyish life,' Oscar wrote at the time: 'the wings of the angel of Death have almost touched him: their purple shadow lies across his way, for the moment: I am perforce the sharer of his pain.' What was particularly poignant was that Drumlanrig had just become engaged to be married to a general's daughter and his fiancée was one of the house party at Quantock.

Oscar was later to recall the occasion in his *De Profundis* letter to Bosie:

> On your return to town from the actual scene of the tragedy to which you had been summoned, you came at once to me very sweetly and very simply, in your suit of woe, and with your eyes dim with tears. You sought consolation and help, as a child might seek it. I opened to you my house, my home, my heart. I made your sorrow mine also, that you might have help in bearing it. Never, even by one word, did I allude to your conduct towards me.... Your grief, which was real, seemed to bring you nearer to me than you had ever been. The flowers you took from me to put on your brother's grave were to be a symbol not merely of the beauty of his life, but of the beauty that in all lives lies dormant and may be brought to light.[71]

Drumlanrig's death meant that Queensberry's second son Percy, Lord Douglas of Hawick, now became the heir to the family titles and property. But his father had also quarrelled with him, partly because he had married a clergyman's daughter in Cornwall, a match of which Queensberry disapproved as an anti-Christian, and partly, in Queensberry's words, because of Percy's taking sides with 'this miserable brother of his' against their father. Percy Douglas, who was always very friendly with Bosie, could not attend Drumlanrig's funeral, as he was in Australia at this time trying, without much success, to make some money from the current 'gold rush' in Coolgardie. Nor apparently did Queensberry himself go to the funeral in the family burial ground at Kinmount, as he was involved in the nullity proceedings brought by his second wife, which were heard in London on 24 October.

In November 1893, Queensberry had married a good-looking young girl called Ethel Weeden, who lived in Eastbourne and whom Queensberry may possibly have picked up on the Eastbourne parade when he was staying there. The marriage took place in the Eastbourne Register Office, the only witnesses being a man named

Hillman, who was probably the Registrar's clerk, and Queensberry's valet Gill, who had given evidence of his adultery in his divorce from Sibyl. The nullity proceedings took place *in camera* so that no details appeared in the press. However, Oscar heard them from the second Lady Queensberry's solicitor, describing them in a letter to Bosie as 'quite astonishing', but adding no particulars.[72] The grounds for the nullity decree which was granted by the President of the Divorce Court in London could either have been that Ethel was under age when the marriage took place – Bosie states that she was only seventeen at the time – or else that the marriage was never consummated. According to Bosie, his father left her the day after the wedding and they never lived together, which may well be true, since although Bosie was given to exaggerating, he made this statement only a few months after the nullity hearing.[73]

On December 1894 there appeared the first and only issue of another Oxford undergraduate magazine *The Chameleon*, edited by John Francis Bloxam of Exeter College.[74] The initial contribution was Oscar Wilde's *Phrases and Philosophies for the Use of the Young*, later republished in Wilde's collected works as well as separately. It also contained two homosexual poems by Bosie, 'In Praise of Shame' and 'Two Loves', besides an unsigned story, 'The Priest and the Acolyte'. This story, about a priest who fell in love with an altar-boy, was wrongly attributed to Wilde: in fact it was written by the editor. All these features were later to be introduced in Wilde's trials. However, the reason for *The Chameleon*'s short life, despite the fact that its prospectus indicated that future contributors would include Max Beerbohm, Lionel Johnson, Charles Kains-Jackson and others, was that the publication was strongly attacked for 'the undesirable nature of some of the contents' by Jerome K. Jerome in his journal *To-Day*.[75]

In his *De Profundis* letter Oscar reminded his friend of how he came to write *Phrases and Philosophies* for *The Chameleon*:

> One day you come to me and ask me as a personal favour to you, to write something for an Oxford undergraduate magazine, about to be started by some friend of yours, whom I had never heard of in all my life, and knew nothing at all about. To please you - what did I not do always to please you? – I sent him a page of paradoxes originally designed for the *Saturday Review*. A few months later I find myself standing in the dock of the Old Bailey on account of the character of the magazine. It forms part of the Crown charge against me. I am called upon to defend your friend's prose and your own verse. The former I cannot palliate; the latter I, loyal to the bitter extreme, to your youthful literature as to your youthful life, do very strongly defend, and will not hear of you being a writer of

indecencies. But I go to prison, all the same, for your friend's undergraduate magazine and 'the Love that dares not tell its name.'[76]

Of course, Wilde did not go to prison because of *The Chameleon*. He went to prison, as will later be seen, because he was convicted by a jury at the Central Criminal Court of offences under the Criminal Law Amendment Act, 1885, section 11. But the fact that his contribution to the magazine appeared alongside 'The Priest and the Acolyte' as well as Alfred Douglas's two homosexual poems prejudiced the jury against him in all three trials in which Wilde was the principal figure, notwithstanding that he had no knowledge of the story prior to its publication, that he told the editor that he disapproved of it and that he thought it 'bad and indecent.'

An Ideal Husband opened at the Theatre Royal, Haymarket, on 3 January 1895 and was an immediate success. The Prince of Wales occupied the Royal Box and sent for the author after the final curtain to congratulate him. Bosie and Constance were also present and were both delighted with Oscar's triumph. Meanwhile George Alexander was beginning to rehearse *The Importance of Being Earnest* at the St James's, where it was due to open on 14 February. There had been some difference of opinion about the latter play since Alexander thought it was too long and in the event induced the author to compress it from four to three acts. Since he was not over-anxious that the author should attend the rehearsals where he imagined there might be further argument, he raised no objection when Oscar told him that he was going off with Bosie for a short holiday in North Africa. Nor did Constance object. 'Did I tell you that Oscar has gone to Algiers for a fortnight?' she wrote to her brother on 22 January.

'There is a great deal of beauty here,' Oscar wrote to Robert Ross from Algiers. 'The Kabyle boys are quite lovely. At first we had some difficulty in procuring a proper civilised guide. But now it is all right, and Bosie and I have taken to hashish: it is quite exquisite: three puffs of smoke and then peace and love. Bosie wakes up at night and cries for the best hashish.'[77] In a postscript Oscar added: 'The most beautiful boy in Algiers is said by the guide to be "deceitful": isn't it sad? Bosie and I are awfully upset about it.' From Algiers they went on to Blidah where they ran into André Gide, who was staying in the same hotel. After dinner on their first night they found a guide whom Wilde told that they wished to see some young Arabs. Gide was homosexual but he wished to conceal this fact from Wilde. One thing, however, which Gide remembered, was that as they began to walk along the street with the guide, Bosie took Gide's arm and said to him:

'All these guides are idiotic: it's no good explaining – they will always take you to cafés which are full of women. I hope you are like me. I have a horror of women. I only like boys. As you are coming with us this evening, I think it's better to say so at once.'[78]

Next day they all three returned to Algiers, but not before Bosie had met an Arab boy in Blidah whom he invited to go to Biskra with him. While Oscar went back to London for the the final rehearsals and opening of *The Importance of Being Earnest*, he left Bosie and Gide behind. Gide states that his description of Biskra had captivated Bosie who went on with his plan. 'But to run away with an Arab is not such an easy thing as he had thought at first,' Gide added: 'he had to get the parents' consent, sign papers at the Arab office, at the police station etc; there was work enough to keep him at Blidah for several days.' However, Bosie succeeded in accomplishing his desire, since he wrote to a homosexual friend in England, possibly Kains-Jackson, from Biskra: 'I am staying here with a marvellous boy. You would adore him.'[79] However he had to cut short the delights of his stay in Biskra when he got a telegram from his brother Percy suggesting he should return to London immediately since their father had tried to create a scene in the St James's Theatre on the strikingly successful first night of *The Importance of Being Earnest*. When Bosie reached Paris, there was a letter from Oscar with some details of the behaviour of the 'Scarlet Marquess' who tried to gain admission to the theatre but was refused entrance. 'He left a grotesque bouquet of vegetables for me! This of course makes his conduct idiotic, robs it of dignity.' Queensberry arrived, as usual, with a prize-fighter. But the playwright had twenty police guarding the theatre, while Queensberry 'prowled about for three hours, then left chattering like a monstrous ape.' Oscar added: 'Percy is on our side.'

> I had not wished you to know. Percy wired without telling me. I am greatly touched by your rushing over Europe. For my own part I had determined you should know nothing.
>
> I will wire to Calais and Dover, and you will of course stay with me till Saturday. I then return to Tite Street, I think.
>
> Ever, with love, all love in the world, devotedly your Oscar.[80]

On his arrival Bosie bought a sword-stick which he gave Oscar to use as a defence in case Queensberry should meet him again and try to assault him.*

---

*The sword-stick, which was later acquired by a collector of Wildeana, eventually turned up at Phillips auction rooms in London where it fetched £1,700 at a sale on 20 October 1982. It now belongs to Mr John Aspinall the zoologist.

Bosie stayed with Oscar in the Avondale Hotel in Piccadilly for ten days and for the last two or three days invited a companion, no doubt a youthful one, to join them, to which Oscar weakly agreed, the bill for the whole ten days amounting to £140. Bosie eventually left with his companion about 26 February. Two days later, Oscar called at his club, the Albemarle, where the hall porter handed him an envelope which he said Lord Queensberry had left there ten days previously. When he opened the envelope, he saw it contained a card from Queensberry with the words 'For Oscar Wilde posing as Somdomite' scrawled across it, the last word having been misspelled by the Marquess in his fury.

Oscar returned to the Avondale Hotel and wrote a note to Robert Ross telling him what had happened and asking him to come to the hotel at 11.30 that night after he had seen Constance in Tite Street. Bosie he asked to come next morning when Ross would probably be there again. 'I don't see anything now but a criminal prosecution,' he told Ross. 'My whole life seems ruined by this man.... I don't know what to do.'[81]

III

The Exile

1

Robert Ross came to the Avondale Hotel late on the evening of 28 February 1895 as Wilde had asked him, and the two men discussed at some length the course to be taken in view of Queensberry's offensive card. According to Ross, he advised Wilde to take no action against Queensberry. However, Bosie, who came to the hotel next morning, urged Oscar to see his solicitor and apply for a warrant for Queensberry's arrest. Wilde agreed to this course. Consequently, Oscar, Bosie and Robbie Ross together called at Charles Humphreys's office in Holborn Viaduct. The solicitor, who recalled his previous meeting with Wilde ten months previously, was amazed when he heard the details of Queensberry's recent conduct. He asked Wilde point-blank whether there was any truth in the libel. Wilde solemnly assured him that there was not. 'If you are innocent,' said Humphreys, 'then you should succeed.'

On the strength of this assurance, Humphreys agreed to apply for a warrant for Queensberry's arrest on a charge of criminal libel. This he did immediately and Queensberry was arrested next morning, 2 March, at Carter's Hotel, Albemarle Street, when he was brought before the sitting magistrate at Great Marlborough Street police court. On hearing a brief statement of the facts from Humphreys, the magistrate remanded Queensberry for a week and released him on bail of £1,500. Queensberry was represented by Sir George Lewis. However, immediately after this hearing, Lewis told his client that he could no longer act for him and he must find another solicitor. No doubt this was because Lewis knew Wilde socially and he was unwilling to appear for the defence in a sensational private prosecution brought by a man in whose house he had been a guest.

An important question which arose during the first conference with

Humphreys was the cost of the proceedings against Queensberry. At this time Oscar was considerably in debt. He therefore told his solicitor that he had no funds immediately available and that he doubted whether he could afford the 'terrible expense' of prosecuting the obnoxious marquess. At this point, according to Oscar, Bosie interposed, saying that his family 'would be only too delighted to pay the necessary costs,' since his father 'had been an incubus to them all,' that 'they had often discussed the possibility of getting him put into a lunatic asylum so as to keep him out of the way,' and that he was a constant source of annoyance and distress to his divorced wife and to everyone else. Bosie himself scraped up all the ready money he could – about £360 – which he handed over to Oscar on the same day as his father's arrest. Some time later Oscar was able to borrow £500 from Ernest Leverson, a relatively rich man, whose father was a diamond merchant and whose literary wife Ada, whom Oscar called 'the Sphinx', was a particular friend. This loan was made on the basis of Wilde's assurance that Bosie's brother Percy had volunteered to pay half the costs and his mother Sibyl had 'promised to pay any amount required.'

The day of the magistrate's hearing was a Saturday and when Sir George Lewis returned his brief to Queensberry, the latter set about finding another solicitor to act for him. The only solicitor's offices which he found open on that day were those of Day & Russell in Norfolk Street. Charles Russell, whom Queensberry saw, agreed to act, after consulting his father Lord Russell of Killowen, the Lord Chief Justice, who advised him to brief Edward Carson, QC, MP, as leading counsel for the defence. However, Carson returned the brief, since he disliked the prospect of appearing against a former classmate at Trinity College, Dublin, although they had never been particularly friendly there.

Russell was now in a quandary. To establish a successful defence to a charge of criminal libel, his client had to prove to the jury's satisfaction that the words he had written were true and that they were 'published' for the public benefit. The law required that the substance of this defence be embodied in a written plea of justification, a copy of which had to be delivered to the prosecutor before the trial. Russell realised that on the evidence available it would be far from easy for Queensberry to justify the libel. So far, this consisted of the two letters to Bosie from Oscar and the latter's published writings, so that the ability to prove immoral tendencies would indeed be formidable. It is true that there were ugly rumours going round London about Oscar Wilde's private life and for some time past Queensberry had been employing a private detective in an attempt to discover evidence of practices which would show that Wilde had gone far beyond mere 'posing'. These inquiries had led the detectives to the rooms of young Alfred Taylor, which, it appeared were the centre of an extensive homosexual circle. It transpired that Oscar had been in the habit of visiting these rooms, but as yet there was no evidence linking him criminally with any of the young men, mostly in the humbler walks of life, who were also known to frequent them. Nevertheless, Russell considered that if only one of the youths whose names were found there could be induced to come forward, evidence incriminating Wilde was bound to be forthcoming. He felt that this development justified him in asking Carson to reconsider his decision and accordingly he went round to Carson's chambers in the Temple again.

Whatever it was that Carson learned during his second consultation with Russell, it was sufficient in his own mind to justify his appearance at the adjourned hearing before the Great Marlborough Street magistrate on 9 March. It is said that at this consultation Carson had been strongly inclined to advise his client to plead guilty but that he changed his mind at the last moment before leaving his chambers for Great Marlborough Street, on being informed that Russell had obtained, or was about to obtain, a statement incriminating Oscar Wilde from Charles Parker. Parker, who was to be the first Crown witness called in the subsequent proceedings against Wilde, was then serving as a gunner in the Royal Artillery, and Russell had considerable difficulty in persuading him to come forward, since, of course, the solicitor was not instructed by the Crown and consequently could not confer immunity on a witness whose testimony, being that of an accomplice, might lead to his own prosecution.

The launching of a libel prosecution by a successful and popular dramatist against a well-known peer and sporting character was bound to create widespread public interest. It was hardly surprising that the small court in Great Marlborough Street should have been packed with inquisitive spectators at the adjourned hearing. When the case was called shortly after eleven-thirty on the morning of 9 March, there was hardly even standing room, and numbers of prominent people who had endeavoured to obtain seats beside the magistrate on the Bench were disappointed. Oscar Wilde, who had driven up to the court in a carriage and pair, was accompanied by Queensberry's two sons, Percy (Lord Douglas of Hawick) and Bosie. As soon as his name was called Queensberry entered the dock. On looking round, the magistrate then recognised Bosie and directed him to leave the court at once. Bosie accordingly withdrew.

Wilde was then briefly examined about his relations with Queensberry and the occasion on which he received Queensberry's card. He formally identified the card when it was passed up to him in the witness box and marked 'A' as the first exhibit in the case. Carson did not cross-examine.

The magistrate then turned to the defendant and asked him whether, having heard the charge, he had anything to say in answer to it.

'I have simply, your worship, to say this', replied Queensberry, who appeared a diminutive figure as he stood up behind his tall counsel. 'I wrote that card simply with the intention of bringing matters to a head, having been unable to meet Mr Wilde otherwise, and to save my son, and I abide by what I wrote.'

'Then,' said the magistrate, 'you are committed for trial and the same bail will be allowed you as before.'[1]

2

The next Old Bailey sessions were due to open in less than three weeks from the date of Queensberry's committal, so that neither side had much time to lose before the trial. For the role of leading counsel for the prosecution, Humphreys determined to cast one who was at the top of his profession and would in every way be a match for Carson. Accordingly, within the next few days, the solicitor went along to the Temple and offered the brief to Sir Edward Clarke, QC, MP. Then in his early fifties, Clarke was a veritable titan at the Bar, a Former Law Officer of the Crown and a man of the highest personal integrity as well as great forensic ability.

Unlike Sir Frank Lockwood, the Solicitor-General who had enjoyed some measure of Wilde's friendship and hospitality and was ultimately to appear as his leading prosecutor in the last trial, Clarke had never met Wilde before he was instructed in this case. All he knew about him was what was common knowledge among theatregoers, namely, that he was a brilliant playwright who had two successes running at the same time in the West End. Nevertheless, the case was not one which on the face of it appealed to him. Indeed, he hesitated before accepting the brief, just as Carson had done with his, though for a different reason. He asked the solicitor if he might first see his prospective client.

Next day Humphreys brought Wilde to Clarke's chambers, and after some conversation a remarkable scene took place between them. 'I can only accept this brief, Mr Wilde,' said Clarke, 'if you can assure me on your honour as an English gentleman that there is not and never has been any foundation for the charges that are made against you.' The fact, apparently overlooked by Clarke in the gravity of the moment, that he was an Irishman did not deter Wilde from standing up and solemnly declaring on his honour that the charges were 'absolutely false and groundless.'

It was on the strength of this assurance, so solemnly and emphatically given, that Clarke consented to appear against Queensberry. As events were to show, the further the case proceeded the less Clarke relished it. In after years he preferred to forget about it, and it is significant that there is no mention of it in his published memoirs. He did, however, place on record his personal attitude in the case. From the notes discovered among his papers after his death, it is clear that he simply did what he conceived to be his duty towards the client who must have assuredly been one of the most embarrassing he had to represent in the whole course of his career. 'I need hardly say,' he wrote, 'I had nothing to do with the institution of that prosecution.' But once briefed, the great leader turned all his attention and energies into the case, along with the two junior counsel instructed with him.

Meanwhile, in the nearby solicitors' offices of Day & Russell, the defence was busily building up a formidable case against Wilde. For some time past Queensberry had been employing private detectives to collect discreditable evidence of Wilde's private life, hitherto with little success. It is a curious fact, which does not seem to be generally known, that the most damning clues were provided by an entirely voluntary agent who received no fee for his services. This was Charles Brookfield, an actor and writer who had conceived a violent hatred of Wilde, although at this time he had a part in Wilde's play *An Ideal Husband* at the Haymarket theatre. It is all the more surprising since Brookfield was a man of cultured upbringing who had benefited in various ways from Wilde's theatrical successes. He put Inspector Littlechild, one of the detectives employed by Queensberry, in touch with a prostitute whom he knew to possess information about Wilde and his disreputable male associates. This woman frankly attributed the falling off in her business to the unfair competition promoted by Oscar Wilde and his life. Pressed for further details, the prostitute told the detective that he had only to visit the rooms of a man named Taylor in a certain house in Chelsea and he would find the evidence he needed. The detective immediately hastened to 3 Chapel Street, and pushing past the caretaker, who vainly tried to prevent his entrance, he found a kind of post-box which contained the names and addresses of numbers of young male homosexuals, mostly in the humbler walks of life, as well as other documents linking them with Wilde. These damning particulars were forwarded to the defendant's solicitors, who now proceeded to amend their client's plea of justification accordingly.

For the time being, Oscar who had gone off with Bosie Douglas to the south of France to enjoy a short breathing space before the trial, remained ignorant of how the shades of the prison house were beginning to close in round him.

An incident now occurred which caused perhaps the greatest sensation abroad of the whole case. Since it involved a name far more illustrious than Wilde's – that of Lord Rosebery, now Prime Minister – it was destined at a later stage to result in a critical misfortune for Wilde as prosecutor of Lord Queensberry. As a further necessary preliminary to his appearance in the dock at the Old Bailey, English criminal procedure then required the charge which had been brought against the marquess to be considered by a grand jury. Grand jurors were usually well-to-do men with substantial property qualifications. On this occasion a distinguished French journalist who had lived in England for many years was empanelled in error. He went down to the Old Bailey intending to excuse himself from attendance on the ground of his French citizenship; but, when he found that Oscar Wilde's prosecution of Lord Queensberry for criminal libel was among the bills before the jury, he decided to remain and say nothing. In due course, a true bill was returned on the strength of evidence, which included, *inter alia*, Queensberry's insulting letters to his son; these Wilde's solicitors had referred to in the Police Court proceedings but not read. However they named Lord Rosebery, against whom, it will be remembered, the defendant had conceived almost as violent an antipathy as he had expressed against Wilde.

A grand jury's deliberations were invariably private and its findings never reported in the newspapers. The French press, however, fully acquainted its readers with what had happened on this occasion, and the information thus imparted was not only spread throughout the Continent but was openly discussed in London bars and clubs. Brookfield and his friends were incited to fresh efforts in the cause of public morality. The fact that the Prime Minister's name had been mentioned in connection with the case was all the stronger reason that nothing should be hushed up. Hostile feeling about Wilde was increasing, and it seems to have reached as far as the south of France, since Wilde and Bosie were refused admission by the manager of the one hotel in Monaco.

Afterwards, writing from prison to Bosie, Wilde made the following comments on this interlude:

The warrant once granted, your will, of course directed everything. At a time when I should have been in London taking wise counsel and calmly considering the hideous trap in which I had allowed myself to be caught – the booby trap, as your father calls it to the present day – you insisted on my taking you to Monte Carlo, of all revolting places on God's earth, that all day and all night as well you might gamble as long as the Casino remained open. As for me – baccarat having no charms for me – I was left alone outside to myself. You refused to discuss even for five minutes the position to which you and your father had brought me . . .

On our return to London those of my friends who really desired my welfare, implored me to retire abroad, and not to face an impossible trial. You imparted mean motives to them for giving such advice and cowardice to me for listening to it. You forced me to stay, to brazen it out, if possible, in the box by absurd and silly perjuries. At the end, of course, I was arrested, and your father became the hero of the hour.[2]

The precise circumstances of their visit to Monte Carlo together are obscure, but what happened when the two men returned to London is fairly clear. They arrived about a week before the Old Bailey proceedings were due to begin. A consultation was immediately held in Clarke's chambers, at which Wilde and Bosie were both present, in addition to solicitor and counsel; and the opportunity was taken of going through all the particulars of Queensberry's amended plea of justification. In spite of all this new evidence for the defence – the truth of which he persisted in denying – which must have come as an unpleasant surprise to him, Wilde remained outwardly unmoved.

Thanks to the activities of Brookfield and the rest of Queensberry's eager band of assistants, much of this evidence was clearly common knowledge in London, with the result that during the next few days Oscar was besought by his friends on all sides to leave the country. But to all their entreaties he turned a deaf ear, and in this course he needed no prompting from Bosie. A perverse and foolish sense of obstinacy, amounting indeed to bravado, induced him to stay at all costs to himself and see the thing through. This is amply confirmed by the testimony of a number of independent witnesses.

For instance, two nights before the trial opened, he took his wife and Bosie to a box at St James's Theatre, where *The Importance of Being Earnest* was playing to crowded houses. In the interval between the acts he went backstage to see George Alexander, the theatre's manager, who was also acting the lead part in the play. Alexander reproached him for coming to the theatre at such a time, as people would be sure to consider it 'in bad taste'. Wilde laughingly replied that he might as well accuse every member of the audience of bad taste in coming to see the play. 'I would consider it in bad taste,' he added, 'if they went to see anyone else's play.'

Alexander then proffered this piece of advice: 'Why don't you withdraw from this case and go abroad?'

'Everyone wants me to go abroad,' replied Oscar in the same jesting mood. 'I have just been abroad, and now I have come home again. One can't keep on going abroad, unless one is a missionary or, what comes to the same thing, a commercial traveller.'

It was the last occasion on which Bosie saw Constance Wilde. 'She was very much agitated,' he recalled, looking back long afterwards, 'and when I said good-night to her at the door of the theatre she had tears in her eyes. I felt dreadfully sorry for her, [and] though I then believed that Oscar would beat my father, and had not the slightest anticipation of the frightful catastrophe that was imminent, I knew that at the very best the whole business must be a terrible ordeal for her.'

About this time – possibly earlier that same day – Oscar had received similar advice to Alexander's from Frank Harris, formerly editor of *The Fortnightly Review*, to which Oscar had been a contributor. He asked Harris if he would be a witness for him at the trial and testify that in his opinion *The Picture of Dorian Gray*, one of the works which had been singled out for attack by Queensberry in his plea of justification, was a moral story. Harris declined, urging his friend to flee, but on being implored to reconsider his decision, he asked Wilde to join him next day at the Café Royal, where he had a luncheon engagement with Bernard Shaw. The story of this celebrated encounter has been told by Harris, Shaw and Bosie (who was also present) and though they differ as to minor details, they are agreed on the main outlines.

> First of all [argued Harris] we start with the assumption that you are going to lose the case against Queensberry. You don't realise what is going to happen to you. It is not going to be a matter of clever talk about your books. They are going to bring up a string of witnesses that will put art and literature out of the question. Clarke will throw up his brief.... You should go abroad and, as ace of trumps, you should take your wife with you. Now for the excuse. I would sit down and write such a letter as you alone can write to *The Times*. You should set forth how you have been insulted by the Marquess of Queensberry and how you went naturally to the Courts for a remedy, but you found out very soon that this was a mistake. No jury would give a verdict against a father, however mistaken he might be. The only thing for you to do, therefore, is to

go abroad, and leave the whole ring with its gloves and ropes, its sponges and pails to Lord Queensberry. You are a maker of beautiful things, you should say, not a fighter, whereas the Marquess of Queensberry takes joy only in fighting. You should refuse to fight with a father under these circumstances.... But don't stay here clutching at straws like testimonials to *Dorian Gray*.... I know what is going to happen.... I know what evidence they have got. You must go.

Shaw, when appealed to, agreed with the force of this argument, and like Harris he was surprised at the attitude of sulky intransigence which it provoked on the part of the other two. 'Your telling him to run away shows that you are no friend of Oscar's,' said Bosie, getting up from the table. 'It is not friendly of you, Frank,' added Oscar, as he followed the younger man out of the restaurant.

There can be no doubt that their line of conduct was reckless in the extreme. Although neither Harris nor Shaw was aware of it, both Oscar and Bosie had already seen Queensberry's amended plea of justification and must have realised that the defendant's tactics at the trial would take the court far beyond the relatively innocent realm of the prosecutor's published writings. The only possible explanation has been given by Bosie himself. He was most anxious that the case against his father should proceed and resented any arguments in favour of its abandonment. During the meeting in the Café Royal, he was, as he put it in a letter which he wrote to Harris many years later (1925), 'terribly afraid that Oscar would weaken and throw up the sponge.' Hence his desire to get him out of the restaurant as soon as possible. 'I did not tell you our case for fear I might not convince you,' he continued in this letter, 'and that you and Shaw might, even after hearing it, argue Oscar out of the state of mind I had got him into.'

What Bosie described as 'our case' was really his private case against his father, and he failed to see, at this stage or at any time, that the evidence he wished to give would not be admissible in any English court of law. It rested on the mistaken belief that Sir Edward Clarke would begin by launching a violent attack against Queensberry. In later years Bosie liked to assert that he had obtained a promise from Clarke that he would put him into the witness box to prove his father's true character – a claim emphatically denied by Sir Edward Clarke. ('I made no such agreement or promise.') Bosie certainly appears to have expected that he would be allowed to depict Queensberry as outwardly pretending to be a solicitous father trying to save his son, whereas in fact he had behaved like an inhuman brute towards every member of his family. Bosie did not appreciate – indeed he never grasped the point as long as he lived – that such evidence as this had nothing to do with the issue to be decided at the trial, and that, even if he did go into the witness box, he would never be permitted to give it, 'The question of Lord Queensberry's character was quite irrelevant to the case, and was never mentioned in my instructions or in consultation,' wrote Sir Edward Clarke in answer to Oscar's friend and first biographer, Robert Sherard, who raised the point when Bosie's autobiography was published in 1929; 'and if an attempt had been made to give such evidence, the judge would of course have peremptorily stopped it.'[3]

The sole issue which the jury would have to decide was a simple one of fact. Did Oscar Wilde pose as a sodomite? If the jury found that he did not, then Queensberry was guilty of libel. On the other hand, if they found that he did, Queensberry was not guilty.

3

Queensberry's trial for criminally libelling Oscar Wilde opened at the Old Bailey on 3 April 1895. This and the two subsequent trials in which Wilde figured have been fully described by the present writer and others, so that it is unnecessary to repeat these accounts in any detail except insofar as they directly concerned Alfred Douglas. The case was tried before Mr Justice Henn Collins and a jury, while the prosecution was led by Sir Edward Clarke and two junior counsel of whom one was the solicitor's son Travers Humphreys, and the defence by Edward Carson and two juniors. 'Watching briefs' for Alfred Douglas and his brother Percy were held by another Queen's Counsel and a junior. This was because one of the youths named Ernest Scarfe, who was mentioned in Queensberry's plea of justification as having had homosexual relations with Wilde in his rooms in St James's Place, was known to both Alfred and Percy, having been introduced to Alfred by Taylor at a skating rink and having later met Percy when they both travelled out on the same ship to Australia. However this precaution proved unnecessary since the defence did not intimate that Scarfe would be called as a witness.

In his opening speech for the prosecution, Sir Edward Clarke related the unsuccessful attempt to blackmail Wilde on account of his letter to Douglas quoting the first letter, of which copies had been sent to Beerbohm Tree and Queensberry. The text of that letter, he told the jury, to the amusement of the spectators in court, might 'appear extravagant to those in the habit of writing commercial correspondence'. But Mr Wilde was a poet, counsel pointed out, the letter was considered by him to be a 'prose sonnet', and he was not ashamed to produce it anywhere as the expression of true poetic feeling, and with no relation to the hateful and repulsive suggestion put upon it by Lord Queensberry.

After the porter at the Albemarle Club had formally proved 'publication' of the libel by describing how he had received Queensberry's card, Douglas expected to be called, being under the mistaken impression that Clark had agreed to put him in the witness box before Wilde so that he could make an all-out attack on his father. However, Clarke called the prosecutor, and in his examination-in-chief Wilde answered his counsel's questions with an easy assurance, relating how he had first met Douglas, how an attempt had been made to blackmail him on account of the letters Douglas had unfortunately left in a pocket of the suit of clothes he had given to Wood, how Queensberry had called at his house in Tite Street and what passed between them, and finally how he had gone to his club and been handed Queensberry's card by the porter.

It was now Carson's turn to cross-examine the witness. So long as Carson confined his questions to Wilde's literary work such as *Dorian Gray* and *Phrases and Philosophies*, Wilde held his own with his fellow countryman, amusing the court with his repartees. It was only when Carson passed to the individuals specifically mentioned in the plea of justification that Wilde began to feel less sure of himself. Carson's most devastating question, which completely disconcerted Wilde, concerned the youth named Walter Grainger who had been a servant in Bosie Douglas's rooms in The High at Oxford and whom he subsequently brought with him when he stayed at The Cottage in Goring with Wilde shortly after he came down. It was here that Wilde was alleged to have had immoral relations with Grainger.

'Did you kiss him?' asked Carson.

For a moment, a fatal moment, Wilde was off his guard. 'Oh, dear no,' he replied unthinkingly. 'He was a peculiarly plain boy. He was, unfortunately extremely ugly. I pitied him for it.'

Quick as lightning Carson pressed home his advantage. Was that the reason Wilde had never kissed him? 'Oh, Mr Carson, you are pertinently insolent.' Why had he mentioned his ugliness? 'I do not know why I mentioned he was ugly,' said Wilde, now on the verge of breaking down, 'except that I was stung by the insolent question you put to me and the way you have insulted me throughout this hearing.' But Carson continued remorselessly in a sharp staccato repetition: 'Why? Why? Why did you add that?' Wilde began several answers inarticulately. At last he managed to blurt out: 'You sting me and insult and try to unnerve me, and at times one says things flippantly when one ought to speak more seriously. I admit it.'

A few more questions on minor matters and Carson gathered up his papers and sat down, to the witness's intense relief. Sir Edward Clarke then began his re-examination, first of all putting to his client the letters written by Queensberry to his son containing statements about Wilde which the witness swore were quite unfounded. Clarke also sought to show that Wilde's associations with Taylor and the various youths whose names had been mentioned were perfectly innocent. But it was too late. The damage had been done, and the foolish slip about the boy Grainger which caused it could not be covered up.

Wilde's case collapsed on the morning of the third day of the trial, Friday 5 April. Clarke had on careful consideration told Wilde before the court sat that 'it was almost impossible in view of all the circumstances to induce a jury to convict of a criminal offence a father who was endeavouring to save his son from what he believed to be an evil companionship,' and he advised his client in his own interest to allow him to make a statement to this effect in court and withdraw from the prosecution. Wilde listened quietly and gravely and told his counsel that he agreed with his advice. 'I then told him that there was no necessity for his presence in Court while the announcement was being made,' Clarke subsequently wrote in his unpublished recollections of the trial. 'I hoped and expected that he would take the opportunity of escaping from the country, and I believe he would have found no difficulty in doing so.'

However Wilde chose to remain in court while Clarke made his statement and the jury found Queensberry not guilty. He afterwards left the Old Bailey by a side door with Douglas and Ross, who had both been present throughout, thus avoiding the ribald scenes of prostitutes dancing on the front pavement. The victorious defendant immediately sent a characteristic message to his unsuccessful adversary, on whom the tables were now to be savagely turned. 'If the country allows you to leave, all the better for the country!' said Queensberry. 'But if you take my son with you I will follow you wherever you go and shoot you!'

Oscar, accompanied by Bosie and Robbie Ross, drove from the Old Bailey to the nearby Holborn Viaduct Hotel, where they had lunch, and Wilde wrote a letter to the *Evening News* explaining his conduct at the trial, after he had had a word with Humphreys, whose offices were nearby. The text was jotted down by Ross on the back of two of the hotel envelopes and signed by Oscar before being given to a reporter from the newspaper so that it could appear in the late afternoon editions. 'It would have been impossible for me to have proved my case without putting Lord Alfred Douglas in the witness box against his father,' the letter read. 'Lord Alfred Douglas was extremely anxious to go into the box, but I would not let him do so. Rather than put him in so painful a position I determined to retire from the case, and to bear on my shoulders whatever ignominy and shame might result from my prosecuting Lord Queensberry.'

The possibility of Oscar going abroad without delay was also discussed. While Ross went off to cash a cheque for £200 with this object in view, the others left to call at the offices of the solicitors Lewis & Lewis in Ely Place where they saw Sir George Lewis and Wilde asked him if he could suggest anything. 'What is the good of coming to me now?' exclaimed this shrewd old lawyer. 'I am powerless to do anything. If you had had the sense to bring Lord Queensberry's card to me in the first place I would have torn it up and thrown it into the fire and told you not to make a fool of yourself.'

Oscar and Bosie now went on to the Cadogan Hotel in Sloane Street where Bosie was now staying. Bosie, who arrived there shortly afterwards, gave Oscar his £200 and advised him to catch the next train for Dover and thence try to get over to France. Other friends apparently repeated this advice in the course of the afternoon. Even Constance Wilde, when Ross went to tell her the outcome of the trial said between sobs, 'I hope Oscar is going away abroad.' But unfortunately Oscar could not make up his mind what to do until it was made up for him by the force of events. He remained in a pathetic state of indecision, lamenting that 'the train has gone' and that 'it was too late.' Soon after five o'clock, Thomas Marlowe, who was then a reporter on *The Star*, called at the hotel and asked to see Wilde. Wilde refused to see him, but sent Ross instead to speak to him in another room. The journalist declared that he had just seen a message come through on the tape to the effect that a warrant for Wilde's arrest had been issued. Bosie, unable to stand the tension any longer, had gone off to the House of Commons to find out from his cousin George Wyndham, MP, whether Wilde's prosecution was inevitable and he learned that it was. Meanwhile Oscar sat on with Ross and Reggie Turner, who had joined them, in Bosie's room in the Cadogan Hotel, glumly waiting for the blow to fall and drinking glass after glass of hock and seltzer in an attempt to steady his nerves.

In fact the warrant had been applied for at Bow Street magistrate's court about 3.30 pm. But the Chief Magistrate Sir John Bridge adjourned the application for an hour and a half, in order, so the late Travers Humphreys told the present writer, to enable Wilde to catch the last boat train for the Continent. The authorities would have been relieved if Wilde had done this, but he did not do so, as we have seen.

At 6.30 he was arrested by two police officers in Room 53 of the Cadogan Hotel. On being shown the warrant he asked whether he could have bail. The detective replied that that was for the magistrate to decide. They added that he would be taken first to Scotland Yard and then to Bow Street. Since Bosie had not yet returned from the House of Commons, Wilde asked if he could write him a note. He was told he could, so he sat down and wrote asking his friend to see his brother Percy Douglas and the theatrical managers George Alexander and Lewis Waller, at whose theatres *The Importance of Being Earnest* and *An Ideal Husband* had been running, to attend Bow Street police court to give bail. He also asked Bosie to send a telegram to Humphreys asking him to appear for him in court. 'Also,' he added, 'come to see me.'[4]

On receiving this note, Bosie hurried off in a cab to Bow Street, where he learned that Oscar had already been formally charged and locked up in a cell for the night. Bosie was not allowed to see him and asked if he could not bail him out. He was much distressed when informed by the inspector on duty that on no consideration could his request be granted. Even if bail were subsequently granted by the magistrate, the inspector added, other sureties besides himself would certainly be required. Bosie then went on to the Haymarket and St James's theatres, where he saw their respective managers Waller and Alexander, whom he asked to give bail for Wilde. Both refused, as also did Constance Wilde's cousin Adrian Hope, when Bosie saw him next day in the course of 'a most painful interview.'

Wilde appeared before the magistrate Sir John Bridge next morning, the Crown being represented by Charles Gill, who had been Carson's junior in the Queensberry trial, and the defendant being represented by Travers Humphreys. After hearing evidence for the Crown, the magistrate remanded Wilde in custody until 11 April, refusing the prisoner bail. When he came up again, this time with Taylor who had also been arrested, he was again remanded in custody, bail again being refused, as it also was on 19 April when Wilde and Taylor were both committed for trial at the next Old Bailey sessions. Meanwhile Sir Edward Clarke agreed to represent Wilde as did Humphreys, this time without fee. There were twenty-five counts in the indictment against the prisoners jointly, alleging acts of gross indecency, procuring and conspiracy to procure. On 23 April the Grand Jury returned a 'true bill' against both prisoners and their trial was set down to open five days later at the Old Bailey before Mr Justice Charles.

Meanwhile it was widely thought that Alfred Douglas would also be arrested. But the authorities had no acceptable evidence against him, a fact revealed in an interesting letter written by Bosie's cousin George Wyndham, MP, to his father the Hon Percy Scawen Wyndham who was a son of Lord Leconfield.

Sunday, 7 April 1895

... I ought to tell you that I know on the authority of Arthur Balfour, who has been told the case by the lawyers who had all the papers, that W[ilde] is certain to be condemned, and that the case is in every way a very serious one, involving the systematic ruin of a number of young men. Public feeling is fiercely hostile to him, among all classes.

There is no case against Bosie, but he has associated himself with W[ilde] up to the last moment; and is spoken of as having known the witnesses who will be called. Men like Arthur [Balfour] and Lord Houghton, who have spoken to me, speak in kind terms of him; but are unanimous in saying that he had better go abroad for a year or two.

Bosie took it very well. He thought I was going to ask him to go at once, and began by saying that nothing on earth would make him leave London until the trial was over. You may be sure that nothing will: he is quite insane on the subject.... If W[ilde] was released, Bosie would do anything he asked, and no entreaty from you or his mother would weigh with him.

But W[ilde] is humanly speaking, sure to be imprisoned. I told Bosie so; and he agreed that it was almost certain....

Whatever is proved, it is common knowledge in London that there was a sort of secret society around the man Taylor.[5]

'Can you do anything or suggest anything at this terrible moment?' Bosie wrote next day to Kains-Jackson. 'I have lived through what seems like countless aeons of anguish since Friday. Can *nothing* be done? Do you know no strong fearless man who will stand up? Do try to help me if only with sympathy.'[6]

Alas, there was nothing that the former editor of *The Artist* could do except to see Bosie and try to comfort him, since with the exception of Frank Harris and Bosie himself Oscar had been deserted by all his friends, including Robbie Ross, most of whom had deemed it prudent to cross to France and remain there until Wilde's trial was over, and they considered it safe to return to England, since with the prevalent anti-homosexual atmosphere in the press they feared that if they stayed they might share Oscar's fate. With regard to Ross it is only fair to record the circumstances of his departure from England. 'My relatives were naturally distressed at my connection with a very disgraceful scandal,' he wrote afterwards. 'My name had appeared in the papers as being with Wilde when he was arrested. In consequence I was obliged to leave some of my clubs. My mother promised that if I would go abroad for a few weeks she would contribute to the expenses of Wilde's defence, which she did; and that she would assist Lady Wilde (who was entirely dependent on her son Oscar) which she did until Lady Wilde's death in February 1896.'[7]

As for Bosie, so long as he could he visited Oscar every day in Holloway prison, to which he had been removed from Bow Street. 'I thought but to defend him from his father,' Oscar wrote to Ada Leverson: 'I thought of nothing else, and now –' To his friend Robert Sherard in Paris, Wilde wrote at the same time: 'I am ill – apathetic. Nothing but Alfred Douglas's daily visits quicken me into life, but even then I see him under humiliating and tragic conditions.'[8]

Bosie has described these visits in his autobiography, how they sat facing each other in a kind of box separated by a long corridor about a yard wide, which was patrolled by a warder.[9] As Oscar was slightly deaf, he had considerable difficulty in hearing what Bosie said, owing to the confused babel from the adjoining boxes, where similar meetings were taking place. As Oscar looked at Bosie, and Bosie looked at him, the tears would roll down Oscar's cheeks. Oscar was further depressed by his counsel Sir Edward Clarke's expressed wish that Bosie should go abroad, since he felt that his continued presence in London would prejudice his client's chances of acquittal. To this Oscar reluctantly agreed. 'I don't know what to do,' Oscar wrote at this time: 'my life seems to have gone from me. I feel caught in a terrible net.... I care less when I think he is thinking of me – I think of nothing else.'[10]

Their last meeting before Bosie's departure took place in Newgate, the old prison adjoining the Old Bailey, to which Oscar had been brought while the grand jury were considering his case along with Taylor's on 23 April.

4

Bosie left London for France on the following morning, 24 April. This was the same day as Oscar's creditors had put the bailiffs into his house in Tite Street and he was sold up, the auction being conducted in scandalous conditions, valuable pictures such as Aubrey Beardsley's portrait of Mrs Patrick Campbell and first editions of books being knocked down for trifling sums, and other possessions, including the manuscript of *A Florentine Tragedy* actually being pilfered. While this was going on Bosie arrived in Calais where he booked into the Hotel Terminus in the Gare Maritime. He then telegraphed Robert

Ross who was in Rouen to join him in Calais, which he did, and since
the English newspapers came over every day on the ferry they were
able to read the reports of the five-day trial at the Old Bailey at which
Oscar and Alfred Taylor were tried jointly, both pleading not guilty.
Before leaving London Bosie had sent Taylor's solicitor £50 as a
contribution to the costs of his defence.[11] In fact Bosie only knew
Taylor slightly and had never been to his notorious rooms in Little
College Street, but he felt sorry for him, solitary and penniless as he
was; he also knew that Taylor, to his credit, had been offered
immunity from prosecution if he gave evidence against Wilde and that
he had indignantly refused to do so, preferring to risk the maximum
sentence of two years' imprisonment with hard labour – which like
Oscar's was to be his fate.

The trial was fully reported in the papers so that Bosie and Ross
were able to follow Oscar's defence when he was cross-examined by
Charles Gill for the prosecution on the subject of Bosie's two
controversial poems, *In Praise of Shame* and *Two Loves*, which had both
appeared in *The Chameleon*. It was on this occasion that Oscar made
his oft-quoted speech on 'The Love that Dare not Speak its name',
which caused the spectators in the gallery, including Max Beerbohm,
to applaud. ('He never had so great a triumph, I am sure', Max wrote
afterwards to Reggie Turner.)

About the third day of the trial, before the prosecution had
concluded its case, Bosie telegraphed to Sir Edward Clarke, offering
to give him 'certain information', although it was compromising to
himself, and again offered to give evidence. In reply he received a
stern rebuke from Oscar's solicitors, informing him that his telegram
was 'most improper' and that Sir Edward Clarke had been greatly
upset by it. At the same time Bosie was adjured not to attempt any
further interference, 'which can only have the effect of rendering Sir
Edward's task still harder than it is already.'

In the end the jury were unable to agree and were discharged,
while Wilde was remanded to come up at the next sessions. His
counsel, Sir Edward Clarke, applied for bail and although it was
initially refused by the trial judge, it was granted by another judge
in chambers in the sum of £5,000, of which half was to be on the
prisoner's personal security and the other half to be by two other
sureties. There were Bosie's brother Percy and the Rev Stewart
Headlam, a kindly Church of England clergyman, who, although
he hardly knew Wilde, had admired his bearing during the trial
and sympathised with him on account of his treatment by the press
and public generally. For this he was strongly attacked, but he
justified his action by stating that 'by the laws of England everyone

is reckoned innocent until he is proved guilty.'

Most of the time he was out on bail Wilde spent in the shelter of Ernest and Ada Leverson's hospitable London home in Courtfield Gardens. While he was there, friends like Frank Harris urged him to 'jump' his bail and go abroad, while Percy Douglas assured his co-surety that he would hold himself responsible for Headlam's amount should Oscar take this course. Frank Harris went so far as to borrow a yacht which he anchored off Erith in Kent and ready to sail at a moment's notice, and one night he got Oscar into a carriage with a pair of fast-trotting horses and started to drive him to Erith; but when he gathered that this was the purpose of the exercise Oscar absolutely refused to go and made Harris turn back. Describing this action in his autobiography, Bosie wrote that he received a very touching letter from Oscar giving the reasons for his refusal:

> It made me weep at the time, and even now (1929) I don't like to think of it, but I have thought since, a hundred times, that it was an insane thing not to go, and that it would really have been a braver thing to do. Oscar said in his letter that he could not 'run away' and 'hide' and 'let down' his bails (but my brother wanted him to go on my account, and Mr Headlam would not have been affected in the least.) He wrote: 'A dishonoured name, a hunted life are not for me to whom you have been revealed on that high hill where beautiful things are transfigured'. He also, pathetically, thought that he had a 'good chance of being acquitted' at the second trial.[12]

Bosie evidently thought that Oscar would follow Percy's advice, judging by a letter Bosie wrote to Oscar while he was still on bail, one of only three from Bosie to Oscar which have survived. 'My own darling Oscar, Have just arrived here,' Bosie wrote on 15 May from the Hotel des Deux Mondes in Paris, where they had previously stayed together. 'They are very nice here and I can stay as long as I like without paying my bill, which is a good thing as I am quite penniless. The proprietor is very nice and *most* sympathetic; he asked after you at once and expressed his regret and indignation at the treatment you had received.... Do keep up your spirits, my dearest darling. I continue to think of you day and night, and send you all my love. I am always your own loving and devoted boy Bosie.'[13]

There had been twenty-five counts against the two prisoners when they were tried jointly. In the second trial, which began on 20 May before Mr Justice Wills and in which the prisoners were tried separately, the counts against Taylor were reduced to fourteen and those against Wilde to eight, this being due mainly to the dropping of the conspiracy counts by the prosecution. It was as the result of Sir Edward Clarke's application that the judge ordered the prisoners to be tried separately. On the other hand, the prosecution insisted on Taylor being tried first, which the prosecution had the right to do. But since Taylor's guilt was clear this was bound to prejudice Wilde's chances of an acquittal, although of course he was tried before another jury. Also instead of Charles Gill leading for the prosecution the authorities brought in the Solicitor-General Sir Frank Lockwood in Gill's place. Carson, who had refused the Crown brief when offered to him, now went to Lockwood and said: 'Cannot you let up on the fellow now? He has suffered a great deal.'

'I would,' replied Lockwood, 'but we cannot: we dare not: it would at once be said, both in England and abroad, that owing to the names mentioned in Queensberry's letters we were forced to abandon it.'[14] The most important name, of course, was that of the Prime Minister Lord Rosebery.

As generally expected, Taylor was convicted on the second day and stood down to await sentence until after Wilde's case had been heard. This led Queensberry, who was in court during Taylor's trial, immediately afterwards, to take a cab to St James's Street, Piccadilly, where he went into a post office and sent Minnie, his son Percy's wife, the following characteristically offensive telegram: 'Must congratulate on verdict. Cannot on Percy's appearance. Looks like dug up corpse. Fear too much madness of kissing. Taylor guilty. Wilde's turn tomorrow.'

Queensberry then crossed the street to return to his hotel when he saw his son Percy, Lord Douglas of Hawick. What happened then is not altogether clear. Apparently Percy approached his father and asked him if he intended to cease writing filthy letters to his wife. The marquess then struck out and hit his son in the eye, a scuffle ensued, a crowd collected, and finally a police officer separated them and arrested them both. Next morning they were charged with disorderly conduct at Marlborough Street police court, and since it was not evident to the magistrate who began the quarrel they were both bound over to keep the peace for six months in the sum of £500. The incident was widely reported in the press in this country and in America, while Percy was asked by the committee of his club, the Army and Navy, to explain his conduct. He did so in a letter which satisfied the committee that he was not to blame for the fracas and that in retaliating as he did he had acted under 'very grave provocation'. He added, for the committee's information, that feeling had been aroused against him because he had acted as bail for Wilde. 'Painful as it is to me to have to mention that matter,' he added, 'it is but common justice to myself that I should inform the committee that I did so with my mother's consent, solely because my brother [Alfred] made that the condition of his leaving the country, which all our family were exceedingly anxious he should do.' Consequently Percy was not asked to resign his membership of the Army and Navy Club.[15]

In his summing up of the evidence to the jury in Wilde's trial, the judge was obliged to mention Bosie in the context of the two letters to him from Oscar, which Bosie had left in the pocket of the suit of clothes he had given Wood in Oxford and on which Allen and Clibborn had attempted to blackmail him. 'Now, Lord Alfred Douglas is not present and is not a party to these proceedings,' said Mr Justice Wills, 'and it must be remembered in his favour that if neither side called him, he could not volunteer as a witness.... I am anxious, too, to say nothing, in the case of a young man like this who is just on the threshold of life, which might to a great extent blast his career.'

> I do not desire to comment more than I can help either about Lord Alfred Douglas or the Marquess of Queensberry, but I must say that the whole of this lamentable inquiry has arisen through the defendant's association with Lord Alfred Douglas. It is true that Lord Alfred's family seems to be a house divided against itself. But even if there was nothing but hatred between father and son, what father would not try to save his own son from the associations suggested by the two letters you have seen from the prisoner to Lord Alfred Douglas? I will avoid saying whether these letters point to actual criminal conduct or not. But they must be considered in relation to the other evidence in the case....

The foreman of the jury rose and interrupted the judge's summing up. He asked: 'In view of the intimacy between Lord Alfred Douglas and Mr Wilde, was a warrant ever issued for the apprehension of Lord Alfred Douglas?'

'I should think not,' Mr Justice Wills replied. 'We have not heard of it.'

'Was it ever contemplated?' the foreman went on to ask.

'Not to my knowledge,' said the judge. 'A warrant would in any case not be issued without evidence of some fact, of something more than intimacy. I cannot tell, nor need we discuss that, because Lord Alfred Douglas may yet have to answer a charge. He was not called. There may be a thousand considerations of which we may know nothing that might prevent his appearance in the witness box. I think you should deal with the matter upon the evidence before you.'

'But it seems to us,' the foreman persisted, 'that if we are to consider these letters as evidence of guilt, and if we adduce any guilt from these letters, it applies as much to Lord Alfred Douglas as to the defendant.'

'Quite so,' remarked the judge somewhat testily. 'But how does that relieve the defendant? Our present enquiry is whether guilt is brought home to the man in the dock. We have got the testimony as to *his* guilt to deal with now. I believe that to be the recipient of such letters and to continue the intimacy is as fatal to the reputation of the recipient as to the sender, but you have really nothing to do with that at present.'

> There is a natural disposition to ask [Mr Justice Wills continued] why should this man stand in the dock and not Lord Alfred Douglas? But, gentlemen of the jury, the supposition that Lord Alfred Douglas will be spared because he is Lord Alfred Douglas is one of the wildest injustice. The thing is utterly and hopelessly impossible! I must remind you that anything that can be said for or against Lord Alfred Douglas must not be allowed to prejudice the prisoner, and you must remember that no prosecution would be possible on the mere production of Mr Wilde's letters to Lord Alfred Douglas. Lord Alfred Douglas went to Paris at the request of the defendant, and there he has stayed, and I know absolutely nothing more about him. I am as ignorant in this respect as you are. It may be that there is no evidence against Lord Alfred Douglas. But even about that I know nothing. It is a thing we cannot discuss, and to entertain any such consideration as I have mentioned would be a prejudice of the worst possible kind.

Meanwhile Ross had returned to Rouen when Bosie went to Paris. About this time Bosie left Paris to rejoin Ross in Rouen, so that they were there when they read the news of Oscar's conviction and his sentence, the maximum of two years' imprisonment with hard labour. The same sentence was also passed on Taylor by Mr Justice Wills, who described the trials as the worst case he had ever tried. When he learned of his friend's fate, Bosie wrote to Sir Edward Clarke. His letter, which was found amongst Clarke's papers by his son after his death and shown to the present writer, indicates how Bosie really felt and how grateful he was to Clarke for his brilliant defence of Oscar Wilde for which the great counsel charged no fee.[16]

Hotel de la Poste,
Rouen
Sunday May 26th 1895

Dear Sir Edward,
    You will forgive me I am sure for writing to you now to thank

you from the bottom of my heart for your noble and generous and superb efforts on behalf of my friend.

It seems almost an impertinence for one so miserable as myself, so broken in heart and spirit, so defamed and ruined to offer you my poor gratitude, but believe me I shall never cease to think of you but with the profoundest gratitude and admiration. That you were unable to get a verdict seems to me, a layman, a piece of monstrous injustice, and the sentence was worse than I would have thought possible after the first disagreement.

Forgive this intrusion from one who is lying in the lowest hell of misery, and believe me to be

> Yours ever gratefully and sincerely,
> Alfred Douglas

Less wisely during the succeeding month, when he was still at Rouen, Bosie wrote letters to two journalists extolling the merits of homosexuality. The first was to W.T. Stead, editor of the *Review of Reviews*, who had commented on the Wilde case. The second was to Henry Labouchere, MP, the editor of *Truth* and the member who had moved the amendment to the Criminal Law Amendment Act under which Wilde had been convicted. Stead refused to publish Bosie's letter. But Labouchere published part of the letter sent to his journal. 'Certainly this exceptional moralist has the courage of his opinions,' he commented, 'but these opinions, being what they are, it is to be regretted that he is not afforded an opportunity to meditate on them in the seclusion of Pentonville [prison].'[17] The letter to Labouchere did Bosie considerable harm at the time and later when it was to be cited against him on a number of occasions in court.

On 25 June Bosie addressed a petition to Queen Victoria from which the following is an extract:

> I appeal to you to exercise your power of pardon in the case of Oscar Wilde, the poet and dramatist who now lies in prison, unjustly convicted by the force of prejudice; a victim not to the righteous indignation of abstract justice but rather to the spite and unscrupulous cunning of another man, the Marquess of Queensberry, whose son I have the misfortune to be. Your Majesty cannot be ignorant of the true character of this man, for he has not scrupled to speak of you in letters, which have been read in open court, in terms which not many years ago would have cost him his head or at least his liberty. Your Majesty will not have been deceived, as were the ignorant public, by his pretension to righteous motives but will have seen that his sole object in attacking

his son's friend was to dishonour that son and to add yet more misery, shame and sorrow to the load which he had already heaped on the head of the gentle misfortunate lady who was his wife.

The Queen's Private Secretary at Windsor intercepted the petition and did not show it to the Queen, who never saw it. Instead the Private Secretary sent it to the Home Secretary's Private Secretary, who showed it to the Home Secretary and the minister had a formal letter of rejection sent to Bosie in Rouen, as in the circumstances he was bound to do.[18]

5

Queensberry, who had stopped Bosie's allowance, now relented to the extent of writing to his son and telling him that he would restore the allowance and add to it if Bosie would renounce Oscar. He went on to suggest that Bosie should go to the South Sea islands for a time, since he would find 'plenty of beautiful girls' there. Not unnaturally Bosie ignored this communication, since, as he told More Adey, a discreet homosexual and a Catholic, who was spending a week or two with him at Rouen at this time, he had 'nothing on earth to live for except Oscar.' Meanwhile Sibyl Queensberry, although not herself a Catholic, had asked Father Sebastian Bowden, an old friend who was a priest at Brompton Oratory, if he could find 'some steady and trustworthy friend to look after her son' and to prevent him as far as possible from rushing into any wild courses 'through a mistaken sense of standing by one who is down, and generally to draw him into a good and sensible mode of life.' By a coincidence Father Bowden already had Adey in mind and had written to him asking him to undertake 'a work of real charity'. Lady Queensberry also offered to pay Adey's expenses if he would prolong his stay and 'look after' Bosie without letting him know the nature of his role. To this Adey agreed, although he made it clear that he could not stay with Bosie indefinitely. Bosie apparently had thought of going to Florence and staying with Lord Henry Somerset, which Father Bowden thought would be 'a great mistake'. At the same time Robbie Ross's family forbade him to stay any longer with Bosie, so Ross was obliged to remove himself to Dieppe and to return to England in July 1895. Indeed, as the priest wrote to Adey, 'my fears are that AD is at present so self-willed and blinded as to be humanly speaking beyond Redemption.' Bosie also engaged in an occasional homosexual intrigue, since, when Ross was in Dieppe, Bosie sent him 'a gourmet of great personal beauty'. The 'gourmet' is only referred to by his first name, Maurice, in a letter from Bosie to Ross, but he was almost certainly Maurice Gilbert, who became a great friend of Oscar in his last years in Paris and whom Ross no doubt introduced to him there.

From Rouen Bosie and More Adey moved on in July to Havre, where Adey left him in 'nice rooms' facing the sea in the Hotel Continental. Here Bosie was able to rent a boat, and engaged two young sailors as crew. But he had not been out more than two or three times with them when the local paper, the *Journal de Havre*, heard of these voyages and accused Bosie of corrupting the youth of the town. 'It is already too evident that the world has the right to insult and injure me because I am Oscar Wilde's friend,' he wrote in French to the editor who published his letter on 1 August. 'That is my crime, not because I was his friend, but because I will be until my death, and even after that if God wills.'

Bosie then left France for Italy where he stayed at the Villa Tarnasse in Sorrento which he took for a month. 'Dear More,' he wrote to Adey from there, 'if you could only come out here a little I can't tell you what it would be to me. I am utterly wretched for want of a kindred spirit.... Do come and save me from despair. I need hardly say the place is supremely lovely, and the weather perfect.' But Adey could not manage it, and Bosie moved on again, this time to a small villa, the Villa Caso in the Strada Pastano in Capri, which he took for a year. 'I am very unhappy,' he wrote to André Gide on 22 September 1895. 'Yesterday I had some terrible news of Oscar. I am told that he is suffering terribly, that he cannot sleep and that he has not enough to eat.'[19] This news came from the journalist Robert Sherard, who had come over from Paris where he was working and visited Wilde in Wandsworth prison, to which Wilde had been transferred from Pentonville. At the same time Sherard had given some of the details of his condition to the London *Daily Chronicle* which published them.

On his way from Havre to Naples, in August 1895, Bosie had to change trains in Paris. Apparently he spent a day or two in Paris and while he was there he was asked by the well-known monthly literary magazine *Mercure de France* to write an article giving his version of the Oscar Wilde affair. He accepted and when he reached Sorrento he sat down and wrote the article in English, since he did not think his French was good enough, although judging by his letters to André Gide his command of that language was already adequate. The article included three affectionate letters which Oscar had written to him from Holloway prison while he was on remand there, and the whole was translated into French by a member of the magazine's staff, Henry D. Davray. Sherard, who heard about this from Davray with whom he was friendly, accordingly informed Wilde at their meeting and asked him if it was his wish that the article with the letters should appear. Considering that it was due to Bosie's carelessness that two of the more compromising examples of their correspondence had been produced by Queensberry with deadly effect at Wilde's trials, it was hardly surprising that the prisoner should have been 'greatly taken aback and much annoyed,' to use his own words, and have asked Sherard to 'have the thing stopped at once.' This was the original cause of Oscar's turning against Bosie in prison. As he was later to write to him:

> You had left my letters lying about for blackmailing companions to steal, for hotel servants to pilfer, for housemaids to sell. That was simply your careless want of appreciation of what I had written to you. But that you should seriously propose to publish selections from the balance was incredible to me. And which of my letters were they? I could get no information. That was my first news of you. It displeased me.[20]

When Sherard returned to Paris, he wrote to the editor of the *Mercure de France* asking him not to publish the letters, but without telling Bosie that he had done so, conduct which Bosie described in a letter to Sherard when he heard of it as 'exceedingly impertinent and in the worst possible taste.' In the result the *Mercure de France* asked Bosie to omit the letters from the article. But Bosie refused since he considered that 'it was useless to publish the article without the letters,' feeling strongly as he did that the letters with the article would contribute to Oscar's rehabilitation, at any rate in France. Consequently the project was dropped and neither article nor letters appeared. When Ross later asked Bosie to give him the letters for Oscar, Bosie again refused and subsequently destroyed the letters, an action which he later regretted.

Meanwhile Ross had come out to Capri and stayed with Bosie in his villa. Although Ross's visit cheered him up, as before that he had been alone, Bosie was upset by what he learned of Oscar's feelings towards him. Consequently he wrote to More Adey whom he had heard was going to see Oscar soon:

> Of course, I *know everything* and I know from what I have heard from Bobbie that my instinct was right and that Oscar has changed about me. I am writing to you now, dear More, unknown to Bobbie, to beg you to do what you can for me with Oscar. If only

you could make him understand that though he is in prison he is still the court, the jury, the judge of my life and that I am waiting hoping for some sign that I have to go on living. There is nobody to play my cards in England, nobody to say anything for me, and Oscar depends *entirely* on what is said to him, and they all seem to be my enemies. . ..

I am not in prison but I think I suffer as much as Oscar, in fact more, just as I am sure he would have suffered more if he had been free and I in prison. Please tell him that. Can't you tell him this and tell him to send me some message? If you could only show him a photograph for a minute I think it might give him back his soul again. Do try and do this; there is a little photograph of me in cap and gown at Oxford that Bobbie had. How can he expect anything from his wife, what did she do for him when he was in trouble and how can he have changed so?

The only thing that could make his life bearable is to think that he is suffering for me because he loved me, and if he doesn't love me I can't live and it is so utterly easy to die. Do work for me, More, and even if you cut him to the heart and make him unhappy you will only be doing him good if you can only make him love me again and know that he is being martyred for my sake. It is such a joy for me to suffer anything for him. Tell him that I know I have ruined his life, that everything is my fault, if that pleases him. I don't care. Doesn't he think that my life is just as much ruined as his and so much sooner? I am drivelling now, so good-bye and do something for me.[21]

In fact Adey had seen Oscar shortly before he got Bosie's letter, and some time must elapse before he would be allowed another visit. He could only send a conciliatory reply telling Bosie that he understood what Oscar's change of attitude must mean to him, but he believed it was no more than a kind of passing delirium of jail moral fever. He had told Oscar that Bosie would not write again – Bosie had written to the Governor asking him to secure the prisoner's assent to the publication of his letters in the article for the *Mercure de France*. 'You must try to show the love which I know you have for him,' Adey concluded, 'by the most difficult of all things – *waiting*.'

Ross was still with Bosie in Capri in the first fortnight of January 1896 when the weather became so bad, wet and stormy, that they were obliged to migrate to Naples where they put up temporarily at Parker's Hotel Tramontano in the Corso Vittorio Emanuele, then much frequented by English visitors. Shortly afterwards Ross left him to return to England, while Bosie found a pension kept by an Englishwoman in Posilipo, the Villa Capella, into which he moved in February, since he could live there for 6 to 8 francs (lire) a day. Meanwhile he wrote to André Gide on 14 February 1896 to tell him how pleased he was to read in the papers that *Salome* had been successfully staged at the Theatre de l'Oeuvre in Paris by the actor-manager A.M. Lugné-Poe, who also played the part of Herod with Lina Munte as Salome and Max Barbier as Jokanaan. ('It is something that at a time of disgrace and shame I should still be regarded as an artist,' Wilde wrote to Ross from Reading prison, to which he had now been transferred.) In another letter from Posilipo, Bosie, who was alone in the apartment, wrote to Gide: 'I spend my time meditating and playing Bach.' (Gide was also a great Bach enthusiast.)

In the first letter to André Gide Bosie quoted a sonnet he had dedicated to those French men of letters 'who refused to compromise their spotless reputations or imperil their literary exclusiveness by signing a merciful petition in favour of Oscar Wilde.' The petition was organised by Stuart Merrill, an American poet who lived in Paris and wrote in French, and was a plea for clemency addressed to Queen Victoria, as Bosie's had been. Those who refused to sign included Emile Zola, Alphonse Daudet, Francois Coppée, Victorien Sardou and others. Bosie's sonnet, which was not published at the time, read:

> Not all the singers of a thousand years
> Can open English prisons. No. Through hell
> Opened for Thracian Orpheus, now the spell
> Of art and song and art is powerless as the tears
> That love has shed. You that were full of fears
> And mean self-love, shall live to love full well
> That you yourselves, not he, were pitiable.
> When you met mercy's voice with frowns and jeers.
>
> And did you ask who signed the plea with you?
> Fools! It was signed already with the sign
> Of great dead men, of god-like Socrates,
> Shakespeare and Plato and the Florentine
> Who conquered form. And all your petty crew
> Once, and once only, might have stood with these!

Bosie sent the sonnet to *The Savoy*, the *avant-garde* journal started by Arthur Symons and Aubrey Beardsley in London, after Beardsley had been dismissed as art-editor of *The Yellow Book*. But Bosie's letter was not even acknowledged, and the manuscript of the sonnet of which he had omitted to keep a copy was not returned to him. 'To do the French justice,' Bosie wrote long afterwards, 'there were at least one or two reviews published at that time in Paris which would have printed the sonnet if I had asked their editors to do it, but as in those days not one Frenchman in five thousand spoke or understood a word of English, I did not think it worth while to ask them.' He went on:

> This was, I now feel, a piece of foolishness on my part, as although they did not understand English (Mallarmé and Verlaine were notable exceptions), French men of letters *were* interested in my poetry, as is proved by the reviews I got and by the fact that a thousand copies of my poems, published in Paris in 1896 by the *Mercure de France* with a prose translation in French, were sold, and that a few years later I was twice asked by Alfred Vallette, the Editor of the *Mercure*, to let him bring out a new edition; but this I would not agree to do, because some of the poems in the collection were considered by English critics and friends to be improper and the rest had by that time been published in London. There was really nothing much wrong about these suppressed poems, and when the latest edition of my poems appeared two years ago [1935] (in two volumes, *Lyrics* and *Sonnets*) they were all reprinted.[22]

6

Another French journal, less generally known and with a smaller circulation than the *Mercure de France*, although more *avant-garde* in its opinions, was the *Revue Blanche*. The editor had published five of Bosie's poems, and then asked him if he would add some reflections on the Wilde case in the form of an article in the next issue. Bosie agreed, and as he had done with the draft of the unpublished *Mercure de France* article, he wrote his piece in English, after which it was translated into French by one Felix Féneon. Bosie's original draft has been preserved and an extract follows, which it will be observed gives some credence to the Solicitor-General Sir Frank Lockwood's reply to Carson's plea for leniency quoted above.

'It is curious to reflect that had I the good fortune to live in Athens in the time of Pericles,' he wrote, 'the very conduct which at present has led to my disgrace would then have resulted in my glory. Today I am proud that I have been loved by a great poet, who, perhaps, esteemed me because he recognised that besides a beautiful body I possessed a beautiful soul.' For the reversal of public opinion and the 'ignorant persecution of the excellent persons who are in very truth the salt of the earth,' he blamed the Roman Catholic Church.

> I am confident that the Government did not wish to let the prosecution of Oscar Wilde take its regular course. My readers will

recall that the first criminal trial resulted in a disagreement of the jury and the question is consequently pertinent – why did the Crown take the very irregular course of having a second trial – why was the prosecution conducted with this extraordinary animosity; briefly why did the Crown manifest so eager a desire to obtain a verdict of guilty? The reason is very simple. The Government was intimidated; the second trial was the result of a political intrigue. I would wish to ask Mr Asquith, the then Home Secretary and an old friend of Oscar Wilde, if he was not threatened by Lord Rosebery that if a second trial was not instituted and a verdict of guilty obtained against Mr Wilde, the Liberal party would be removed from power. The fact is that the Liberal party then contained a large number of men whom I have referred to as the salt of the earth. The maniacs of virtue threatened a series of legal actions which would have created an unprecedented scandal in Europe – a scandal in political circles. If Oscar Wilde was found guilty the matter would be hushed up. This was the cause of the second trial, and the verdict of guilty. It was a degrading *coup-d'état* – the sacrifice of a great poet to save a degraded band of politicians.

The conviction of Oscar Wilde was one of the last acts of this disgraceful and discredited Liberal Party who is now in an exceptional minority in the House of Commons.

There is nothing more to say. Oscar Wilde is in jail and will remain there till the expiration of his sentence. A national crime has been committed, a crime from which no element of morbid intrigue, sensuality, cruelty and hypocrisy is wanting. ...

In English politics the Liberals had been succeeded by a Conservative administration headed by Lord Salisbury, with Mr Arthur Balfour as Leader of the House of Commons. Douglas pointed out in the final paragraphs of his article that Balfour was a man of culture and a philosopher who had been a friend of Wilde's and was an admirer of his genius. This was the person who might help. Accordingly, Douglas appealed to the leading writers in France, in particular to Henri Bauer, Paul Adam and Octave Mirbeau, whom he mentioned by name, to write personally to the Conservative leader and urge him to release the prisoner. The new Government had shown solicitude for Dr Jameson and his band of filibusters in the Transvaal. Certainly a poet and an artist had an equal claim to their protection. And now, asked Douglas in conclusion, who would play the part of Nicodemus to Mr Balfour?

Opinion in France at this time as expressed in the literary journals was unanimous in condemning the sentiments expressed in this article. Writers such as Henri Bauer, who had been prominent for their sympathy towards Wilde in the hour of his tragedy, stigmatised

Douglas's intervention as clumsy and sensational. The repercussions were not slow in making themselves felt on the editor's head; and it is significant that, in the following issue of the *Revue Blanche*, Douglas was at pains to point out in the course of an explanatory statement that '*l'amour de mon ami pour moi était platonique, c'est-à-dire pur.*' But there is no doubt that the article did Douglas a great deal of harm, and it made his stay in France much more difficult and embarrassing for him than it otherwise might have been.

However he may have continued to feel about Lord Rosebery and the late Liberal administration, it must always be remembered in justice to his reputation that Lord Alfred Douglas lived to modify very considerably his views on the controversial subject of homosexuality. Nevertheless, for many years after the publication of the notorious *Revue Blanche* article these views remained unchanged.[23]

Towards the end of March 1896 Bosie left Naples for Paris to arrange for the publication of his poems. It is true that they contained such homosexual efforts as 'In Praise of Shame' and 'Two Loves' ('I am the Love that Dare not Speak its Name'), which had appeared in *The Chameleon* and been quoted in the Wilde trials, as well as 'In an Aegean Port', which Kains-Jackson had originally published in *The Artist*. Hence Bosie's unwillingness to include them in *The City of the Soul* and other collections of his poems which appeared from time to time in England during the ensuing forty years. He spent six months in Paris, correcting the text as well as the French prose translation on the opposite page. The translation was the work of Eugene Tardieu, 'a man of considerable talent and charming personality, who was on the staff of the *Echo de Paris*,' and who according to Bosie, wished to dedicate the poems to Oscar with the translation. He told Ross this, and Ross relayed the news to Oscar when he and Robert Sherard together visited him at Reading in May. In the circumstances Oscar's reaction was predictable. 'Will you write at once to him and say he must not do anything of the kind,' Oscar told Ross. 'I would not accept or allow such a dedication. The proposal is revolting and grotesque.'[24] The result was that the poems eventually appeared without any dedication. On 30 October 1896 they were published in book form by the *Mercure de France* at 3 francs 50 centimes for the ordinary copies and 10 and 25 francs respectively for the fifty *de luxe* copies and the twenty-five *de grand luxe* copies on Japanese vellum. All the copies are now great rarities. Bosie gave so many away that when he came to write his autobiography in 1929, he did not possess a single copy of any of the editions. Nor, somewhat surprisingly, did he send his mother a copy, although she was paying him a generous allowance; she had to write to Adey asking him to get one for her.

For most of this period Bosie was not without company, since besides Adey and Ross, his brother Percy and his mother visited him in Paris. 'We left Bosie this morning,' Sibyl Queensberry wrote to More Adey on 16 May 1896. 'He is well now but looks very white and thin. I hope you will try and get him to take care of himself. ... You must draw on me further if you find living in Paris too expensive, but I hope Bosie will not have to be there much longer.' She had previously written to Adey about Percy: 'I hope very much that Lord Douglas is not to be asked to come forward in any way or do anything further for your friend. He has already done himself a great deal of harm and sacrificed himself for his brother to the utmost and he ought not to be expected to do any more.' Apart from his short visit to Bosie in Paris, Percy did not further associate himself with Bosie, or Oscar for that matter. Since his return from Australia his finances were very shaky due to unsuccessful speculations on the Stock Exchange, and he was already borrowing from moneylenders on the expectation of his succession to the Queensberry title and what was left of the family estate.

Sibyl Queensberry also told More Adey at this time that she had seen her lawyer and he had given her an important piece of advice. 'He assured me that he had the best possible authority for saying that it would be highly dangerous for Bosie to come back to either England or Scotland,' she wrote: 'he was *most emphatic* on the subject so that I am sure he has good reason for what he says and he assured me that on no account must he think of returning at present or for a long time to come, so I hope you will impress this on Bosie.'[25]

Bosie decided to disregard this advice, and proposed to go to England and visit Oscar at Reading. 'I wrote informing Robert Ross of my intention,' he has recorded, 'and in reply he told me that he had just come from Wilde and that, as his correspondence and visitors were strictly limited, he (Wilde) desired that I should neither write nor visit him. ... I was very upset on receiving this news, and I had some thought of trying to obtain an interview with Wilde through influence which I possessed; but I was told that it would be bad for Wilde if I did so, and I accordingly determined to follow out his wishes and to wait until he could write or send [someone] to me.' (The influence Bosie mentioned was no doubt his cousin George Wyndham, MP.)[26] In his action Robert Ross showed duplicity. He had been Wilde's lover long before Douglas – indeed there is good reason for believing that it was Ross who initiated Wilde into homosexual practices. While outwardly remaining on friendly terms with Bosie and staying with him as his guest, he was really jealous of him and in his correspondence and meetings with Wilde in prison probably he ran down Douglas and emphasised his comfortable lifestyle in Naples and Capri compared with Wilde's in Reading.

On 27 September 1896, Bosie wrote from Paris to More Adey: 'Lugné-Poe told me the other day that he had seen the Leversons at their house in London and that they had abused me very much and told him that I prevented Oscar from going away when he was out on bail. I wrote a very nice letter to Leverson telling him what Lugné-Poe had said and asking for a denial or some explanation, but I have had no reply at all. Can you do anything to elucidate the mystery? I am *very fond* of the Leversons, very fond of both and I am much distressed at their quite inexplicable conduct.' Here again it is not difficult to see Robert Ross's malevolence at work. Finally, on 31 January 1897, Lady Queensberry, who was wintering in Italy with her daughter Edith, wrote to More Adey from Rome where Bosie had joined them:

> I have been so pleased to find Alfred looking so much better than I have seen him for a long time and very bright and cheerful. He tells me Mr Ross is urging him to advertise his poems in London papers and is trying to get them reviewed even if they are to be slated. I think this would be a great mistake and from what Bosie said to me I don't think he quite likes the idea himself.
>
> I find the English people here very kind to him and he has many nice friends and I am *sure* it would be a great pity to bring him prominently before the public now; it would make it more difficult for him and for us all in every way.*
>
> The poems have sold wonderfully well without any pushing or advertising which is surely much better and more dignified – everyone admires them and they are sure to make their way in time. Later on he can bring out an English edition with a few additions.
>
> Please do not tell Bosie I have written or Mr Ross unless you can trust him not to mention it, but try and persuade him to stop urging him into publicity. I fear, too, rousing his Father again. I am sure his talents will be recognised in time, and I think it wonderful that the 1st edition is so nearly sold out.

On one point Bosie was adamant, that his feelings towards Oscar had not changed, whatever Oscar might now be thinking or saying about him. 'The last time I saw him,' Bosie told More Adey at this time, 'he kissed the end of my finger through an iron grating at Newgate, and he begged me to let nothing in the world alter my attitude and my conduct towards him.'

*'It may interest your husband and disgusted me,' Constance Wilde wrote to a friend at this time, 'to hear that A[lfred] D[ouglas] is received in society by the embassy at Rome and by private persons at Nice. So much it is with a bourgeois nation to be of the aristocracy!'

He wrote to me in the same strain many times and he warned me
that all sorts of influences would be brought to bear upon me to
make me change; but I have not changed. From first to last I have
been absolutely consistent and absolutely the same. I shall not
change now. I decline to listen to anything he says while he is in
prison. If he really means what he says and if he is really not mad,
he is not the same person that I knew and he is not Oscar, the
Oscar to whom I shall always be faithful and who belongs to me
quite absolutely. When lovers quarrel, they return to each other
their letters and presents. I and Oscar were lovers, but we have not
quarrelled, and as I have not asked for a return of my letters and
presents he cannot ask for his. If Oscar really meant what he says
now, I should despise him utterly, for no meanness could be lower,
and I should be obliged to think that what many people have over
and over again told me about him is true.

But I do not believe that he means what he says, and I regard
what he says as non-existent. I ignore the cruel insults and the
unmerited reproaches which I am told his lips have uttered against
me. I attribute them simply to an evil and lying spirit which at
present inhabits Oscar's body, a spirit borne in an English prison,
out of English 'prison discipline', and which I hope in spite of
everybody and everything to ultimately cast out of him. But even if
I shall never cast it out, even if Oscar's body is always to be
inhabited by this thing, even if the last time I saw Oscar I really
said goodbye to him for ever and ever (at least in this world), I
should still love and be faithful to my own Oscar, the real one, *and* I
should always refuse to take any notice of English prison spirits. I
daresay you think I am talking nonsense, but I mean every word I
say, and that is enough on this subject.[27]

7

Early in 1897, in late January or early February, More Adey visited
Oscar in Reading prison, after which he wrote to Bosie and told him
that Oscar was writing to him and in fact had already begun his letter.
This was the *De Profundis* letter, parts of which Ross was to publish
five years after Wilde's death. In its complete and unexpurgated form
the letter began 'Dear Bosie' and ended 'Your affectionate friend
Oscar Wilde.' In fact much of the letter was neither affectionate nor
friendly, although Adey appears to have advised Oscar to avoid
recriminations – advice which Oscar largely ignored. 'You have
suggested that at least as a matter of policy it is useless to curse and
insult me,' Bosie wrote to Adey on 8 February 1897, 'and for that I am
mildly grateful to you. You know I have never been able to

understand either your or Bobbie's point of view in this matter, or your extraordinary and sudden change of front and complete abnegation or what you said before.' In short he accused Adey and Ross of having 'at least to a great extent gone over to the enemy' and were now really playing Queensberry's cards for him.

> In the early part of the proceedings I was, as you know, absolutely deceived in the most complete way as to the real state of affairs, no doubt with the best of intentions but with as a matter of fact the most deplorable results. For had I the least idea of Oscar's real state of mind towards me, I would never have sent him that unfortunate message about the dedication of my book [of poems] which brought the actual storm on my head. But perhaps you don't think that deplorable.
>
> What you are working for I don't know and I don't understand, but the inconsistencies of both you and Bobbie I may tell you quite frankly I put down to the baleful influence of the Catholic Church. The fact of belonging to and really believing in that institution puts such a gulf between you and Bobbie on the one hand and real pagans with a real sense of the supremacy of Greek love over everything else such as Oscar and I, that it is impossible for you to understand what I think about it, and what Oscar would think if he were in his normal condition. I feel I have been out-witted and out-intrigued all through, and *sans amertume* I tell you both that when I get the chance I will fight with any weapons I can find.... It requires all my previous knowledge of you to refrain from saying that all this about it 'being better for Oscar and I not to meet' et cet is canting humbug. But as it is, I am content to call it Popish weakness coupled with social cowardice.
>
> I look forward without excitement to Oscar's letter. Indeed I wonder he writes. What he can have to say to me unless one thing I cannot understand, and if he is going to abuse me I would rather not see it. In all his life he has never written me a letter that was unkind or at least unloving and to see anything terrible in his handwriting written directly to me would almost kill me. However he must do as he pleases, and I will write [back] again only what I think will be agreeable to him.

Finally, he asked Adey, first, when he might expect Oscar's letter, and secondly, the exact date of Oscar's release.[28] Adey's reply has not survived, but whatever he wrote was probably to the effect that he could not say when Bosie might expect the letter, but that it would be despatched by Adey himself in accordance with Oscar's instructions to Ross. As for Oscar's release this was fixed for 19 May 1897, two years to the day since his conviction; in those days no remission for good conduct was allowed and the petitions to the Home Secretary for an earlier release had come to nothing. Before Oscar's release, which took place on that date from Pentonville, his wife's solicitors had executed a deed of arrangement by which Oscar agreed to surrender his life interest in his marriage settlement in return for an annual allowance of £150 from her, provided he did nothing which would entitle Constance to a divorce or a decree of judicial separation, or 'be guilty of any moral misconduct, or notoriously consort with evil or disreputable companions.'

'I have no doubt that you or Mr Ross or some other one of his friends will be seeing him before his release on the 19th,' Constance's solicitor wrote to More Adey on 10 May, 'and I do hope you will impress upon him, as Mr Hansell [Wilde's solicitor] has already done, how absolutely fatal to him any further intercourse with Lord Alfred Douglas will be: apart from the fact that Lord Alfred Douglas is a "notoriously disreputable companion" Lord Queensberry has made arrangements for being informed if his son joins Mr Wilde and has expressed his intention of shooting one or both. A threat of this kind from most people could be more or less disregarded, but there is no doubt that Lord Queensberry, as he has shown before, will carry out any threat he makes to the best of his ability.'

On the day of his release Oscar together with More Adey took the night boat to Dieppe, where they were met by Robbie Ross and Reggie Turner. They spent a week in a hotel, the Sandwich, after which Oscar and Ross moved to the Hotel de la Plage at Berneval, a seaside village about eight miles from Dieppe. Here Oscar used the name Sebastian Melmoth, and when Bosie learned he was there, probably from More Adey, he wrote to him addressing his letter with this pseudonym. 'Bosie has written, for him nicely – on literature and my play [*Salome*],' Oscar wrote to Ross on 3 June. At the same time he replied to Bosie in friendly terms though not with particular affection:

> The production of *Salome* was the thing that turned the scale in my favour, as far as my treatment in prison by the Government was concerned, and I am deeply grateful to all concerned in it. Upon the other hand I could not give a play for nothing, as I simply do not know how I shall live after the summer is over unless I at once make money. I am in a terrible and dangerous position, for money that I had been assured was set aside for me was not forthcoming when I wanted it. It was a horrible disappointment: for I have of course to begin to live as a man of letters should live – that is with a private sitting room and books and the like. I can see no other way

of living, if I am to write, though I can see many others if I am not. ...

I hear the *Jour* has had a sort of interview – a false one – with you. This is very distressing: as much I don't doubt, to you as to me. I hope however it is not the cause of the duel you hint at. Once you get to fight duels in France, you have to be *always* doing it, and it is a nuisance. I do hope that you will always decline a duel, unless of course some personal fracas or public insult takes place. Of course you will never dream of fighting a duel for me: that would be awful, and create the worst and most odious impression.

Always write to me about your art and the art of others. It is better to meet on the double peak of Parnassus than elsewhere. I have read your poems with great pleasure and interest: but on the whole your best work is to me still the work you did two years and a half ago – the ballads. ... You have real sympathy with the Ballads. ... The recurring phrases of *Salome*, that bind it together like a piece of music with recurring *motifs*, are, and were to me, the artistic equivalent of the refrains of the old ballads. All this is to beg you to write ballads.

I do not know whether I have to thank you or More for the books from Paris, probably both. As I have divided the books, so you must divide the thanks.[29]

No doubt the books included the *Mercure de France* edition of Bosie's poems, which had come out in the previous year. As for Bosie's interview, this appeared on the front page of *Le Jour* on 28 May and was signed Adolphe Possien. In it Bosie described Oscar's sufferings in prison and blamed English hypocrisy. However the editorial comment was hostile declaring that in Paris the name of Oscar Wilde was synonymous with '*pathologie passionelle.*'

'The interview is quite harmless,' Oscar wrote to Bosie next day when he had read it, 'and I am sorry you took any notice of it. I *do* hope it is not with the low-class journalist that you are to fight, if that absurd experience is in store for you. Let me know by telegram if anything has happened.' At the same time he added in a note to Ross on the subject of a duel in France: 'Though it is not dangerous, like our English cricket or football is, still it is a tedious game to be always playing.' Anyhow Bosie took Oscar's advice and the duel was called off.'[30]

Oscar's letters soon became more affectionate, 'Don't think I don't love you,' he assured Bosie on 4 June. 'Of course I love you more than anyone else. But our lives are irreparably severed, as far as meeting goes. What is left to us is the knowledge that we love each other, and every day I think of you, and I know you are a poet, and that makes you doubly dear and wonderful.' Soon he was writing to 'My dearest Boy,' as he used to, and eventually he invited Bosie to come and stay with him in his chalet at Berneval on 19 June using the name Jonquil de Vallon. But two days before he was due to leave Paris, Bosie got a telegram putting him off and telling him to await a letter. The letter arrived next day and was to the effect that Oscar's solicitor had written to him telling him that it would be dangerous for him to come as Queensberry was having Oscar watched.

> Of course it is impossible for us to meet [Oscar wrote]. I have to find out what grounds my solicitor has for this sudden action, and of course if your father – or rather Q, as I only know him and think of him – if Q came over and made a scene and a scandal it would utterly destroy my possible future and alienate all my friends from me. I owe my friends everything, including the clothes I wear, and I would be wretched if I did anything that would separate them from me.
>
> So simply we must write to each other: about the things we love, about poetry and the coloured arts of our age, and that passage of ideas into images that is the intellectual history of art. I think of you always, and love you always, but chasms of moonless night divide us. We cannot cross it without hideous and nameless peril.
>
> Later on, when the alarm in England is over, when secrecy is possible, and silence forms part of the world's attitude, we may meet, but at present you see it is impossible. I would be harassed, agitated, nervous. It would be no joy for me to let you see me as I am now.[31]

Meanwhile Bosie was carrying on a somewhat acrimonious correspondence with Robert Ross, whom he had accused of being responsible with More Adey for an arrangement with Constance Wilde which would result in Oscar losing his allowance of £150 if he and Oscar were to consort together. On 23 June Ross wrote to Bosie from London:

> If you want to know what I suggest as a way out of the ridiculous position in which you say More and I have placed Oscar (I repeat that I am far more responsible than More) I suggest that you contribute something to Oscar's support or that you get your brother to fulfil his promise to give Oscar £500 as soon as he is able and in a position to do so. I am well aware that he is able and in a position to do so. You are much better off than any three of us and you have not contributed a penny either to setting Oscar up or giving him money for immediate use or providing an income for him.

At all events I should have thought you had good taste enough *under these circumstances* not to write the sort of things you do, though I can easily understand and sympathise with your irritation and annoyance at any arrangement which deprives you of seeing Oscar. However you are not the sort of person to allow £150 a year to stand in the way of your wishes. Provide £150 on your own account, and then let Oscar choose which he likes. With your £150 he will have the added pleasure of your perpetual society and your inspiring temper for the future. £150 is not much of a sacrifice – you spend more at the races every year in Paris. And when you have found the £150 it will be your opportunity to revile Adey and myself for having lost you £150 a year with which you have to support Oscar, your dearest friend. Until you have done this it would be more seemly to be silent.[32]

Bosie sent Ross's letter to Adey with one from himself, in which he reproached Ross for going out of his way 'to let me know that he is responsible for what has happened, and in the letter I read behind the words his own satisfaction that after all I have been baffled of my long hope and long expectation.' Bosie's letter to Adey, dated 4 July from Nogent-sur-Marne, where he was staying in a little cheap inn, continued:

As for what Bobbie says about money in his letter, it doesn't affect me much. It seems to me so very unimportant and (as I have made him enraged by saying) he and I look at money from two different natural points of view. I have no money.

Bobbie says I am richer than any three of you. Of course even as a matter of the strictest fact and allowing for the ridiculous exaggeration of bad temper, this is *most grossly false*. I have about £350 a year, but with that I have to pay everything and I am alone. I don't know what you have, but I know Bobbie has £200 a year, that he and you have a sort of ménage together (which makes an enormous difference) and that besides that he lives when he likes at home [with his mother] and has all the necessaries of life for nothing. Therefore he is *at least* as well off as I am. His money is mere pocket money, and it is his own fault if he has not more as it is only sheer indolence that prevents him from earning at least £150 more a year [from writing] as he used to. But even apart from all that, it is no use reproaching me with my failure ever to have any money. I know I am frightfully extravagant, but nobody except people of the Lady Henry Somerset type reproach people for that sort of thing.

Although it makes Bobbie very angry, I must repeat that I was brought up differently from him, and my views and ways about money are the result of my breeding and my blood. The idea of my being able to send any money to Oscar out of my own pocket is simply comic to me. It would only mean that I should have to try to get more out of my own people to cover the deficit, as *I have no money of my own.* Instead of doing that, I prefer to try to procure money for him at the primary source, that is through my own people, and that I have done and will continue to do. On the other hand if we lived together, I should simply like him to have all my money paid to him, as to be dependent absolutely on him. It would be a very good thing for me.

Bosie added that he had already spent his July allowance although it was only the 4th of the month. Also he owed a bill for six weeks for his rooms in Paris as well as a week's bill at Nogent and at the moment he possessed exactly 4 francs 75 centimes. 'When or how I am hoping to get more I haven't the least idea!'

When he heard of what Bosie had written on the subject of social differences, Oscar expressed himself vigorously to Ross:

As regards Bosie, I feel you have been as usual, forbearing and sweet, and too good-tempered. What he must be made to feel is that his vulgar and ridiculous assumption of social superiority must be retracted and apologised for. I have written to him to tell him that *quand on est gentilhomme on est gentilhomme,* and that for him to try and pose as your social superior because he is the third son of a Scotch marquis and you the third son of a commoner is offensively stupid. There is no difference between gentlemen. Questions of title are matters of heraldry – no more. I wish you would be strong on this point; the thing should be thrashed out of him. As for his coarse ingratitude in abusing you, to whom, as I have told him, I owe any possibility I have of a new and artistic career, and indeed of life at all, I have no words in which to express my contempt for his lack of imaginative insight, and his dullness of sensitive nature. It makes me quite furious. So pray write, when next you do so, quite calmly, and say that you will not allow any nonsense of social superiority, and that if he cannot understand that gentlemen are gentlemen and no more, you have no desire to hear again from him.[33]

It appears that Sibyl Queensberry had recently been in Paris and taken an apartment for her son in the Avenue Kléber with a *femme-de-ménage* called Marie. She wrote to More Adey asking him if he knew anything about Oscar's movements, as she was thinking of going to a small seaside place somewhere in Normandy and hoped that Oscar would not be in the neighbourhood. 'I suppose he has definitely taken up his residence in Paris,' she added. 'I had unfortunately just settled

Alfred in rooms there and I hear they are together. It is most heartbreaking.'[34] What seems to have happened is that Bosie offered the apartment to Oscar and thought he was actually there, judging from the following letter, one of only three from Bosie to Oscar known to exist.

> Grand Hotel des Parisiens,
> Villerville,
> Calvados.
> 22 July 1897

Dearest Oscar,

I was very glad to get a letter from you *at last*. It is a week tomorrow since I left [Paris] and the time seems ages being here by myself. I really don't know what to do about everything. I am penniless again. I suppose it is no use asking you to send me a louis (which I think you owe me), but if you happen to have it I wish you would send a mandat postale or even ten francs. I am sorry now I left Paris so soon as my people don't seem able to come just yet and it is wretchedly dull here by myself. If I had enough money I would come straight back to Paris leaving my things here.

I had another letter from Albert [the innkeeper at Nogent] yesterday to which I replied. I wish you would ask Strong [*The Observer* Paris correspondent] if he could send his servant Leon down to fetch my things from Nogent. I have written to Albert about it so it will be all right and it is such a bore having my things there in case I want to come to Paris. I shall write by this same post to Strong asking him to lend me a couple of louis, and if I get that I will come back to Paris. On second thoughts I shall wire him, so I may be in Paris on Sunday or even tomorrow.

[Later] I have just wired Strong asking him to telegraph me 50 francs, so if you get this tomorrow (Saturday) morning, do go round and see him and explain that I must get back to Paris to settle up these people and also explain to him that if he can lend me 50 francs it is no use sending a mandat postale as his letter would arrive on Sunday and I should not be able to get it changed. Perhaps between you you may be able to raise 50 francs!

I simply can't stand being here now that the weather has turned bad and my people aren't coming for ages. When I get back to Paris I will wire home for £10 and settle up all these people, stay another week in Paris and then come on here to wait until my mother comes. Don't you think this is the best thing? I can't get away from here however with less than 50 francs with my journey et cet to pay. Of course I shall leave the bill till I return.

I am furious with Bobbie for coming to Paris in that idiotic way, and I am convinced that he purposely waited till I had gone in order that he might make an ass of himself with Maurice. This was quite unnecessary and very unfriendly of him. Of course I don't for an instant believe that Silk's registered letter only contained £5, but I don't mind at all!!

It is stupid of the absurd Marie to excite herself. All the same I'd rather you didn't run up the tradesmen at Avenue Kléber any more just at present.

Do try and manage to get strong to send me enough to get back. Otherwise I shall have nothing till Wednesday.

With love

Yours always

Bosie[35]

Bosie evidently got back to Paris with money from Strong, but Oscar did not join him in his flat in the Avenue Kleber. He told Bosie that 'he could not face Paris yet' and suggested they meet at Rouen. However Bosie was still in money trouble and told Oscar he could not manage the journey. This annoyed Oscar and they did not correspond again for about a month. On 24 August Oscar wrote to Ross: 'Since Bosie wrote that he could not afford forty francs to come to Rouen to see me, he has never written. Nor have I. I am greatly hurt by his meanness and lack of imagination.' However a few days later, Bosie raised some money and they met after all in Rouen where they spent a night and a day (28–29 August) at the Hotel de la Poste. Since Bosie had previously stayed there and was known, he consequently could not use the assumed name of Jonquil de Vallon, which he thought was 'a cause of great disappointment to Oscar.' On the other hand, the meeting was a great success. 'I have often thought that if he or I had died directly after that, our friendship would have ended in a beautiful way,' Bosie later wrote in his autobiography. 'Poor Oscar cried when I met him at the station. We walked about all day arm in arm, or hand in hand, and were perfectly happy.'[36]

They arranged to meet six weeks later in Naples, where Bosie hoped to get another villa where they could live together. Meanwhile Oscar returned to Berneval, while Bosie went back to Paris, whence he joined his mother and sister at Aix-les-Bains, where they had decided to spend a month or five weeks in preference to Normandy.

Bosie telegraphed Oscar affectionately from Paris. 'My own Darling Boy,' Oscar replied by letter, 'I got your telegram half an hour ago, and just send you a line to say that my only hope of again doing beautiful work in art is being with you.'

It was not so in old days, but now it is different, and you can really recreate in me that energy and sense of joyous power on which art depends. Everyone is furious with me for going back to you, but they don't understand us. I feel that it is only with you that I can do anything at all. Do remake my ruined life for me, and then our friendship and love will have a different meaning to the world.

I wish that when we met at Rouen we had not parted at all. There are such wide abysses now of space and land between us. But we love each other.[37]

8

Oscar was so lonely after Bosie had left that, as he told Robert Ross, he was on the brink of killing himself. The weather was so bad in Berneval that he went to Rouen for a few days where the weather was worse. He returned to Dieppe and he wrote to Carlos Blacker, a friend of Constance: 'I don't mind being alone when there is sunlight, and a *joie de vivre* all about me, but my last fortnight at Berneval has been black and dreadful, and quite suicidal. I am trying to get some money to go to Italy ... but the expenses of travelling are frightening. ... I am greatly disappointed that Constance has not asked me to come and see the children. I don't suppose now that I shall ever see them.'[38] (In fact, he never did see them nor his wife.) Meanwhile he decided to go to Paris and he wrote to several acquaintances from whom he hoped to raise some money, including the journalist Rowland Strong and the Irish-American poet and novelist Vincent O'Sullivan. He arrived in Paris on 15 September and got a room in the Hotel d'Espagne, a cheap little hotel in the Rue Taitbout, off the Grand Boulevard. Vincent O'Sullivan called for him there a day or two after his arrival and found him waiting for Strong. But as Strong failed to turn up, they left and lunched together in a restaurant in Montmartre. 'It was a kind of restaurant where nobody would recognise Wilde,' O'Sullivan wrote afterwards, 'and he did not want to be recognised.'

It appears that in fact Oscar had enough money to get to Naples, since he had already arranged to take the train which stopped at Aixles-Bains where he was to pick up Bosie. However, when O'Sullivan asked him about his plans, Oscar replied: 'I shall go to Italy tonight. Or rather I would go, but I am in an absurd position. I have no money.' O'Sullivan asked him how much he needed and Oscar told him. On leaving the restaurant they drove to a bank where O'Sullivan had an account, and while Oscar remained in the cab, O'Sullivan went into the bank and brought him out the sum he wanted. 'It is one of the few things I look back on with satisfaction,' was O'Sullivan's comment on this incident. 'It is not every day that one has the chance of relieving the anxiety of a genius and a hero. I think he left Paris the same evening; certainly very soon.'[39]

At all events Bosie was waiting for him at Aix-les-Bains and they continued the journey together, stopping for a day at Genoa, where, unknown to her husband then, Constance was to die unexpectedly in 1898 and to be buried in the Protestant cemetery. On arriving in Naples they went to the fashionable and expensive Hotel Royal et Etrangers in the Via Partenope facing the sea and the Castello dell'Ovo. 'I celebrated the occasion by running up a bill for £68 in the fortnight we were there,' Bosie afterwards recalled in his autobiography.

> This bill remained unpaid right up to the time when I left Oscar at Naples, about two or three months later, when my dear mother sent me £200 to give to Oscar and also the money to pay the hotel bill and enable me to get back to Paris via Rome. I must explain that the proprietor, or manager of the Hotel Royal, being of course under the usual impression that obtains, or used to obtain on the Continent that an 'English Lord' is invariably a millionaire, seemed quite undisturbed by my request that he should let the bill stand over. He expressed himself enchanted to oblige me, and beyond sending in the bill again after about two months he made no kind of demonstration. I would not have the cheek to do a thing like that nowadays (1929), but in the year 1897 I still lived under the pleasing illusion that life more or less belonged to me, and that money was not a thing to take seriously.[40]

'My going back to Bosie was psychologically inevitable,' Oscar wrote to Robbie Ross from the hotel on 21 September. 'I cannot live without the atmosphere of Love: I must love and be loved, whatever price I pay for it. . . . When people speak against me for going back to Bosie, tell them that he offered me love, and that in my loneliness and disgrace, I, after three months' struggle against a hideous Philistine world, turned naturally to him. Of course I shall often be unhappy, but still I love him: the mere fact that he wrecked my life makes me love him.'

> We hope to get a little villa or apartments somewhere, and I hope to do work with him. I think I shall be able to do so. I think he will be kind to me; I only ask that. So do let people know that my only hope of life or literary activity was in going back to the young man whom I loved before with such tragic issue to my name.[41]

In fact they found 'a lovely villa over the sea', the Villa Giudice in

Posilipo, which had 'a nice piano', on which Bosie played Bach and Chopin and Mozart, while a young Italian poet named Rocco, who knew French and wished to translate *Salome*, gave Oscar lessons in Italian conversation. They had a cook, Carmine, a maid, Maria, and two boys called Peppino and Michele who waited on them at table. Servants cost little more than their keep in those days, and Bosie reckoned that the cost of feeding Oscar and himself and the servants only came to about twelve francs a day, so that they could just about manage on Bosie's weekly allowance of £8 from his mother and Oscar's 'pittance' of £3 a week from Constance. French currency was then generally accepted in Italy, francs being the equivalent of lire. There was one snag about the villa when they moved in. Although it was charmingly situated in the Via Posilipo with a terrace and marble steps leading down to the sea, it was infested by rats, so much so that at the outset of their stay Bosie had to hire a room in a house opposite the villa to sleep in. However the rats were eventually got rid of, partly through the operations of a professional rat-catcher and partly – chiefly, according to Oscar – through the ministrations of a 'potent witch' who was recommended by Michele and who came and 'burned odours' and muttered incantations which she declared that no rats could resist. Anyhow the rats disappeared and Bosie was able to come back to sleep in the villa.

'I daresay that what I have done is fatal, but it had to be done,' Oscar wrote to Ross on 1 October. 'It was necessary that Bosie and I should come together again; I saw no other life for myself. For himself he saw no other: all we want now is to be left alone, but the Neapolitan papers are tedious and wish to interview me, etc. I want peace – that is all. Perhaps I shall find it.' He did, and Bosie likewise, but for barely two months.

During this period Oscar revised *The Ballad of Reading Gaol* and added several more stanzas to the ballad, while Bosie wrote a number of sonnets, including the four comprising *The City of the Soul* and three which Oscar called 'lovely' and entitled *The Triad of the Moon*.

> Only to build one crystal barrier
> Against this sea which beats upon our days;
> To ransom one lost moment with a rhyme!
> Or if fate cries and grudging gods demur,
> To clutch Life's hair, and thrust one naked phrase
> Like a lean knife between the ribs of Time.

These were all published in Bosie's first volume of poems to appear in England anonymously in 1899 under the title of *The City of the Soul* and the imprint of Grant Richards.

Bosie also wrote a sonnet on Mozart, inspired by what is perhaps the most beautiful number in *Don Giovanni*, the trio *Ah taci, ingiusto core!* (Ah be quiet, foolish heart!) between Donna Elvira, Leporello and Don Giovanni in the balcony scene outside Donna Elvira's house in Act II. On Oscar's advice, Bosie sent the sonnet to Stanley Makower, a young music critic who was running *The Musician*, a short-lived weekly. 'Of course it should be headed by the whole of the first thirteen bars of the trio in question, but I was too lazy to write it all out,' Bosie wrote in his covering letter, which he concluded by praising Makower's novel *The Mirror of Music* as 'quite wonderful.' ('I have read no book so good for a very long time.') In a patronising reply rejecting the sonnet, Makower, who was two years younger than Bosie, admitted that he had 'no knowledge of this form of poetry' but added that he considered Bosie's poem to be 'full of promise'. This annoyed Oscar but Bosie forgot all about it with the result that the sonnet never appeared in any collections of his verse. Nevertheless it seems worth reproducing, and here it is:

> O wonderful delightful melody!
> O drops of clear white water! pearls and stars
> Strung on a silver string! no passion mars
> Thy perfect beauty. Realised agony
> In its excess leaves me both cold and free
> Nor can I ever bleed at pictured scars;
> But I have never heard those thirteen bars
> But that my tears paid tribute unto thee.
>
> The beauty of perfection makes me weep
> With helpless ecstasy. O rare Mozart!
> Prince of the sweet untroubled countenance.
> Exquisite shepherd that hast, for flock of sheep,
> Live troops of notes that run and trip and dance
> In the green pastures of eternal art.[42]

'Alfred Douglas has shown me your letter to him, with its nice message to me [about *The Ballad of Reading Gaol*]' Oscar wrote back to Makower. 'The rest of your letter, however, pained me a good deal: because it showed that you did not understand or appreciate, in the smallest way, the reason why he sent you his sonnet on Mozart.'

He was charmed and fascinated by much in your book, which I had lent him, and wrote to you to express his pleasure in your work, and, as a sign of his pleasure in it, sent you a sonnet of his own, not as a corpse for a callous dissecting table, but as a flower to gild one grey moment in a London day.

He is a little in years, and a little in literature, your senior.... His poems place him at once quite in the front of all the young poets of England: I know no young poet who is in any way his equal, or even near him.... Full of promise is an expression quite meaningless in even the most elementary criticism....

I may say finally that Alfred Douglas was merely amused at your letter: the one who was pained was myself, as I had the pleasure – and it was a great pleasure – of knowing you personally and had often spoken to him about you, and it was a grief to me to find that, even without meaning it, you could be ungracious, and lacking in recognition of a charming compliment from a poet of the highest distinction.

This 'bombshell', as Oscar called his rebuke, produced a grovelling apology from Makower and he was forgiven. But apparently it was too late to publish the sonnet in *The Musician*, since it ceased publication before this could be done. Oscar good-naturedly dismissed the whole affair as 'a mere misunderstanding on your part', and when *The Ballad* was published, the author sent Makower a complimentary copy.[43]

Repeated telegrams to *The Ballad*'s publisher produced an advance of £10, and this enabled Oscar and Bosie to go to Capri for a few days. 'I want to lay a few simple flowers on the tomb of Tiberius,' said Oscar. 'As the tomb is of someone else really, I shall do so with the deeper emotion.'*

Besides this exercise they both lunched in his 'lovely villa' with Dr Axel Munthe, the Swedish doctor who was to write *The Story of San Michele*. Oscar thought Munthe was 'a great connoisseur of Greek things' and 'a wonderful personality.' However the sirocco and the rain drove Oscar back to Naples a day early, but Bosie stayed on an extra day in order to dine with Mrs Snow, an American who lived on the island and on whom Bosie's namesake Norman Douglas was to base the character of the Duchess of San Martino in his novel *South Wind*.

The news, reported in the Italian press, that Bosie and Oscar were living together in Naples, was noted by the British Embassy in Rome, with the result that one of the attachés, Beauchamp Denis Brown, whom Bosie had previously met in the Embassy, was sent down to Naples to let Bosie know that the renewal of their association in this form was very *mal vu* in the embassy. Worse still, when Constance Wilde heard about it, and also that they planned to visit Capri,

---

*According to local tradition the Roman Emperor, who died in 37 AD, was buried in the villa in Capri which had been the scene of his orgies. However, in fact after his death his remains were taken from Capri to Rome where they were cremated with the usual ceremonial.

always popular with homosexuals, she was furious. She immediately stopped Oscar's allowance on the ground that he had broken the terms of the deed of arrangement. This unpleasant news was conveyed to Oscar by his solicitor. Oscar was further upset to learn that both Robbie Ross and More Adey had agreed with Constance's action. Bosie was also concerned, since his mother threatened to stop his allowance as well if he went on living with Oscar. 'The terms of Oscar's agreement are that he should forfeit his allowance if he lived with disreputable people in such a way to cause a public scandal,' Bosie wrote to Adey on 20 November.

> I am not a disreputable person and there has not been the smallest vestige of a scandal. And yet you and the wretched Bobbie, who are supposed · to be trying to represent Oscar's interest quietly, acquiesce in and approve of the proposal to deprive him of all his money which is as much his own by right and equity as the clothes I wear on my back are mine.... The reason I went to live with Oscar in Naples was not to prove that I always got my own way, but firstly that he asked me to do so, and secondly, that I naturally wanted to go. That is all. Of course if Oscar and I are to be starved to death for living together, it does make a reason for not doing so; but it is odd to find you and Bobbie quietly acquiescing in this system of abominable tyranny.[44]

A few days later Oscar also wrote to More Adey, telling him he wished to know whether some compromise could be made:

> I am quite ready to agree not to live in the same house with Bosie again. Of course to promise to cut him, or not to speak to him, or to associate with him would be absurd. He is the only friend with whom I can be in contact, and to live without some companion would be impossible. I had silence and solitude for two years: to condemn me now to silence and solitude would be barbarous.
>
> It is not a matter of much importance, but I never wrote to my wife that I was going 'to keep house with Alfred Douglas.' I thought 'keep house' was only a servant-girl's expression.
>
> I do think that, if we engage not to live together, I might be still left the wretched £3 a week – so little but still something. How on earth am I to live?
>
> Do, if possible, try to arrange something. I know you all think I am wilful, but it is the result of the nemesis of character, and the bitterness of life. I was a problem for which there was no solution.

That is what happened. At the beginning of December Bosie left Oscar for Paris via Rome. After some delay Constance Wilde restored Oscar's £3 weekly allowance, and through a codicil to her will it continued to be paid by her trustees after her death in April 1898. Meanwhile Lady Queensberry did not cut off Bosie's allowance. On the contrary, before he left Naples she sent him the money to pay the bill at the Hotel Royal and three months' advance rent of the villa in Posilipo, in the event of Oscar wishing to go on living there without Bosie. She also sent Oscar £200 through More Adey at her son's request.

'You mustn't misunderstand me,' Bosie wrote to his mother from Rome on 7 December 1897 asking her to send Oscar the £200. 'Don't think that I have changed my mind about him or that I think him bad or that I have changed my views about morals.'

> I still love and admire him, and I think he has been infamously treated by ignorant and cruel brutes. I look on him as a martyr to progress. I associate myself with him in everything. I long to hear of his success and artistic rehabilitation in the post which is his by right at the very summit of English literature, nor do I intend to cease corresponding with him or not to see him from time to time in Paris and elsewhere. I give up nothing and admit no point against him or myself separately or jointly.
>
> Do not think, either that he has been unkind to me or shown himself to me in an unfavourable light.... He has always behaved *perfectly* to me. The only thing that happened was that I felt and saw that he didn't really wish me to stay and that it would really be a relief to him if I went away. So at last I was able to get away, with a clear conscience. It was the most lucky thing that ever happened. If I hadn't rejoined him and lived with him for two months, I should *never* have got over the longing for him. It was spoiling my life and spoiling my art and spoiling everything. Now I am free.[45]

About three months later, probably on 2 March 1898, Oscar wrote Robbie Ross an extraordinary letter from Paris which Bosie was to characterise in his autobiography as 'one of the most astonishing products that the history of literature has ever recorded.'[44] Bosie, who was also living in Paris at the time, knew nothing of the letter until fourteen years later when he read *Oscar Wilde: A Critical Study* by Arthur Ransome, in which the letter was quoted, and as a result Bosie sued Ransome for libel.

> The facts of Naples are very bald and brief.
>
> Bosie, for four months, by endless letters, offered me a '*home*.' He offered me love, affection and care, and promised that I should never want for anything. After four months I accepted his offer, but when we met at Aix on our way to Naples I found that he had no money, no plans, and had forgotten all his promises. His one idea was that I should raise money for us both. I did so, to the extent of £120. On this Bosie lived, quite happily. When it came to his

having, of course, to repay his *own* share he became terrible, unkind, mean and penurious, except where his own pleasures were concerned, and when my allowance ceased, he left. . . .

It is, of course, the most bitter experience of a bitter life; it is a blow quite awful and paralysing, but it had to come, and I know it is better that I should never see him again. I don't want to. He fills me with horror.[46]

There is much that is incorrect or misleading in this letter. There were no 'endless letters' extending over four months. Their decision to go to Naples was agreed at their reunion in Rouen in August 1897 and there is nothing in Oscar's letters to Ross and others when he and Bosie were living in the villa at Posilipo to suggest that Bosie was not paying his 'share' of the expenses, while through his mother he paid the cost of their stay at the Hotel Royal before they moved into the villa.

Many years later, in 1930, when Bosie was living at Hove with his mother, she wrote him a hitherto unpublished letter setting out the facts of the Naples incident:

My recollection of the time when you left Oscar Wilde at Naples is quite clear. When I found out that he was staying with you in your villa at Posilipo, I wrote saying that I could not possibly go on providing you with money to support him and that unless you left him I would not go on paying your allowance.

You were very upset at my letter and declared that you would not leave him; but a few days later I got a letter from you in which you said you would agree to leave him provided that I would send him £200 as it was impossible for you to leave him without money. I gladly agreed to do this and telegraphed that I would do as you wished. You then left Wilde and went to Rome on your way back to Paris.

I wrote to Mr More Adey whom I knew was a friend of Oscar Wilde's as well as yours and told him what had happened. I enclosed a cheque for £100 made payable to Mr Adey and asked him to give or send this money to Wilde and said I would send the other £100 in a few days. A few days later I sent Mr Adey another cheque for £100. Mr Adey acknowledged my cheques and sent them on to Wilde.

I have seen a copy of the letter Wilde wrote to Ross at this time. It is a wicked and abominable letter, and it seems almost impossible to understand how any man however degraded could sink to the level which would permit him to write such a letter. Still less is it possible to understand how this letter could be used against you as it was at the time when it was first made public in 1913 at the trial of the Ransome action and by Ross who was perfectly aware of its falsity and treachery.

When you left Oscar Wilde at Naples, you did so with the utmost reluctance and your one thought was for the comfort and well being of your friend. I had warned you before that if you had anything more to do with him you would bitterly regret it.... It was your loyalty to this bad man that caused all the sorrows and troubles of your life. You were blamed for your attachment to an utterly unworthy man and also abused for deserting him when as a matter of fact you expended yourself in serving and helping him all his life and have always been generous and highminded and forgiving.

Yet at the time Oscar wrote the 'wicked and abominable letter' to Robbie Ross, he was outwardly on affectionate terms with Bosie, choosing furniture for him from the Paris branch of Maples, the London store, for his new flat in the Avenue Kléber and accepting money and hospitality when Bosie could afford them. 'As regards Bosie,' Oscar wrote to Ross on 11 May 1898, 'he has been very nice to me indeed, but for the last week he has been at Nogent, with Strong, as he had no money at all. But when he had money he was very hospitable and generous in paying for things when we were to-gether.'[47]

9

The last three years of Oscar Wilde's life, which he spent mostly in Paris with occasional visits to Italy and Switzerland, were by no means unhappy. It is true that he led a somewhat aimless existence, since he had lost the power or the will to write, and after the publication of *The Ballad of Reading Gaol* he wrote nothing except two long letters in the *Daily Chronicle* on prison conditions and penal reform. However, he remained a superb conversationist and, if anything, was more brilliant than in the earlier period of his social success before his imprisonment. In his old age Bosie recalled their dinners together in Paris when he held his audience spellbound as he discoursed in his exquisite voice on all things in heaven and earth, sometimes making his listeners rock with laughter and sometimes bringing tears to their eyes. 'Such talk as Oscar's now no longer exists, as far as my experience goes,' Bosie wrote forty years after his death. 'I have never known anyone to come anywhere near him.... He talked better, if possible, after his downfall than he did before. As Shaw rightly points out, after he could no longer write but could still talk as no other man ever did, he was entitled to all the money he could get.'

And this he did not scruple to do. For instance he sold the scenario of a projected play to at least half a dozen purchasers including Frank Harris. He had originally written the scenario for George Alexander, but it was Harris who was to expand it into a drama using Wilde's real or imagined dialogue and who was eventually to produce it in London as *Mr and Mrs Daventry*.[48]

Oscar also continued both to defend homosexuality and to practice it. 'A patriot put in prison for loving his country, loves his country, and a poet in prison for loving boys, loves boys,' he wrote to Ross in February 1898, shortly after his arrival in Paris from Naples. 'To have altered my life would have been to have admitted that Uranian love is ignoble. I hold it to be noble – more noble than other forms.'

When the present writer first met Bosie in 1931, Bosie assured him that it was Robbie Ross who 'dragged' Oscar back to homosexual practices when they were staying together at Berneval. 'Oscar told me this one night after dinner in Paris when he had had a great many drinks,' Bosie claimed. 'I did not mention it in my autobiography because I thought everyone would think I was inventing it to get even with Ross.' As for Oscar's last years in Paris, Bosie went on, the manner of his life there was notorious and he was quite open about it. 'He was hand in glove with all the little boys on the Boulevard. He never attempted to conceal it. Oscar believed, as many other eminent people do, that he had a perfect right to indulge his own tastes.'

When Bosie said this, he had become a sincere convert to the Roman Catholic faith and in consequence had forsworn his own former homosexual activities. Otherwise his statement might be regarded as a case of the pot calling the kettle black. In fact, when Bosie took his flat in the Avenue Kléber, which Oscar helped to furnish, he was just as much attracted by the Boulevard boys as Oscar himself was. For example, Oscar wrote about Bosie to Ross in these terms at the time:

> He is devoted to a dreadful little ruffian aged fourteen whom he loves because at night, in the scanty intervals he can steal from an arduous criminal profession, he sells bunches of violets in front of the Café de la Paix. Also every time he goes home with Bosie he tries to rent him. This, of course, adds to his terrible fascination. We call him '*Florifer*,' a lovely name. He also keeps another boy, aged twelve! whom Bosie wishes to know, but the wise 'Florifer' declines.[49]

A fortnight later Oscar wrote that Bosie had got tired of the 'Florifer' but was thinking of using the word in a sonnet. 'All romance should end in a sonnet,' Oscar added. 'I suppose all romances do.' Although Bosie and Oscar continued to meet from time to time, the old spell was broken and they never resumed their former intimacy. Also there was a touch of malice in Oscar's remarks about Bosie to Ross. 'Bosie has no real enjoyment of a joke unless he thinks there is a good chance of the other person being pained or annoyed,' he told Ross. 'It is an entirely English trait, the English type and symbol of a joke being the jug on the half-opened door, or the distribution of orange peel on the pavement of a crowded thoroughfare.' And again: 'He apparently goes to the races every day, and loses, of course. As I wrote to Maurice today, he has a faculty of spotting the loser, which, considering that he knows nothing at all about horses, is perfectly astounding.'[50]

Bosie had been out of England for more than three years and was anxious to go back, but Oscar and Ross both understood that he had 'apprehensions' about doing so. 'Personally, I think it would be wiser for him to wait until he is sixty,' Oscar told Ross. When the weather became warmer, Oscar and Bosie went to Nogent, partly for the change and partly because Oscar dared not go back to his hotel, where he owed several weeks' bills, while at Nogent he had credit. 'It is a lovely place, and we have had some charming days,' Oscar told Ross, 'but Bosie goes up to Paris daily, and only returns for dinner. He goes and sits in his rooms. He says it is absurd to have rooms and not to sit in them.' There, according to Oscar, Bosie preyed on his *femme-de-ménage*, 'who now pays for everything including cigars.' When the weather became really hot, Bosie joined his mother in Trouville. 'Paris is a fiery furnace,' wrote Oscar in mid-August. 'I walk in streets of brass. And even the bad boys have left for *les bains de mer.*... Bosie is at Trouville still. But as the doctor won't let him bathe, and his mother won't let him baccarat he is dreadfully bored. He goes to Aix next month.'[51]

It was from Aix that Bosie wrote the last of his three letters to Oscar which have survived, although the end is missing:

> Pavilion des Bains,
> Aix-les-Bains
> 20 September 1898

My dear Oscar,
    I was very glad to hear from you at last. As you never wrote, I thought you must be offended about something, for I wrote to you 3 times from Trouville without an answer, and went up to Paris a day earlier on purpose to see you. I spent the whole evening

hunting for you, and when I finally went to your hotel they told me that you had gone to Nogent. I was on the point of going there. But luckily I didn't, as I should have been very disgusted to find no one but Albert and Snatcher.*

I got your telegram afterwards. I saw Maurice [Gilbert] who stayed with me one night at 112 [Avenue Kléber].

How extraordinary of Strong to go to England just when all the excitement about Dreyfus is on. I am still unshaken in my anti-Dreyfus beliefs, but I must admit that things look rather bad and the '*vieux père J'accuse*' must be triumphing!†

I have heard nothing more about my poems. I can't make it out. George Wyndham wrote as if it was practically settled, but a month has elapsed and I have heard nothing more.

A letter was received from Asquith saying that no steps had ever been taken against me by the Treasury and that, as it was impossible for anything to have occurred since I left England, it was obvious that there was nothing to prevent my return. His letter began 'I have communicated privately with the director of public prosecutions and I learn' et cet: so that it is quite official information. However, on the top of this Cuffe, the public prosecutor, has written to my uncle George Finch (his cousin) saying that he hears that I think of coming back and that he thinks it would be *very inadvisable*. So it is rather contradictory.

It was all settled that I was to go to Clouds, a party had been got up there to meet me, and now it is all off. My mother is going to see Cuffe personally and ascertain whether there....[52]

'Bosie is back from Aix,' Oscar noted on 3 October: 'his mother on leaving gave him £30 to go to Venice with. He of course lost it all at the Casino, and arrived in Paris on the proceeds of his sleeve-links. For the moment he is penniless.' He added that Frank Harris had arrived from London and that he had breakfasted and dined with him frequently, along with Bosie, to whom Frank was 'very nice'. He also

---

*Albert was the inn-keeper at Nogent. 'Snatcher' may be Reginald Turner whom Wilde called 'the boy snatcher of Clement's Inn', where Turner lived. Turner, who was a Jewish homosexual and worked on the *Daily Telegraph*, was in France throughout much of 1898 in connection with the Dreyfus case in which he was naturally interested.

†Strong had gone to London where on 18 September he had published an article in *The Observer* stating that Commandant Esterhazy had important disclosures to make. A week later Strong printed a further piece in which Esterhazy confessed to having forged the controversial *bordereau* on the strength of which Dreyfus had been convicted. The '*vieux père*' was 48-year-old French writer Emile Zola, whose famous letter to the newspaper *Aurore* beginning with the words 'J'accuse' was a fierce denunciation of those responsible for hounding down Dreyfus at this time.

reported to Ross that Frank had bought a hotel in Monaco and hoped to make a lot of money.

Meanwhile the complication over Bosie's return to England had been sorted out between his mother and Hamilton Cuffe. In November Bosie accordingly returned to London where he stayed at his mother's house in Cadogan Place until after his sister Edith's marriage to Sir George Fox-Pitt in March 1899. Oscar was very keen to know how he was being received in London and what he was doing. 'I suppose that London takes no notice at all: that is the supreme punishment.... He has only written to me once – a brief scrawl – not very charming.' In fact, Bosie spent a considerable time with two publishers, who were bringing out his poems. The first was Edward Arnold, who published his *Tails with a Twist*, a book of nonsense rhymes, very well-illustrated with colour drawings by E.T. Reid, which for some reason Bosie did not like. The work came out in December 1898 under the pseudonym 'A Belgian Hare', and Bosie foolishly sold the copyright to Arnold for £50. 'Never on your life part with a copyright,' Bernard Shaw told Bosie years later when he heard about it. 'Always hold on to it and *license* publication or performance.'[53]

There were twenty-eight poems in *Tails with a Twist* beginning with 'The Hyaena' and ending with 'The Cod.' The author explained in his preface how they came to be written:

> Some years ago, at a certain country house party, a lady happened to quote to the author of these lines portions of a little poem entitled 'The Leopard', which that strong and melodious poet, Mr Wilfrid Blunt, had written many years previously for a magazine brought out by some English children of his acquaintance in India. The poem so delighted the present author that, taking it as a model, he produced 'The Lion', the first *animal rhyme* proper to see the light; the others followed in due course, and the present collection is the result of efforts scattered over the space of about four years.
>
> The author has called 'The Lion' the first animal rhyme proper for the reason that, while Mr Blunt's poem serves as a model and suggested an idea, it was not an *animal rhyme* in the sense that these are. It differed in that it was simply a poem describing in language suited to the comprehension of very young children the savage and treacherous actions of the leopard. The intention of these rhymes is entirely different.

The lady was Bosie's cousin Pamela Wyndham, who married Edward Tennant later Lord Glenconner in 1895. The house party was probably at Clouds which was Pamela's home.

THE LION

The Lion is an awful bore,
He comes and dabbles in your gore.

And if he wants to have a feed,
He bites your leg and makes it bleed.

Although the tears stream from your eyes,
He takes no notice of your cries.

In vain you argue or protest,
He finishes his meal with zest.

Nor will he take the least rebuff
Until he feels he's had enough.

Tails with a Twist had a considerable success, although the author was often accused of having plagiarised Hilaire Belloc's *The Bad Child's Book of Beasts*, which had appeared in 1896. But, as Bosie was to record in subsequent editions of his work, most of the rhymes contained in it had been written at least two years before Belloc's, and were widely known and quoted at Oxford, where Belloc was Bosie's contemporary, and in other places.

The other publisher whom Bosie saw at this time, and who had agreed to bring out an English edition of his collected poems entitled *The City of the Soul*, was Grant Richards, a young publisher who had previously worked for W.T. Stead on *The Review of Reviews* and had recently started on his own. 'I hear he is daring, and likes to splash in great waters,' wrote Oscar, who thought of sending him a novel after Grant Richards had published Bernard Shaw's *Plays Pleasant and Unpleasant*. *The City of the Soul* appeared anonymously in May 1899, by which time Bosie was back in his Paris flat. Oscar was dining with him there when *The Outlook* which contained its first review, a glowing one, headed 'A Great Unknown' by Lionel Johnson, arrived. 'Among crowds of clever versifiers here comes a poet,' wrote Johnson, who was apparently unaware of the poet's identity. The collection, which was later published under Bosie's name, went through three editions in the next dozen years, but it omitted some of the poems published by *Mercure de France*, such as 'In Praise of Shame' and 'Two Loves', the reason for their omission being, as Bosie subsequently wrote, that, 'although there is no actual harm in them, they lend themselves to evil interpretations, and the fact that they have been so interpreted by those whose interest it has been to attack and defame me, and that they have actually been used against me in the law courts by the very persons who most applauded them at the time they were written, has given me a distaste for them which such poetical merits as they may possess are insufficient to dispel.'[54]

Bosie returned to London in the autumn of 1899, primarily to arrange for the publication of another nonsense rhyme *The Duke of Berwick*. This was to appear under the imprint of Oscar's publisher Leonard Smithers, who had published *The Ballad of Reading Gaol* besides his plays *An Ideal Husband* and *The Importance of Being Earnest* when no other English publisher would touch anything by Wilde. *The Duke of Berwick* was to have twelve coloured illustrations by a young artist Anthony Ludovici, who recalled his first meeting with Bosie and the publisher for tea at Lady Queensberry's house in Cadogan Place: 'After tea, Lord Alfred Douglas read *The Duke of Berwick* to us. I listened enraptured and immensely amused whilst in his melodious light baritone voice he half-read and half-recited his delightful skit on his father – at least that is what at the time I understood the verse to be.'[55] Bosie and Smithers both liked the artist's illustrations and the work duly came out, but it had practically no sale since Smithers' firm went bankrupt about a week later.

It should be added that this nonsense rhyme was not a skit on Lord Queensberry but referred to a minor character in Wilde's *The Picture of Dorian Gray*, the Duke of Berwick, who, to show disapproval, left a club room 'in a marked manner' as Dorian Gray entered it. The faintly-drawn character of the Duke amused Bosie, who elaborated him into a legendary figure of fun (a sort of male Mrs Grundy) somewhat to the annoyance of Wilde, whose sense of humour according to Bosie rather boggled at the turning into ridicule of anything connected with his own literary work. The key to the satire, as Bosie later told the novelist Hugh Walpole, was in the verse:

> He and the Duchess always turned their backs
> On those whose conduct was in the least bit lax.
> Where-e'er they went they waved a moral banner
> And constantly left rooms 'in a marked manner.'

Hearing that his father was ill, Bosie went to see him at Bailey's Hotel in Kensington where Queensberry was staying. They met in the hotel smoking room, when Queensberry embraced his son, wept copiously, called him his darling boy, and promised to give him back his allowance. However, a week later he wrote Bosie an abusive letter, saying that he did not intend to give him a penny until he knew what his son's relations with 'that beast Wilde' then were. As usual Bosie replied in kind and they never saw each other again. Queensberry died a few weeks later, on 31 January 1900. When Sibyl Queensberry went to see him on his death-bed, he told her that she was the only woman he had ever loved, but when Percy, his heir, appeared he sat up in bed and spat at him. To the last he kept saying that he was being persecuted by the 'Oscar Wilders'. At the end he was received into the Catholic Church by his uncle, the Very Rev Canon Lord Archibald Douglas, having confessed all his sins, renounced his atheism and professed his love for and faith in Jesus Christ. Evidently he had no time to cut Bosie out of his will, since Bosie inherited £15,000, of which he received £8,000 immediately. After the funeral at Kinmount, Bosie went back to Paris accompanied by Percy. 'Bosie is over here with his brother,' Oscar wrote to Robbie Ross on 22 February 1900. 'They are in deep mourning and the highest spirits. The English are like that.'

Two days before Queensberry's death, Bosie's boyhood friend, Wellington Stapleton-Cotton, was killed during the siege of Lady-smith in the South African war. When he heard the news, Bosie tried to enlist as a trooper in a cavalry regiment 'Paget's Horse', but the commanding officer advised him to apply to join the Duke of Cambridge's Corps, a volunteer cavalry unit, which was being recruited by Lord Arthur Hill entirely from gentlemen prepared to pay for their horses and equipment. Bosie went to the depot and after passing the riding, shooting and medical tests, was told that he was accepted. He thereupon left a cheque for £250 to defray the cost of his horse and equipment. Shortly afterwards, somewhat to his surprise, his cheque was returned to him with a curt note to the effect that his services were not required.[56] This was a stinging blow, the second he had received in six months, the first being when Sir Herbert Warren, the President of Magdalen, returned the copy of *The City of the Soul* which Bosie had sent him. Bosie now relieved his feelings by writing to Lord Arthur Hill, who was an uncle of another of Bosie's boyhood friends, 'Artie' Downshire, telling Hill what he thought of him and the Duke of Cambridge. It was clear that the association between 'Queensberry's boy' and Oscar Wilde had not been forgotten by the military Establishment and Bosie was consequently unwelcome in the army.

With part of his inheritance Bosie bought some racing stables at Chantilly, near Paris, together with several horses, for which he found a good trainer in George Woodhouse. Ross had suggested that Bosie should give Oscar £2,000 so that he could have an annuity which would bring him in an additional £140 a year. Bosie refused to hand over such a large sum, although he regularly sent Oscar cheques for various sums ranging from £10 to £125, as the entries in his pass-book show for the year 1900. It is likely that when Ross suggested it he knew that nothing would come of the idea, while at the same time relishing the effect on Oscar of Bosie's refusal. 'He really is, now that he has money, become mean, narrow and greedy,' Oscar complained to Frank Harris, who passed this on to Bosie one night shortly afterwards when Harris visited him at Chantilly. 'Bosie I have not seen for a week,' Oscar wrote to Ross about the end of June. 'I feel sure he will do nothing. Boys, brandy, and betting monopolise his soul. He really is a miser: but his method of hoarding is spending, a new type.' It irked Oscar a little that after Bosie had had two successful wins, he did not give him more than in fact he did, but the fact remains that Bosie was not ungenerous with his cheque book as proved so far as Oscar was concerned. Anyhow Oscar, who was well aware of this, did not press the matter and they continued to meet on quite friendly terms.[57]

With the end of that year's racing season, Bosie and his brother Percy took a shoot at Strathpeffer in the Scottish Highlands. Before leaving Paris, Bosie invited Oscar to dinner at the Grand Café in the Boulevard des Capucines. Oscar was in good spirits and amused at Bosie's anxiety to reach Strathpeffer by 12 August, the traditional date for the start of grouse shooting. For a few minutes before they parted, Oscar suddenly became depressed and told Bosie he did not think he would live to see the new century. 'If another century began and I was still alive,' he said, 'it would really be more than the English could stand.' Bosie brushed this aside as a piece of gloomy nonsense, and as he said good-bye he promised to send Oscar another cheque from Scotland. He kept his word and did so on 16 August.[58] For the last two months of Oscar's life, which he spent mostly in bed suffering from ear trouble finally complicated by cerebral meningitis, Bosie was shooting in Scotland. However he sent Oscar another cheque at the beginning of November, which he enclosed with 'a very nice letter', according to Ross, who added that Oscar wept a little on receiving it. Ross then departed for the south of France to join his mother who was wintering in Menton, leaving Reggie Turner to look after Oscar. On 27 November, when Oscar's condition had deteriorated to such an extent that his death appeared to be a matter of days, if not hours, Turner telegraphed Ross who arrived at the Hotel d'Alsace on the morning of the 28th. Turner would also have telegraphed Bosie but he did not know his address. It was therefore left to Ross to do this, so that Bosie learned on 1 December that Oscar had died the previous afternoon. He had previously had a letter from Ross to the effect that Oscar had been taken ill but that the illness was 'nothing serious'.

Bosie arrived at the hotel in time to pay Oscar's funeral expenses, but he did not see his body, since the coffin had already been nailed down; the undertaker had advised that decomposition had begun to set in shortly after death. Ross told Bosie that Oscar had been received into the Catholic Church and the last rites had been administered while he was still conscious, although Bosie did not believe that Oscar was conscious at the time, nor that he wished to become a Catholic, since 'he was as a matter of fact the most complete sceptic imaginable, and would never have bowed his intellect to any dogma or any form of religious belief however fine.' Ross also mentioned, quite casually, that he had been through Oscar's papers and had not found anything of importance, although in fact they contained a number of Bosie's letters to Oscar. Bosie, who did not show any particular interest, told Ross to do what he thought best, and dismissed the matter from his mind, having thus accepted Ross as Oscar's self-appointed literary executor.[59]

Bosie was the chief mourner at the funeral which took place on 3 December 1900 at the cemetery at Bagneux, after a Low Mass and the burial service had been conducted in the Church of St Germain-des-Près. 'I am miserable and wretched about poor darling Oscar,' Bosie wrote to More Adey when he returned to Scotland. 'It seems so beastly that I couldn't have seen him before he died, and nobody told me a word about his illness till the day before his death when it was too late.... I suppose Bobbie is consoled by the R. Catholic tomfoolery.... I did so loathe the idea of his 'being received' on his death-bed à la Aubrey Beardsley. It was so utterly unlike him.'[60]

IV

Racing, Marriage and Journalism

1

Bosie was an inveterate gambler whether on or off the racecourse or in the casino. He was also a keen sportsman, being an excellent shot, a good rider to hounds, with a genuine love of horses, and an enthusiastic owner during the eighteen months he had his racing stables at Chantilly.[1] His most successful horse was a six-year-old gelding called Hardi, a beautiful chestnut, who had belonged to Edmond Blanc, the owner of the casino at Monte Carlo and which Bosie bought for £250 after he had won a selling race. The initial race where he was first past the winning post when Bosie owned him was at Lille. But Bosie was not there to see his victory, since he was Frank Harris's guest at Monte Carlo and spent the afternoon of his last day in the casino. Here he had an astonishing run of luck, winning close on £2,000 in four days. He started with 25 louis and began by putting a louis (20 francs) on number 13, which promptly came up. He doubled his stake *en plein* and the number came up again. In those days if you won *en plein* with a gold louis, you were paid 10 gold louis (200 francs) plus a 500 franc note. Each time Bosie won, and he was backing *en plein* haphazard, he kept the gold louis and put the note in his pocket. It was only at the end of his last day that he lost the initial 25 louis. He then took the train for Paris, stopping the night at Marseilles – there was no Blue Train then – and there he found a telegram from his trainer saying Hardi had won at Lille at 6 to 4 against, and although the prize money was only 3,000 francs Bosie had backed him to win another 1,500 francs. Hardi won several other races for his owner, including a £500 handicap at Maisons-Lafitte, where the Pari Mutuel (Tote) odds were 68 to 1 for a win and 17 to 1 for a place. He won other races with Hardi and two other horses in his stable.

Frank Harris's hotel in Monte Carlo was called Cesari's, since it was being run by the celebrated *maître d'hôtel* of that name. It was a small hotel consisting entirely of beautifully furnished and ultra-expensive suites, each with a sitting room and bathroom – an unusual luxury for those days. It was an 'hotel for millionaires' Frank Harris told Bosie, whom he volunteered to let in at the rock bottom if he invested £2,000 as he would soon be getting 100 per cent on his money. Frank also motored Bosie to the Reserve restaurant at Eze – he was a pioneer motorist. Here they had an excellent lunch on the terrace overlooking the sea to the music of a Hungarian band. Over the liqueurs and cigars Harris told Bosie that the restaurant belonged to him. 'You see for yourself the sort of business we are doing,' said Harris. 'This is my gold mine.'

'Well, it seems a good sort of speculation,' commented Bosie, 'but I don't quite see where the hundred per cent profit you spoke of is going to come in.'

Harris leaned across and clutched Bosie's arm. 'My dear man, this is nothing,' he declared. 'The real gold mine is this. I have a concession from the French Government allowing roulette and trente-et-quarante to be played here!'

Bosie was much impressed. Afterwards he admitted that, if Harris really had such a concession it would have been a veritable goldmine, but he was too young and inexperienced to reflect that in this event Harris would hardly have been so anxious and taken so much trouble to secure Bosie's modest investment. Anyhow Bosie wrote cheques for that amount and in return received two thousand shares in the '*Cesari Reserve Syndicate.*'

In fact Bosie never got sixpence. He later discovered that the restaurant was mortgaged up to the hilt and – what he should have realised – Harris's story about the concession was a pure invention, since no such concession had been granted by the French Government during the previous half-century, roulette and trente-et-quarante being illegal under French law which of course did not extend to the independent principality of Monaco. Ashamed, perhaps, for being taken for a ride and being a mug, Bosie told few people of what had happened but he never bore Frank Harris any grudge for his action. When Harris admitted that he had 'been done out of the promised concession' and would 'make it up' to Bosie in another way before long, Bosie simply shrugged his shoulders and said: 'All right, old chap'. It was only after Harris had told lies about him in his *Life and Confessions of Oscar Wilde* that Bosie recounted the true facts in the magazine *Plain English* which he was editing at the time. Nor did Bosie's racing fortunes prosper after what happened to Hardi, his favourite horse. One frosty morning in winter he bolted at exercise, threw off the boy who was riding him, and ran away for about five miles down the La Morlaye road at Chantilly. The road was like iron, and when Hardi was caught he was found to be badly broken down and never became sound enough to race again. Eventually when Bosie sold the stables, he reluctantly had Hardi put down, since otherwise he would have ended up in a cab. 'It was a pity, as if I had known anyone who would have given him a good home, I would have gladly handed him over for nothing,' Bosie recalled afterwards, 'He might still have been hacked about and even hunted, though of course he was rather a handful to ride for anyone who was not used to riding thoroughbred racehorses.'

From a financial point of view Bosie's racing career in France was disastrous, since he lost a good deal of money through betting. On the other hand, he was well up in his gaming at the casino in Monte Carlo. 'Although I lost a lot of money and acted very foolishly,' he was to write in his autobiography, 'I have never regretted it.'

The eighteen months or two years during which I had the horses were the happiest days of my life. After all the misery and beastliness of the Oscar Wilde affair it was a grand thing to get back to the clean, wholesome atmosphere of my entirely sporting little racing stable. Getting up for two hours before breakfast to ride glorious gallops in the splendid morning air made me so fit and well that I renewed my youth like a phoenix. The sort of life I had been living in London, Naples and Paris was very unhealthy. Up till the time when I bought the horses I had not been on a horse's back, fired off a gun, or played a strenuous game of any kind, for at least six years. Oscar Wilde, who, during those years, even when I was not in his company, completely overshadowed my life, hated sport and games of all kinds. He had no patience with my love of horses and racing.... He resented my spending money on racing instead of giving it to him.

I, for my part, have always had two distinct sides to my nature. I love literature and poetry and art and music with a passionate love. But I am equally fond of sport. If I had my life to live again I might even go in more for sport and less for literature. Even now (1929) I am not quite sure that I would not rather have ridden the winner of the Grand National than have done anything else. Anyhow, I believe that my eighteen months, on and off, at Chantilly added twenty years of health and vigour to my life; while my trainer, Woodhouse, whom I always regarded and treated as a personal friend, was one of the best and most loyal natures I have ever come across.[2]

Bosie also admits that it never occurred to him to live on the interest from the £16,000 he had inherited from his father, which with his mother's allowance would have come to £600 a year, a comfortable sum for a bachelor to exist on in those days of negligible taxation. Instead he gaily went through the whole of his inheritance, having decided, though he afterwards blushed to admit it, that before it was all gone he would marry an American heiress.

In order to go to America for this purpose Bosie needed £800, since he had already exhausted most of his inheritance in his racing venture at Chantilly. He therefore had recourse to a moneylender, who did not oblige. 'My moneylender has not come off,' he wrote to Frank Harris on 13 March 1901, 'so my departure to sunny climes is postponed.' In the same letter he enclosed a sonnet which he had written to Oscar Wilde's memory and which he hoped Harris would publish in his new journal, *The Candid Friend* ('I hope I don't bore you with my sonnets?') It was subsequently published in various editions of Bosie's collected poems as 'Forgetfulness.' It is given here since it is not so well known as the other poem which he wrote on the same subject called 'The Dead Poet.'

To O.W.

Alas! that Time should war against Distress,
And numb the sweet ache of remembered loss,
And give for sorrow's gold the indifferent dross
Of calm regret or stark forgetfulness.
I should have worn eternal mourning dress
And nailed my soul to some perennial cross,
And made my thought like restless waves that toss
On the wild seas's intemperate wilderness.

But lo! came Life, and with its painted toys
Lured me to play again like any child.
O pardon me this weak inconstance.
May my soul die if in all present joys,
Lapped in forgetfulness or sense-beguiled
Yea, in my mirth, if I forget not thee.*[3]

It was during this period, either shortly before or shortly after Wilde's death in 1900 that Robert Ross, knowing that Bosie had inherited a considerable sum when his father died, made Bosie a

---

*The wording of the last line was suggested by Psalm 137 verse 1: 'If I forget thee, O Jerusalem: let my right hand forget her cunning ... yea, if I prefer not Jerusalem in my mirth.'

remarkable offer. According to the account which Ross gave Wilde's future biographer, Hesketh Pearson, in 1916, he asked Bosie to pay off Wilde's debts, thereby discharging his bankruptcy and acquiring the copyrights in his writings and plays wherever possible. Ross offered as Wilde's *de facto* literary executor to administer the Wilde estate on Bosie's behalf until the estate became solvent and Bosie could recoup his financial outlay. However, Bosie turned down Ross's offer. 'The function which I set myself in 1900,' Ross told Pearson, 'was to try and get the books and plays a fair hearing and a fair reading, and to obtain some benefit from their sale for Wilde's children.... But Douglas never forgave either himself or me for having rejected such a very good business proposal. As years went on he became frankly jealous at the prestige which I obtained for having rescued Wilde's estate from bankruptcy, and he was envious at the not inconsiderable proceeds which, if he had accepted my offer, would have been his. That was the real basis of our final quarrel.'[4] The details of the quarrel are related later in this chapter.

2

In the spring of 1901, about the same time as Bosie sent his sonnet on Wilde to Frank Harris, Bosie received a fan letter from a young lady who signed herself Olive Custance. She turned out to be a twenty-seven-year-old poetess, whose first book of verse had been published in the previous year by John Lane under the title *Opals*. Indeed she was known to her friends as Opal since she had a passion for opals, although they are supposed to bring bad luck. But Bosie, who may have been superstitious, always called her Olive. She had been a regular contributor to *The Yellow Book*, the famous quarterly of the Nineties, and her work had been enthusiastically received by the editor, Henry Harland. 'I know that comparisons are odious,' Harland wrote to her in 1896, 'but shall I tell you that of all the poetry we have published in *The Yellow Book*, it is yours which moves me most, which seems to me most poetical?'[5]

Olive's father, Colonel Frederic Custance, who had been in the Grenadier Guards, owned Weston Old Hall, about nine miles north-east of Norwich, the local village being Weston Longeville. Colonel Custance was also chairman of the local bench of magistrates, besides being a keen sportsman, who was often invited by King Edward VII to shoot at Sandringham. The family was an old county one, Olive being descended on her father's side from Francis Bacon, the Elizabethan lawyer and essayist, and on her mother's from William

Jolliffe, Lord Hylton, secretary to the treasury and a privy councillor early in the nineteenth century. The Custance family had owned the Weston Longeville estates for several centuries.

To Olive's letter Bosie replied politely and they arranged to meet in the South Kensington (now the Victoria and Albert) Museum. But owing to some mistake, they went into the museum by different doors and missed each other, and Bosie went back to his rooms in Duke Street, Portland Square, whither Olive who was chaperoned by her maid promptly followed him. When they met Bosie was struck by what Richard Le Gallienne described as her flower-like loveliness, and it was a case very nearly of love at first sight. They discovered that they had met when she was a bridesmaid of ten at the wedding of one of Bosie's cousins. At first she seems to have been the more enthusiastic lover, sending Bosie a copy of her *Opals* together with a bunch of red roses. 'I have been wondering how to write and thank you,' Bosie replied. 'But first I wanted to read your poems, I have just read them. They are wonderfully beautiful. I have not seen anything so good for years. I am so glad they are *really* good!' He sent her a photograph of himself taken several years before – probably the one in Cairo – but he did not think he had altered much. 'Send me yours,' he concluded. They arranged to meet again, this time surreptitiously, in the Carfax art gallery which Robert Ross and several others were running in Ryder Street, St James's. She called him her 'Prince' while she was his 'Page' and soon they were writing passionate love letters to each other.[6]

In an undated letter from Weston to Bosie at this time she wrote:

> Beautiful Prince,
>   I must send a few words to you by the early post just to thank you for your sweetness to me. It was so lovely to look into your clear brave eyes and to talk to you and hear your voice and your laugh. It was so lovely that I can hardly believe it was not all a dream.
>   When shall I get another letter from you and tell me you are pleased with your little Princess? No! I am not your Princess. *She* will be very beautiful. But meanwhile love me a little please, kind and beautiful Prince.
>
>   Opal

It was at this period, in the spring of 1901, that Olive went to Paris with her mother and a Norfolk neighbour, the Hon Frederick ('Freddie') Manners-Sutton, twenty-one-year-old son and heir of Viscount Canterbury. In Paris they met the notorious lesbian writer

Natalie Barney, who had also written to Olive Custance admiring her poems. Olive replied to Natalie with a daring verse:

> For I would dance to make you smile, and sing
> Of those who with some sweet mad sin have played,
> And how Love walks with delicate feet afraid
>   'Twixt maid and maid.

Although here and there Olive's poems have a hint of lesbianism in them, she was not attracted to Natalie as Natalie was to her. When Olive told her that Freddie Manners-Sutton had taken a fancy to her, Natalie replied: 'Tell him I'm in love with you!' When he heard this Freddie did not seem to mind, as long as he could see Olive, even if she were with Natalie. But Natalie wished to have Olive to herself, and contrived to persuade Mrs Custance to agree to her and Olive going off to Venice together, provided Olive was chaperoned by her maid, while Freddie Manners-Sutton and Mrs Custance returned to England. In Venice Olive hung a picture of a statue of Antinous, the Roman Emperor Hadrian's favourite, over her bed, confessing to Natalie that it reminded her of Lord Alfred Douglas with whom, she said, she was really in love. Natalie now tried to 'rescue' Olive by proposing that she (Natalie) should marry Bosie, and the three of them would live happily ever after in a *ménage à trois*. But this idea did not appeal to Olive, who now went back to Norfolk, while Natalie returned to Paris, where she rejoined her lesbian lover Renée Vivienne, a francophile English girl whose real name was Pauline Tarn. Later in the summer, Natalie, who was the daughter of rich American parents, took Renée with her to Bar Harbour for the social season. While she was there Natalie heard that Bosie was coming to America and she wrote to him, perhaps still hoping for a *ménage à trois*.[7]

Bosie was very much given to sending telegrams which were extremely cheap in those days. One which he sent to Olive at Weston nearly got him into trouble. 'A dreadful thing happened to your last wire!' Olive wrote to him. 'It was opened by Daddy! However 'Bosie' conveyed nothing to him. So I said it was from Natalie and soon after sent myself a wire from her to say she was going to Italy as Mummy doesn't like her! I think you will laugh at all this. But why, oh why, does fate make it so difficult for us to meet?' She added that she was coming up from Norfolk to London and would be staying with her parents in their flat in Dover Street, where she asked Bosie to write to her but to get a friend to address the envelope, not forgetting to address it to Miss *Olive* Custance, otherwise it might be given to her mother.[8]

While Olive was in Norfolk during the summer, Bosie spent August and part of September with his brother Percy, now 10th Marquess of Queensberry, who had taken the beautiful Hebridean island of Colonsay for a year. There was a charming house there called Killwan in which they lived and the shooting was excellent, there being plenty of grouse, partridges, woodcock and any amount of duck and snipe, not to mention coverts of pheasants. Meanwhile Bosie had been trying to raise enough money to visit the United States, and he eventually succeeded, although the operation was not an easy one. On his arrival in Colonsay he wrote to Olive: 'I was very much harrassed in London by the crude behaviour of money lenders and others, but as Oscar Wilde said, "It is only by not paying one's debts that one can hope to live in the memory of the commercials." '[9] He wrote again on his return to London in September: 'I am going to America next month. I am rather dreading it. I heard from your friend there Natalie by the way. She had heard I was coming to America. Why can't you dress as a boy and come with me? Much love, Prince.' He had arranged to sail by the Dominion Line on 1 October for Portland, Maine, since he had been advised to stay first in nearby Boston in order to avoid the newspapers in New York. 'This is just what I expected and it upsets all my plans. I hate America and the whole thing. I don't know what to do now.' This is in fact what he did. In the same month Olive was having a short holiday with her cousin Lady Angelsey in Dinard. Bosie wrote suggesting that they should all meet in Paris. Lady Angelsey, who was far from being straight-laced – her husband whom she divorced shortly afterwards was a well-known transvestite homosexual – was agreeable, and they all met in the Hotel Rastadt in the Rue Danou, where the 'children', as Lady Angelsey called them, had a separate table. Whether or not Bosie and Olive slept together is uncertain, but they spent all their waking hours in each other's company and they went out to Chantilly one day to see Bosie's racing stables which he still kept going. Before embarking he sent her a heart-shaped locket with a piece of his hair. She wrote to him characteristically:

> My own Prince,
>   The little heart is sweet and I shall always wear it even when you have forgotten me and married the beautiful rich princess who will give you all those lovely things you ought to have.
>   I miss you more than I can say for I love you beyond everything in the world and I think we shall never be happy together again. Write to me soon and tell me you love your little

Page, and that one day you will come back to 'him', my Prince, my Prince.

I found Mummy rather unhappy as 'Tannie' [Olive's former governess] had told her we met that time in London. Wasn't it horrible of her? However Mummy has forgiven us and all will be well if she doesn't find out about Paris. She would never forgive any of us *then*, I am afraid.

Good-bye, my darling. May all your dreams come true.

I cannot write more. Good-bye,

Olive

'I hate going to America,' he wrote from the ship after he went on board, 'and you know I shan't have anything to do with any horrid princess or anybody at all. How could I after I have known the dear little Page?'

Olive replied a few days later:

Weston Hall,
Norwich.

My own Boy,

What a joy to get that last little letter from you. But now at last I feel you have really gone and I am miserable without you. Last night I dreamed of you and woke to find my pillow wet with tears and I stretched out my empty arms to you and called you, my Prince, very softly, but you were too far away to hear.

Oh how I miss you, your sweet golden head, your small red mouth – always it seems a little shy of my kisses – and above all your great blue eyes, the most beautiful eyes a boy ever had, like two blue flowers under water (as I told you once) and those 'carved lids fringed with lashes thick and long' (I think I wrote that poem to you). How my lips love them. . . . If only I might kiss them tonight. But if I were to write for ever I should not be able to tell you how much I love you. . . .

I will send you the photographs as soon as they are ready and I will also send you to New York a little cigarette case for your birthday on the 22nd (isn't it?). I seem to be scribbling dreadfully, but I forget even to write well when I write to you. I forget everything except that I love you.

See! What a child I am! But you will understand because you are a child too, my Darling, my own Bosie whom God made for me I think.

Good night my Poet (and you must write a poem to *me* I think?). I dream beautiful dreams tonight and I will pray that they all come true.

Your loving
Olive

The equinoctial gales must have set in early that year, since Bosie had a very rough passage to Portland, with storms and heavy seas throughout the voyage. However, he liked Boston where he met 'some nice boys from Harvard.' From Boston for some reason he took the train to Buffalo, via New York, as he wished to see the Niagara Falls, which he did from the Canadian side. On 19 October he wrote to Frank Harris from the Queen's Royal Hotel at Niagara, about eight miles from the Falls, 'I have come to this place from Buffalo for a couple of nights. Have you got any pal over here you could give me a letter to? I have heaps of social introductions, but I should like to meet some of the literary people?'[10] Buffalo he disliked. 'I have been deeply wounded (stupidly because I ought to be beyond that now),' he wrote to Olive from Buffalo 'to find that people here simply don't want to know me or avoid me.' The people in New York were better and he enjoyed Washington best of all, except that his visit to the federal capital was marred by one unfortunate incident. On 2 December he wrote from 10 East 30th Street, New York.

> I have got back here from Washington where I had a fairly nice time, and where I also had a disagreeable experience which I will tell you about when I see you. All the embassy people were charming to me especially the dear old ambassador Lord Pauncefoote who is a perfect dear.
>
> I know that you will be pleased to hear that I am coming back.... I can't think why I ever came and I think on the whole my visit has been rather a failure. However I have met *some* nice people. The women here are charming, but the men are with scarcely an exception the most awful cads....
>
> I told you the way George Montagu treated me. He used to be very nice. I am sorry to think he should be capable of such meanness....
>
> This is a beastly country really. I feel quite two years older since I left England. It will be a nice place to live in in about 500 years time when the people have got civilised and when they have built up a few traditions of conduct and manners. I am sorry I didn't go only to Canada. The people there are really delightful and it really is a much finer country.
>
> You will gather from my letter that I am rather depressed and feel that I have wasted three months and a good deal of money without getting anything....
>
> You see my only idea in coming was entirely the heiress, and then meeting you and our week in Paris completely knocked that on the head, and I ought to have realised that it was no use my coming here and simply wandering about with no object. I have met quantities of heiresses but I have treated them only with bare civility!

Bosie's unpleasant experience in Washington occurred at the Metropolitan Club, of which he had been made an honorary member, having been proposed by his cousin Percy Wyndham, who was Second Secretary at the British embassy. He had been frequenting the club for about a fortnight, when unknown to him, someone in the club raised the question of his honorary membership with the committee in view of his 'connection with a disgraceful scandal'. The next occasion on which he went into the club for a drink, he was recognised, and a member who was sitting with a group of other members made an offensive remark about Oscar Wilde in a loud voice, evidently intending that Bosie should hear it, which he did. He thereupon finished his drink, left the club and went straight to his cousin's rooms and told him about it. Percy replied that he had just received a letter from the committee asking for an 'explanation' of his introduction of Lord Alfred Douglas as an honorary member. Percy Wyndham told Bosie that he had replied to the effect that no explanation was necessary, since Lord Alfred Douglas was his cousin and guest, that he was on intimate terms with the British ambassador and Lady Pauncefote, and that he was a member of White's, London's oldest and most exclusive club. He added that in view of the Metropolitan Club committee's attitude, it was unlikely that Lord Alfred would have any desire to enter their club. To this the committee made no answer. The matter would have rested there, if the incident had not been leaked to the press with the result that it made headlines in the *New York Herald* and other newspapers, much to Bosie's embarrassment. The ambassador sent for Bosie and told him that the Metropolitan Club was a 'pot-house', whose members never lost any chance of being rude to anyone who was on friendly terms with Lord Pauncefote and his staff. At the ambassador's request he escorted Lady Pauncefote to a public concert, and attended a large dinner party at the embassy on the same evening. He received other invitations including one from Senator Cabot Lodge. But he felt the atmosphere was getting on his nerves and that his cousin, who like all young English diplomatists did not wish to act in any way which might prejudice his promotion in the service, was anxious for him to leave. Hence Bosie took the hint and went back to New York. Bosie was bitterly hurt and disappointed, but, as he afterwards put it, it was just one of the numerous occasions on which he had to pay for his association with Oscar Wilde.[11]

The reference to George Montagu in Bosie's letter requires clarification. Montagu, heir presumptive to his unmarried uncle the 8th Earl of Sandwich, had been at Winchester and Magdalen with Bosie, and they were friends there and later, although George was four years younger than Bosie. After Bosie's return from France in 1898, they resumed their friendship, but two years later George's family secured his nomination as Conservative candidate for South Huntingdon in the next General Election. Again because of Bosie's association with Oscar, George Montagu was obliged to 'drop' him. Montagu was duly returned as MP at the so-called 'Khaki election' in October 1900, whereupon Bosie wrote him two letters of protest followed up by a sonnet 'The Traitor' which he also sent him.

Before Bosie left the United States another incident occurred which deserves a brief mention. In one of the hotels in which Bosie stayed, he rang the bell in his bedroom for 'room service'. To his utter amazement the floor waiter who answered the bell was none other than Alfred Taylor. After serving his sentence Taylor had emigrated to Canada on the understanding that his family or relatives would make him a quarterly allowance of £60. He drew this for about two years from a Canadian bank, after which he made no further withdrawals and the bank could give no information as to what had happened to him. Nor is there any record of their conversation when Taylor and Bosie met in these unusual circumstances, but no doubt it was a nostalgic occasion for both.[12]

Bosie returned to London in January 1902 to find his mother had just given up her town house in Cadogan Place and taken another in Wilton Street. While this move was going on, they both went to stay at Clouds, the Wiltshire home of Sibyl Queensberry's uncle Percy Scawen Wyndham and his wife Madeline. 'Just back from shooting,' Bosie wrote to Olive early in February. 'It poured all day. However I shot very well and enjoyed it. No news. The Duchess of Somerset came over to lunch, and Mr and Mrs [Rudyard] Kipling. Lady Airlie [Lady of the Bedchamber to the Princess of Wales] has just arrived... Uncle Percy has just discovered that he was a great friend of your grandfather Hylton Jolliffe. They were in the Crimea together.' As soon as Olive received this letter she wrote to Bosie:

> 19 Dover Street,
> London, W1.
>
> Darling Prince,
>   When are you coming to London? I am so *longing* to see you. I have taken two stalls for *The Importance of Being Earnest* for next Saturday afternoon. Could you come? It would be a way of meeting. I shall say I am going with George, so that will be all right.
>   My Beautiful London is very dark without you. Come out of 'The Clouds', my sunbeam.
>   Your Page.

George Alexander had revived Wilde's play after an interval of seven years, but it only made a small profit for the actor-manager and had a short run. Evidently the public was not ready for Wilde revivals – the next one, again *The Importance* which took place seven years later, after the publication of Wilde's collected works by Robert Ross, was much more of a success. Whether Bosie came up from Clouds for the matinée in February 1902 and met Olive is not known. But what is known is that a few weeks later Olive became engaged to be married to George Montagu. Olive's mother, who deplored her infatuation with Bosie, was delighted, as also was her father, who had just returned from the South African War, where he had commanded the Norfolk Regiment. Olive later admitted that she did wrong to become engaged to George, although when she accepted him she fully intended to marry him. 'But she says, quite rightly,' Bosie added, 'that to have gone on with the marriage when she found out, as she did afterwards, that I really wanted to marry her, and in view of the fact that she loved me and did not love George, but only "liked him very much", would not have been right to him or to me or to herself.'[13]

As soon as he learned the news of Olive's engagement, Bosie invited her to dinner at Kettner's in London, a curious choice in view of its associations in the Wilde trials. But it was an excellent discreet restaurant, and Bosie no doubt chose it as he felt they were unlikely to be recognised there. Over the meal, Olive told Bosie that she had agreed to marry George Montagu, only because she thought that Bosie did not wish to marry her, and that he had 'irrevocably' made up his mind to go for an American heiress. Bosie replied that she must know from his letters that he adored her, that he had given up the idea of the American heiress and had come back to England because he could not live without her. He had always wanted to marry her, he went on, but he did not think it fair to ask her because he had no money and in future would be almost entirely dependent on his mother. In the end he asked her to elope with him, since it was the only possible way by which they could get married 'as if her people got wind of it such pressure would be brought to bear that we would inevitably be separated for ever.' They arranged to meet a few days later in Robert Ross's art gallery so as to work out the details.

At this meeting Olive said that she was due to go down to Hinchingbrooke, Lord Sandwich's place in Huntingdonshire, to meet George's family and stay the weekend. She also said that her mother had, that morning, received a letter from the King congratulating her on her daughter's engagement. Bosie's reaction was to tell her that, while she was away at Hinchingbrooke, he would get a special licence and if she was 'game' they would meet in St George's Church, Hanover Square, at ten o'clock the following Tuesday morning, 4 March 1902, and get married on the quiet. To this she agreed.

Until the last moment Bosie was uncertain whether she would turn up at the appointed time. However she did and explained that she had been staying with her mother in Dover Street, and had told her she was going to spend the day with Tannie, her old governess who lived somewhere in the suburbs. Meanwhile she had taken her maid into her confidence and she had packed a small portmanteau which the maid had managed to take with her undetected and had gone to Victoria Station to await the arrival of the boat train for Paris. Bosie had arrived at the church ten minutes early with his sister Lady Edith Fox-Pitt in her carriage and pair. The only other witness who signed the register after the ceremony besides the registrar was a young barrister friend of the bridegroom, Cecil Hayes, then private secretary to Lord Denbigh and subsequently to appear for Bosie on several occasions in the courts.[13] Robert Ross in whom Bosie had also confided, sat in the back of the church, since Bosie felt he had to let him into the secret because of his meetings with Olive in the Carfax gallery. 'For some extraordinary reason Ross always seemed to resent my marriage,' Bosie wrote afterwards. 'All the same I continued to be on good terms with him for several years after it took place, and he professed to be devoted to Olive, and made every effort to ingratiate himself with her. My wife, who sometimes has wonderful intuitions about people, never liked him or trusted him.'[14] Bosie's mother was not present, but he had told her about it the night before in her new house in Wilton Street where he had been staying and she gave him her fondest blessing, a diamond ring for her future daughter-in-law, a cheque for £200 and the promise of an increased allowance.

Before boarding the boat train at Victoria, Olive sent her mother a telegram saying that she had become Lady Alfred Douglas and that she and her husband were spending their honeymoon in Paris, staying at the Hotel Rastadt in the Rue Daunou. The same evening Sibyl Queensberry wrote to Bosie from 31 Wilton Street:

> I followed in my prayer book through the service and could imagine you two dear things standing up together, and I hoped and prayed for you both. I know I shall love Olive....
>
> I suppose they [the Custances] all know by this time and I feel very nervous. I don't know what they can do, but I imagine the irate father telegraphing to the Embassy to have you both arrested at the station, but that is not possible I know....
>
> Wilfrid [her cousin Wilfrid Scawen Blunt] arrived all excitement; he was so sorry he was away and he would certainly have been

there. He spoke of sending you some money. He was delighted at the whole thing....

Wilfrid was very much against, and so am I, having it announced in the papers *at once*. He thinks it would put the family's backs up more than anything, so I hope you wont mind Darling but we have told Hayes not to do it just yet if there is time to stop it. We think they ought to be given two or three days to let different members of the family know and not to let them read it suddenly in the papers. Wilfrid wanted me to write to Mrs Custance and perhaps I will. I wish I had asked you about it. Send me a telegram early tomorrow to say 'All well' as you know how ingenious I am in conjuring up things.... Bless you both, your devoted Mother. Tell Olive I love her so much for loving you.... We called at Percy's club to tell him, of course you will write to him.

'I have written to Colonel Custance,' she wrote to Bosie a few days later, 'to say I am giving you £500 a year and that I will supplement this by paying rent on anything else to begin with, but I hope you may later be able to earn something by literary work.'[15]

While they were in Paris having what Bosie called 'the time of our lives,' their runaway marriage caused a great rumpus in England. King Edward was said to be 'very angry', though 'what on earth it had to do with him' Bosie was never able to make out. The Montagues also gave tongue, with the exception of the jilted George who remained sorrowful but dignified. The Custances were naturally upset, particularly the Colonel who immediately went along to Scotland Yard, hoping to find something against his son-in-law and was surprised to learn that nothing whatever was known against him and that so far as the Yard's information went he was a model of every virtue. Indeed years later when Colonel Custance went to the Chancery Court to obtain custody of his grandson, Bosie's only child, the only charges he managed to make against his son-in-law was that he was 'very bad tempered' and that he 'attached far too much importance to religion!' Nor did Bosie blame him for going through what he called all the usual motions which were proper to the outraged father of an absconding daughter. He realised that it was a frightful blow to him that Olive, on whom the Weston Longeville estates had been entailed by her Custance grandfather, should have thrown aside a very eligible young man like George Montagu, who expected to succeed to an earldom and £30,000 a year, to run away with the penniless younger son of a notorious marquess and a son moreover who was under a cloud for having been mixed up in about the worst scandal which had occurred in London for a century.

However, Colonel and Mrs Custance eventually accepted the

inevitable fact of the marriage and within a few weeks the Colonel declared that he had 'forgiven' them and invited them to spend a fortnight at Weston. The visit was a great success, since Colonel Custance was surprised to discover that his new son-in-law had other interests besides poetry, notably such field sports as hunting, shooting and racing. The only sport that Bosie had never indulged in was fishing so that Colonel Custance taught him how to cast a fly and catch the trout which abounded in the stream at Weston. The result was that Bosie quickly became an enthusiastic angler.

3

'Alas, our marriage ended in misery for both of us, whatever Bosie may say,' Olive was to write years later. 'But, at least, it did have a radiant beginning.'[16] For ten years or so they lived happily enough together. Their eventual separation was due to Colonel Custance's attempts to obtain the custody of their only child. But, although they never again lived together as man and wife after 1913, they saw and visited each other frequently and generally remained on good terms. In her last letter to Bosie shortly before her death in 1944, she wrote that she was 'ready to agree to anything as regards my life that could please you.... I wish still to be a good wife to you.'

At first they lived in London in a house which Bosie took in Carlyle Square, Chelsea, although they often visited friends and relations in the country. In August 1902, when Olive was about six months pregnant, they were invited to Clouds. Bosie had gone down to Brighton to visit his mother, who was staying there and he wrote to Olive on 28 August:

> Of course you wont go if you don't feel well enough, but I should like you to go if possible as the Wyndhams are such dears and Clouds is the sweetest house to stay in I know. Everyone does exactly as he likes and Aunt Madeline will devote herself to looking after you. Her great joy in life is to get someone to stay with her who wants looking after and petting, and she has a splendid effect on one's nerves if one is not feeling very well.[17]

In the event Olive had a son who was born on 17 November 1902 at 39 Carlyle Square, Chelsea, and christened Raymond Wilfrid Sholto. Olive's friend Freddie Manners-Sutton was godfather. From the first the Colonel took a more than usual grandfatherly interest in the infant, whom he designed eventually to become his heir. But Bosie

and Olive did not regard this as anything out of the ordinary and
certainly not a cause for unease or alarm, until much later when
Olive, looking back, wrote to her husband: 'Everything was different
after Raymond was born. Mummy and Daddy were so dreadful about
him too. They seemed to think we ought to give him up to them.' In
the same year as Raymond's birth, John Lane published Olive's
second book of poems, *Rainbows*. One of these, 'The Girl in the Glass',
is of particular interest, since it seems to be a self-portrait and was
almost certainly written shortly after her wedding.

> Girl in the glass! you smile, and yet
>   Your eyes are full of vague regret;
> For dreams are lovely, and life is sad,
> And when you were a child what dreams you had!
> Now, over your soul life's shadows pass,
>   Girl in the glass.
>
> Girl in the glass, an April day
>   Looks not more tearful, looks not more gay
> Than your rose-flushed face with the wistful mouth.
> For your soul seeks Love as a swallow flies south,
> So, into your eyes Love's sorrows pass,
>   Girl in the glass.

In his autobiography, which was published during Olive's lifetime
Bosie analysed the essence of their relations during their marriage:

> After we were married, I was more in love with her than she was
> with me. Then, of course, the moment that happened I was,
> comparatively speaking, lost as far as my supreme position in her
> eyes was concerned. It was a dreadful business, but I could not see
> that I could help it or was to blame. Moreover, even if I had known
> what I know now, I could only have prolonged the agony of our
> love. But how could I know or guess that the very thing she loved in
> me was that which I was always trying to suppress and keep under:
> I mean the feminine part in me?
>
> The more manly I became the less attractive I was to Olive. I
> can see now, looking back on it all, that she was always desperately
> trying to recapture the 'me' that she had guessed and seen and
> loved, and only occasionally finding it concealed under various
> cloaks. If we had never married, we would have gone on for ever
> adoring each other. But marriage ... gradually destroyed our love.
> When I say destroyed our love, I only mean that it destroyed our
> passionate love; another kind of love still remains. My only

consolation, now that I at last understand, is that if she had
married anyone else, her disillusion would have been ten times
more rapid and quite as complete.[18]

'Darling sweet beloved girl,' Bosie wrote to his wife after they had
been married for some months and she had to leave him for a night or
two, probably to see her parents. 'The house is quite empty without
the darling little mouse.' He added that he was going to sleep in her
bed and dream about her.

During the next two or three years Bosie and Olive with their baby
son lived in Chelsea, first in Carlyle Square and later at 41 Walpole
Street, off the King's Road, with frequent country visits to Olive's
parents and Bosie's relatives, punctuated by trips to the Continent,
Belgium, Corsica and the Riviera. In 1903 they were in Ostend where
Bosie played a system of roulette starting with £50 and ending up with
£350. But he found the strain too great for his nerves to stand and he
never played it again. Then, in the following year they moved more or
less permanently to the country to a beautiful old farm house called
Lake Farm, six miles from Salisbury on the road to Amesbury,
although they continued to rent a London house, latterly 99 Church
Street, Chelsea. Lake Farm belonged to an amiable old gentleman
named Lovibond who lived in nearby Lake House in Lake village.
They had met him through Bosie's cousin Pamela Wyndham, who
had married Edward Tennant, later Sir Edward and Liberal MP for
Salisbury, and later still Lord Glenconner. They lived at Wilsford
Manor, about half a mile from Lake Farm, both being on the river
Avon, one of the best trout streams in England. Further along the
river towards Amesbury there was Amesbury Abbey, a magnificent
Palladian house, which incidentally had been built by Bosie's
ancestor the third Duke of Queensberry who with his wife, the
celebrated 'Kitty' had been patrons of John Gay and other eighteenth-century dramatists, as mentioned in the first chapter. It was
now the home of Sir Edmund Antrobus, baronet, who owned about
8,000 acres in the neighbourhood including Stonehenge and had
previously commanded a battalion of the Grenadier Guards.
'Strobus', as he was called and his eccentric wife, known as 'Wavie',
got on well with Bosie and Olive, as did the tenants and other 'county'
neighbours. The shooting and fishing were a great attraction for
Bosie, particularly the fishing, since in addition to the stretch of water
by Lake Farm he could also fish the waters at Wilsford, Amesbury
and others, so that he had several miles of first-class fishing.

For Bosie and Olive the years at Lake Farm were perhaps the
happiest in their married life. Like Olive, Pamela Tennant had

literary talent and with Bosie they were all regular contributors to *The Academy*, a highbrow literary weekly edited by Harold Child and belonging to the *Country Life* group of periodicals owned by the publishing firm of George Newnes. While Olive occasionally pined for London, Bosie hated tearing himself away from the fishing. 'Up to the time of my marriage I had never fished at all,' he later recalled; 'but I ended by loving it quite as much as shooting. I believe I caught one day, with dry fly, the second-largest basket of trout ever secured on the Amesbury Abbey water. As far as I remember I got eighteen fish, all over a pound and a half, eleven of them over two pounds, and one of three pounds. In addition to that I put back quite a dozen just under a pound and a half, the rule of the water being that you kept only fish over a pound and a half.[19]

Olive had some trouble with her health and on one occasion had to see a specialist in London, which she was inclined to prefer to Wiltshire in the winter. She had some differences with her husband over this, but they always made it up, since Bosie was still passionately in love with her, as the following letter written from the country shows:

Salisbury
22 January 1906

My precious darling,
    I can't say how much I love and adore you. When you came back from that specialist and cried like that, my heart ached with love for you. I can hardly bear to be away from you for one night. I feel quite ill for the want of you. Every day I love you more.
    My blessed sweet, you shan't go to the country unless you like. But you know I sometimes am a better judge and in this case I *know* it is the right thing to do and I know I can make you happy here and I do want you to come even if we are not certain of keeping on the house.
    I am going to try myself to try [sic] and make you happy, my darling good little girl. I have often been selfish and horrid, but not really in my heart, and I have always tried to do what was best and tried to think of you before myself. But I know I fail and London is bad for me morally and physically if I have too much of it. I love it for a few months. I am longing to get back to you.
    It is dreadful that you should be so tormented by illness and troubles. Every wound to you is a sharp knife in my heart. I hate to think that I cannot bear your hurts for you.
    My darling dearest darling sweet,

Your loving devoted,
Boy.

Olive had recently published a third volume of her poems, *The Blue Bird*, with the following dedication 'To My Husband':

> I sing the joy and sorrow of the world,
> The strange and secret histories of the heart;
> I am a dreamer, and each day my dreams
> Go out to kiss the eyes of lovely grief,
> The laughing mouth of Love. I have bowed down
> Before the light of beauty all my life,
> And now, O poet passionate and brave,
> O lover with the beautiful sad face,
> Like a shy child I bring you all my songs.

'They are quite beautiful and some are better than any you have ever done,' Bosie wrote to her after he had received the proofs. 'It will make a beautiful little book.'

He responded by writing six sonnets 'To Olive' which first appeared in *The Academy* in 1907; they were published in book form with a selection of Bosie's other sonnets two years later, and were subsequently reprinted in his *Collected Poems* (1919). Bosie seems to have preferred the fifth, since he quoted it in his autobiography:

> When we were Pleasure's minions, you and I,
> When we mocked grief and held disaster cheap,
> And shepherded all joys like willing sheep
> That love their shepherd; when a passing sigh
> Was all the cloud that flecked our April sky,
> I floated on an unimagined deep,
> I loved you as a tired child loves sleep,
> I lived and laughed and loved, and knew not why.
>
> Now I have known the uttermost rose of love;
> The years are very long, but love is longer;
> I love you so. I have no time to hate
> Even those wolves without. The great winds move
> All their dark batteries to our fragile gate:
> The world is very strong, but love is stronger.

The Blue Bird appeared under the imprint of the Marlborough Press, unlike her previous two books of poems, *Opals* and *Rainbows* which had been published by John Lane. The Marlborough Press published *The English Review*, a short-lived weekly edited by an eccentric and cantankerous Yorkshireman, Thomas William Hodgson Crosland – it only lasted from 21 October 1905 to 17 February 1906. It is probable that Olive chose him as a publisher because some of the poems first appeared in Crosland's journal, besides which her husband also contributed a weekly poem or nonsense rhyme to *The English Review*. Neither Olive nor Bosie ever got paid anything for their contributions, and when *The English Review* went out of business and its editor was made bankrupt which happened shortly afterwards, Olive was able to buy the unsold copies of *The Blue Bird* for £3, although Crosland wanted £5 for them. But Olive bore the bankrupt editor no malice. 'A thousand thanks for those charming little birds!' she wrote to him, acknowledging receipt of the books, at the same time inviting him to dinner, since she heard he had been ill. 'Do come and dine tonight – no dressing! I hope you are better.'[20] Bosie's nonsense rhymes which appeared in *The English Review* were afterwards published in book form, under Bosie's name, as *The Placid Pug*, to which was added a reprint of *The Duke of Berwick*; while similar rhymes, which he wrote later, first saw the light in *Vanity Fair*, then edited by Frank Harris, and were afterwards published as a book entitled *The Pongo Papers* (1907) by Greening – the same firm which had brought out Robert Sherard's biography of *Oscar Wilde: The Story of an Unhappy Friendship*, the first biography of Wilde to be written.

It was also in *The English Review*, under Crosland's brief editorship, that Bosie's sonnet on Wilde, 'The Dead Poet', first appeared, although it had been written five years before in Paris, about a year after Wilde's death.

> I dreamed of him last night, I saw his face
> All radiant and unshadowed of distress,
> And as of old, in music measureless,
> I heard his golden voice and marked his trace
> Under the common thing the hidden grace,
> And conjure wonder out of emptiness,
> Till mean things put on beauty like a dress
> And all the world was an enchanted place.
>
> And then methought outside a fast locked gate
> I mourned the loss of unrecorded words,
> Forgotten tales and mysteries half said,
> Wonders that might have been articulate,
> And voiceless thoughts like murdered singing birds.
> And so I woke and knew that he was dead.

Bosie was an early – if not a pioneer – motorist. For that reason, recalling his association with Oscar, the editor of the magazine *Motorist and Traveller* sent him *De Profundis* to review when the original version was published by Methuen with a preface by Robert Ross on

23 February 1905. It was sympathetically reviewed, among others by Max Beerbohm, Hamilton Fyfe, William Archer, and Cunningham Graham under their own signatures. Bosie's notice which appeared under his initial, was critical, and in view of the controversial question as to whether or not he received the typed copy which Robert Ross stated that he sent him in August 1897, it is quite clear from the review that if he did receive the copy he did not read as far as the passages which appear in the published version. The reviewer began by describing the work as 'this interesting posthumous book' which 'takes the form of a letter to an unnamed friend,' whom Bosie assumed to be Ross who had prefaced and edited it. Bosie certainly had not the faintest idea when he wrote the review that the 'unnamed friend' was himself. While conceding that 'there are fine prose passages in it, and occasional felicities of phrase which recall the Oscar Wilde of *The House of Pomegranates* and *Prose Poems*, and here unexpectedly comes an epigram,' as well as 'much that is profound and subtle on the philosophy of Christ as conceived by this modern evangelist of the gospel of Life and Literature', he described the book as 'rather pathetically ineffective', since 'the mood which produced it was generated by suffering and confinement which culminated in the death of its gifted and unfortunate author a few years later.' He concluded:

> He says that if he had been released a year sooner, as in fact he very nearly was, he would have left his prison full of rage and bitterness, and without the treasure of his new-found 'Humility'. I am unregenerate enough to wish that he had brought his rage and bitterness with him out of prison. True, he would never have written this book if he had come out of prison a year sooner, but he would almost certainly have written several more incomparable comedies and we who reverenced him as a great artist in words, and mourned his downfall as an irreparable blow to English Literature would have been spared the rather painful experience of reading the posthumous praise now at last so lavishly given to what certainly cannot rank within measurable distance of his best work.[21]

The twenty-two-year-old budding novelist Compton Mackenzie, who kept a diary at this time, wrote in it on 22 May 1905 that he went to see Robert Ross that evening in his rooms in Hornton Street, Kensington, and that More Adey and Reggie Turner were there:

> Robbie read some of the letters he had been getting from people about *De Profundis*. George Alexander had written to say that after reading it 'he was bound to confess that he shed tears'. Robbie said

he hoped he would shed more tears and pay royalties to Wilde's estate if he revives the plays whose acting rights he bought for almost nothing when Wilde went bankrupt.* At this moment Bosie Douglas came in and stood on the fender fidgeting, and scratching himself as usual and kept sliding off it. Then Robbie read a letter from G.B. Shaw to point out that *De Profundis* was Wilde's final score off the British public, and that it was a gigantic *blague*, the final pose even in prison. Douglas said Shaw was probably right and Robbie got angry. Douglas criticised Wilde's life in Paris and Robbie said the one most to blame for that was Douglas himself.

Douglas lost his temper, kicked the fender and marched out of the room. He came back for a moment and told Robbie he did not know what he was talking about. Then he slammed the door, and presently downstairs we heard the front door slam. More Adey was walking about looking more vague than ever and Reggie Turner said Bosie was so impossible that he should have to put him in his next novel when all the reviewers would say that Mr Turner's characters were far from true to life....[22]

Later in the same year, in July 1905, Bosie was in London staying in his Chelsea house in Church Street, when Olive's ex-fiancé, George Montagu, married an American girl from New York called Alberta Sturges. 'I suppose you saw an account of George's wedding in the papers,' he wrote to Olive. 'I didn't think it half as smart as I expected. Phipps [a friend of their Winchester schooldays] with whom I dined last night, told me he had met Alberta and that it was quite a shock. He said she was not only ugly but very common!'

Although the Custance property was entailed on Olive, she did not get much money from her father at this time, while the allowance her husband received from his mother sometimes proved insufficient for their needs. Thus they were constantly hard up and Olive twice pawned her diamond ring. On the second occasion, after it had been redeemed, for some reason it was sent to Bosie, who happened to be staying with his cousin Wilfrid Scawen Blunt at Newbuildings Place, one of Blunt's houses in Sussex. 'I couldn't make out what the little package was for me,' Bosie wrote to his wife on 21 September 1906, 'and I was rather horrified to find the ring. I shouldn't like to pawn it again I think Damus [Bosie's mother] was very much hurt when we did it before. You know she has not many things and it was the best

*George Alexander did pay a half share of the royalties during his lifetime and under his will left the rights in the plays in question, *Lady Windermere's Fan* and *The Importance of Being Earnest*, to the Wilde estate for the benefit of Wilde's two sons Cyril and Vyvyan Holland.

diamond ring she had and she gave it to me the night before our marriage to give to you. I think if it is necessary to pawn anything you might have chosen something else.'

Some time during the earlier part of the year 1907, Harold Child resigned from the editorship of *The Academy* to join the staff of *The Times*, and Bosie's cousin and neighbour Pamela Tennant learned that the journal, which then shared an office with *Country Life* in Tavistock Street, could be bought quite cheaply. According to Robert Ross, it was he who wrote to Bosie and suggested that he should get his cousin's husband, Sir Edward Tennant, Bart, as he had now become, to purchase the paper and make Bosie editor. Ross adds that he was invited down to Wilsford Manor to discuss the matter and he advised the Tennants with regard to the price and saw their solicitors on the subject, 'as I have some knowledge of the value of newspaper property.'[23] In his autobiography Bosie does not mention Ross as having had anything to do with it, but gives the credit entirely to his cousin Pamela for having induced her husband to buy *The Academy* and appoint him editor, thus as it were keeping *The Academy* in the family since she would continue to contribute to it as well as Bosie.

When he found that he could get it for £2,000, Pamela's husband bought it. Bosie was consequently installed as editor at a salary of £300 a year, while the office moved from Tavistock Street to 63 Lincoln's Inn Fields, the staff besides the editor consisting of a twenty-year-old editorial secretary, Miss Alice Head, and an office boy. The printing, advertising and circulation were to be the responsibility of the newsagents, W.H. Smith & Son. Both Pamela and Edward Tennant considered that it would be an ideal occupation for her cousin and that it would remain essentially literary in content rather than political, since Bosie's politics, in so far as he had any, were demonstrably right-wing Tory and viewed as something of a joke at Wilsford Manor.

So the arrangement was concluded, and Bosie and Olive with five-year-old Raymond gave up Lake Farm as well as their Chelsea house and moved into a charming Queen Anne house in Hampstead, 26 Church Row, where their landlords were the Provost and Fellows of Eton College. Unknown to either Bosie or Olive at the time the move was to presage a host of troubles for the new editor of *The Academy*.

4

At first all went well on the editorial side of Bosie's new literary venture. In addition to contributions from his cousin Pamela Tennant as well as Olive and himself, new contributors included a group of young and hitherto unsuccessful writers who regularly met in a pub and called themselves the New Bohemians. Leader of the group was Arthur Machen, an essayist and short story writer, who nearly became great and well-known, although he was to die in poverty, his work such as *The Ghost Ship* largely unrecognised. Other members of the group were Randal Charlton, Louis McQuilland, Michael (Tommy) Pope and Richard Middleton. Machen was a militant Anglican High Churchman, and Bosie tended to follow his line in religion, which in so many instances had led to conversion to the Roman Catholic faith. Other contributors included Bernard Shaw, St John Hankin, Siegfried Sassoon, Robert Ross, Reginald Turner and More Adey, as well as Oscar Wilde's friend Ada Leverson ('The Sphinx') and two brilliant young poets James Elroy Flecker and Rupert Brooke. Although there were occasional squabbles with members of the public who objected to some literary article, initially *The Academy* flourished. It was certainly good value at threepence for eighteen or twenty pages of letterpress.

T.W.H. Crosland, to whose defunct journal *The English Review* both Bosie and Olive had contributed, did not allow his bankruptcy to prevent him starting a new periodical entitled *The Future*. The first issue, which like the others was entirely written by Crosland himself, came out on 23 November 1907 and contained an article headed 'Distinguished Journalism'. The article attacked *The Academy* in the following terms:

> Since Lord Alfred Douglas took over the editorial chair of *The Academy* we have seen what we have seen. With a millionaire at the back of it who has obviously no axes to grind, and whose wife, Lady Tennant, is a woman of great literary perception and endowed with the best intentions towards humanity, and with an editor of Lord Alfred Douglas's undoubted talents and large experience, we believed and still believe that we had a right and have a right to look at *The Academy* for something approximating to ideality in the matter of literary papers. Lord Alfred Douglas is a militant defender of the arts and a proficient executant in at least one of them; he has at his elbow, as it were, Lady Tennant, and at his bank Sir Edward Tennant. Yet what do we find? So far from establishing itself as a literary journal of broad literary dispositions and quality, *The Academy* under Lord Alfred Douglas's editorship, has exhibited a distinct tendency to deteriorate into a feeble organ of the feebler and lesser cults, and at the present moment it is of no more use to the serious principles it might have served than the proverbial headache.[24]

Bosie evidently paid heed to this criticism, since within a few months he accepted Crosland as a regular contributor, and a little later, towards the end of 1908, as assistant editor. It turned out to be an unfortunate choice for Bosie, since, although Crosland was an able journalist who taught the editor a great deal about the techniques of journalism, their association led to various troubles and quarrels. 'I could never understand why two men of such wholly alien natures should become such close friends,' commented Alice Head, who later became editor of *Good Housekeeping*. 'He (Crosland) could not possibly have provided a greater contrast to Lord Alfred's exceptional beauty. Lord Alfred had blue eyes, perfect teeth, a schoolgirl complexion and a smile of infinite charm. Crosland, on the other hand, was pot-bellied and obstreperous with a gruff manner and a constant scowl on his face; he also suffered from diabetes.'

> He angered me very much by the way he alienated most of Lord Alfred's friends and tried to run the business on dubious lines as his own, but I recognised at all times that he was a poet and writer of peculiar achievement. He influenced Lord Alfred most unwisely, and led him into all sorts of difficulties. Lord Alfred gave me a taste for good literature, and I am everlastingly grateful for his many kindnesses.[25]

It was due to Crosland that a political polemical element was introduced into what purported to be 'an independent, uncommercial journal conducted in the interest of literature and for the maintenance of a high standard of fearless and independent criticism.' Not unnaturally it made many enemies in the literary field, particularly among writers whose works were reviewed unfavourably. 'Nobody likes *The Academy*,' Bosie wrote to his wife on 29 October 1908, shortly after Crosland became assistant editor; 'It appears to annoy and infuriate everybody, but *on the other hand* they all read it, and I don't care how angry it makes people as long as they read it. The circulation goes on rising, we are printing extra copies this week, and we have more adverts again.'

At the end of 1908, in a letter to Ada Leverson ('The Sphinx'), who had asked whether she could write a critique of Somerset Maugham's latest play *Penelope*, the editor explained the journal's policy in the matter of dramatic criticism and book reviewing:

> You can do the Maugham play if you like, it being understood that on the *Academy* we write absolutely without favour. Nobody is allowed to write 'something nice' about a book or a play because the author happens to be a friend, or to attack because he happens

to be an enemy. It is necessary to say this because I find that on most if not all other papers, log-rolling and its contrary are taken for granted. I must warn you also that the pay, under the present regime, is exiguous in the extreme, and as nobody signs there is not even much honour and glory.

An effort is being made to run a paper which will do good to letters instead of advertising any given person or set of persons. It is of course a very old-fashioned or obsolete idea, but strange to say it seems to be working out well.[26]

One would-be contributor at this period was Michael Field, whose poem Bosie rejected. Evidently he did not realise that Michael Field was a pseudonym for two poetesses, Katharine Bradley and Edith Cooper, who collaborated on lyric poetry and poetic drama, since he replied to their letter 'Dear Sir' and went on: 'I am sending back this MS as I do not consider it up to your very high level. In view of the terms in which I spoke of you in an article "A Neglected Poet" signed A.D. last year, I think it would be unfortunate to print in this paper any poem of yours which was not fully worthy of your great genius. I hope my returning this poem entirely in what I consider to be your own interests will not prevent you from giving me an opportunity of printing others.'[27]

Although Bosie's editorial letters were mainly literary, he occasionally wrote a business one, as instanced by the following dated 14 December 1908 to John Lane of The Bodley Head, who had been Wilde's publisher as well as Olive Douglas's. It controverts the accepted view that Bosie had no head for business and was not interested in it.

> You will please understand that the prices which you have lately been paying for your advertisements are quite exceptional and I cannot allow them to be taken as precedents. It seems to me that you are taking an unfair advantage of the fact that I have had personal friendly relations with you to try to beat me down in a really outrageous manner.
>
> I should be sorry not to have your advertisements at all, but I cannot consent to allow you to make use of my paper at prices which are less than half those paid by any other publisher in London. I must say that I think that this continual bickering about money is not worthy of the reputation of The Bodley Head. Considering that the circulation of THE ACADEMY is double what it was when I first took over, it is not reasonable that you should pay less for advertisements than you paid before. I do not expect you to advertise to oblige me, but simply as a matter of business, and on the same basis as other publishers.

> If you want to know how the paper is going and what its value as
> an advertisement medium is, I refer you to Messrs W.H. Smith &
> Son's Newspaper Department. They can give you even better than
> I can convincing evidence of the way the paper is going.[28]

According to John Lane's biographer Lewis May, Lane was keen
almost to the point of meanness where business was concerned.[29] No
doubt that was a cause of his success as a publisher, since he had
started from very modest beginnings with the antiquarian book
collector Elkin Mathews. However, his difference with *The Academy*
over the question of his firm's advertisements seems to have been
settled to the editor's satisfaction, since The Bodley Head continued
to advertise in the journal.

There is no record of Somerset Maugham having complained about
the critique of *Penelope*, since Ada Leverson's notice was a friendly
one. But Bernard Shaw expostulated about the criticism of his play
Getting Married in May 1908. 'For shame, Mr Shaw!' was the title of
The Academy notice. 'Not a play at all,' the critic wrote, 'but a
conversation': two ladies, a waiter and a general talking about
marriage. The play should never have been passed by the censor, the
critic went on. Mr Shaw, the vegetarian, teetotaller, non-smoker and
someone 'who does not possess a masculine intellect,' had no right to
give instructions in sociology and morality. In short Bernard Shaw
was 'beginning to make serious inroads on the British home,' and 'the
sooner Mr Shaw learns that he is not in a position to preach the better
it will be for him.'

'Who on earth have you been handing over your dramatic
criticisms to?' Shaw wrote to the editor. 'Your man, who must have
been frightfully drunk, has achieved the following startling libel.'

> The waiter, disguised as a butler, told us, among other things, that
> his mother was very fond of men and was in the habit of bringing
> them home at night.

'You will see that the writer gives himself away hopelessly at the
beginning by saying that he left the house at the end of twenty-five
minutes,' Shaw went on. 'Later he describes a scene which he did not
wait for, and contrives to get both a libel and a flat mis-statement of
fact into his reference. However, it is really this howler about the
man's mother which makes the article entirely indefensible.' This
statement was 'pure invention' Shaw added, telling the editor that *The
Academy* would have the producers, the theatre manager and the actor
concerned all demanding damages at the rate of £2,500 apiece. The
author suggested that the best thing that the editor could do was to

admit the notice was a misdescription and withdraw it in the next issue 'unreservedly'.

Bosie replied that he had received Shaw's letter with the greatest surprise. 'I strongly resent the accusation of being drunk which you bring against the writer of the article,' he wrote. 'It seems to me that it is characteristic of the feminine quality of your intellect, to which reference was made in the article, to make such an outrageous suggestion. As a matter of fact I wrote the article myself. If I misheard any particular sentence in the dialogue the error was, on your own showing, a trifling one, and it is ludicrous to suggest that it is libellous. That part of the play which I heard simply teems with indecencies, and I should be delighted to go into the witness-box in any court and say so.'

> You may be perfectly aware that I am not actuated by any malice towards you. You have had nothing but praise from the *Academy* during the whole time that I have edited it, and now on the first occasion when I find it compatible with my duty as a critic to find fault with you, you resort to the rather mean expedient of asking me to throw over a supposed contributor. I confess that I am surprised that a man of your intellectual attainments should exhibit such pettiness.

The editor added that Shaw was at liberty to take what action he chose in the matter, and he gave him the name and address of his solicitors.

'Thank goodness it was you, and not some poor devil whom it would have been your duty to sack,' Shaw retorted. 'You MUST have been drunk – frightfully drunk – or in some equivalent condition; no normal man behaves like that. . . . I feel pretty sure that your solicitors will advise you to admit the blunder and withdraw it. If they don't, change them.' He himself, Shaw added, did not propose to take any action, since he had only intervened 'to get you out of a scrape.' But others were not so inclined to take the libellous sentence so amiably.

'Your letter is a piece of childish impertinence,' Bosie rejoined, 'but as it was evidently written in a fit of hysterical bad temper, I shall not count it against you. I am immensely amused by your professed desire to "get me out of a scrape". I do not consider that I am in any scrape at all, and I think that you will find that I am a person who is very well able to look after himself without any assistance from you.'

'I asked you for a friendly reparation: you have given me a savage revenge.' Thus the author of *Getting Married* characteristically ended the correspondence. 'However, perhaps it was the best way out. As you have owned up, we are satisfied; and the public will forgive you for the sake of your blazing boyishness.' He concluded:

> There is always the question – Who is to edit the editor? Fortunately in this case there are two Douglases – A.D. the poet and – shall I say? – the hereditary Douglas. Make A.D. the editor. It needs extraordinary conscientiousness, delicacy and Catholicism to criticise unscrupulously, brutally, and free-thinkingly, as the *Academy* is trying to do, and, indeed, derives all its interest and value from so doing. The hereditary Douglas, when he gets loose from A.D., is capable of wrecking a paper – even of wrecking himself. Most people are – hence the need for editors. Excuse my preaching; I am a born improver of occasions. *Sans rancune.*
>
> G. Bernard Shaw[30]

A more serious literary difference, which really put an end to their friendship, was with Robert Ross. Crosland, who had a horror of homosexuality, disapproved of Ross as a contributor. He had heard, he told Bosie, that Ross was 'an unsavoury person' and 'not the kind of man to be writing for us.' This view was shared by Pamela Tennant who also told Bosie so. It so happened that Bosie had sent Ross a book to review. When Ross's review came in to the office, Bosie handed it to Crosland and asked him to edit it. Crosland interpreted this request as a licence to alter the review in any way he wished. 'When the review was published,' Ross subsequently stated, 'I found that a perfectly ordinary criticism of the book in question had been turned into vulgar and violent abuse of a great personal friend of mine who was dragged into the article and mercilessly attacked.' Bosie wrote to Ross admitting that he had been obliged to take liberties with the article. Ross did not reply to Bosie's letter, but when he received a cheque in payment for the article he returned it to the editorial secretary Alice Head, saying he did not wish to accept payment for an article which he considered was no longer his.[31] The amount of the cheque was then handed over to the Royal Literary Fund.

By this date Robert Ross had become much better known than he was during Wilde's lifetime. His edition of *De Profundis* had been widely praised when it first appeared in 1905, as had his edition of Wilde's collected works which appeared three years later under his general editorship. He had also by arrangement with the Official Receiver in Wilde's bankruptcy become Wilde's literary executor *de jure* as well as *de facto* when the Wilde estate was discharged from bankruptcy, which it was in 1906, all the creditors including the

Douglas family being paid 20 shillings in the pound with 4 per cent interest. On the 1 December 1908 a number of Ross's friends entertained Ross to dinner in The Ritz in London, with Sir Martin (later Lord) Conway in the chair, to mark their appreciation of Ross's achievements in the matter of Wilde's literary and pecuniary rehabilitation. Bosie did not attend the function which he described as being rather snobbish, although he was invited to do so by Reggie Turner who had formed the committee to organise the dinner.

A few weeks later Olive Douglas invited Ross to lunch. He replied formally that he was engaged on that day. 'It was so kind of you to write,' Olive replied, 'but Oh what a stiff letter! What have I done? Do come and see me one day soon. You must know I always love to see you.' She repeated the luncheon invitation adding 'Because I am afraid you and Bosie are not friends just now, I am sorry.'

Ross wrote back that it was because he did not wish to quarrel with Bosie again that he had avoided and would continue to avoid meeting him in the future. 'We should inevitably differ,' he went on.

> I am with the opposite side on every controversial matter discussed by the *Academy*, which moreover attacks all the people who are my personal friends and most of the books and authors I happen to admire. . . .
>
> Alone of all my former friends, or I may say of Wilde's friends, he sent me no message of felicitation on the public celebration of the conclusion of what had been my chief occupation for eight years. . . .
>
> I have no hostile feelings whatever because I know Bosie too well and have known him too long. But I decided some time ago to deny myself the privileges coincidental to friendship with him. I do not wish to reopen unnecessarily matters quite unimportant now to anyone but myself; I merely wish to explain an attitude which otherwise might have seemed churlish to yourself for whom my regard may more adequately be described as homage.[32]

Ross concluded by suggesting that they might meet 'under the hospitable roof' of their mutual friend Mrs Carew, the anonymous donor of £2,000 to defray the cost of the Epstein memorial over Wilde's grave in Père Lachaise cemetery in Paris.

Olive showed this letter to her husband, who wrote to Ross on 1 March 1909 characterising Ross's letter as an 'extraordinary farrago of impudent rubbish.' Bosie went on:

> As to your absurd dinner to meet the Duchess of Sutherland and other people who have nothing whatever to do with Oscar or

literature, I certainly did not feel inclined to go to a function to meet Frank Harris, Robert Sherard and about 20 other people with whom Oscar was not on speaking terms when he died. I said nothing about it except in a letter to Reggie in response to one asking me to attend the dinner ... but I think it was indiscreet of Reggie to show it to you or repeat its contents.

As to your determination to forego my friendship, as you have raised the point, I may say that the boot is on the other leg. I gave up going to your house because I disapproved of your views, your morals and most of your friends. My own views have changed and I do not care to meet those who are engaged in active propaganda of every kind of wickedness from anarchy to sodomy....

I agree with you that it is better that we should keep apart. I don't consider that you have ever been a real friend of mine, in the sense that More [Adey] and others have been my friends. And I may tell you frankly that I don't think your character has improved with age.

Ross was somewhat alarmed by the reference to his morals and sodomy in Bosie's letters and he consulted his solicitor Sir George Lewis. Lewis advised him that, while Bosie's letter was undoubtedly actionable, it would be very unwise of him to take the matter to court, because it would revive 'a very unpleasant scandal' and that in view of Ross's well-known intimacy with both Oscar Wilde and Alfred Douglas it was unlikely that he would obtain much relief from a jury. On Lewis's advice Ross did not reply to Bosie's letter and they had no further communication for three years when Bosie wrote to him again, this time about *De Profundis* in the context of Arthur Ransome's recently published critical study of Wilde. On this occasion Bosie's letter did lead to a legal action with unfortunate consequences for himself, as will be related in due course.

Meanwhile, Ross had begun to hear stories that Bosie was repeating to various people the charges which Bosie had brought against him in his letter of 1 March 1909 quoted above. For example, he told More Adey that Ross was being watched by detectives; that he had seduced one of the servants in the Hotel Dieudonné in Ryder Street, St James's, close to the Carfax Gallery, where Ross had stayed in 1908; and that he also had had improper relations with one of the waiters in the Royal Automobile Club in Pall Mall. Ross informed Sir George Lewis of all these accusations, but Lewis again advised Ross to take no action. Anyhow, as Ross put it, 'beyond ordinary annoyance it did not cause me any uneasiness as the charges were perfectly untrue.'[33] Eventually, in October 1914, as will be seen, Ross prosecuted Bosie for criminal libel, after he had similarly proceeded against Crosland and Bosie for criminal conspiracy.

More unfortunate than such literary differences as the *Academy*'s editor had with individuals like Shaw and Ross was the political line of the paper which became increasingly Tory in complexion, in opposition to Mr Asquith's Liberal government; this included Lloyd George and Winston Churchill, whom Bosie regarded as jointly responsible for the ruin of the country and the 'smash up' of everything that used to make life in England worth living. Some member of Bosie's family, probably Algie Bourke, remarked to him one day that it appeared to be 'rather rough on Eddie Tennant' that Bosie should be using Tennant's paper and his money to attack his political party and in particular the Prime Minister, who was his brother-in-law. (Mrs Margot Asquith was Tennant's sister.) Bosie thereupon wrote to the proprietor of *The Academy* asking him if he objected to the political line of the paper. 'If so, I will drop it,' Bosie assured him. 'I cannot, of course, change my views or those of the paper, but if you wish it I will drop politics altogether and stick to literature alone.' According to Bosie, Tennant replied to the effect that he did not mind at all. ('In fact I think it very lively, and a great deal of what you say I entirely agree with.')[34]

Unhappily, about a fortnight later, in September 1908, Bosie wrote a very strongly worded attack on Mr Asquith for his action in suppressing the procession or, to be strictly accurate, the form of the procession, as a feature of the Eucharistic Congress which was being held in London in that year. It was intended that the Host should be carried through the streets round Westminster Cathedral, attended by dignitaries of the Roman Catholic Church in their vestments. Although the Chief of the Metropolitan Police, himself a Catholic, had given permission for the procession to take place in this form, it was not generally realised at first that as such it was contrary to the Catholic Emancipation Act. When Mr Asquith, who was holidaying in Scotland, had his attention drawn to the matter in certain sections of the press which had voiced vigorous protests, he appreciated that if the Host were publicly exhibited in this way it might well provoke a riot by objecting Protestants in the community. Accordingly, a few days before the procession was due to take place, Mr Asquith and his Cabinet decided that the Archbishop of Westminster must be asked to omit the illegal elements from the procession – such as the public display of the Host – and bring the procession into conformity with the law. The Archbishop was understandably annoyed at being obliged to change his plans at the last minute but he had no option but to comply. The nub of Bosie's attack upon the Prime Minister was that the procession should have been allowed to take place as originally conceived.

To Bosie's great surprise and indignation, he received a letter from Edward Tennant, stating that he considered the article was 'in the worst possible taste'. Tennant went on to state that he had decided to sell *The Academy* and to sever all connection with it. This reaction from a public figure whose wife's cousin had attacked a Prime Minister from whom he hoped to get a peerage, was understandable. In the event Bosie left the ensuring negotiations in Crosland's hands. The result was that Bosie was given *The Academy* by its proprietor as a present together with £500 to keep it going, although Tennant did not think it would last for more than a few months. In exchange Bosie gave Tennant a bill for £500 which he had no intention of meeting and in fact did not do so. The whole incident soured Bosie's relations with his cousin Pamela and her husband and they were never the same again.[35]

5

Bosie soon found that, in spite of the paper's rising circulation, the costs of running *The Academy* once Edward Tennant had withdrawn his support were more than he could personally sustain unaided. That he was able to carry on as editor for the next two years until he eventually sold it was due to the intervention of his cousin George Wyndham, who persuaded Lord Howard de Walden to put up £2,000 covered by a debenture. In addition, Crosland's conduct was a constant source of worry, not to mention Colonel Custance's behaviour over Raymond.

'Although Crosland did a lot for *The Academy*,' as Bosie was to write in his autobiography, 'and, although its undoubted success at this time was due really more, I believe, to him than to me, he let me and the paper in for all sorts of trouble which would never have come our way but for him.'

> He involved me personally, as well as the paper, in all sorts of rows and feuds, which were really his own and not mine at all. He was not over-scrupulous about using the paper to fight some of his private battles, under the guise of attending to the 'public interest', and I as editor got all the 'credit' for what he did and wrote. The articles were nearly always unsigned, and, of course, I willingly accepted responsibility for everything that appeared in the paper. The result was that I drew upon myself a pretty large volume of anger and hatred.

For instance, Crosland wrote a series of articles entitled 'The Monopoly and the Muzzle', in which he commented adversely on W. H. Smith and Son's position and power in the news business. This was the height of folly, since Smith's had originally agreed with Edward Tennant to print and distribute *The Academy*. Consequently they no longer did this and furthermore refused to have it on their bookstalls, withdrawing it in July 1909 'as a matter of public duty'. Yet in spite of their rows, Bosie had a genuine regard for Crosland, whom he allowed to lunch at his expense on most days and gave him money when he was ill and hard up. Once, after a fracas, the editor wrote to his assistant (5 March 1909):

> I am awfully sorry I lost my temper this afternoon. I really had no excuse, and I am ashamed of having done it. My palliation is that my nerves were on edge and that (as it never rains but it pours) I have had for the last three or four days private troubles of which you know nothing. However, they are all cleared up now. So please forgive me for my ungrateful petulance. It was these troubles that made me impotent to write anything this week. The paper is splendid. I think it is the best number we have ever had.
>
> Ever affectionately yours
> Alfred Douglas[36]

No doubt the private troubles referred to in this letter related to Bosie's father-in-law Colonel Custance, whose wife had died recently and who now kept his daughter and grandson more and more in his Norfolk home, leaving Bosie alone in Hampstead.*

At the same time, it would be idle to deny that *The Academy* made its editor a great many unnecessary enemies by reason of his assistant's activities. 'Almost the worst turn that Crosland did me,' Bosie later recalled, 'and one which let me in for an enormous amount of unpleasantness, grief and regret, was that he forced me into a terrible fight with poor Freddie Manners-Sutton (afterwards Viscount Canterbury) which ended at the Old Bailey in a triumph for Crosland and myself, but which was, all the same, too dearly bought at the price of the sacrifice of my friendship with Freddie, who had been a great friend of my wife's before I married her, and who had, by the time I had got *The Academy* become one of my own greatest friends.'[37] In addition, Manners-Sutton was Raymond's godfather.

When Crosland became assistant editor of *The Academy* and the paper was turned into a limited company, with Bosie and Crosland as the sole directors (The Wilsford Press), Manners-Sutton told Bosie

*Mrs Eleanor Custance died on 14 November 1908.

that if he was short of money at any time he might be able to find someone who would produce it. This situation predictably arose in June 1909, and Bosie sent Crosland down to Norfolk to see Manners-Sutton, who lived at Brooke House, Norwich. Crosland asked for the loan of £500, and when this was refused he suggested £150. Manners-Sutton again turned this down, contending that Bosie was drawing £15 a week as the paper's editor and he was not prepared to advance any money until this amount was reduced. Crosland then returned to Lincoln's Inn Fields and reported the unsuccessful outcome of his mission. On 9 June Bosie wrote from his house in Hampstead an abusive letter to Manners-Sutton, in which he upbraided him for having accompanied his refusal of Crosland's request for a loan 'with gross impudence and brutal insolence,' although Manners-Sutton subsequently stated in court that he and Crosland had parted on perfectly friendly terms. 'Consequently', Bosie concluded, 'I beg to inform you that neither I nor Olive will ever speak to you again, and that I forbid you to come to this house. Furthermore, I will tell you quite plainly that I consider you to be a low, huckstering, Jew-minded pimp.'

Manners-Sutton ignored Bosie's letter, but he could not ignore an article which appeared in *The Academy* three days later, referring to 'a certain scion of a noble house who in the intervals of exercising his feudal propensities is not above turning a humble penny.'

> The bright young man is connected with two publishing firms which carry on two very different classes of business, for while one firm, of which he is the principal shareholder, is engaged in publishing various works and translations of various Christian liturgies, the other has gone in chiefly for dubious stories of a highly spiced character and anything else that will bring grist to the mill without actually compelling the intervention of the police.

To anyone with any knowledge of publishing at that period, it was clear that the scion of a noble house was Manners-Sutton, who was a director of Cope & Fenwick which published religious books; he was also a shareholder in Greening & Co, which had published two allegedly 'naughty books,' but had also published Robert Sherard's biography of Wilde as well as Bosie's *Pongo Papers*. Manners-Sutton consequently instructed his secretary to write to *The Academy* requesting a statement in the next number that the Hon Frederick Manners-Sutton was not the gentleman referred to and that further references should cease. The letter was moderate in tone, as was a further one to the effect that the paragraph in *The Academy* of 12 June was a libel on

Manners-Sutton and should be withdrawn, failing which legal proceedings would follow. To this Crosland replied in a letter signed by himself on behalf of The Wilsford Press Limited:

> With regard to the action you threaten, we have only to remark that in our view Mr Manners-Sutton is a person whom it would be difficult for reasonable people to libel. At the same time, if he wishes to make a fool of himself, we shall be quite pleased to receive his writ.

The only course now open to Manners-Sutton was to prosecute Crosland for criminal libel, and a summons was accordingly issued returnable at Bow Street magistrates' court. 'That little beast Freddie has summoned Crosland for libel and the case comes on today,' Bosie wrote to his wife on 21 July 1909. 'The papers are sure to be full of it and Freddie has not a leg to stand on. Newton [Bosie's solicitor who was acting for Crosland] says he can get the case dismissed right off.'

The matter came before Sir Albert de Rutzen at Bow Street, where Crosland pleaded not guilty. But after he had heard the prosecutor's evidence, the magistrate suggested an apology and a withdrawal, which would have satisfied Manners-Sutton and his solicitors and put an end to the case. But it did not satisfy either the defendant nor Bosie. 'Justify, justify up to the hilt!' Bosie shouted at the man in the dock, and at Manners-Sutton 'Take him to the Old Bailey!' Crosland was accordingly committed for trial at the next convenient sessions of the Central Criminal Court.[38]

Meanwhile in August, Bosie wrote to his kinsman Wilfrid Scawen Blunt saying *The Academy* was in financial straits and that he must have £500 within the next few days to keep it going and would require £3,000 to set it on a business footing. He suggested that Blunt should take debentures to that amount and help him. 'To this,' Blunt noted in his diary for 23 August that, as he 'had no mind to keep the *Academy* from a death it well deserves, for it has become an entirely disreputable paper,' he telegraphed the following answer: 'Just leaving for Clouds. You must not count on me in this matter. Blunt.'

'Many thanks for your kind and considerate telegram just received,' Bosie replied. 'Did not count on you. I never count on anyone who can't write sonnets. Douglas.'

Blunt went on to comment in his diary:

> I read this as a threat of the blackmailing kind, and paid no attention to it. And today it is followed up by an abusive letter which I suppose is of the same nature. He seems to have been playing this game all round with his friends, for he did it with

George Wyndham in the Spring, and I see a case before the magistrate in London where something of the same sort seems to have been attempted with Manners-Sutton. Blackmailing is the only explanation unless indeed he is out of his mind. But there is too much method in his madness for that excuse.[39]

On 10 February 1910, Crosland was charged at the Old Bailey before the Common Serjeant, Sir F.A. Bosanquet, familiarly known by a coincidence as 'Old Bosie', with 'having written and published a false, scandalous and defamatory libel of and concerning the Honourable Henry Frederick Walpole Manners-Sutton.' Mr (later Sir) Edward Marshall Hall, KC, MP, led for the prosecution, while Mr J. P. Valetta was the principal counsel for the defence. Crosland repeated his plea of not guilty and that what he had written to Manners-Sutton was published for the public benefit.[40]

In his written plea of justification, which a defendant in a case of criminal libel was obliged to put in, Crosland referred to an incident in Manners-Sutton's private life, with which both Bosie and his solicitor Arthur Newton were connected. Some time in the year 1905 Bosie had introduced his friend Freddie Manners-Sutton to a foreign gentleman, presumably French, named Boudemont, who occupied a flat in or off Buckingham Gate which was used as a brothel. Manners-Sutton visited the flat twice, on the first occasion with Bosie and on the second alone, when he met a girl called Maggie Dupont, with whom presumably he had sexual intercourse. Later a man purporting to be the girl's father got in touch with Manners-Sutton, claiming damages on the ground that she was under the age of consent and that Manners-Sutton had ruined her character. Although it was improbable that the man was her father and equally improbable that she was under age, while it was practically certain that she had no character to ruin, Manners-Sutton was naturally perturbed. He went to see Bosie who had been responsible for his original visit and asked what he should do. Bosie allegedly replied that if the claim was not met, it would lead to an action into which Manners-Sutton would be dragged, not to mention Bosie himself who already had sufficient scandal in his life. Bosie went on to advise that he should take his solicitor Arthur Newton's opinion. In the event they both went to see Newton who told Manners-Sutton that in the circumstances there was nothing for it but to pay up. This Manners-Sutton did to the tune of £1,000 for the 'father' and 'daughter' together with £200 by way of costs to Newton.

In his examination-in-chief Manners-Sutton did not deny the facts of what Marshall Hall referred to as the 'incident' in his private life, but in cross-examination by Valetta he strongly rebutted the suggestion that he had ever seen Maggie Dupont since his second visit to the flat. Incidentally she and her 'father' had disappeared and could not be traced, so that they did not appear at the trial.

Cross-examined by Marshall Hall, Crosland was characteristically defiant. He admitted that he was a bankrupt, but said he could earn a great deal more money if he chose. He denied personally writing the article to which Manners-Sutton objected, apart from the letter, but added that it would have appeared, so far as he was concerned, even if Manners-Sutton had lent *The Academy* the £500 for which he had asked.

'You say *The Academy* is used for literary purposes?' Marshall Hall went on to ask.

'Literary and political,' Crosland replied.

'*The Academy* is never used to fight its private battles?'

'Certainly: it is occasionally.'

'Are you responsible for what appears in *The Academy* or is Lord Alfred Douglas?' Marshall Hall continued.

'He is the master and I am the man,' replied Crosland to the accompaniment of laughter in court.

'Who rules?'

'Wait till you see Lord Alfred Douglas and you will see who rules.' Crosland's answer produced a further outburst of mirth.

At one point Marshall Hall was unwise enough to comment: 'Your solicitor tells me you are a difficult man to handle.'

'I am,' Crosland snapped back. 'And *you* can't handle me!'

Counsel then held up a poster on which was printed in large type: WHERE'S MAGGIE DUPONT? This poster was admittedly issued by *The Academy* – 'a paper dealing with intellectual and literary matters,' Marshall Hall quoted sarcastically – and done so with Crosland's knowledge and concurrence, and exhibited outside Newton's office.

'Your gang knows where she is!' the defendant shouted at Marshall Hall. 'And Manners-Sutton knows. And then you come here and get a big fee to make me look like a liar!'

For this outburst Crosland was sternly rebuked by the judge, who told him to confine himself to answers to counsel's questions. These covered a wide field of monetary dealings into which it is unnecessary to enter.

Crosland was followed in the witness box by Bosie, who was examined and cross-examined, denying much of what Manners-Sutton had said about the 'incident'. He proved a good witness, although the Common Serjeant described him as 'disagreeable'.

In his cross-examination, Marshall Hall managed to get in a

reference to Oscar Wilde, although it was hardly relevant. 'Was there ever anything to be ashamed of in your relationship with him?' Marshall Hall demanded.

'No, there was not,' Bosie answered without hesitation.

It was an unfortunate case with more than a hint of blackmail in it. Also a great deal of dirty linen was washed in public, the newspapers splashing such headlines as 'Amazing Incidents of Smart-set Life' and 'Peer's Son Tells of Visit to West End Flat.'

As the case progressed the jury became more and more sympathetic towards the defendant and in the result Crosland was acquitted.

One outcome of the case for Bosie was that he and Freddie Manners-Sutton were eventually reconciled. Some years later, Manners-Sutton, by then Lord Canterbury, admitted that the responsibility for the case was not Bosie's and that his attempt to send Crosland to prison for criminal libel made Bosie's support for his assistant editor a matter of honour. They became friends again and in fact Bosie stayed with him a fortnight or so before he died in 1918.

Meanwhile Crosland had hit back at Marshall Hall in a characteristic article on the Manners-Sutton case in *The Academy*. 'English justice has not yet come to such a pass,' he wrote, 'that the conviction of innocent persons can be procured by the specious loquacity and verbose venom of King's Counsel.' He went on:

> Mr Marshall Hall should now, it seems to us, be entirely convinced of this fact, and for the future should do his best to refrain from imagining that his gifts as a cross-examiner or as a pleader can be of the smallest use to his clients unless he exercises them in a reasonable and high-minded manner. He may also learn from this unfortunate affair that the Buzfuz method, while no doubt excellent when you are dealing with unintelligent policemen or frightened widows, is apt to get you into serious trouble when persons of average pluck and intelligence happen to come along.
>
> Both for the present writer and for Lord Alfred Douglas Mr Marshall Hall prepared what Bunyan called 'the grievous crabtree cudgel.' To his own great surprise and consternation he got cudgels in return. The spectacle of the most relentless cross-examiner at the Bar appealing to the Common Serjeant for protection against a couple of literary persons such as ourselves and Lord Alfred Douglas is one which is long likely to be remembered in the humorous annals of the Old Bailey.[41]

6

In June 1910, Bosie, on behalf of *The Academy*, brought an action against the Rev Dr R.F. Horton, a well-known Nonconformist

minister and the *Daily News*, in respect of an article by Horton which
had appeared in that paper on 16 March 1909. The article contained
the following:

> Some well-known organs, eg *The Academy*, have passed into Roman
> hands. That once-famous literary paper now passes its verdict on
> current literature with a bias to Rome. Good books are those which
> favour Rome. Books which criticise or oppose Rome are, *ipso facto*,
> bad. This paper, therefore, is to be read, though the public does not
> know it, with *The Tablet*, *The Month* and *The Universe*.
>
> This is all quite legitimate, but the public should know that the
> paper has become an organ of Catholic propaganda.

The action came before Mr Justice Darling in the High Court, with
Lord Robert Cecil appearing for *The Academy* and Sir Edward Carson
for the defendants.[42]

It is doubtful whether the action should have been brought at all,
particularly since the *Daily News* had published an apology. However,
it was, and Bosie made quite a good showing as a witness. He began
by denying, in reply to his counsel, that he or any member of the staff
of *The Academy* was a Roman Catholic.

Asked by Carson, whose appearance must have reminded him of
his father's trial in 1895, whether *The Academy* was not strongly anti-
Protestant, Bosie replied that it had been very strongly against
nonconformity – 'if you call that anti-Protestant.'

'More than that,' Carson insisted. 'Very strongly against Protestantism in the English Church?'

'Yes,' Bosie agreed.

'Strongly against the Reformation?'

'I won't admit that,' said Bosie. 'But against the way that the
Reformation has been distorted.'

'Do you call yourself a Protestant?' Carson continued.

'No,' Bosie replied. 'I strongly object to the word. I call myself a
member of the Holy Catholic Church.' After which, he added,
somewhat unwisely, 'I presume *you* don't go to church?'

'Please don't presume anything about me at all,' Carson answered
sharply.

'I won't presume,' said Bosie. 'I will take it so.'

Carson let this pass, and went on: 'Protestant is a horrible word,
isn't it?'

On Bosie agreeing, Carson continued: 'And you don't hesitate to
insult people who are Protestants?'

At this point the judge intervened with a question of his own. 'You
object to calling yourself a Protestant?'

'I don't protest against anything,' Bosie answered. 'Surely you can be a loyal member of the Church of England without hating or detesting the Church of Rome?'

'Nobody asked you to do anything of the kind,' commented Carson.

'You ought to hate the devil and all his works,' the judge again addressed the witness, this time causing some laughter in court.

Carson then referred to a book review by Arthur Machen in which Machen had remarked:

> I cursed the Protestant religion with all my heart and soul, and still do. I curse it and hate it and detest it with all its works and all its abominable operations, internal and external. I loathe it and abhor it as a most hideous blasphemy, the gravest woe, the most monstrous horror which has fallen upon the hopeless race of mortals since the foundation of the world.

'Those are the words of the man you employed to give an independent review?' Carson queried.

'Yes,' the witness agreed.

'Aren't those disgraceful words?'

'Certainly not.'

'Offensive words?'

'You may take them to be offensive,' said Bosie. 'But I don't see anything offensive in them.'

Carson again quoted another piece about a certain Dr Aked: 'He provides weekly doses of heresies and imbecilities. . . . He deserves the same kind of notice that one cannot help giving to a peculiarly foetid drain as one passes by.'

'Did Mr Machen write that?' the judge asked.

Bosie agreed that he did.

The Academy's assistant editor also gave evidence. 'What is your religion?' asked Carson.

'Ah'm a Methodist,' Crosland intoned in a broad Yorkshire accent. This was strictly speaking true since Crosland's father had been a Methodist preacher in his native Leeds, although Crosland was not known to have been inside a Methodist place of worship for the past twenty-five years. This reply gave rise to more mirth from most of those in court.

In his summing up, Mr Justice Darling regretted, what was a matter of general knowledge, that after four hundred years religious differences should still be so acute in this country. So far as the evidence went, he dealt with it in an uncontroversial way, explaining to the jury that it was open to them to find that the words complained of were fair comment on a matter of public interest and that they were published without malice.

The jury retired and after an absence of about fifteen minutes returned to say that they could not agree upon a verdict. The judge told them to try again and they did so. After another quarter of an hour they came back with a finding in favour of the defendants, though they added a rider to the effect that Dr Horton should have taken more care in verifying his facts.

In order to meet the costs of this action, Bosie felt that he had no alternative but to sell *The Academy*. Again Lord Howard de Walden came to the rescue, not only surrendering his debenture but along with Lord Fitzwilliam buying the paper with its stock for a further £2,000. Thus Bosie and Crosland bowed out and as from the beginning of July 1910 there was a new editor and a new assistant editor. The paper was described in the first issue as being 'Edited by Cecil Cowper Esq, JP, Barrister-at-law'. Although he was a member of the Bar and a Justice of the Peace, Mr Cowper, according to Bosie, was utterly without experience in journalism or letters, and Bosie believed 'he was by profession a land agent.' The assistant editor was Mr Ellis Ashmead Bartlett, 'a conceited self-advertising ass,' who had been a war correspondent in the South African War when Howard de Walden served in that campaign.

'*The Academy* of last week is too appalling for words,' Bosie wrote to Crosland on 5 July after the first issue under the new dispensation had appeared.

> The 'Esqre, J.P. Barrister-at-Law' business has produced howls of laughter in the town. It is all very sickening, and I think we have grave cause of complaint against H[oward] de W[alden] and Fitzwilliam. When we sold them the paper we hardly supposed that it was going to be made the laughing-stock of London. We really would have done better to have sold it to Harmsworth or Alfred Mond at once! Fitzwilliam, of course, knows no better, and he is a decent chap. Nevertheless I have told him fairly straightly what I think of it all.[43]

Although he claimed that he had put £2,000 of his own money into the paper, which he raised on his reversionary interest in his mother's property, Bosie always said that at the end of the day he was out of pocket and that in spite of his efforts and those of Crosland in increasing the circulation the paper always ran at a loss. This may well have been due to his own fault since he tended to leave things more and more in Crosland's hands while he went racing or stayed in country houses. But when all the paper's overdraft at Cox's Bank had been paid off and things had been cleared up, Bosie was able to give Crosland £250 out of the purchase money. But the paper did not prosper under the new ownership and some years later it was offered to Bosie for the nominal sum of £25. When he refused this, *The Academy* ceased publication after a life of half a century.

7

The eighteen months which followed Bosie's sale of *The Academy* continued to have their business and personal preoccupations for both husband and wife. Bosie had more time for sport, particularly horse racing and shooting. A lucky wager made at the time of the sale of *The Academy* when he backed a winner at 14 to 1 enabled him to settle the remainder of the paper's debts. He liked to shoot pheasants and snipe, the former in Worcestershire to which he went by the still unreliable motor car, and the latter in Scotland, as far north as the Orkneys. 'We got here late last night after many mishaps,' he wrote on one occasion from Tenbury. 'Stringer's car broke down badly on the way, the main driving rod smashed. We had to drive 9 miles to Worcester in a carrier's cart. There we hired another car to do the remaining 22 miles. First one back wheel was punctured and then a few minutes further on the other. However we shot today and got 200 pheasants.'

Bosie had given Olive a cocker spaniel which they called Winston, probably after the Liberal minister on account of his pluck. He took the dog with him to Kirkwall, where he wrote to Olive:

> Winston is thoroughly enjoying himself and is becoming more sporting every day. He now always accompanies me shooting and utters piercing yaps every time I shoot a snipe. He retrieved one today that fell into a stream with a very fast current. He was carried down the stream about 50 yards with great violence and I thought he would be drowned. But he never let go of the snipe and returned safely to shore to the great admiration of the keeper.

The autumn of 1911 found Bosie in Paris trying to arrange with a French publisher for the translation of *The City of the Soul*. 'Everyone is so charming to me and they make a great fuss of me,' he wrote to Olive who had stayed at home or gone to Weston. 'If only we lived in Paris, we could do what we liked and have what we liked. It is rather sickening to think of the way I am treated in England and to contrast it with what we are like here. Last night I dined at Natalie'[Barney]s. It was most charming. The other guests included the poet Remy de

Gourmont and the Duchess of Clermont Tonnère.'[44]

In England Bosie arranged with John Lane to reprint *The City of the Soul*, while the same publisher brought out Olive's fourth and last volume of verse, *The Inn of Dreams*. On Lane's request that he should write some more sonnets for The Bodley Head, Bosie commented: 'It is easier to talk about it than to do it. I have as you know written very little poetry in my life and I would rather not write another line than fall below my standard.'[45] As for Olive, she seems to have sensed impending disaster in her domestic life as reflected in her poem 'The Prisoner of God'.

Once long ago and long ago I knew delight
God gave my spirit wings and a glad voice.
I was a bird that sang at dawn and noon,
That sang at starry evening time and night;
Sang at the sun's greatest golden doors and furled
Brave things in the white gardens of the moon;
That sang and soared above the dusty noon.

Once long ago and long ago I did rejoice,
But now I am a stone that falls and falls.
A prisoner, cursing the blank prison walls,
Helpless and dumb, with desperate eyes, that see
The terrible beauty of those simple things
My soul disdained when she was proud and free.
And I can only pray: God pity me.
God pity me and give me back my voice!
God pity me and give me back my wings!

'I sent a rather nice notice of your poems in a Dublin paper in Raymond's letter to you this morning,' Bosie wrote to his wife after *The Inn of Dreams* had been published. '*The Academy* on your poems I thought rather idiotic but what can you expect from the sort of people who have got it now? They only praise *The City of the Soul* because they think it is the thing to do.'[46]

Early in 1911, to his father-in-law's intense annoyance, Bosie became a convert to the Roman Catholic faith, thus following the example of such contemporaries as Beardsley and Wilde. Colonel Custance shared the mistrust of Catholicism and Catholics ('those priests') then common among certain sections of English upper-class society. His only sister had married a Catholic and became one herself, and besides this he particularly resented his grandson being brought up in what he regarded as an alien religion. Bosie's action is remarkable in view of his anti-Catholic sentiments expressed in some of his writings quoted above. He had been thinking about it carefully for some time and it appears that what finally caused his conversion was Pope Pius X's encyclical 'Against Modernism.' The encyclical promulgated in 1907 was of course originally written in Latin. But an English translation was duly made and a copy of this was sent to *The Academy* by the Catholic authorities in Britain. Bosie thought of sending it out for review by someone like Arthur Machen, but on picking it up and reading a few lines he became interested in it himself and took it home to read through. 'It had the effect of convincing me that the Catholic Church, in communion with the see of Peter in Rome, is the only true Church,' he later wrote in his autobiography. 'I definitely made up my mind to become a Catholic, but I put it off chiefly because, as appears from what I have just written, my conversion had come entirely through the intellect. I felt no emotion about it. . . .'

> When I had been a Catholic for about eighteen months I underwent the most violent persecution, which lasted on and off, for at least ten years. The result of this persecution was to force me deeper and deeper into my religion. For years it was my only support and consolation in a succession of almost unbearable miseries. Instead of being cold I became very devout and mystical. I lived on reading *The Lives of the Saints*, and such mystics as St Teresa and St John of the Cross. I got to the stage of glorying in the persecution I was undergoing, and regarding it as a special sign of grace, which, of course, it undoubtedly was. . . .
>
> The persecution began with the attack on me in Ransome's book inspired by Robert Ross.[47]

One individual who was shocked by Bosie's conversion was his cousin Wilfrid Scawen Blunt, who made some acid comments in his diary. On 7 June 1911 he wrote:

> That scoundrel Alfred Douglas has become a Catholic, after bringing a libel action not a year ago against a parson who stated that he had done so – and he now writes me an apology for his abusive letters in a penitential mood which would have more effect with me if he did not go on with his nonsense about 'the point of view from which he regarded *The Academy*' and 'the motives which compelled him to conduct it as he did.' He adds‛ 'I daresay you know I have become a Catholic.'
>
> I have answered him as follows: 'Dear Alfred, Your trespass against me was a small matter and easy to forgive, but your sins against others of your friends in the last two or three years have been less forgivable, and you must not expect me to condone them

Ham Hill, Powick, Worcester
Birthplace of Lord Alfred Douglas. From a lithograph by W. Wood

Kinmount
The Queensberry family home in Dumfries, Scotland

John Sholto Marquess of Queensberry
About the time of his marriage to Sibyl Montgomery in 1866

Sibyl Marchioness of Queensberry
From the painting by Johnstone Douglas in the possession of Mr Edward Colman

Alfred Montgomery
Father of Sibyl Queensberry

below left
**Alfred Douglas
aged eight**
From the watercolour by
the Hon Richard Graves in
the possession of Mr
Edward Colman

below right
**Francis Viscount
Drumlanrig
as a Lieutenant in
The Coldstream Guards**
He left the army at the age
of twenty-four to become
private secretary to the
Foreign Secretary Lord
Rosebery who took a fancy
to him and persuaded
Queen Victoria to create
him an English peer as
Lord Kelhead so that he
could become a Lord-in-
Waiting and speak for
Gladstone's Liberal
Government in the Upper
House. He died unmarried
in 1894, having supposedly
been killed by the
accidental explosion of his
gun at a shooting party.
From a posthumous
painting in the possession of
Mr Edward Colman

Entrance to Magdalen College, Oxford

below left **Herbert Warren** President of Magdalen

below right **Alfred Douglas** As an undergraduate at Magdalen

above left **Lionel Johnson** The poet who introduced Douglas to Wilde

16 Tite Street The Wildes' London home in Chelsea

Oscar and Constance Wilde

from Oscar

To the gilt-mailed Boy.

POEMS.

at Oxford,

in the heart of June.

above left **Half-title page of 1892 edition of Wilde's Poems** Inscribed by Wilde and given by him to Douglas when Wilde was staying with him in Oxford, June 1892

above right **Alfred Douglas and Oscar Wilde** At Felbrigg Farm, near Cromer, Norfolk, in September 1892

Babbacombe Cliff

Wilde rented this house near Torquay from Lady Mount Temple during the winter of 1892–93. In the room above the arch on the right, which Wilde called Wonderland, he completed *A Woman of No Importance* and wrote most of *A Florentine Tragedy*, while Douglas studied Plato in another room with his tutor. The house is now a hotel

above left **Oscar Wilde and Bosie at Oxford** Summer, 1893

above right **Robert Ross and Reggie Turner**

Caricature by Max Beerbohm Given to Douglas by the artist

above left **Alfred Douglas in Cairo** Spring, 1894

above right **The Earl of Rosebery** Foreign Secretary and Prime Minister

below left **Lord Queensberry** at the time of the Wilde trials

below right **Queensberry's card with its offensive inscription**
which he left at Wilde's club 18 February 1895

Lord Queensberry attacks his son Percy 21 May 1895

below left **Aged twenty-five** From a drawing by Walter Spindler
used as a frontispiece to the 1896 Paris edition of Douglas's *Poems*

below right **Title page of Paris edition of Douglas's Poems**

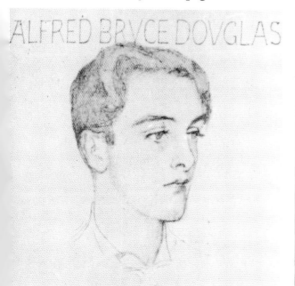

ALFRED BRVCE DOVGLAS

LORD ALFRED DOUGLAS

—

POEMS

PARIS
PUBLISHED BY THE MERCVRE DE FRANCE
XV, RVE DE L'ÉCHAVDÉ-SAINT-GERMAIN, XV

—

M DCCC XCVI

André Gide

Oscar and Bosie lunching in Naples
Autumn 1897

Hardi at Chantilly
Douglas's most
successful horse
with which he
won many races

Olive Custance
Lady Alfred Douglas

Raymond aged nine
Only child of
Alfred and Olive Douglas

above left **T. W. H. Crosland** *above right* **Herbert Moore Pim**

below left **Arthur Ransome** with his wife Ivy outside the Law Courts, April 1913

below right **Frank Harris**

Douglas leaving the Old Bailey
during his trial for criminally
libelling Winston Churchill,
December 1923

Wormwood Scrubs Prison
Douglas served his six-month
sentence here after his
conviction for criminal libel

above left **Aged forty-eight** with Winston

above right **In his sixties** as the author remembers him

Regency Square Brighton from the West Pier
Hove can be seen beyond the houses in the square
From John Piper's *Brighton Aquatints* to which Douglas wrote an Introduction

At Norbury Park with Marie Stopes
Left to right: Keith Briant, Marie Stopes,
Humphrey Roe (her husband) and Alfred Douglas

below left Richard Rumbold *below right* Donald Sinden

Old Monk's Farm, Lancing
Douglas spent the last three months of his life here as the guest of his literary
executor Mr Edward Colman and Mrs Sheila Colman. She is sitting in the car while
her husband stands at the entrance. Douglas had a suite of rooms on the left of the
doorway.

Old Monk's Farm
Easter, 1944. The last photograph, with Sheila Colman, taken by Edward Colman

or give you any further countenance. I am sorry but I cannot decide otherwise. Your affect cousin W.S.B.'

'Of what value has your countenance ever been to any man?' Bosie replied. 'To be known as your friend or associate has always been something in the nature of a social handicap.' What was Blunt, Bosie went on, but 'a contemptible cad, whom most people considered a half crazy old gentleman, with a bee in his bonnet'?

'Alfred Douglas writes me another abusive letter, which is what I expected and indeed intended,' Blunt noted in his diary three days later, 'for I had rather have him as an enemy than a friend. His letter shows that, whatever he may have done by becoming a Catholic, it has not brought him to the point of repenting his sins. He is a swindler, a blackguard of the lowest type – the aristocratic swindler.'

Next day there was another entry:

> 11 June 1911.... A third letter has come from Alfred, this time containing threats, and I have got Dorothy [Carleton, Madeline Wyndham's niece with whom Blunt was living] to copy me out the correspondence to send to George [Wyndham], who I think is in some way responsible for his attack on me by receiving him into his house after the Manners-Sutton affair and so allowing him to pose as anything but the proved blackguard he is.
>
> The Bellocs dined with us and Cecil Chesterton with whom he [Hilaire] is collaborating on *The Witness*. Told them of Alfred's latest escapade, and they told me that among other of his blackmailing attempts with *The Academy* he threatened the other Chesterton [G.K.] which caused them to get up the dossier of Alfred's connection with the Oscar Wilde trial and that armed with this they reduced Alfred to silence. They have got the dossier by them still. It was through Belloc that George negotiated the sale of *The Academy* last year to Howard de Walden. They agreed that it would have been wiser to let him go bankrupt. But they consider him quite harmless to effect anything except annoyance.[48]

As already noted, the Custance Weston Longeville estates had been entailed by Colonel Custance's father on Olive, while the Colonel had a life interest in the property. Early in 1911 Colonel Custance proposed to his daughter that she should break the entail and agree to a resettlement by which she voluntarily surrendered her rights in return for an annual income of £600 during her father's lifetime, and a life interest at his death with remainder to her son Raymond. Bosie objected to this arrangement and strongly advised his wife not to sign the resettlement documents without her father giving a written undertaking to provide her with the stipulated £600 a year. However, when Olive went down to Weston she found all the documents had been prepared by Custance's solicitors Lewis and Lewis with the exception of any provision for the £600 a year. When Olive pointed this out to her father, he replied that his 'word was good enough'. Thus she weakly consented to the resettlement, being as things were badly served by the solicitors who should not have allowed her to sign the documents without any binding agreement on the part of Colonel Custance to pay her £600 a year.

No sooner were the documents signed than Colonel Custance, who was paying Raymond's fees at a preparatory school in Seaford, did exactly what Bosie had warned Olive's solicitors that he would do. He wrote to his daughter, saying that unless the boy were handed over to him he would not pay her 'allowance', adding that the moment her husband took the boy away 'all payments to you will cease.' Bosie's response was to remove the boy from Seaford and to take him to Sibyl Queensberry's house. This naturally upset Olive whom Bosie blamed for having agreed to the resettlement. They quarrelled but later made it up. 'I do still love you and for a short time I really did hate you,' Bosie wrote to her in a letter marked 'very important' on 3 June 1911. 'But I do understand that what you have done has been forced on you by your father and that villain Lewis and I forgive you. Your loving Boy.'

Meanwhile Bosie wrote to Colonel Custance and continued to write to him until Custance replied that any further letters from his son-in-law would be 'thrown unopened into the back of the fire'. Bosie then had resort to postcards and telegrams. 'There is no doubt,' Bosie telegraphed on 12 February 1912, 'that Olive was induced to sign the settlement by fraudulent promise of consideration which is now being withheld from her. Am seeing lawyer this afternoon. The whole matter will have to be fought out in the law courts.' Bosie followed this up with several more postcards. In one of these postcards in which Bosie bitterly reproached his father-in-law for depriving Olive of the money he had promised to give her, despite the fact that he had inherited £30,000 from his late wife who had died in 1908, he described Colonel Custance as 'a despicable scoundrel and a thoroughly dishonest and dishonourable man'. He threatened to send similar statements to the Colonel's London club, the Carlton, his club and bank in Norwich, and the tenants on the Weston Longeville estate. Unable to stand any more of these attacks, Custance instructed his solicitor, Sir George Lewis, to issue a summons charging Bosie with criminal libel.[49]

While these proceedings were pending, Custance and Lewis began another action, this time in the Chancery Court, designed to obtain custody of Raymond, who had recently been received into the Roman Catholic Church and who had now gone to Ampleforth, the well-known Catholic public school in Yorkshire. The Chancery proceedings were to drag on for several years and eventually led to an order to the effect that Raymond should spend three-fifths of his holidays with Colonel Custance and the remaining two-fifths with his father. Although it is anticipating events a little, it is convenient to record here that Bosie appeared in the Marylebone magistrates' court on 26 February 1913 on the charge of criminally libelling Colonel Custance, and the defendant was committed for trial and released on bail. On 6 March the case came before the Central Criminal Court but was adjourned in order to allow time for Bosie to put in the customary written plea of justification. When the case came up again at the Old Bailey on 24 April before the Recorder, Sir Forest Fulton, Bosie, on the advice of his solicitor, for some reason did not attempt to justify the libel. Consequently the jury found him guilty without leaving the jury box. However, his counsel who was his old friend Cecil Hayes, made such a powerful plea in mitigation of sentence that the Recorder did not send him to prison but simply bound him over to be of good behaviour for six months in the sum of £500.

'What beat me at the Custance libel prosecution at the Old Bailey,' Bosie was later to write, 'was simply that my nerve went and I was demoralised.' As will be related, he had just lost his libel action against Arthur Ransome and had been made bankrupt on the petition of a moneylender. To crown everything Olive left him and went back to Weston. This happened while Bosie and Raymond were on a visit to Bosie's sister Edith's brother-in-law, Alexander Fox-Pitt-Rivers, at the Manor House, Hinton St Mary, near Sturminster Newton in Dorsetshire, where their host was the local squire.[50] When Bosie got back to his house in Hampstead, he found it half-dismantled, as Olive had taken much of the furniture and other personal possessions when she departed.

As Bernard Shaw was to put it shortly afterwards, 'it is rather a humorous stroke of Fate's irony that the son of a Marquess of Queensberry should be forced to expiate his sins by suffering a succession of blows beneath the belt'.[51]

V

The Litigant

1

It will be recalled that the original edition of *De Profundis* was published by Methuen & Co in 1905, and it was reviewed by Bosie in the *Motorist and Traveller*. Methuen's pre-publication announcement of the work as having been edited by Robert Ross came as a surprise to Bosie, who went to see Ross. Each has left a different account of the meeting.

According to Bosie, he asked Ross why he (Ross) had not told him about the manuscript of *De Profundis* before, and also why Oscar had not told him about it. 'I wanted to keep it as a surprise,' said Ross. To which Bosie replied: 'Wilde was hard up and keen on selling anything he could get rid of. Why should he not have published it himself?'

'He didn't do that because the manuscript consists of a long letter,' Ross retorted. 'It contains a lot of disagreeable writing about you and other people, but I have cut this out, and what is left makes a nice little book.' Bosie then said that it seemed very extraordinary that nobody should have heard of this before, but Ross assured him that 'he would publish nothing that would hurt Wilde's reputation and that the book would do him good, and there the matter ended.'[1]

Ross's account, in a statement prepared for his solicitors, Lewis & Lewis, is rather different:

> When the book was announced, Douglas (whom I used to see from time to time when he was in London), asked me what it was. I replied quite truthfully that it was the letter which Wilde had written to him from prison and had asked me to publish at some future date. I added that it was the same document of which Douglas had told both Wilde and myself he had thrown into the fire, the typewritten copy, on receiving it from Wilde.
>
> I assured Douglas that no passage would be published which reflected in any way on himself and his family.

Besides mentioning the fact that Bosie had reviewed the book in the *Motorist and Traveller*, Ross also added that Bosie had discussed the book with several friends. 'He never asked to see the original manuscript.'[2]

In this context it should be noted that nowhere in the numerous letters, postcards and telegrams, amounting to eighty-eight in all, addressed by Wilde to Ross after his release from prison, is there any change in the instruction in the letter written by Wilde from prison to Ross on 1 April 1897 that the original of the whole of the *De Profundis* letter should be sent to Bosie, nor is there any request as stated by Ross above that he should publish it 'at some future date.' On the other hand, Ross has stated definitely that Bosie received a typed copy of it in Wilde's lifetime, to be precise on 8 August 1897. It is known that Ross was staying with Wilde at Berneval at this time and it is not inconceivable that Wilde changed his instructions orally, possibly at Ross's suggestion, and in the result one of the two typed copies which Ross had had made was sent to Bosie who was then staying at Nogent-sur-Marne, and after he had read a page or two with their reproachful language, he destroyed the whole typescript. 'Long before the publication of *De Profundis*', Ross wrote in the statement about Bosie receiving the typescript, 'I had taken counsel's opinion as to the ownership of the copyright. It was declared that I was the sole owner and this was recognised by Wilde's Official Receiver. Douglas has no claim because the MS never passed into his possession.'[3]

This statement requires some qualification. At the time of the original publication of *De Profundis*, the legal copyright was, strictly speaking, not vested in Ross but in Wilde's Official Receiver in bankruptcy, who, in view of the fact that the publication had had a considerable success, claimed the proceeds from the sales of the six editions published in 1905 for the English creditors in the bankruptcy. At first Ross resisted this claim, but when he realised its legal validity he proposed a compromise. While not foregoing his own claim to the copyright of *De Profundis* as 'beneficial owner', he proposed to allow the proceeds of the sales, already amounting to a considerable sum, to be employed in liquidating Wilde's bankruptcy. In return Ross as Wilde's literary executor was to be made administrator of the Wilde estate after all the creditors had been paid. The Official Receiver agreed to this compromise, and, after the creditors had been paid in full in 1906, the guardian of Wilde's two children Cyril and Vyvyan Holland petitioned for Ross to be appointed to administer the Wilde estate for the benefit of his sons. This was also agreed, and Ross was given control of all the literary and dramatic copyrights which had not already been disposed of by the Official Receiver, while he was authorised to try to recover the copyrights which had already been sold, such as those to George Alexander. He was thus confirmed as the owner of the copyright of *De Profundis*.

It was in these circumstances that Ross who was on friendly terms with Sir Frederic Kenyon, the Director of the British Museum, offered the MS of *De Profundis* together with drafts of four of Wilde's plays and his poem *The Sphinx* to the Museum. First, he showed the material to Kenyon who wrote to him on 29 October 1909:

> I have at last been able to finish reading the MS of *De Profundis*, and I have since had an opportunity of speaking with the Archbishop of Canterbury [Randal Davidson] whose opinion will carry great weight with the Trustees.
>
> My own feeling is that, although the suppressed portions of *De Profundis* cannot be made accessible to the public for at least the present generation, there is no reason why the Trustees should refuse the offer of the MS of a remarkable work by a writer who, whatever estimate different people may form of his genius, was unquestionably a remarkable figure in the literary history of his time. Indeed I would go further and say that the British Museum is the best place for a work which cannot be made public for a considerable time, but which may be of great interest to future generations.
>
> I was glad to find that the Archbishop spontaneously and unhesitatingly took the same point of view. With the assurance of his support, I think you might well let your offer be laid before the Trustees. I have no doubt they will recognise, as I do, the generosity and disinterestedness of your action in the matter and I certainly expect that they will accept the trust you offer to them....
>
> As to the exact terms of the offer, I should be inclined to suggest that the *De Profundis* MS should be sealed up for 40 years (till 1950), it being understood that the Trustees would again consider whether the time was ripe for its being made accessible to the public. I see no reason why the plays should not be made accessible at once.[4]

Ross made his formal offer of the MS to the Museum on 5 November, accompanied by a short statement of its history:

> ... Wilde was not permitted to send the letter when he was incarcerated: it was handed to me on the day after his release – May 19, 1897 – with a request that I should keep the manuscript for possible publication after his death, and cause two typewritten copies to be made; one of which was to be sent to him and the other to Alfred Douglas.
>
> In 1905 I issued about two-thirds of the manuscript giving it the

title 'De Profundis'. Blue pencil marks indicate passages which are published.

The unpublished parts, while not in any way scabrous could not possibly be published during the lifetime of the present generation; at the same time they have great interest for future generations from a psychological point of view, explaining as they do the otherwise inexplicable conduct of Wilde in taking action against Lord Queensberry. If any future generation is sufficiently interested in Wilde's life or writings, this complete manuscript is the only authentic document which elucidates his career from the year 1893 until his arrest in 1895.[5]

The Trustees accepted the gift on 13 November, subject to the condition, with which Ross and Kenyon agreed, that it was to be locked up for fifty years (not forty as suggested by the Director), and should be opened on 1 January 1960. In a subsequent minute it was noted that 'the Trustees certainly have never had any reason to suppose that the manuscript was ever the property of Lord Alfred Douglas.'[6]

Bosie's quarrel with Ross came to a head following the publication of *Oscar Wilde: A Critical Study* by Arthur Ransome in February 1912. At this date Ransome was a young writer of twenty-eight, whose father was Professor of History at Leeds University, and although he had not begun to write the children's books and books on fishing by which he made his name, he was by no means unknown as an author in 1912. He had already written several books including a *History of Story-Telling* and a work on Edgar Allen Poe; he had also translated Remy de Gourmont's *Une Nuit au Luxembourg* into English with a critical essay on the French writer. The Wilde book was commissioned by Martin Secker, an enterprising young publisher who was building up an impressive list of promising young writers which included such names as D.H. Lawrence, Compton Mackenzie and Norman Douglas. When they first met, Secker suggested that it would be helpful if Ransome could get an introduction to Ross as Wilde's literary executor, and this he was able to do through Laurence Binyon, who was then working in the British Museum. In the result Ross helped Ransome by answering questions about Wilde and supplying him with relevant documents; in return the author dedicated the book to Ross, although Ross had not expected this.

According to Ross in the statement to Sir George Lewis already quoted, he 'did not show Ransome any documents or letters reflecting on Douglas' but 'simply assisted him with regard to dates and showed him some early drafts on Wilde's plays and his other literary work.' This statement is quite disingenuous. He showed Ransome at least one of Wilde's letters to him, from which Ransome quoted; it was the one in which he described Douglas's conduct in leaving him at Naples after their reunion in 1897 when there was no more money, since Constance Wilde had stopped his allowance, as 'the most bitter experience of a bitter life.' Ross, according to himself, told Ransome that he could not show him the manuscript of the *De Profundis* letter since he had given it to the British Museum. He did not add that he lent Ransome his typed copy and allowed Ransome to take it away with him to his home in Wiltshire.[7] Ransome confirms this in his own autobiography, and it is clear from his book on Wilde that he had read it, since he remarks that 'its complete publication would be impossible in this generation.' Ransome goes on:

> The letter, a manuscript of 'eighty close-written pages on twenty folio sheets' was not addressed to Mr Ross but to a man to whom Wilde felt that he owed some, at least, of the circumstances of his public disgrace. It was begun as a rebuke to this friend, whose actions, even subsequent to the trials, had been such as to cause Wilde considerable pain. It was not delivered to him, but given to Mr Ross by Wilde, *who also gave instructions as to its partial publication.*[8] (My italics.)

When he had read this, Douglas wrote to Ross on 6 March 1912 as follows:

> It is true that the man Ransome does not mention my name but anyone reading the book carefully with a full knowledge of the circumstances would be led to infer that I was the 'friend' referred to. I now write to ask you whether it is true that the MS of *De Profundis* consists of a letter addressed to me, and if so why you have concealed this fact from me for all these years. I should also like to know why you published the letter as a book without my knowledge or consent.
>
> Hitherto I have always been under the impression that *De Profundis* was a letter written by Wilde to *you* but containing abusive or scandalous references to me which you had suppressed. Of course if this latter version of the affair is correct there is no more to be said. But if Ransome's version is correct, matters assume a very different and very serious aspect.

Ross handed this letter to his solicitor Sir George Lewis who replied to Douglas on the following day:

> The manuscript of *De Profundis* consists of a document in the form of a letter addressed to you, the original of which was entrusted by

Mr Oscar Wilde to Mr Ross *with directions that he should not part with it but that he should send you a copy of the letter*, which he did in the year 1897; so that you are already aware of this fact which has never been concealed from you. The manuscript was published after Mr Oscar Wilde's death *in accordance with his directions to Mr Ross* and the reason why it was published without your name was out of consideration for you. This was also why Mr Ross decided that many passages in the manuscript should be omitted from the form it which it was published, and this your letter shews was within your knowledge.

On receiving this letter Douglas telephoned Sir George Lewis and asked to see him. Following their meeting, Douglas again wrote to Ross (9 March) explaining why he had seen Lewis:

I merely wished to put on record that I had been shamefully deceived by you over the *De Profundis* matter. As you must be perfectly well aware, I have never, until I saw it stated in Ransome's book, had the slightest inkling that the MS of *De Profundis* was a letter addressed to me by Wilde or that there was any connection between the letter you sent me in 1897 (which I destroyed after reading the first half dozen lines) and the book. Had I been aware of this I should have used every endeavour to prevent the publication of the book by appealing to the sense of decency and honour which at that time I did not doubt you possessed. Failing that I should have applied for an injunction.

Wilde, after his release from prison, only once referred to the letter sent by you to me at Nogent-sur-Marne in 1897 and on that occasion he implored me to forgive him for having written it.... You now ask me to believe that Wilde was so base and so vile as to have left you in the possession of the original letter (of which I burnt the copy) and to have agreed with you that it was to be published in whole or in part after his death, and this at a time when he was on terms of the most affectionate friendship with me and was receiving large sums of money from me. Whether it is true or not that Wilde was a party to your action (and I prefer to believe that it is not true and that in spite of his degradation he was not quite as bad as that) there can be no question as to your part in the matter. You admit it and positively glory in it and you have made a lot of money by it.

A few days later, on Crosland's advice, Douglas issued writs for libel against Ransome, his publisher Martin Secker, and the Times Book Club, which had circulated copies of Ransome's book. Secker, who was just beginning his career as a publisher, apologised and withdrew, since he had no further financial interest in the book, having already sold his rights in it; but Ransome and the Times Book Club both accepted service of the writs and so the case proceeded against these two defendants, who apparently on Ross's advice instructed Sir George Lewis's firm to act on their behalf.

During the interlocutory stage prior to the hearing of the case, Douglas was granted 'discovery' of two important documents relevant to Ransome's alleged libel, namely the text of the whole of the *De Profundis* MS and that of the letter from Wilde to Ross dated March 1898 complaining of Douglas having deserted him at Naples when there was no more money. Henceforth it was to be the bitterest and most malicious struggle with no holds barred between two homosexuals over a man they had both loved.

> I am well aware that I have to thank you for handing to Ransome for production at the trial of his action the manuscript of the letter Wilde wrote to me the copy of which you profess to have sent to me.... But don't imagine that the production of this MS will make the slightest difference to my line of conduct. I am going straight ahead with my action and my only hope is that you will go into the witness box and give me a chance of having you cross examined.

Thus Douglas wrote to Ross on 1 November 1912. He concluded this letter by threatening to horsewhip Ross 'within an inch of your dirty life.'

'You filthy bugger and blackmailer,' Douglas wrote to Ross again a few days later.

> My libel action against Ransome henceforth becomes an action against you and it will be so conducted. Now that I have proof positive that all this business has been engineered by you and that Ransome has been relying simply on what you told him and the documents you gave him, I have not got any particular animus against Ransome. I consider him to be your dupe and though his translation of the disgusting and blasphemous work of Remy de Gourmont and his prefix to it prove that he is a filthy rotten sort of person I do not forget that he is only a young chap and may live to repent his early follies and foulnesses. But *you* are and have been all your life a filthy bugger and unspeakable skunk.... You have corrupted and debauched hundreds of boys and young men in your life and you have gone on doing it right up to the present time.[9]

2

The trial of *Douglas v Ransome and the Times Book Club* for libel opened before Mr Justice Darling and a special jury in the King's Bench

Division of the High Court on 17 April 1913 and lasted for ten days.[10] For the plaintiff, who was on the verge of bankruptcy and could not afford to employ fashionable or expensive counsel, there appeared Mr Cecil Hayes, who had been 'called' to the Bar for less than two years and was relatively inexperienced – he was a friend of Bosie's and, it will be recalled, was a witness at his wedding. On this occasion he represented the plaintiff for a nominal fee or more likely no fee at all. The defendants, on the other hand, were represented by the best and most experienced legal brains of the day – Mr Ransome by Mr J.H. Campbell, KC, (later Lord Glenavy) and Mr H.A. McCardie (later Mr Justice McCardie), and The Times Book Club by Mr F.E. Smith, KC, (later Lord Birkenhead). Bosie subsequently complained that Mr Hayes was intimidated by his opponents' brilliant combination of advocates. To some extent this was true.

The issues which the jury had to decide were, first, was Lord Alfred Douglas the cause of Wilde's disgrace? And secondly, did he live on him and then desert him when he was penniless? If the defence could show that the answers to these questions were in the affirmative, then the plaintiff must fail in his action.

Actually Bosie had quite a strong case. Far from deserting Wilde he had stuck to him when he came out of prison, inviting him to join him in his villa at Naples, and paying his fare there from Dieppe. He only left him at his mother's urgent entreaty; and, when he did so, as we have seen, he persuaded Lady Queensberry to send Wilde £200. During the remainder of his life he gave him further sums amounting to £1,200, and on Wilde's death in the same year he paid for the funeral in Paris. As for the suggestion that his influence had brought about Wilde's ruin, it could be argued that this was absurd, since he was only twenty-four at the time of the scandal, while Wilde was over forty, and an experienced man of the world who, as Mr Hayes pointed out in his opening speech, had lived in the Latin Quarter of Paris and had lectured and travelled all over America.

In his examination in the witness box Bosie produced his bank book, which showed that in the year 1900 he had given Wilde cheques to the value of £380 and he swore that Wilde had had at least twice that amount from him in cash. 'Wilde was very extravagant,' he added. 'If I gave him £100 on Monday, he would have spent it all by Saturday, and would not even then have paid his bills.'

'How did he spend it?' asked the judge.

'I cannot say,' replied Bosie.

Unfortunately, as the trial proceeded, the desertion issue, which was the core of the case, became progressively obscured. Letters written by Wilde to Bosie in extravagant language, the same letters including the notorious 'prose poem' which had been produced by Edward Carson with such deadly effect at the Queensberry trial in 1895, were now put to Bosie in his cross-examination by Mr Campbell; also the article defending homosexuality which he had written for the French journal *La Revue Blanche*, and in which he had described Wilde's conviction as 'the greatest romantic tragedy of the age.' It was in vain for the witness to repudiate this article, whose effect when read out in Court was to prejudice him irremediably in the eyes of the jury. The main issue thus tended more and more to be not 'Did Douglas desert Wilde?', but rather 'Had Douglas been addicted to the same vicious practices as Wilde?'

Having dealt with the plaintiff's own writings, Mr Campbell then left it to his junior, Mr McCardie, to read from the MS of *De Profundis*, a document written on eighty folio pages of prison notepaper. Before doing so he handed up the MS to Douglas, who stated that he could recognise it as being in Wilde's handwriting, but that, contrary to a statement previously made by Robert Ross, he had never received a copy of it before the present trial. When the first published and greatly expurgated edition appeared in 1905, he said he thought it was part of a letter which Wilde had written to Ross.

Hayes immediately objected to its being read, but since it had been expressly mentioned in the written pleadings as part of the justification on which Mr Ransome relied, the judge ruled that it could not be excluded. Mr Campbell said that only such parts of it as concerned the plaintiff need be read, but Mr Hayes wanted the whole read so that the jury might see that Wilde was a man of moods, that at one moment he appeared to be full of forgiveness and in the next full of venom and anger and that his account of affairs could not be trusted. The judge directed the reading to begin.

This was the first intimation which the public had of the contents of the unpublished portion of *De Profundis*. What was read out by Mr McCardie consisted of a devastating attack on Bosie's character, accusing him of greed, selfishness, superficiality and so on, and it created a considerable sensation, both on the audience inside the Court and the wider public outside. After counsel had been on his feet for about half an hour, Bosie asked if he could sit down. Mr Justice Darling said he could, adding that he did not wonder why he wanted to do so. Bosie then begged permission to leave the box. Darling asked if he was unwell, and on being told that he was not but merely wished to avoid hearing any more of the reading, he was directed to stay where he was.

The reading was continued when the Court sat next morning. After a while the judge noticed that the plaintiff was not in the box and enquired if he was in Court. Mr Hayes said that he was not. This considerably amazed the judge. 'The very object of this reading,' he remarked, 'is that the plaintiff may be cross-examined upon it. Let him be sent for.' Ten minutes later Bosie reappeared to receive a sharp reprimand from the Bench. 'If you leave the Court again while you are a witness,' said the judge, 'I will give leave for judgment to be entered against you.'

Eventually the jury interposed to say they had heard enough, and Mr Campbell went on with his cross-examination. Soon he was involved in a brush with the witness. Complaining of his interrupting him, Bosie said, 'You must allow me to finish my answer if you wish to get the truth. But perhaps you don't wish it.'

MR JUSTICE DARLING: Don't be impertinent to the learned counsel.

LORD ALFRED DOUGLAS: I accept your Lordship's rebuke.

MR JUSTICE DARLING: You will not only accept my rebuke, but you will act upon it.

More of Bosie's own writings were put to him, including some of his letters, in one of which he had boasted of being a 'bone of contention' between Wilde and his wife and in another of which he had referred to borrowing considerable sums of money from Wilde in the heyday of the dramatist's success. 'I remember the sweetness of asking Oscar for money: it was a sweet humiliation.'

MR CAMPBELL: Is not the plain truth of the *De Profundis* letter that you were the ruin of Wilde's life?

LORD ALFRED DOUGLAS: Yes.

MR CAMPBELL: Did you not admit that to be true?

LORD ALFRED DOUGLAS: Through a sense of Quixotic generosity I let it pass.

The only other witness called for the plaintiff was More Adey. He said that he had conveyed the £200 from Lady Queensberry to Wilde when the household at Naples broke up in 1897. But he admitted in cross-examination that he had thought it was in the interests of both men that they should not meet again and in this he had been assisted by Ross. The £200, he later explained to the judge, really formed part of a 'debt of honour' in respect of the costs of the criminal libel prosecution of Lord Queensberry which Bosie's elder brother Lord Douglas had undertaken to meet.

For Mr Ransome only two formal witnesses were asked to testify – a Frenchman, M Didier, who had translated the notorious article in the *Revue Blanche*, and the Chief Librarian of the British Museum, Sir Frederick Kenyon, who stated that he had the original MS of *De Profundis* in his keeping and identified the passages which had been read out. He added that under the terms of its gift the MS was to remain sealed up for fifty years and was not to become available to the public until 1960.

The manager and librarian of The Times Book Club then successively went into the box. They indicated the precautions which had been taken to see if Mr Ransome's book contained anything objectionable, and on their behalf Mr F.E. Smith submitted that, having regard to these precautions, no responsibility should be held to rest with The Times Book Club.

In his closing speech to the jury Bosie's counsel commented strongly on the fact that Robert Ross was sitting in Court and had not been called. If he had been, said Mr Hayes, he could have explained how the letter which Bosie claimed to be his, since it was addressed to him, came into his possession, and how it subsequently passed to the British Museum.

MR JUSTICE DARLING: You may call him now if you wish.

MR HAYES: But the onus of proving their justification lies on the defendants.

MR JUSTICE DARLING: Mr Ross is not a party to this action, and the decision of the question as to whether he should be called does not rest with him.

MR HAYES: He ought to have been called by the defendants. I could not cross-examine him as my witness, and should be bound by his answers.

Mr Hayes then turned to Mr Ransome. Why had he not likewise given evidence? His solicitors had delivered sixty-three pages of particulars of justification, not one of which he had gone into the witness box to substantiate.

MR CAMPBELL: This is very unfair. The particulars themselves show that he could not himself have proved any of them.

MR JUSTICE DARLING (to MR HAYES): Your object in trying to get Mr Ransome into the box was not to prove these particulars, but to enable you to put questions to him which you did not care to put to your own witnesses.

Mr Ransome's book related to a very bad man of genius, said Mr Justice Darling in his summing-up. But was nobody to write about him because his moral character was bad, or read his plays or see them? He asked the jury whether they ought not to look at works of art or statues by artists whose lives were bad. 'Benvenuto Cellini was an assassin who, when he was making a brooch for the Pope, asked the Pope to give him absolution for a murder he had committed, and absolution for crimes he might commit in the future, which the Pope granted. That was no reason for not studying the works of Cellini.'

The book was published, the judge went on, because Wilde was a great literary artist and manager of words. Whether they liked his work or not, whether they considered his paradoxes too laboured or not, he was nevertheless a great artist in written words, and he wrote plays which were being performed at the present day. Among other things which Wilde wrote was *De Profundis* and he came to write that because his vices had brought him into Reading Gaol for two years. Now in his opinion *De Profundis* was a most remarkable and interesting document. It must be read as a study of what a bad man, but a man of genius, went through in prison, and what the effect of prison was upon him as written from day to day. However, it must not all be taken as gospel truth, though it did not follow that it was all false. It was for the jury to determine what parts were true of that letter as well as the other letters which had been put to the plaintiff in cross-examination.

Darling's summing up was on the whole against the plaintiff, who, it must be admitted, had done his best to antagonise the judge by his conduct and demeanour in the witness box.

It took the jury just under two hours to find that the words complained of constituted a libel and moreover that they were true. With regard to The Times Book Club they found that there had been no negligence in the circulation of the book.

It would have been wiser if Bosie had not revived interest in the Wilde scandal by launching this action, but having done so, it is impossible not to feel some sympathy with him. Had the fact of the financial help which Wilde actually received from Bosie after he came out of prison, particularly the fact of the cheque payments supported by the entries in Bosie's bank book, been put more strongly to the jury, the verdict might have been different. Above all, the jury could not fail to have been impressed if Bosie had produced letters in his possession from Wilde shortly after he left Reading, in which Wilde wrote that 'It is only with you that I can do anything at all,' and begging his friend to 'remake my ruined life for me.' But because of the affectionate expressions which Wilde used in these letters Bosie was reluctant to put them in evidence.

Mr Ransome, to whom these proceedings with their accompanying publicity were most distasteful, subsequently behaved with characteristic generosity to the unsuccessful litigant. The case naturally led to a considerable public demand for his book and a new edition was necessary. In bringing this out he considered the question of reprinting the text in its original form, as he had a perfect right to do. However, as he put in the preface to the new edition, which was published by Methuen, Mr Ransome came to the conclusion that the libellous passages were not 'essential to the critical purpose of the book', and he therefore decided 'in order to spare the feelings of those who might be pained by the further publication of these passages, to omit them from this edition.' Nor have they appeared in any subsequent edition of Mr Ransome's book.

The fact that More Adey had testified for the defence had the effect of terminating Bosie's friendship with him, as shown by the following letter to him from Bosie written at the end of the trial.

> 26 Church Row
> Hampstead.
> 23 April 1913

Dear More,

I see that yesterday when you were recalled by the Judge to give evidence, you, too, played the Judas Iscariot to me, your old friend. You deliberately misled the jury.

You know perfectly well, for I have discussed the matter with you a dozen times, and you discussed it with my solicitor, that the £200 was sent to Wilde in November, 1897, within a week of my leaving him at Naples, and you also knew perfectly well that this £200 formed no part of any debt of honour.

I wish you joy of what you have done, knowing as you do that I have for years led a clean, straight life, and have struggled hard to be a good Christian and a good Catholic, and knowing that Ross, who put up Ransome to write the book is a filthy beast and to this day a habitual sodomite and corrupter of young boys.

Our friendship is at an end. I shall never speak to you again. It is no business of mine to seek for revenge on you or on Ross, but the reckoning will surely come sooner or later.

> Alfred Douglas.

P.S. I am sending a copy of this letter to the Judge.[11]

The unsuccessful plaintiff appealed against the decision in the libel action to the Court of Appeal, but was later given leave by the Court to withdraw his appeal when it was clear that owing to his bankruptcy he would be unable to give security for the costs of the appeal. But this further set-back did not prevent him from pursuing his vendetta against Ross whom he was determined to bring to justice. 'I swore the day after the Ransome trial,' he said, 'that I would never rest till I had publicly exposed Ross in his true colours.'

3

This period – to be precise, the first five months of 1913 – was Bosie's darkest. On 14 January of that year a Receiving Order had been made against him in the Bankruptcy Court on the petition of a money-lender. On previous occasions he had had recourse to money-lenders but they had always given him time to pay. However, on this occasion in anticipation of the Ransome case, which it was thought he might lose, the money-lender was adamant. Then Olive left him and returned to Weston; at the same time he was prosecuted for criminally libelling his father-in-law and convicted a week after losing the Ransome case. Meanwhile he continued to live alone in the barely furnished house in Hampstead, miserable and lonely and deserted by all his friends except George Wyndham who had always stood by him in the past.

Then he had some unexpected relief. On 23 April, the day before he was due to appear at the Old Bailey on the charge of criminal libel brought by Colonel Custance, a beautiful girl, an American whose first name was Doris, arrived at Bosie's house in Church Row. She had heard of his troubles and she produced a pearl necklace and other jewels which she wished him to accept and sell in order to raise money for the costs of the defence. Bosie was greatly touched by her kind offer but he felt he could not accept and told her so. Nevertheless she came down to the Old Bailey and was waiting outside to welcome him when the Recorder had bound him over and he was released, in spite of Custance's counsel Richard Muir begging the judge to impose the 'most severe sentence possible'.[12]

Bosie now began by explaining to Doris, whom he saw every day, that being a Catholic he could never consent to lead an immoral life, and for several weeks he went about with her 'in a perfectly innocent way,' as he put it. 'In the end, however, I deeply regret to have to admit that I succumbed,' he added in his account of the affair. He raised some money by selling the inscribed books which Wilde had given and the letters Wilde had written to him which he had not destroyed, as well as the advance royalties on the book *Oscar Wilde and Myself* which he had agreed to write, but which in fact was to be almost entirely written for him by Crosland. This enabled him to go on living in the Church Row house and also to carry on the fight in the Chancery Court over his son Raymond's custody, as well as taking Doris 'all over the place in London to restaurants and similar resorts.'

I did this partly out of bravado and as a demonstration against my enemies, and against my wife, whom at that time I never expected to see or speak to again. I had burnt all her photographs and everything else in the house that might remind me of her. Her father and George Lewis had me followed continually by detectives. Doris and I used to see them waiting outside my house or her flat, and laugh at them. Colonel Custance and Lewis moved heaven and earth to induce Olive to start divorce proceedings against me. But this she absolutely refused to do.

Less than four months after our separation Olive rang me up one day on the telephone. I answered, not knowing who it was. The sound of her voice on the telephone completely finished me, and I went straight off to see her and 'we made it up'. This of course caused a breach with Doris, and my irregular life came to an end for ever.[13]

On 3 June 1913, Bosie wrote to Olive that he was going over to Paris that day and would be back on the 10th or 11th 'for a few days' after which he might go back to Paris. The reason for his brief return to London, which he did not tell his wife, was that he had been directed to appear at the Bankruptcy Court in Carey Street on 12 June for his Public Examination. This revealing letter continued:

I am glad in a way that you telephoned to me and I am glad that I have cut out of my heart the hatred and contempt I felt for you. I can never think that you treated me otherwise than abominably, but it is wrong to hate anyone and I do not hate you now or wish you anything but good.

But you have done a dreadful thing to me, and perhaps the most dreadful of all, in fact certainly the worst thing of all, is that you drove me out of the state of grace and holiness into mortal sin. I was good and in spite of all the suffering and persecution I was going through I was happy. I went every morning at 6 or 7 o'clock to Communion and used to feel lifted right up to Heaven and I had no hate for anyone in my heart. I used to pray every day for your father and for Ransome and Ross and even George Lewis, and I really meant it.

Then when that Chancery case came on and you appeared against me, I turned bitter, for the first time, but even then I did not let go of the sacraments, and although I had met and known Doris for some time I utterly refused to do wrong with her. After that [the Chancery case] was over I went to France and she came over to me and we spent a week together, but we were living in separate hotels and perfectly innocent and very happy. It was simply on my part the ache of the void of love of a woman. I had got used to you 'loving' me and making a fuss of me, in the intervals of hating and abusing me, and I could not refuse love when it came to me. Now I have fallen into living in sin and I am utterly miserable.

It is like going back into a hot blazing desert after being in a cool shady wood.

I can't stand it any longer and I am going away alone. Doris is perhaps coming over later to be with me or near me as I can't live utterly alone. But we are going to be simply as we were when we first met. She suggested this herself. You know I am not like other men and that it is possible for me to have a Platonic friendship with a pretty woman.

Then as regards you and me, there is nothing to do but to wait and see what happens. Things may come right in the end somehow or other. I do still love you. I thought I had got over it, and for a short time I did really hate you. But I do understand now what you have done has been forced on you by your father and that villain Lewis and I forgive you. Your loving Boy.[14]

At Bosie's public examination in the Bankruptcy Court, when he was adjudicated bankrupt, it appeared that since the receiving order had been made accounts had been filed showing that he had unsecured liabilities amounting to £2,076 and that his assets consisted in the copyrights of five books. These were *Tails with a Twist, The City of the Soul, The Placid Pug, The Pongo Papers* and *Sonnets*. Some of the copyrights might become valuable after his death, he said, in reply to the Official Receiver, but he did not place any value upon them for the present purposes. Of his liabilities he thought about £1,650 represented the case advanced by the money-lender with interest. Asked by his counsel, Mr Harold Benjamin, who had paid the costs in the Ransome action which amounted to some £1,500, Bosie replied that these had been met by his family.

'With regard to the manuscript from which the book *De Profundis* is extracted', his counsel asked, 'would you say that that is of any value?'

'I should think it is of great value – probably worth £5,000.'

He added that he had never received the manuscript which was in the form of a letter addressed to him by Oscar Wilde. 'I never received it and heard nothing about it until recently.' He went on to say that he was advised that the letter, which 'appeared now to be in the possession of the British Museum,' was his property, but he had not attempted to obtain possession of it. He added that he would give any information which might be of interest to his creditors in the matter.[15]

The fact that he had been made bankrupt meant that he automatically ceased to be a member of White's, London's oldest and most exclusive gentlemen's club. However there was a rule that any member against whom a receiving order had been made might be readmitted without ballot if he could show that no blame attached to him financially and that there was no suggestion of fraud or dishonesty. This covered his case and he was told by the Receiver that he could get his discharge without any difficulty. Afterwards he always felt that the committee of White's, which included certain members of his family, should have made a move to readmit him. Consequently, as he was to write in his autobiography fifteen years later, 'I have determined that I will never apply for my discharge in bankruptcy any more than I will ask my relatives in White's Club to put into force the spirit of the rules which govern their select establishment.'[16] Thus he was still a bankrupt when he died.*

Bankrupt and embroiled as he was in litigation, culminating in Colonel Custance's repeated attempts in the Chancery Court to obtain custody of Raymond, Bosie was thoroughly unhappy. Only his mother stood by him and his cousin George Wyndham, who had him to stay at Clouds. On top of his legal troubles, Olive left him again, barely two months after their 'reconciliation' and went back to her father. She wrote to Sibyl Queensberry at this time:

> Bosie was cruel to me before I went to Weston, but I have often been very unhappy with him. But I love him above everything, and would never have left him if he had not taken away Raymond. Everybody I know takes my father's part, and, God help me I don't know where to turn for advice and comfort. My father is angry all the time because I love Bosie still – and I am utterly miserable. But would it do Bosie any good if I am turned out to starve? I am utterly helpless since I made those settlements. Perhaps it would be better for Bosie to divorce me for desertion? I only wish I had the courage to kill myself!'[17]

The following three letters which Bosie wrote to his wife within a few days of each other from Church Row in September 1913 show how he felt about her conduct towards him after their second separation:

> *15 September.* I got your curious letter without proper beginning or end, but I suppose that part of the condition of abject slavery and submission to your charming father under which you now live is that you are not even allowed to show natural affection to the husband whom you treated so basely and whose forgiveness you were so anxious to obtain a month or two ago.
>
> I confess that I now take very little interest one way or the other

---

*The bankruptcy was eventually annulled on 17 August 1981 at the instance of Bosie's literary executor Mr Edward Colman after Bosie's debts had been paid in full from the royalties earned by his writings.

in your moods. It is quite evident that money and self-interest are the only motives that sway them, and I can only hope you are satisfied with the state of affairs that you have brought about.

I am glad that you have at last discovered that Raymond is a 'clever and interesting child.' That is at any rate a welcome change from your usual way of abusing him and saying how much you hate him and wish he had never been born.

17 September. It is, alas, quite true that the great love I had for you, the love that made me write for you the best sonnets that have ever been written to a woman in the English language, is no longer what it was. I still care for you and often think of you with sorrow and agony and miss you terribly. But of course I can't pretend to feel the same about you. How could I after the way you have treated me? For one thing it is difficult if not impossible to love whole-heartedly what one despises and the worst part of the whole business is that I cannot help despising you.

After you asked me to forgive you and explained in a sort of way why you had behaved as you did I *did* feel that I could forgive you and my old love for you came back for a short time. But when I found that your pretended remorse was more or less a sham and that you were quite ready at a moment's notice to behave just as badly all over again, I realised bitterly that your desire for my forgiveness was only the result of a selfish care for your own comfort and a natural wish to put yourself right in the eyes of the world, and also and chiefly the result of jealousy and pique because you heard I was fond of another woman.

Well, I lost her through making friends with you, but I don't regret her and though she is always writing to me now and wants to come back I don't propose to make myself miserable with any more women. At the same time in view of the way you have behaved to me since our 'reconciliation' and the letters you have written to me, it seems almost a pity that you couldn't have left me alone when I had got a woman (and a very beautiful woman) to love me. The dog-in-the-manger attitude is the least lovely and the least dignified of all attitudes and your adoption of it was no more to your credit than your other manoeuvres.

19 September. I am getting a little bit tired of your continual libellous and slanderous assertions that I have been 'cruel' to you. You know perfectly well that it is a damnable lie to say so. So far from being cruel to you I have been extraordinarily good and long-suffering and patient with you. Having treated me in a most abominable way you try to put yourself right by slandering me and telling lies about me. It is a mean and despicable dodge and it is worthy of you, but it will do you no good in the long run.

Everyone who knows us and who knows what I have had to

endure from you and your horrible family knows that I have always been kind and loving and generous to you. What you call being 'cruel' is my refusing to let you make a public exhibition of yourself with Jack Stirling, Filson Young (you wanted to go and stay in an hotel with him in the west of Ireland and I was 'cruel' enough to prevent you) and other men.

So far from my ever having been cruel to you the boot is entirely on the other leg. *You* have been brutally cruel and heartless in your treatment of *me* and you have admitted it over and over again, and what is more all the world knows that it is a deliberate and wicked lie to say that I have ever been cruel to you.[18]

For her part Olive was upset by these letters and she turned to her mother-in-law for comfort. 'I have told Daddy that you spoke to me,' she wrote to Lady Queensberry. 'He will be angry perhaps, but he knows I shall always love Bosie, though I am afraid to live with him at present. I don't think Bosie loves me any more. I trust you. I have done all this for Raymond's sake, though you know I love Bosie.' The affections of this sweet-tempered but highly-strung boy were torn between his father and his grandfather, while his mother sided first with one and then the other.

4

In spite of the financial advantage Frank Harris had taken of Bosie over the Cesari Reserve Syndicate on the Riviera, the two men kept in touch, since, although Harris as an editor and journalist was in his decline, he was still of some consequence in Fleet Street. Harris gave Bosie some literary introductions in 1900 when Bosie paid his abortive visit to America in search of an heiress; he also published several of Bosie's sonnets which he was running a journal called *The Candid Friend* and later when without any great success he revived *Vanity Fair*. 'I have been offered the opportunity of writing on *Country Life* and *The Academy*,' Bosie had written to Harris from Lake Farm in 1906. 'But I am not a very prolific writer and would much rather write for you. But of course I must think of money a little. I am as usual in abject poverty but hope to get a good bit from *The Placid Pug*. I never got paid a penny by Crosland for all the rhymes, articles and sonnets which I contributed to the *English Review*.'[19] He added that he had twice lent Crosland the money for the printers' bill in order that the magazine should appear. However, whatever his faults – and it cannot be denied that he had many – Bosie tended to forgive his enemies and those who had injured him no matter how violent were their quarrels. Indeed, he had done this with Crosland and gone to the extent of making him assistant editor of *The Academy* after Crosland had attacked him, as we have seen. He was to do the same with Frank Harris, with whom he had such a violent quarrel in the autumn of 1913 – perhaps the worst year in Bosie's fortunes – that they actually came to blows.

At this period Harris was running a weekly called *Modern Society*, of which he was managing director as well as editor. It was a shady, scabrous production, full of malicious gossip in doubtful taste. The cause of Bosie's row is unknown, but it probably concerned Lord Fitzwilliam, who had employed Harris for a short time on *The Academy* after he had bought it with Lord Howard de Walden from Bosie in 1910, and after a time dismissed Harris. Harris revenged himself by printing some offensive paragraphs about Fitzwilliam after he had been cited as a co-respondent in a divorce action. These appeared while the case was part heard and therefore *sub judice*, as a result of which Fitzwilliam's lawyer applied to the court to have Harris committed to prison for contempt of court, which he eventually was by Mr Justice Horridge.

This is what Bosie wrote to Harris from his house in Hampstead on 2 November 1913:

> You are entitled to all the honour and glory you can extract from the fact that as you weigh about 3 stone more than I do and as I made no attempt whatever to hit you first you succeeded in grabbing me by the collar and forcing your thumb into my wind-pipe, thereby reducing me to impotence. All this I cheerfully concede to you. But would it not be more to the point if you could pretend even to yourself that you have behaved otherwise than a blackguard.
>
> Can you even pretend to deny that you swindled me out of £2,000 when I was young and foolish and trusted and even admired and liked you? Can you deny that I forgave you the injury you did me so completely that I never even reproached you with it? Can you deny that the moment I had the *Academy* and (as you thought) a millionaire to back me up you immediately tried to blackmail me? And can you deny that you have joined with all that you know to be the foulest and lowest in London to defame and insult (when you thought he was down) the man who, according to your own written words, is one of the few authentic poets of his day?
>
> If you can deny all these things, then you must be even more clever at deceiving yourself than you are at deceiving other people. If you cannot (and you know in your own heart that you cannot)

deny them, then your own conscience must be your own punishment. It is ill fighting with a dying man and it is borne in on me that you will not be alive very much longer and so I leave you

> To what disaster of malign Despair,
> Or terror of unfathomable ends?

The last two lines of this letter were quoted from Bosie's sonnet 'Dies Amare Valde' written in 1902. Harris thought it the best sonnet Bosie ever wrote, indeed describing it as 'the best sonnet ever written in English,' the last four words being 'as sublime as anything in Dante'. Bosie, on the other hand, considered he had written twenty as good but none better than this one.[20]

Nor was it the last that Bosie had to do with Frank Harris, who was then engaged in writing his vivid but unreliable *Life and Confessions of Oscar Wilde*, which libelled Bosie to such an extent that Harris was afraid to publish it in his lifetime in England and it originally appeared in America. As will be seen, Harris was to agree to write a preface expunging the libels but reneged at the last minute, so that Bosie had to bring out the letter and new preface as a separate publication. Meanwhile, if any English bookseller unwittingly sold a copy of the American edition, which Harrods was to do on one occasion, the litigious Bosie sued for libel and won damages.

5

Their son Raymond was the root cause of the trouble between Bosie and Olive. Twice in 1914 Bosie applied to Mr Justice Eve in the Chancery Court for full custody of the boy, the application in each instance being opposed by Colonel Custance and his daughter, the result being that Custance was to have Raymond for three-fifths of his school holidays and Bosie two-fifths. Bosie had got him into Ampleforth College, a fine Catholic school in Yorkshire, although Custance, who now agreed that he should be educated at a Catholic college, would have preferred him to go to Downside in Somerset as being an older and more exclusive institution of its kind. 'The only basis on which I can resume friendly personal relations with you is that my son is handed back to my sole custody,' Bosie wrote to his wife on 18 December 1914.

The present application was only in respect of these holidays. The main question will come on before the same judge after the Xmas holidays are over. Until it is settled one way or the other it would only lead to further bitterness and misery for us to meet. . . . As long as I do not see you I can at least keep alive a sort of ghost of my old love for you which enables me to sign myself Your loving Bosie.

'Of course it is not your fault *this time* that your father has behaved so vilely, so don't worry about it,' he wrote a few days later. 'He is simply cutting his own throat.'[21]

Olive now changed sides, and when the matter again came before the Chancery Court, which it did on 30 June 1915, she joined Bosie in his application for full custody of Raymond. Somewhat surprisingly Mr Justice Eve refused to vary the original arrangement, although on the face of it there is some difficulty in appreciating why a judge should deny a father and mother complete control of their son. However, the judge was probably prejudiced against Bosie when Custance's counsel read out some of Bosie's more violent letters to his father-in-law. Also Mr Justice Eve seems to have been shocked by the fact that for no apparent reason a picture of Raymond as a boy of eleven should have appeared in Bosie's *Oscar Wilde and Myself*. At all events, while expressing some sympathy for Bosie and his wife, the judge remarked that he needed stronger reasons for varying the original order, and he dismissed the application with costs. Lady Queensberry made a similar application a few weeks later and this met with a similar decision. It was a pity that the application should not have been granted as it would have resulted in Bosie and Olive coming together again on a permanent basis. As things turned out, they drifted apart with intermittent reconciliations and differences for the next few years, although they continued to correspond.

Bosie was so exasperated by Mr Justice Eve's decision that he took Raymond to Scotland, which was outside the jurisdiction of the Chancery Court. Raymond was accordingly removed from Ampleforth to the Benedictine Monastery and College of Fort Augustus at the southern end of Loch Ness, where Sir David Hunter-Blair, known as 'Dunsky' from his Galloway home, was Abbot; he had been a friend of Wilde's at Magdalen where he became a Catholic and almost succeeded in converting Wilde at the same time when they visited Rome together. Bosie took a house nearby and hoped that Olive would join him there but she did not do so, although she no longer lived with her father while Bosie had given up the house in Hampstead. Before the term began at Fort Augustus, Bosie and Raymond stayed at the hotel in the nearby village of Whitebridge, since scarlet fever had broken out at Fort Augustus.

'Raymond is very well and happy,' his father wrote to Olive on 14 August 1915. 'He loves Scotland. We go fishing on various lochs every day and he is very keen on it. Lady Encombe is at Killin Lodge 4 miles from here with her boys and we see a lot of them. . . . All here is Lovat's property. . . . Raymond sends his love. He has given me the mumps and I have had it for the last 5 days. It hurts like anything but I expect it is nearly over by now. I take no notice of it!'

In a less friendly tone in the same letter Bosie reviewed his relations with Olive since their separation:

> It is more than two years since you deserted me and ever since you have fought against me in every possible way from the Ransome case onwards, and have put the public insult on me of assisting your father to try to make out that I was unfit to have charge of my own son. Long before that however you treated me with cruelty and brutality. For the last two years we lived together you practically lived with another man. . . . Day after day and night after night I was left alone while you spent your time dining and lunching and supping with and going to theatres with Stirling or Clonmel. And as to my having been unfaithful to you I was never so till you drove me to it (and as you know all that has been over for 4 years) by repeatedly telling me in the most insulting language that you were tired of me and that your marriage to me had been one long misery. . . .
>
> I refuse to argue with you about Raymond. Only an abnormal and unnatural woman would ever *desire* her husband to put up with the hideous and humiliating position which you and your father have created for me in that regard. I think you will vainly search history for another example of a woman writing to her husband and offering to come back and live with him *if he will agree to give up his son.* The whole thing is a nightmare. . . .
>
> But I am not capable of ceasing to love you. Even if I desired to do so (as I sometimes have) I could not do it altogether, at least not when you appeal to me as you have done. But I can keep myself in control and I would far rather never see you again than try to patch up an ignoble reconciliation with you by surrendering my duties and my rights as a father. . . .
>
> I could only live with you now on the old basis of goodness and morality and religion which we flouted when we married. I believe you would not like it, you would be bored and you would want all sorts of things that I can't give you. But you shall never have the right or the chance to say that I 'cast you out'. I haven't got a home at present and I am wretchedly poor. But when I have one, you have only to come to it. But you don't really care enough for me to pay the price. You never did. . . . I like to *think* that you really love me but I expect you love me a great deal more absent than present and I fear that the waters of separation must still be between us.[22]

To his friend Sorley Brown, editor and later owner of the *Border Standard*, then on active service in the army, he wrote from White-bridge on 22 August: 'You will be interested to hear that I have taken my boy Raymond out of the jurisdiction of the Chancery Court and brought him to Scotland, thus defying the odious order of the Chancery judge. Last Monday, the 16th, was the day I was supposed to send him to that old beast Custance, but my mother and I decided that the injustice and iniquity of the whole thing was too much to be borne any longer, so I have taken the bull by the horns. As a Scotsman and the son of a Scotch peer I can rely on the laws of this country which are quite different from those of England. I have had advice on the subject from an Edinburgh lawyer and my position is quite secure, though of course if I went back to England I should be imprisoned for contempt of Court. Words cannot express the con-tempt I feel for the Court and for the loathsome little worm of a judge, so that really I am thoroughly enjoying the situation.'[23] Indeed he was to express his contempt in writing a biting satire on Mr Justice Eve which he called *Eve and the Serpent*.

But Bosie had not reckoned with Custance and Lewis. After barely a term at Fort Augustus, when Bosie was on the point of moving into the house he had taken there and Olive had agreed to join them, Raymond went fishing and failed to return. Bosie and the monks were distraught, fearing that he might have been drowned in the loch. After an agonising couple of days Bosie had a telegram from his wife saying that Raymond was safe at Weston. Custance had succeeded in establishing some means of secret communication with Raymond and arranged with him that he should be picked up at a certain point on Loch Ness where a car and a private detective would be waiting for him. Thus it happened, to Bosie's intense annoyance. Custance's next move was to reapply to the Chancery Court for Raymond's custody. The application was made in February 1916 and Bosie returned to London to contest it in person. The matter came before another judge, Mr Justice Peterson, who did not order Bosie to be arrested for contempt of court but merely affirmed the previous ruling that Raymond should spend three-fifths of his holidays with Custance and two-fifths with his father. Meanwhile he was to return to Ampleforth. At the same time Bosie told the judge that as Raymond had deceived him he washed his hands of him and would have nothing further to do with him. The result was that they did not meet for nearly ten years.

'I was at that time intensely devoted to my son,' Bosie was to write in his autobiography. 'His loss, and the horrible circumstances of it, completed my sense of the cruelty and injustice of the world.'

I gave up all idea of happiness in this life, and clung to Catholicism as my only consolation, in spite of the fact that I was very badly treated by most of the Catholics with whom I had dealings, including the monks of the Ampleforth Benedictine School, where I had placed my son. The monks had supported me all through my fight for the custody of the boy, but when I definitely renounced the boy they made terms behind my back with Custance and Lewis. I wrote a sonnet about this which appears in my *Collected Poems*.

'The end of the whole story,' Bosie concluded his account of the affair, 'is that my son, when he was of age and his own master, wrote and asked my forgiveness, which I of course gave him. Since then we have been on terms of deep affection. This action of my son was a bitter blow to Colonel Custance, and he did not long survive it.'[24]

6

We must now return to the year 1914, the year in which the Great War began and in which Bosie was involved in further legal troubles. Unfortunately he had by his behaviour forfeited his recognisances after he had been bound over for criminally libelling his father-in-law. For instance, as he told Sir George Lewis, he had written to King George V informing him of 'the foul way' he had been treated by Colonel Custance 'who has with your assistance broken up my home and deprived me of the society of my wife.' He had also sent copies of Olive's letters to the King as well as to members of Colonel Custance's family and 'to people of importance who are acquainted with him.'[25] Consequently he received an order of the Court to attend the Old Bailey on 6 March 1914 to hear judgment on his case. This he refused to do and wrote to the Recorder of London accordingly, informing him that he was on his way to Paris and was not coming to the Old Bailey since he was 'seriously and conscientiously convinced' that he had 'no chance whatever of obtaining justice or fair treatment at the hands of the Central Criminal Court.' From Paris he went to Boulogne, where Crosland saw him at Easter, and they discussed possible developments on their behaviour towards Robert Ross with whom they were both completely obsessed. Meanwhile Crosland had written to Ross accusing him of 'creating for Oscar Wilde a literary and general reputation which is to a great extent a fraudulent one and of dishonestly dealing with *De Profundis*.'

From the public point of view it is the highly respectable Ross labouring generously for the much maligned and greatly suffering

Wilde and bringing him into his own. You have flooded the book-stalls with Wilde's works to the great detriment of the public mind.... My own efforts to bring you to book have not been personal to yourself and therefore it is that I propose to you that you should withdraw your prefaces and other sophistications from publication and resign your executorship of Wilde's literary estate, and that you should further make some public statement which would help in the false and dangerous conception of Wilde you have been the means of spreading abroad.

In a second letter to Ross, Crosland stated that 'a letter nailing you down has been sent by Lord Alfred Douglas to Mr Justice Darling and two other judges, the Prime Minister, the Director of Public Prosecutions, Sir George Lewis, Mr John Lane and others. 'If these letters do not contain the truth about you,' Crosland added, 'there can be little question that you would have taken a certain and obvious legal remedy.'[26]

Goaded beyond endurance Ross now took the hint and prosecuted Crosland for conspiring with Bosie and others to bring a false charge against him (Ross) in respect of his alleged immorality with a youth named Charles Garratt. During the preliminary police court proceedings at Marlborough Street, the magistrate, Mr Paul Taylor, announced that he had received a communication from Lord Alfred Douglas in France, saying that if he was given an assurance that no steps would be taken against him to appear before the Recorder in the matter of Colonel Custance until the Crosland trial was finished, and also if no obstacle was put in his way to his being granted bail, he would at once return to England and answer the conspiracy charge. It was obvious, the magistrate commented, that it would be quite impossible for him to give such an undertaking. Hence the trial in its various stages continued with Crosland alone in the dock.

During the protracted police court proceedings which eventually led to Crosland being committed for trial Bosie kept in touch with him and they used to meet at weekends in Boulogne, for which Lady Queensberry paid Crossland's expenses. 'You know I was a good and faithful friend to that filthy beast Wilde when he got into trouble,' Bosie wrote to Crosland on 27 April; 'so that it would be a poor thing if I couldn't do as much and more for you, who are the only real friend I have ever had and especially as you are in all this through me. In view of all you say I shall not return to England until I can do so with safety.'[27]

Meanwhile Crosland tried to get the editor of the *London Mail* committed for contempt of court for prejudicing a fair trial by stating in a paragraph under the heading 'Things we want to know':

Whether all people would not heave a sigh of relief if the Government decided to deport the unspeakable Mr Crosland and the more unspeakable Lord Alfred Douglas.

The matter came before a Divisional Court consisting of three High Court judges. 'Avory was for us – Shearman and Rowlatt against us,' Crosland wrote to Bosie. 'I couldn't have believed that the *London Mail* should be allowed to get off without at least a severe reprimand. Rowlatt said the contempt was really not so very bad and they must pay the costs – that was all. It will now I hope be quite plain to you – as it is to everybody and has long been so – that we are not popular in judicial or legal circles. Avory said that any common sense person could see that the paragraph complained of was calculated seriously to hurt and prejudice persons over whose heads a criminal charge was hanging; yet though he argued with the other two for quite half an hour in front of all the court he couldn't bring them round, and so in effect we lost.'[28]

Crosland's trial opened at the Old Bailey on 27 June 1914 before Mr Justice Avory and a jury. F.E. Smith led for the prosecution in what was to be his last big case as a private practitioner, while Crosland was defended by Bosie's friend Cecil Hayes. Since Bosie was not present, the trial need only be briefly described here. 'Charlie' Garratt, an auburn-haired effeminate looking youth who was serving a sentence for importuning, stated that he had never met Ross until the present, although he had previously admitted to Crosland's solicitors that they had met before, which was in fact the case. Christopher Millard, alias Stuart Mason, Ross's homosexual private secretary and Wilde's bibliographer, also gave evidence for the prosecution, stating that Douglas had tried to persuade him to make a statement incriminating Ross and Garratt, although according to this witness he knew that Garratt had never met Ross. Robert Ross in the witness box recalled his friendship with Wilde and declared that he had begged him to give up his 'gutter perverts.' Likewise in his examination-in-chief he said he regarded *The Picture of Dorian Gray* as a 'perfectly moral' book. Asked by F.E. Smith whether there was such a thing as an immoral book he retorted: 'Yes, I know heaps of them. Lord Alfred Douglas's *Poems* for instance.' It was a smart reply but it antagonised the judge. When Ross asserted that his reputation was as good as Caesar's wife's, Mr Justice Avory told him to 'leave Caesar's wife alone.' As against this, when Cecil Hayes, in cross-examining Mr Edward Lister, a partner in Lewis & Lewis, Ross's solicitors, put Bosie's letter to More Adey of 27 April 1913 to the witness, the letter in which Bosie had described Ross as 'an habitual Sodomite and corrupter of young boys', and asked him whether any proceedings had been taken against Bosie in regard to that letter, the witness replied that they had not.[29]

Crosland proved a good witness and stood up well to Smith, who cross-examined him for two days. Asked about *De Profundis* the witness declared that Ross had picked out the pious parts of the book and made it appear a religious work and a work of repentance, when in fact it was, as a whole, an immoral and disgraceful work. He also pointed out that the unpublished part containing gross libels on Bosie and his family and had been sent by Ross to the British Museum when Bosie could no longer defend himself. 'I call that treacherous, and not only treacherous, sir, but damned treacherous,' Crosland shouted, 'and posterity will bear me out in this.'

One answer in Crosland's cross-examination particularly amused and pleased the jury when Crosland said that he was anxious that the jury should not be confused.

'The jury can probably take care of themselves,' said counsel.

'I dare say they can,' Crosland replied, 'but I want them to take care of me!'

The judge's summing-up was strongly in Crosland's favour. In essence it was to the effect that when a man gives evidence in his own defence, as Crosland had done, he did not have to establish his innocence; it still remained for the prosecution to prove his guilt. He plainly hinted that the defendant, knowing of Ross's old friendship with Wilde, was entitled to form his own opinion, and this showed a strong hostility to Wilde and all his works.

It took the jury only twenty-seven minutes to find the defendant 'not guilty' and he was discharged amid applause at the back of the court.

Among those who congratulated Bosie on the verdict, which of course included him in the acquittal, was Sorley Brown, who wrote a friendly article in the *Border Standard* on the case. 'I thank you for your good wishes and your faithful partisanship,' Bosie wrote to him from Boulogne on 11 July. 'I have had a dreadful time lately. The persecution has been awful, what with my father-in-law and Ross and George Lewis. Thousands and thousands of pounds have been spent in the effort to ruin me. However the verdict in the Crosland case was a crushing smash for Ross and his gang and for Lewis (who is really the worst of the lot).... I hope to be back in England in a week or two. I have written a scathing poem in rhymed couplets about F.E. Smith, and will send you a copy when it is ready next week.'[30]

The poem, *The Rhyme of F Double E*, of which Bosie had a thousand copies printed for private circulation, was later included in his

Collected Satires. 'In fact it was never really put on sale,' Bosie wrote to a correspondent who asked for a copy, 'and I confined myself to circulating it in the House of Commons, the Bar, the Bench, et cet.'[31] Nevertheless it was grossly defamatory of the great advocate, but Smith chose to ignore it. Its style may be judged from the following extracts:

> Never was such complete disaster,
> The great F.E. had met his master!
> For Crosland tore him limb from limb
> And wiped the dusty floor with him.
> And Cecil upper-cut him sweetly,
> And the Judge finished him completely.
> The Court was full of grins and chuckles
> When Avory rapped him on the knuckles
> And took him down a score of pegs,
> Till with his tail between his legs,
> Like a well-walloped fox-hound pup,
> He bolted at the summing-up
> So much for Smith. He stands revealed:
> The 'gentleman' is hairy-heeled
> Under his patent leather boots,
> His 'get-up' at the ducal 'shoots'
> Of Blenheim's smirking auctioneer
> Is just sartorial veneer
> To hide a very ugly heart
> That's filled up with 'exchange and mart'.
> His sentiments are so much tripe
> And he'll be rotten before he's ripe.
>
> *   *   *
>
> Who'll look at you again, dear Fred,
> Lives there a man with soul so dead?
> Even in Ulster they'll eschew you,
> And in 'the House' askance they'll view you.
> You'll hear them whisper: 'We can't sit
> Upon this honest floor with IT.
> Oh, Smith, you've taken Ross's "thou",
> You'll take the Chiltern Hundreds now!'[32]

'When I wrote these lines in 1914,' Bosie wrote in his *Collected Satires* (1926), 'I did not know as much about the true inwardness of English politics as I know now, or I should not have committed myself to this rash prophecy. I was so far "out" that Lord Birkenhead may truly say that, since he put up his great fight for Robert Ross & Co, he has never "looked back".' Which was true enough, since F.E. Smith became successively Attorney-General, Lord Chancellor, Viscount Birkenhead and Earl of Birkenhead, being the youngest lawyer to hold the Great Seal in modern history.

Bosie stayed on for a few more weeks in France, but with the outbreak of the Great War in 1914, he considered it prudent to return to England. To his surprise he was arrested on landing in Folkestone, as he thought, on the Recorder's Bench Warrant for having broken his recognisances in the Custance case, but in fact on a summons issued by Robert Ross for criminal libel. Owing to some mix-up over his sureties, for which Bosie blamed the machinations of Ross and George Lewis, he had to spend five days in Brixton and two days and a night in Wormwood Scrubs prison, sleeping on a plank bed. Apart from the disgusting and uneatable food, what he particularly resented at Wormwood Scrubs was the removal of his personal belongings. The only thing he was allowed to keep was his rosary, which he was wearing round his neck. While at Brixton, which was a remand prison, he was allowed to wear his own clothes, and keep his other personal effects. Also he was much heartened by Olive who had heard of his arrest and turned up at the police court and accompanied him to the Old Bailey, where he was bound over, ordered to be released on bail and to come up for trial at the next sessions in November. Meanwhile he stayed with his mother at her house in Cliveden Place, off Eaton Square.

Bosie did not have very much time to collect hard evidence against Ross, particularly in view of young Garratt's shilly-shallying. However, he had two strokes of luck. Providentially he found an excellent solicitor in Mr Edward Bell, a Scotsman whose great-grandfather had been hanged for being 'out' in the Jacobite Rising of '45 and whose fighting spirit matched his client's. Together they had a conference with the counsel Bell proposed to brief, Mr A.S. Comyns Carr, who, when he heard what Bosie had to say, remarked: 'If you will undertake to go into the witness box and say there what you have told me I will draw up a plea of justification. But I tell you frankly that, unless you can get a lot of real evidence, apart from your own, you will not have a chance.'[33]*

Bosie got various clues, including one in Guernsey, which he visited without success, besides a dozen others equally fruitless. Finally, an anonymous 'tip-off' led him to an address near Campden Hill where he was given the name of a certain Mr E, the respectable father of a boy who had been one of Ross's victims. He went to the address and asked for Mr E. No such person was known there. His heart sank and he looked down the long street of at least 150 houses. He prayed

*Later Sir Arthur Comyns Carr, K.C., Liberal MP for East Islington.

desperately to St Anthony of Padua, for whom he always had 'a special cult'. He then walked a few yards with his eyes on the ground. Suddenly he heard a voice saying: 'What do you want? Can I help you?' Bosie looked up and saw a beautiful little boy, about ten years old, smiling at him. 'I was looking for someone at a number which was given me in this street, and now I am told there is no such name known there.' He replied: 'Tell me the name and the number.' Bosie did so. 'All right,' said the boy, 'I know where it is. The numbers in the street have been changed.'

The boy took his hand, according to Bosie, and led him right down to the other end of the street. There he stopped in front of a door and said: 'You'll get what you want there.' Bosie let go of his hand and went up to the door and rang the bell. 'Does Mr E live here?' Bosie asked. 'Yes, he does,' was the reply. 'Will you come in?' Bosie did so, but first he looked down the street again for the boy. But he had vanished. There was no sign of him anywhere in the street.

Bosie had considerable difficulty in obtaining a statement from Mr E. This was due to the woman who had admitted Bosie to the house and turned out to be Mr E's second wife and the step-mother of his two sons. 'Don't tell him anything,' she adjured her husband. 'We don't want to have any scandal in the family!'

Bosie made a strong appeal to Mr E. 'The boy himself is dead. After what happened he left home and went to South Africa and died there. His elder brother is a private in the army now at Goring. He will tell you the whole story.' Mr E then gave Bosie the brother's name, rank, and unit.

So far as the boy in the street who had led Bosie to Mr E's house was concerned, Bosie was convinced that his experience with him was supernatural. 'I firmly believe that the child was an angel,' Bosie wrote afterwards, 'or, at any rate, he was supernaturally moved to help me. He was a beautiful little boy, and he had an angelic face and smile. And how did he disappear in the space of time, in a few seconds, between when I let go his hand and when I looked round again?'[34]

Bosie still had trouble in getting the evidence he needed. When he got to Goring, he found that the brother's unit had been transferred to Norfolk. He went there and called at the headquarters of the commanding officer. This was the house of Charlie Tracy, later Lord Sudeley, whom Bosie knew. However Tracy was not there and the commanding officer, whom Bosie called 'odious', was rude and insolent and refused to let him see the man in question. Bosie thereupon told him, in the presence of the adjutant and other officers, that unless he produced the man, for whom Bosie had a sub-poena, he would apply to the court for a bench warrant and that he would publicly expose the colonel as 'a man who was trying to shield Ross and what he stood for. He grew red in the face and stormed out of the room, followed by his officers.' The door was slammed and Bosie was left alone.

About five minutes later, a young subaltern, 'very much a gentleman,' according to Bosie, came in and told him that he had sent for the man and that Bosie could interview him in the subaltern's presence. The young man duly arrived and was told that he need not answer any of Bosie's questions unless he wished. At first he showed considerable reluctance to say anything. 'You don't want to shield the man who ruined your brother,' said Bosie to him, 'and is, indirectly, responsible for his death, do you?' Bosie also told him that unless he told the truth he (Bosie) would be sent to prison for denouncing Ross. The young man then gave Bosie the whole story, which Bosie wrote down in the form of a statement which the man signed. Bosie then handed the man a sub-poena with the statutory fee of three pounds and told him that he would have to attend the Old Bailey on the date fixed for the trial in November, or early December.

After that evidence began to flow in, and eventually Bosie secured more than a dozen witnesses, including a clergyman of the Church of England, who were all prepared to testify against Ross. Subsequent events were described by Bosie in his letters to Olive:

> *9 Cliveden Place, SW 5 November 1914.* . . . The plea of justification was put in yesterday and handed to Lewis & Lewis. It is a long document of six foolscap sheets. I think it will be a staggering blow for Ross. I got a lot of damning evidence. . . .
>
> Have you got the letter Ross wrote to you at the time I broke off with him? If so, please send it to me. If not try to remember more or less what he said in it. Comyns Carr wants to be able to put it to him in cross-examination that he wrote a letter more or less threatening me with reprisals because I would not go on knowing him. You know this is so, but have you kept the letter? It is most important if you have it. . . .
>
> Bell, my solicitor, and Carr both think that we are certain to win. It is doubtful whether Ross will face it. The evidence is overwhelming. He is sure to be arrested after the case is over. . . .
>
> *13 November.* The trial begins on Monday [19 November]. We are all right and ready for them and though of course it is an anxious time and things will not be very agreeable still I am fairly confident. We have damning evidence against Ross.
>
> Bell, my solicitor, saw Lewis and his gang of ruffians at the Old Bailey on Wednesday when both attended to fix a day for the trial. Lister, Lewis's partner, let out to Bell that they 'didn't like the case

at all' and that 'Ross had no more money'. They have got Wild and young Fulton.*

The judge will be Lord Coleridge. He is I believe a very decent chap. I knew his father who was Lord Chief Justice when I was at Oxord. Anyhow he is a gentleman which is a good thing.[35]

7

The trial of Lord Alfred Douglas on a charge of criminally libelling Robert Ross by accusing him of homosexuality and blackmail opened at the Old Bailey on 19 November 1914 before Mr Justice Coleridge and a jury and lasted eight days. Ross was represented by Ernest Wild, KC, and Eustace Fulton and the defence was led by Comyns Carr.

Ross put up a poor showing in the witness box and the judge waited in vain for any condemnation of homosexuality by Ross. Asked whether he had been to a New Year's Eve party several years previously, at which twenty or thirty men danced together, Ross lamely denied it. At the end of his evidence the foreman of the jury wished to stop the case and acquit Bosie but one juryman insisted on sticking it out in favour of Ross.

Bosie called fourteen witnesses including an inspector from Scotland Yard with many years experience of the West End; he swore that Ross was well-known for his homosexual activities, notably for associating with 'sodomites' and 'male prostitutes'. Another of Bosie's witnesses, a boy named Smith, belonged to a church dramatic society, testifying to his association with Ross and admitting to 'painting and powdering' his face. Asked by Ross's counsel in cross-examination whether this was not quite usual for actors, the boy replied, 'Hardly, when they come to church!'

The young soldier broke down at one point when he related how his dead brother had disappeared from home when he was sixteen years old and how he and his father heard that Ross was responsible. He described going to a bar in Copthall Avenue off London Wall which Ross was known to frequent and asking Ross what he had done with his brother. He said that Ross had offered him money to keep quiet and when he refused Ross had threatened to accuse him of blackmail. This frightened him, the witness declared, and so he made off.

Asked by Comyns Carr if he would recognise the man he had conversed with in the bar in Copthall Avenue, he said he was not sure

*Ernest Wild, K.C., was later knighted and appointed Recorder of London. Eustace Fulton, then a junior, later became Chairman of London Sessions.

since it had happened some years ago. He was then told to look round the court room, and after a few moments of breathless silence, he said there was a gentleman sitting at the solicitors' table whom he thought resembled the man. Ross was then asked to stand up which he did. 'That is the man,' the witness declared dramatically pointing at him.

When Bosie gave evidence, Ross's counsel asked him what proof he had of his charge that Ross was a blackmailer. Bosie in reply maintained that there was such a thing as moral blackmail, and that a man who kept old letters of his friends and produced them against him twenty years later was as much a blackmailer as a man who demanded money with menaces. Mr Justice Coleridge sympathised with this view in his summing up, in which he also expressed his surprise at Ross's attitude towards homosexuality in the witness box. 'I waited and waited,' the judge remarked, 'but I waited in vain for any moral expression of horror at the practice of sodomitical vices ... and indeed, to be frank with Mr Ross, when he was asked whether he did not constantly introduce these things into ordinary articles in a magazine, all he could say was that he could not remember. It was certainly not so emphatic a denial as you would expect from a man with no leprosy upon him.... I don't recollect that there is a copy or extract which has been produced indicating that he disapproves or that he views this kind of vice with disgust ... I would say that is the attitude of the man and his mind towards this kind of perversion of sex.'

The jury were out for three hours and failed to agree on a verdict. They were sent out again and again disagreed. The case was therefore adjourned to the next sessions.[36]

Bosie then wrote to his wife telling her what had happened:

> *30 November*. ... I was robbed of my verdict by Lewis squaring one of the jury. He was the man who told the judge that the jury were 'divided into two camps.' Both Bell and I saw Lewis go up to him, touch him on the shoulder and walk out of court with him when the case was over. The foreman of the jury and 8 other jurymen waited for me outside the court when it was over to tell me that they were all in my favour except this one man who said *on the first day of the trial* that he would never bring in a verdict against Ross. The foreman told me that they would have stopped the case after Ross's cross-examination if it had not been for this one man. The judge summed up against Ross on every point.
>
> Lewis had also apparently succeeded in squaring the newspaper reporters, as all the evidence was suppressed (I called 14 witnesses and the charges were one and all proved up to the hilt) and anyone

reading the papers would have imagined that it was simply my word against Ross's. I don't suppose Ross will come on again. If he does his only chance will be to buy another juryman as I have more and stronger evidence since the trial. It was a sickening thing to be cheated out of my verdict. I am having the judge's summing up printed.

Ross is quite finished anyhow and Lewis very severely damaged. I told the jury that he Lewis was a blackmailer and that he had threatened me, *through you*, with the production of other letters if I went on with the case. The judge made no attempt to stop me but glared at Lewis in grim silence. I had things my own way all the time.

Bell and I are preparing affidavits about Lewis squaring the juryman and we are going to have a go to get him struck off the rolls. If you ever consent to speak to him again after this, I shall be surprised. I explained at length how your father had treated me and how Lewis had tried to ruin me by working the two cases together against me. Wild protested and tried to stop me but the judge refused to interfere and I got it all out.

The 9 jurymen all shook hands with me after the case. They were frightfully upset, much more so than I was. If the case had been properly reported it would have been a tremendous triumph for me. However I think it will make no difference. It is ten to one against their offering any evidence at the next trial and then I simply get my verdict as a matter of right.

P.S. Comyns Carr was splendid. His cross-examination of Ross was masterly and he made a brilliant speech.

Wild was very funny. He was all the time trying to propitiate me as much as to say 'Don't hit me, I can't help it, I am only doing my duty.' In his final speech he said 'It would be idle for me to attempt to make any comparison between my unfortunate client, bowed down, crushed and already ruined under the weight of these terrible charges and the *brilliant and fascinating personality of the defendant.* I cannot disguise that my client was a very bad witness and the defendant a very good one. I can only remind you that the best witnesses are not always the most truthful.'!!

I was very polite to Wild all through and we continually bowed and smiled and exchanged amiable compliments. It quite spoilt the picture he had drawn of the sort of man I was supposed to be.[37]

The fresh hearing came on before Mr Justice Avory on 11 December 1914. 'The triumph over Ross and Lewis is complete,' Bosie wrote to Olive when it was over. 'They have to pay my costs (£600).... Avory came up from Birmingham to try the case when he heard there had been a disagreement. He has got his knife right into Lewis and Ross. Lewis is as much ruined as Ross. Your respected father will have to get a new solicitor!'[38] What happened was that Ross's legal advisers represented to Bosie that if he would consent to a *nolle prosequi*, that is the abandonment of the prosecution, Ross would pay his out-of-pocket expenses and also undertake never to produce in any legal proceedings or otherwise make public Bosie's letters to Ross and Wilde in return for an undertaking from Bosie that he would abstain from attacking Ross in the future and repeating the charges he had made against him. 'The only result of their fraudulent manoeuvres,' Bosie wrote to Sorley Brown, 'may be to save Ross from the police prosecution which would almost certainly have followed. Of course, also, in a way, they have succeeded in robbing me of the *éclat* of a win in a crowded and excited court.'

'I don't mind telling you that if I could have afforded it, I would have refused to make any terms at all,' Bosie wrote to Brown a few days later. He continued:

> I had him [Ross] utterly beaten and done for, and I have got even stronger evidence of his filthy practices since the last trial. But I am absolutely *ruined* by all this, and I could not afford to lose the certainty of making sure of my costs. One of the least of the injuries this man has done me is to drive me into the bankruptcy court. Of course the *nolle prosequi* is to all intents and purposes a complete justification for me and carries with it a verdict of 'Not Guilty', but it gives Ross a sort of hole to wriggle out of, and if I could have afforded it I would not have agreed to any compromise. But that is always the way.
>
> Ross seems to be able to command unlimited money from innumerable backers, but nobody has ever offered to help *me* with so much as a five pound note. Socially he is now an outcast as far as decent society is concerned, but I don't suppose he much cares about that as he seems still to have rich and powerful friends. Of course there ought to be a Treasury prosecution, but I should like to bet that it will all be hushed up, though the Treasury has, I hear, sent for the shorthand notes of all the evidence. However that remains to be seen.[39]

Ross was a member of the Reform Club and the committee could not afford to let the result of his case against Bosie pass unnoticed. While they were debating whether or not to demand his resignation, Bosie sent them the following quatrain:

> The question finds the Wilde clique at a loss,
> The controversy's raising quite a storm,
> Is 'The Reform' reforming Robert Ross,
> Or Robert Ross reforming 'The Reform'?

On consideration the committee decided to take no action, and Ross remained a member of that club, besides the Burlington Fine Arts and the Royal Automobile. He also continued to list his recreation in his entry in *Who's Who* as 'editing new editions of Wilde's works.'[40]

As Ross's solicitors made clear publicly, Bosie's costs were not paid by their client personally but 'by relations and friends of his who desire that these proceedings shall be terminated'. This subscription was organised by Ross's close friend Edmund Gosse, who shortly afterwards likewise organised the testimonial to Ross accompanied by a further sum of £700 as a mark of recognition of the recipient's services to art and literature.

In February 1914 Bosie had written to the Prime Minister Mr Asquith, accusing Ross of being 'the filthiest and most notorious Bugger in London, for whom the Prime Minister had created a job carrying with it a large salary,' and threatening to make the whole affair public. On 21 February 1915 Bosie returned to the attack with a further letter to the Prime Minister in which he wrote:

> It is not quite a year since I wrote and gave you very definite information about the man Robert Baldwin Ross, who was then a frequent guest at your house and an intimate friend of your wife, and for whom you created a post as assessor of picture valuations at the Board of Trade carrying with it a salary of, I believe, £1000 a year. You chose to ignore my letter and your wife continued to associate with and countenance Ross and you continued to receive him as a guest in your house.
>
> I am credibly informed that you *still* continue to receive Ross in your house and allow your wife to associate with him. I am loath to believe this however, and I write to give you an opportunity of assuring me that it is not true and partly to give you precise and exact information as to the result of my trial at the Old Bailey for libelling Ross and calling him a Sodomite and a Blackmailer. I do this in order that you may not be in a position to pretend ignorance in the matter.

Bosie went on to give full details of the trial and its result. He concluded his letter with the following:

> I now beg to inform you that, if I can establish it as a fact that you still continue to receive this horrible man in your house and to allow him to associate with your wife, I shall in the public interest and in view of your official position feel it my duty to call public attention to the matter. I am acquainted with more than one editor of a Unionist [Conservative] paper who would be glad to have the

opportunity of taking it up and printing this letter or such parts of it as may seem advisable.

Before proceeding further I wish in fairness to you to give you an opportunity of denying that you have received Ross in your house since my trial, or failing that pledging yourself not to do so in the future.[41]

The Prime Minister passed Bosie's letter to the Director of Public Prosecutions, who sent it to the Home Secretary, then Sir John Simon. 'I return this horrible letter,' Simon wrote on 31 January. 'Bonham Carter [Asquith's private secretary] is of course quite right to leave it unacknowledged.'[42]

Bosie next tackled Winston Churchill whom he may have heard was about to be dismissed from his post of First Lord of the Admiralty. He wrote to him on 21 May 1915:

I send you herewith a copy of a letter I sent the Prime Minister on the 22nd of January of this year. A little more than two months after receiving the letter Mr Asquith signed a public testimonial to the man Robert Ross and subscribed to a present of money to him.

Of the two editors of Unionist papers, to whom I have so far shown the letter, one refused to have anything to do with it, and the other declined to deal with it *at present* from motives of patriotism, but expressed his readiness to take the whole thing up as soon as the war was over.

There is not the slightest doubt that the moment the facts about Asquith's support and backing of Ross (after his public exposure) are made known Asquith is finished. He must be a lunatic to have put himself in such a position and it is ridiculous to suppose that he can go on hushing up the business for ever. For example, I have only got to bring out *one* number of a paper with an account of the whole thing and a copy of my letter and print 10,000 copies to put him out of office for ever. There is no particular hurry and I am quite content to bide my time.

But in the meantime, as you have had nothing whatever to do with the extraordinary Ross-whitewashing movement, why should you not take it up on your own account? When Asquith goes, someone will have to lead the Liberal Party and why should it not be you?

If you feel inclined to discuss the matter with me, I can show you all the documents which are quite conclusive, and on any points you like to raise I can refer you to my solicitors Carter & Bell.[43]

This letter certainly arrived at a crucial moment in Churchill's career, since on the same day as Bosie wrote it Churchill received the unwelcome news from Asquith that he must leave the Admiralty as part of the government changes necessitated by the formation of the Coalition. Nevertheless Churchill remained loyal to the man who had advanced his political career so rapidly, and he accepted the non-departmental office of Chancellor of the Duchy of Lancaster. At the same time there would be no question of his leading the Liberal Party as Bosie suggested, since Churchill had a relatively small personal following in the party. Also there is no record of his having made any response to Bosie's communication. Nor, it appears, did they even meet at this time. Their only meeting, which took place a few years later, was to be a dramatic one and most unfortunate for Bosie.

The testimonial to which Bosie refers in his letter to Churchill consisted of a flowery encomium written by Edmund Gosse in recognition of Ross's 'services to Art and Literature,' particularly praising the 'humour and resource' which had illuminated the expression of his views and 'the generosity with which you have put yourself at the disposal of all those who claimed your sympathy or your help. You have been one of the earliest amongst us to observe new talent and one of the most zealous to encourage it.' The 'address' which was accompanied by the sum of £700, was signed by three hundred persons, including Mr and Mrs Asquith, Bernard Shaw, More Adey, H.G. Wells, William Rothenstein, Ada Leverson, Lady Ottoline Morrell and her MP husband Philip, Sir George Lewis, J.L. Garvin, G. Lowes Dickinson, the Earl of Plymouth, Earl Beauchamp, Algernon Methuen, Robert Sherard, and the Bishop of Birmingham (Right Rev Henry Wakefield).[44]

Shortly afterwards Bosie composed a satire on the Ross affair, *The Rossiad*, and in the explanatory notes which accompanied it he wrote:

> Mr Robert Ross, in accepting the testimonial and gift of money, gracefully intimates that he would like to devote the latter to a 'public object' The Senate of the University of London thereupon gives evidence of 'humour and resource' by accepting the money to found a SCHOLARSHIP FOR BOYS, to be called the 'Robert Ross Scholarship.'[45]

At the same time Bosie wrote a devastating sonnet which he called 'All's well with England':

> Scorn not the 'literary executor'.
> He is officially condoned, for he
> Has lifted Oscar Wilde from obloquy
> And planted him in our hearts' inmost core.
> Behold the signatories take the floor!

Plymouth and Beauchamp, Gosse and Shaw, and see
Budding around the genial Beerbohm Tree,
Schiff, Schiller, Schuster, Spielman and some more.

Out there in Flanders all the trampled ground
Is red with English blood, our children pass
Through fire to Moloch. Who will count the cost?
Since here at home sits merry Margot, crowned
With Lesbian fillets, while with front of brass,
'Old Squiffy' hands the purse to Robert Ross.[46]

Shortly before his prosecution of Bosie for criminal libel, Ross considered it prudent to resign his £1,000 a year post of Adviser to the Inland Revenue on picture valuations for estate duty which he had held since 1912, to which Bosie had referred in his letters to the Prime Minister. The testimonial and gift of money were designed by Edmund Gosse as a solatium for the loss of his paid office. Nevertheless he remained a Trustee of the National Gallery, and shortly before his death he was appointed adviser for the purchase of works of art to the Felton Bequest Committee in Melbourne. Unfortunately he died before he could make the prolonged visit to Australia which he had planned. However, notwithstanding the testimonial from his friends and this fresh appointment, there is no doubt that his reputation was seriously damaged by the trial and he was never the same man afterwards.

Bosie would have done better to forget about Ross, instead of (as he did) continuing to expose and harrass him through the medium of Crosland. 'Ross did not get his testimonial for nothing', Bernard Shaw wrote to Bosie many years later, when Bosie was still obsessed by him. 'Only a great deal of good nature on his part could have won over that distinguished and very normal list of names to give public support to a man who began with so very obvious a mark of the beast on him.... Let Ross alone: the world has had enough of that squabble.'[47]

8

Although he was now forty-five and well over the age to which conscription was to apply, Bosie hoped to undertake some form of military service, particularly since his nephew Bruce, his younger brother Sholto's son, was killed in action in 1915. He offered himself as an interpreter in French, since he now spoke and wrote that language fluently, but he was turned down without any reason given, although he wrote to Kitchener, the War Minister, personally. His wife suggested, no doubt at her father's instigation, that as a last resort he could join the ranks like other poets. Bosie tartly replied that this course was impracticable. He also thought of joining the French Foreign Legion and he obtained a letter of introduction to the Legion's Commanding Officer from a friend Colonel 'Taffy' Lewis who had been an honorary member of the Legion mess, when he was *The Times* war correspondent in Morocco. However Lewis was against it, telling Bosie that it was a 'mad idea' and that he could never stand the conditions, and after some reflection Bosie gave it up and went back to writing. He turned out sonnets and satires and wrote a book, *The Wilde Myth*, covering much of the same ground as *Oscar Wilde and Myself* except that it was in his own words and not 'ghost-written' by Crosland as the other had largely been. The publisher gave him an advance of £200 and it reached the proof stage, but the publisher refused to go on with it for some reason, although the proofs had been read and passed by counsel. 'That scoundrel Crosland was responsible for this,' Bosie wrote to Sorley Brown on 23 March 1917. 'Meanwhile I am left with the book on my hands and don't know what to do about it.... If I had the money I would publish the book myself.... It has been canvassed at all the libraries and booksellers and it is "eagerly expected" according to what The Times Book Club say, and yet I can't get it out.' The book was never published, although the manuscript is in existence as well as several of the proof copies. Perhaps it was as well that the work never saw the public light of day, as Bosie's subsequent shorter work *Oscar Wilde: A Summing Up (1940)* is much better and more objective, the diatribes against Robert Ross which disfigured *The Wilde Myth* being omitted.[48]

In the same letter to Sorley Brown Bosie wrote: 'My wife has become a Catholic (she was received into the Church last Sunday by the Right Rev Monsignor Brown at St Ann's Vauxhall) and in consequence we are now reconciled. She is at Richmond but I see her constantly.'

Bosie's relations with Olive were variable and often divergent. At one moment he was writing to her as 'darling little girl' and at another as 'You miserable woman.' She was restless, and, particularly when she was at odds with her husband, bored and lonely. She lived in four places in as many years. At Richmond, Surrey, she had a house at 16 Queen's Road, and a passionate reconciliation took place in the 'long drawing room' there. For a time she took a temporary job at Harrods but soon gave it up as it was too much for her. She would meet Bosie regularly when they were on good terms, he stayed with her occasionally, and invited her to Shelley's Folly, the house about three miles from Lewes which his mother had taken from Lord Monkbretton. 'You can come here when you like,' he wrote to her in one of their more friendly periods. 'This place is quite amazingly beautiful now. You will be surprised when you see it, I mean chiefly the view and the heavenly country.' A local trainer, who lived close by, lent Bosie one of his horses and he would often ride him on the downs. 'I am very glad now that I did not go to the war, but at the time it was a grievance,' he was to write in his autobiography. 'Beyond a little snipe and duck shooting up in Caithness, which was the nearest I could get during the war to the snipe bogs of the Orkney Isles ... I did nothing but read and take long walks, with an occasional ride.'[49]

On 3 January 1917 he wrote a pathetic letter to Olive from Shelley's Folly about the spaniel Winston he had given her. It will be remembered that he had been an enthusiastic sporting retriever:

Winston died yesterday. I have been away in Caithness for five weeks. While I was away Winston got very bad and old and feeble and as my mother had to go to London she sent him to the vet at Lewes to look after him and try to cure him.

Yesterday when I got back there at 6 o'clock my mother got a letter, posted 3 days before, which had followed her to London and back, to say that the dog could not live for many hours and was asleep all the time as his heart might stop any minute. I rushed off to Lewes on a bicycle and prayed all the way to St Anthony of Padua that the dog might not be dead before I saw him. When I got to the vet's they told me he was still alive and the vet went up to fetch him and carried him into the room where I was and laid him on the hearth rug. He was alive but apparently rigid and unconscious. I called to him and whistled my old whistle and stroked his dear old pathetic head and he woke up and tried to raise his head and moved his paws and opened his mouth and a little foam came out and he died. He knew me and my voice and died I hope happy. He lived less than 30 seconds after he was brought into the room.

It's the last link between us broken. I gave him to you and he was your dog till you got tired of him as you do of everything. I have done nothing but cry ever since. He was the last thing I had except my mother.

Of the many letters Bosie wrote to his wife perhaps the frankest and most revealing was one he sent her shortly before the end of the war:

Shelley's Folly, Lewes. 9 October 1918. My Dear Olive, In spite of all that has happened and in spite of the injuries you have inflicted and are still inflicting on me, you remain my wife. You have from time to time written to me telling me that you 'love' me and though our ideas of love and what it entails are so different yet I suppose it is true that in your own (to me inconceivable) way you are still fond of me.

Well, all my ideals are shattered as far as this world is concerned. My dream of the possibility of a real Catholic married life with wife and child is gone for ever and nothing could bring it back. My son has behaved in an unforgiveable (unless he has repented) manner to me, and on you (and of course also your father) must rest the responsibility of what may result to him here and hereafter. Besides Raymond is no longer a child and I have lost interest in him; he has made his choice and turned his back on the Douglases.

I cannot pretend that I love you now as I used to do (though I am still fond of you in a way) nor would I ever propose to live with you permanently. On the other hand, you are still my wife and if the spiritual bond between us has been strained to the utmost breaking point there still remains the material fleshly bond which we neither of us can dissolve. It is a curious and in some ways a humiliating thing to confess that of all the love I had for you I am not conscious of anything remaining except a strong physical attraction.

The fact is that the inner woman I loved in you never really existed at all. My conception of you which I clung to in the face of all evidence and common sense was a purely imaginary one. It took years for you to destroy it completely. But it is absolutely dead and gone now. That is why I say I cannot pretend to love you as I did, because what I loved was something that never had any real existence outside my own imagination. On the other hand I have got over my anger with you, and I am lonely and unmated!

If I were not a Catholic, of course I should have long since gone to another woman, but I *cannot* do that, though sometimes the effort to keep away from it is almost unbearable. You know I tried it in the first agony of despair and misery which your betrayal and desertion of me brought. I was miserable in my conscience all the time and since then I have lived absolutely without intercourse with women. It is something of a miracle that I have been able to do it, and I don't doubt that if I were a priest I would get all the necessary grace to live a life of complete chastity without any undue suffering. But I am not a priest: I am a married man and my 'vocation' is that of a married man. I was not intended to live like a priest and it is really an unnatural state for me to be in, although it is extraordinary and wonderful how *very* seldom I have any temptation to go wrong (only about once or twice in a year and then I don't give way to it).

You know I am and always have been disconcertingly frank. I always say exactly what I really mean and perhaps what I have told you may annoy you or disgust you. If so I cannot help it. I refuse to have any pretence with you..

If you are to see me, I would like to come and stay with you occasionally as I used to do when you were at Richmond, or you could come here (but I expect you would rather not do that).

This letter is entirely private and I trust to your honour not to show it to anyone. Your loving Bosie.

P.S. Of course you know that Ross died suddenly of heart failure on Saturday. I fear he had no time to put himself right even if he had wanted to. But I hope this may not be as I fear.*

They met during the next few weeks, since the tone of Bosie's next letter is quite different from the foregoing, and it may well be that the 'physical attraction' found expression as one would expect. 'I *do* love you when you are good,' Bosie wrote to her on 1 November. 'I *loved* you when you cried and were sorry and confessed that you had behaved badly. When you did that all the wretchedness of those last seven or eight years rolled away, and I felt towards you just as I used to do when we first married.'

In 1920 Olive settled in a cottage at Bembridge, in the Isle of Wight. On the gate she inscribed the words: 'Safe haven, after a stormy passage.' So it was to prove, although Olive was to move on to several other addresses during the following years, in London and Hove, where she was close to Bosie and saw him nearly every day, although they never lived together except occasionally for a few days at a time. However on this occasion the reconciliation was permanent.[50]

9

Bosie figured in two interesting trials at this period, which deserve mention. The first, in which he was called as an expert witness, was the so-called 'Black Book' trial. The second, in which he was the plaintiff, was the result of his reading his own obituary in a London evening newspaper.

The 'Black Book' Trial, in which Bosie testified for the defence, was one in which an eccentric character, thirty-eight-year-old Noel

*Robert Ross died in his sleep in his rooms in London on 5 October 1918. He was buried in Kensal Green. He expressed a wish that his ashes might eventually be placed beside those of Wilde in the latter's grave in Père Lachaise cemetery in Paris. This was done by his niece Margery Ross at a ceremony at Père Lachaise on 30 November 1950, the fiftieth anniversary of Wilde's death. The present writer was there and spoke with others on this occasion at the graveside ceremony. Bosie's nephew Francis 11th Marquess of Queensberry was also present.

Pemberton Billing, MP, was prosecuted for criminally libelling a well-known classical dancer of the time, Maud Allan, in *The Vigilante*, a patriotic journal which he owned and edited.[51] Tall and good-looking, Pemberton Billing wore a monocle and a long pointed collar without the usual accompaniment of a necktie, and he used to drive about in a light yellow Rolls Royce. At various times in his adventurous life he had been a sailor, a mounted police trooper, an air pilot and an inventor. He had been one of the earliest Englishmen to realise the possibilities of aircraft in war-time, and as a youngster before the Great War he had actually designed one which flew. In 1916 he had succeeded in getting himself elected an Independent MP for Mid-Hertfordshire pledged to support a strong air policy and a more vigorous conduct of the war generally. Besides his speeches on air policy, he drew attention to himself in the House of Commons by addressing the House from the members' gallery, being in fact the last MP to do so. In his journal he described a 'Black Book' which he alleged was kept by Prince William of Wied and was supposed to contain the names of 47,000 British citizens whose sexual vices were known to the Germans who could thus blackmail them. 'It is a most Catholic miscellany' he wrote. 'The names of Privy Councillors, youths of the chorus, wives of Cabinet ministers, dancing girls, even Cabinet Ministers themselves, diplomats, poets, bankers, editors, newspaper proprietors and members of His Majesty's household follow each other with no order of precedence'.

The issue of *The Vigilante* for February 1918 contained the following paragraph:

THE CULT OF THE CLITORIS

> To be a member of Maud Allan's private performances in Oscar Wilde's *Salome* one has to apply to a Miss Valetta, of 9, Duke Street, Adelphi, W.C. If Scotland Yard were to seize a list of these members, I have no doubt they would secure the names of several thousand of the first 47,000.

The above was not written by Billing, who was ill at the time, but by his Assistant Editor, Captain Harold Spencer, an American who had previously worked for the British Secret Intelligence Service but had been invalided out of the service, apparently on mental grounds. As editor Billing was of course responsible and it was a responsibility which he thoroughly relished.

It was not long before this offensive paragraph reached the notice of Maud Allan and the play's producer Mr J.T. Grein, under the auspices of whose Independent Theatre Society two private performances of the play were to be given; owing to the Lord Chamberlain's ban it could not be publicly performed because under the censorship rules in force at that time it was forbidden to introduce biblical characters on the stage. The innuendo that the dancer was a lesbian was sufficiently grave to justify criminal proceedings, and for this reason Miss Allan and Mr Grein were able to obtain leave of the High Court to institute a private prosecution for criminal libel against Pemberton Billing.

The trial began before Mr Justice Darling and a jury at the Old Bailey on 29 May 1918, and lasted six days. Mr Hume-Williams, KC, (later Sir Ellis Hume-Williams, Bart), Mr Travers Humphreys (later Mr Justice Humpreys) and Mr J.P. Valetta appeared for the prosecution. Mr Pemberton Billing preferred to conduct his own defence and was not represented by counsel. He pleaded 'Not Guilty', having already in his written plea of justification described 'the tragedy of *Salome*' as 'a stage play by one Oscar Wilde, a moral pervert' and as 'an open representation of degenerated sexual lust, sexual crime, and unnatural passions and an evil and mischievous travesty of a biblical story.' The presentation of *Salome* on the stage, he stated, would particularly attract many people whose names appeared in the list of some 47,000 persons, which the Germans had compiled in the 'Black Book' for the purpose of blackmail.

In his opening speech for the prosecution Mr Hume-Williams, KC, described the statement about Miss Maud Allan in *The Vigilante* as 'a libel of such a gross kind, so outrageous in form, that the proceedings came within the purview of the criminal law instead of a civil action being brought.' Miss Allan, who was the only witness for the prosecution, then gave evidence identifying herself as the person referred to in the article. In cross-examining her Pemberton Billing referred to the fact that her brother had been executed in San Francisco for the murder of two young girls and outraging them after death, justifying his questions on the ground that vicious practices were hereditary in her family. Although these had the effect of putting her on the defensive, Maud Allan proved a spirited witness. She related how she had danced before the King and Queen of England. She had also been to Downing Street as Mrs Asquith's guest, though she did not dance there. Only in Manchester had her dance 'The Vision of Salome' been forbidden by the Watch Committee, 'a very little body of officials who make themselves very officious.'

'Do you think that everybody who moves in the public interest is making himself officious?' asked the defendant.

'No, certainly not,' replied Maud Allan sweetly. 'It does not apply to you though, Mr Billing!'

In opening his defence to the jury, Pemberton Billing said he proposed first of all to prove that *Salome* was an immoral and impure play, and one which was calculated to be harmful to public morality and to purity in public life generally. He would then show the existence of 'The Cult' to which he had referred, and its political significance. 'I trust above all things,' he went on in characteristic rhetorical vein, 'that you will remember that in your hands rests a most momentous decision. Either you are going to say that beastly trash of this description should not be allowed to appear, or, despite the decision of the censor, and despite the decision that for twenty years this play was never allowed to be put on the stage, you as twelve jurymen are going to give that play a licence, and assist in the propaganda and the spreading of evils which, in my own words, all decent men thought perished in Sodom and Lesbos.'

The defendant's first witness was a pert, attractive young lady who tripped into the box and gave her name as Mrs Eileen Villiers Stuart. She was to reappear some months later in the dock in a charge of bigamy, for which she was sent to prison for nine months. Now she gave evidence about the 'Black Book' which she said she had seen. Among the names in the book, she said, were those of the Prime Minister and his wife, Lord Haldane, and, to the surprise of the court, Mr Justice Darling. Mrs Villiers Stuart was followed by Captain Harold Spencer, who swore that he had discovered the 'Black Book' while serving as ADC to the German Prince William of Wied, who occupied the throne of Albania for a short time in 1914. The book was in the King's private rooms in the Royal Palace at Durazzo, he said, and His Majesty had displayed a 'morbid curiosity' in its contents. The witness confirmed some of the names he had seen in the book including those of Mr Asquith and Lord Haldane.

Two medical witnesses came next, one of whom was the well-known physician Sir Alfred Fripp, who said he had neither read nor seen *Salome*, but he knew that it had been banned and he understood it was boring if not disgusting. He was followed by the dramatic critic of the *Morning Post*, who said he thought it was a 'melodrama of disease', and by Father Bernard Vaughan who said he would not like to trust himself to speak as a priest about 'this abomination' which he looked on as constructive treason against the majesty and sanctity of God. 'But I will speak as an Englishman,' he went on, 'as a patriot who loves his country, and wants to see —' Here the judge interrupted and told him he could say all that tomorrow in the pulpit, but at present he was here to give evidence about specific questions in the play. Father Vaughan begged the judge's pardon. 'I have tried to do my little bit,' he added complacently.

Lord Alfred Douglas was now called as the former friend of Wilde and as the translator of the play which, as we have seen, was originally written in French. The translation, said Bosie, was an elaborate farce, because the author really wrote the play in English, translated it into French, with the assistance of a French writer to correct his numerous blunders, and when he had finished it he asked the witness to translate it into English. 'Then when I finished my translation he revised it and put it back into his own original language.' Oscar Wilde, Bosie thought, was 'the greatest force for evil that has appeared in Europe during the last three hundred and fifty years,' and he regretted intensely having met him. He added that to his knowledge Wilde was studying Krafft-Ebing's *Psychopathia Sexualis*, which he was continually reading and talking about. Sadism and sodomy were dealt with in this work, also incest.

'Did Wilde intend that Salome should actually bite the lips of the Prophet?' asked Pemberton Billing.

'Yes, certainly.'

'Draw blood?'

'Yes.'

'Suck them?'

'Yes. That was the idea.'

'Was it intended by the writer that she should work herself up into a great state of sexual excitement?'

'Yes.'

'Uncontrolled sexual excitement?'

'Yes. A sort of orgasm. It is meant to be the culmination of sexual excitement.'

Hume-Williams for the prosecution began his cross-examination by putting to this witness the notorious 'prose poem' letter and the other affectionate letter written by Wilde and used in his trials and later in the Ransome case, which had also been tried by Mr Justice Darling. 'Every time I come here,' Bosie protested to Hume-Williams, 'this bestial drivel is brought up.... You ought to be ashamed to bring it out here.'

'You are not here to comment on counsel,' the judge observed.

'I shall answer the question as I please,' was the witness's excited reply. 'I came here to give evidence. You bullied me at the last trial, I shall not be bullied and browbeaten by you again. You deliberately lost me the case in the last trial. I shall answer the questions as I choose and not as you choose. I shall speak the truth.'

'You shall not make rude speeches, or you will be removed from the Court,' Darling told him.

'Let me be removed from the Court,' Bosie answered. 'I did not want to come here to be examined to help out this gang of scoundrels they have at the back of them.'

This sally was greeted with an outburst of cheering from the spectators in the gallery, which caused the judge to threaten to have the court cleared.

'When did you cease to approve of sodomy?' counsel asked the witness at one point.

Bosie thought a moment or two before replying. 'I do not think that is a fair question,' he said. 'It is like asking: When did you leave off beating your wife?' Hume-Williams then held up a letter. 'Is that in your handwriting,' he asked.

'If you show me letters in my handwriting, I give you fair warning that I shall tear them up,' answered Bosie testily.

'Is that your handwriting?'

'Show it to me.'

'No,' the judge interrupted. 'Show it to him from a point where he cannot touch it. He says he will tear it up.'

The court usher then held up the letter close to the witness.

'Is that your letter?' counsel went on.

'It is in my handwriting,' Bosie agreed. But at first he thought it was one of his letters to Wilde which Ross had appropriated at the time of Oscar's death. Actually it was the original of the letter which Bosie had written to Henry Labouchere, editor of *Truth*, on 9 June 1895 from Rouen shortly after Wilde's conviction defending his friend and justifying the practice of homosexuality. On having another look at the letter Bosie agreed that in fact it was the one he had written to Labouchere which the prosecution had somehow got hold of.

Hume-Williams thereupon put the contents of the letter to the witness, which included the following:

> When you say that the acts which resulted in Mr Wilde's incarceration are not practised by others you are astonishingly amusing. You may believe it or not as you like, but I assure you on my word of honour that I personally know forty of fifty men who practice these acts. Men in the best society, members of the smartest clubs, Members of Parliament, peers, et cetera, in fact people of my own social standing, or perhaps I should say of what was my social standing until the other day. I don't know what reason you can imagine me to have for saying this if it were not true. I will add that at Oxford, where I suppose you would admit one is likely to find the pick of the youth of England, I knew hundreds who had these tastes among the undergraduates, not to mention a slight sprinkling of dons.

'You were not a decent person?' counsel continued.

'No, I was not,' Bosie agreed, 'and I have said that. It is proved all over the place that Prime Ministers, judges, lawyers, and everyone protected people who committed these acts. The reason they go for me is because I am no longer like that. If I were still on Oscar Wilde's side, I should be getting praise from judges and Prime Ministers, and praise from greasy advocates.' He added that like Ross he would get a testimonial and £700 from Mr Asquith given from people in society saying what a fine person he was; 'Asquith and all these people presented Ross with a testimonial and £700 because he was a sodomite.'

'Are you a sodomite?' Pemberton Billing asked at this point.

'No, of course I am not.'

'Sit down,' the judge ordered Pemberton Billing. 'You have no right to interrupt.'

As the defendant resumed his seat, Hume-Williams asked Bosie whether he had given up the practice of sodomy. But Bosie was not to fall into this trap. 'I never admitted that I practised it,' he declared. 'I do not admit that I practised it, though you may draw any conclusion you like. I am not going to make admissions to please you. I never said I was a sodomite.'

Here the judge again intervened. 'You cannot ask him if he has committed sodomy,' he told counsel, 'because it is an offence punishable by penal servitude, and he is not bound to answer.'

Another relevant document put by the prosecution counsel to the witness was the latter's critical review of *Salome* which Bosie wrote for *The Spirit Lamp*, when he was editing this undergraduate journal in 1893.

I suppose the play is unhealthy, morbid, unwholesome, and un-English, *ça va sans dire*. It is certainly un-English because it is written in French, and therefore unwholesome to the average Englishman, who can't digest French. It is probably morbid and unhealthy, for there is no representation of quiet domestic life, nobody slaps anybody else on the back all through the play, and there is not a single reference to roast beef from one end of the dialogue to the other, and though it is true that there is a reference to Christianity, there are no muscular Christians. Anyone, there-fore, who suffers from that most appalling and widespread of diseases which takes the form of a morbid desire for health had better avoid and flee from *Salome*, or they will surely get a shock that it will take months of the daily papers and Charles Kingsley's novels to counteract. But the less violently and aggressively healthy, those who are healthy to live and do not live to be healthy,

will find in Mr Oscar Wilde's tragedy the beauty of a perfect work
of art, a joy for ever, ambrosia to feed their souls with honey of
sweet-bitter thoughts.[52]

'That is your opinion of the play?' Hume-Williams asked Bosie.

'It is exactly the same opinion as your witnesses now have about it,'
Bosie replied. 'The only difference is that I have escaped from the
influence and your witnesses are still under it.'

'But I understand you to say that your conversations with Oscar
Wilde led you to the conclusion that it was a play full of perverted
sexual passion?' The witness agreed.

'So you knew that when you wrote the article?'

'Yes, of course I did. I have been telling you all the time. I was
defending Wilde then just as you are defending him now.'

The concluding stages of this remarkable trial were heard in an
atmosphere alternating between intermittent uproar and opera
bouffe. The judge summed up against a background of cheering,
hissing and other interruptions. People were removed from the court,
one after another. They included Bosie who objected to what Darling
said about what Bosie had written in his critical review of *Salome*. 'You
have no right to say that I wrote it,' Bosie shouted at the Bench as he
was being ushered out. 'You lie. You are a damned liar. If you say it
outside the court, I will prosecute you!' He added another touch of
comic relief to the proceedings by returning some minutes later to ask
if he could retrieve his top hat, which he had left behind in his hurried
exit.

To do him justice, Darling did his best to disabuse the minds of
the jury that they were trying Oscar Wilde and his play rather than
the libel on Maud Allan. But to no avail. After an absence of an hour
and a half the foreman of the jury announced their verdict – Not
Guilty. Tumultuous cheering broke out which the judge was
powerless to suppress. The ovation was repeated by the crowds
outside when Pemberton Billing emerged after his acquittal. However, but for the unprecedented temper of the times and the prevailing
anti-German war hysteria, it seems safe to say that he would have
been convicted. In the light of all the evidence, the unfortunate Maud
Allan ought to have succeeded, since she had been most grossly
libelled.

As regards Bosie's contribution to the defence it was not perhaps
his most creditable performance in the witness box, in the many trials
in which he gave evidence. On the other hand, he clashed so
vituperatively with Mr Justice Darling that his conduct made him the
most popular figure in the case after the defendant.

10

During the afternoon of 4 February 1921, Bosie slipped out of his London office to buy an evening newspaper. To his astonishment he saw an *Evening News* placard announcing his death. He immediately bought a copy of the paper and on opening it was confronted by the following headlines:

SUDDEN DEATH OF LORD ALFRED DOUGLAS
FOUND DEAD IN BED BY A MAID
HEART FAILURE AFTER A CHILL

The news story underneath these headlines read as follows:

The 'Evening News' learns that Lord Alfred Douglas was found dead in bed to-day, when a maid went to his room at 24, Pembridge Gardens, to call him.

Death was apparently due to heart failure.

Lord Alfred, who was 50, had lately been suffering from a bad chill, but it had not been thought necessary to call in a doctor. He had been exceedingly busy lately in connection with his weekly journal 'Plain English' and for the past week had been working into the night.

This story was accompanied by an anonymous obituary, which Bosie subsequently discovered had been written by Arthur Machen, the journalist whose articles Bosie had published in the days of *The Academy* and who was now on the staff of the *Evening News*. The obituary notice was far from friendly:

A GREAT LIFE SPOILT
HOW THE EVIL GENIUS OF THE DOUGLASES DOGGED
LORD ALFRED

A brilliant and most unhappy career is ended. Lord Alfred Douglas was born, in a sense, under the happiest auspices. He was a Douglas, the son of one of the most ancient families in Britain. He was connected with many of the 'best people' in society, he had brilliant capacities, and showed that he was certainly to be numbered among the poets.

He might have done anything, and, his poetry excepted, he did nothing, and worse than nothing.

The charity which is fitting at all times, but most fitting when we are speaking of the newly dead, urges that much should be forgiven to this poor, bewildered man, who, with all his gifts, will perhaps only be remembered by the scandals and the quarrels in which he involved himself.

It is a great thing, in a sense, to be born a Douglas, but the family inheritance had gifts from evil fairies as well as good ones. It would not be true to say that all ancient races are degenerate, but there were very many marked signs of degeneracy in the house of Douglas.

Many of them were violently eccentric, to put the case mildly.

When he read this, Bosie telephoned a news agency, stating that the report in the *Evening News* was without foundation. 'I am very glad to say that I am in the best of health,' he told the agency which passed on what he said to the paper. The later editions contained an expression of regret that currency had been given to 'the inaccurate statement'. But nothing was said about the obituary which on the face of it was defamatory.

Bosie immediately went to see his solicitor and instructed him to issue a writ against Associated Newspapers, owners of the *Evening News*, for libel. Nowadays a matter of this kind would almost certainly be settled out of court with the addition of a complete apology and the payment of a sum by way of damages by the paper's insurance company, while the writer of the offending notice would be reprimanded for not checking his sources properly. But things were different sixty years ago. Associated Newspapers consulted their solicitors, who happened to be Lewis & Lewis, and Sir George Lewis advised them to plead justification, which, in view of what he knew about Bosie and his relations with Wilde, Ross and Custance, he considered a good defence to the statement that except for his poetry Bosie had done nothing and 'worse than nothing', this statement consequently being true in substance and in fact.

The trial opened before Mr Justice Horridge and a special jury in the High Court on 24 November 1921, and lasted three days.[53] Mr Comyns Carr represented the plaintiff, and the defence was led by Mr Douglas Hogg (later Lord Hailsham). Bosie sat at the solicitors' table with his wife. 'Her presence,' wrote Bosie afterwards, 'and the moral support she gave me, to a large extent paralysed the attack on me with reference to her father, which was one of the chief features of the brief prepared by Lewis & Lewis for Douglas Hogg.'[54]

Comyns Carr decided not to put his client into the witness box since nothing had been alleged by the defence in their pleadings about the plaintiff's past life which had not already been gone into over and over again. Bosie was greatly disappointed by this decision, but as Comyns Carr remarked in his opening speech to the jury, he was going to ask the defendants to prove their plea of justification. The

Evening News had not apologised and was not apologising now but trying to justify its libel by bringing up details of Bosie's past, even recalling that he had not taken his degree at Oxford. If anything appeared in the cross-examination of the defence witnesses which it was necessary for the plaintiff or his friends to answer he would adopt the course of calling evidence to rebut it. At this, the judge who appeared hostile to the plaintiff, remarked that it was for him to decide whether further evidence would be admitted.

When it came to Hogg's turn to open the defence case to the jury he attacked Bosie vigorously and took advantage of his counsel's decision not to call him as a witness. The plaintiff asked for damages for injury to his character by this obituary notice, said Hogg, but he elected to give no evidence as to what his character was so as to enable the jury to judge what injury had been done to it. It was not a question of a boy under the influence of a brilliant playwright, defence counsel went on. This was a man of four or five and twenty, who knew the truth of the charges against Oscar Wilde, and with that knowledge proceeded to write letters to newspapers saying that there was no harm in these indecent offences and that he knew hundreds who habitually indulged in them. Lord Alfred Douglas waited until Oscar Wilde came out of prison, Hogg continued. Oscar Wilde's wife was most anxious that he should not resume acquaintance with Lord Alfred Douglas, as she regarded it as the ruin of her husband. Knowing that, Lord Alfred Douglas proceeded to invite Oscar Wilde and got him to stay with him in his villa in Naples, where they lived together for some months. As further evidence of Bosie's association with Oscar, Hogg quoted not only Wilde's two notorious letters used against him at his trials, but Douglas's letters to him after they parted in Naples.

For instance, on 7 January 1898 Douglas wrote from Paris to Wilde, who was still in Naples:

> The annoyance of living in this town and not having any money to live the way one would like is perpetual. The facilities of Naples are so enormously superior. Here I have simply not the energy of going to the trouble of doing that sort of thing. Since I left Rome, there have only been three occasions, and unbridled chastity is telling on my health and spirits.

In another letter, again from Paris, undated but written to Wilde when the latter was in Rome in April and early May 1900, Douglas wrote:

> When are you coming back? I am glad you are enjoying Rome so much. It is certainly a lively place, and life there was really better

than Naples. I quite agree with you that the boys are far more beautiful there. In fact, I think they come next to English boys.

Was it too much to say, Hogg asked the jury, that the scion of the house of Douglas, who wrote these letters, showed signs of degeneracy from its ancestral standard?

The news editor of the *Evening News*, Mr Arthur Olley, was the only defence witness. In his examination-in-chief Hogg asked him how the newspaper came to announce the plaintiff's death.

'We received a telephone message, which was taken first by a telephone clerk, and then by myself in view of its importance,' the witness replied. 'It was from a woman who said three times to each of us that she was Lord Alfred's private secretary, telling us that he had been found dead in bed that morning; that he had recently been working very hard, had had a cold, and had a weekend at Brighton.'

'Did you believe that statement?'

'I had no reason to doubt the statement,' the witness answered.

'Do you really mean to tell the jury,' Comyns Carr asked in cross-examination, 'that, receiving a telephone message from a woman whose description you had to take entirely from herself, you published a report of a man's death without taking further steps to confirm it?'

'We did take further steps.'

'What did they consist of?'

'The woman gave us a telephone number, of herself presumably, and the name of a doctor,' the witness admitted. 'I handed over the duty of checking the telephone number and finding the doctor to a sub-editor and went to arrange about the writing of the obituary notice. Both enquiries unfortunately drew blank, but in the intense haste to catch the edition the statement made got upstairs to the printing room.'

'The statement made must be the obituary notice that had been written,' the judge interposed. 'That got to the printing office, didn't it?' The witness agreed that this was so.

'Did you consider at all,' Comyns Carr continued his cross-examination, 'before publishing a statement of this kind, apart from the libellous character of the notice, whether or not possible injury might be done to a man's relatives by publishing a statement of his death without confirmation?'

'Yes,' the witness replied with some embarrassment.

The judge again intervened, further embarrassing the witness by his remarks. 'But without waiting for confirmation, and when you had drawn blank this thing was published! It strikes me, you know, as a shocking thing, that a paper, in order to catch the evening edition, should publish the death of a man when they were waiting for confirmation that they had not received.'

Further cross-examined, the witness said the lady gave no address. He could not remember the telephone number, but he thought it was not the telephone number of Lord Alfred's house.

'I hope you will be more careful in future,' Mr Justice Horridge admonished the unfortunate news editor, 'before putting in accounts of people's deaths.'

'Where did you get the information that the death took place at 24 Pembridge Gardens?' Comyns Carr went on to ask.

'From this woman.'

'Did you enquire whether he had ever lived there?'

'That was one of the enquiries we were making.'

'You know that he was never there in his life?'

'Yes.'

'Did you send a representative round to Lord Alfred Douglas's office to see him about it?'

'I did not.'

'Did a man named Macgregor come back and report the result of his visit?'

'I forget.'

'This is a matter of sufficient importance to remember,' the judge addressed the witness. 'Did you make any enquiries before putting in a contradiction?'

This question evidently refreshed the news editor's memory, as he replied: 'I think it is quite possible we did go to Lord Alfred's office.'

'Did you not gather,' the plaintiff's counsel concluded his cross-examination, 'that Lord Alfred was annoyed not only at the statement of his death but at the obituary notice?'

Again the witness's memory failed him. 'I do not remember that,' he replied lamely.

'Did you really believe he was dead?'

'Yes, in my own mind I did believe it.'

Comyns Carr now turned to the judge and asked permission to call rebutting evidence. Douglas Hogg strongly opposed this, but Mr Justice Horridge, who was now coming round to the plaintiff's side, after some hesitation eventually consented that this should be done, since it would be more satisfactory in his view if the jury were to hear what the plaintiff had to say.

Before putting his client into the witness box, Comyns Carr called three more or less formal witnesses to testify to the plaintiff's character and mental state, a doctor and two Roman Catholic prelates. The doctor was Byres Moir, consulting physician at the

London Homeopathic Hospital. He said he had attended Lord Alfred Douglas for slight complaints for the last ten years, and had never seen any evidence of degeneracy, but had found him average, or above the average, in ability, both in body and mind.

'Have you found any signs of moral degeneracy?'

'I have seen no evidence of anything immoral about him. I have found him leading the ordinary life of relationship with his family, mother, wife, sister, and he could not have had relationships such as I have seen if he had been grossly immoral.'

Monsignor F.B. Bickerstaff-Drew, a prelate of the Papal household, said he had known the plaintiff since 1905 or 1906 and had received him into the Roman Catholic Church in May 1911.

'Have you ever seen any signs of degeneracy in him?' asked Comyns Carr.

'Certainly not.'

'You have heard the letters read this morning,' said the judge to this witness. 'Would you have thought they showed degeneracy or not?'

'I certainly should have thought they showed degeneracy in the person who wrote them,' the Monsignor answered, 'but I should not say he is the same person now.'

'I asked you your judgement as a minister of the church,' the judge went on '– about the boys in Rome, for instance?'

'I think my judgement is the same, that they are altogether abominable.'

Finally, the Right Rev George Burton, Roman Catholic Bishop of Clifton, agreed with Monsignor Bickerstaffe-Drew that the letters were abominable. 'I consider that Lord Alfred Douglas is a man who has turned his back absolutely on the past,' the Bishop added. 'I only know about him since his reception into the Catholic Church, and my testimony must be all in his favour.'

'I now call Lord Alfred Douglas,' said Comyns Carr. Bosie got up from his seat at the solicitors' table and strode confidently into the witness box. It had been an immense relief when the judge had given leave for his evidence to be given in rebuttal, as he had told his counsel that if he were not called they might as well throw up the case. He had wished to do so after Carr's opening speech, but, as we have seen, he had been overruled.

Replying to his counsel, he began by stating that his opinion of the letters written by him to Oscar Wilde and received by him from Wilde was that they were 'disgraceful letters' which he was heartily ashamed of having been written. He added that he had said that at least three times in the witness box in previous trials.

'Do you still entertain the views of any of them which are expressed in these letters?' asked Comyns Carr.

'No. I look upon them with utter repugnance and horror, and my whole attitude on all these things is entirely and completely changed.' Regarding the letters he had written to Henry Labouchere, editor of *Truth*, they were private letters and not intended for publication, and still less to be brought up against him after thirty years.

'With reference to the statements in these two letters as to the prevalence of the vices referred to, what attitude since you changed your opinion have you taken up?'

'For many years I have conducted a regular campaign against that form of vice in every possible way, both in papers and by various actions which have arisen out of these questions.'

'Give us some examples?'

'The case of Mr Robert Ross, who is responsible for stealing my letters from Wilde, keeping them all these years, handing them over to his solicitor Sir George Lewis, and which have now been brought into court.'

'What steps did you take in your campaign?'

'I denounced Robert Ross as being the head of the gang in London on whose shoulders the mantle of Wilde had fallen. I forced the matter to the Old Bailey. It took me about five years – the most terrible fight I ever had in my life.'

'You justified that allegation?'

'The jury disagreed and the case was put off until the next sessions. Meanwhile a *nolle prosequi* was entered, and my costs were all paid.'

'In that case, as in the Ransome case,' Comyns Carr went on, 'were many of these letters put to you in cross-examination?'

'Oh, yes,' the witness replied. 'They are always put to me every time I get into the witness box. Whatever the case is concerned with, they are invariably trotted out and read by leering counsel.'

'You are not surprised are you?'

'Well, I think there might be a limit after thirty years perhaps.'

Asked by his counsel about the Pemberton Billing case, in which he had testified under sub-poena, the witness said that he thought Billing had been acquitted largely owing to his evidence.

'Have Lewis and Lewis been the solicitors in every case against you?' Comyns Carr asked, continuing his examination-in-chief.

'In every case – in five or six suits,' the witness replied. Even my father-in-law, who had a solicitor of his own, hearing that the Ransome case was going on and that Sir George Lewis was the solicitor, transferred his business to Lewis in order that he might more effectively hit me and, if possible, get me locked up.'

'What was the cause of the quarrel with your father-in-law?'

'He was very anxious to obtain possession of my son and bring him up in his own house. He wanted to have complete control over him and I did not like it. Also I considered, as I said in my libel, that he defrauded his daughter.'

'Were there differences of religion between you and your father-in-law?'

'Yes. He was a Protestant and I was a Catholic. I became a Catholic in 1911. My son was then quite a little boy, and I naturally brought him up in my own religion.'

Here the judge enquired as to the date of Colonel Custance's prosecution of the witness for libel. The witness replied that it was in 1913, two years after he had become a Catholic and made his son one. 'My wife has become one since,' he added.

Comyns Carr had not concluded his examination-in-chief when the court rose for the day. 'For God's sake be careful,' he said to his client as they left the court room, thinking of Hogg's cross-examination which lay ahead next day. 'Don't worry,' said Bosie. 'I have got the jury already, and the judge is beginning to come round.'

The remainder of Comyns Carr's examinatioon-in-chief, which took place next morning, was mainly concerned with the plaintiff's quarrel with his father-in-law, and the legal proceedings in connection with it which have already been described. In this context the plaintiff said that, unknown to himself or his wife, Colonel Custance had settled £100 on Raymond. The Colonel, or somebody for him, had discovered that under an old Act of Parliament, by settling this amount on the boy he could have him made a ward in Chancery.

'You could do it with a shilling,' Mr Justice Horridge remarked.

In his final answers to his counsel's questions, the plaintiff said that the effect of the libellous obituary had resulted in his loss of the editorship of the weekly paper *Plain English*, which he had founded fifteen or sixteen months previously. Since then he had started a new paper called *Plain Speech*.

11

Douglas Hogg began his cross-examination by asking the witness whether his 'first public appearance' was with some of his verses published in *The Chameleon*, to which Wilde had also contributed. These were the two homosexual poems 'In Praise of Shame' and 'Two Loves', from which counsel proceeded to read extracts. The witness admitted that he had written them and that they had been published in that magazine. He had never republished them, since though really quite innocent they were open to misconstruction.

'At the time of your association with Wilde were you constantly receiving letters from him?'

The witness admitted that he had and that they had frequently appeared in the past, in addition to the press reports of them in defence counsel's opening speech. 'They are idiotic and horrible.'

'It is obvious from other letters which have been read that Wilde asked you to return his letters?'

'It is lucky I did not return them,' the witness replied. 'They would have got into certain hands and we would have had them read today. Whoever stole them took care to take the worst ones. But some of them were very creditable letters, especially those written from Holloway prison.'

Counsel then read the article in the *Revue Blanche* which the witness admitted having written. It referred to homosexuality and described Oscar Wilde as addressing himself to 'twelve retired shopkeepers and a half-imbecile old man called a judge.' The witness said he had written it but he was not defending the article. It was 'rotten and horrible.'

'You were twenty-six at the time?'

'Yes. I did not grow up till I was about thirty.'

'How many suits have you been in?' Hogg persevered.

'I have been twice in the dock at the Old Bailey, once when I beat Ross, and on two occasions I have been a witness and won in each case.' He added to the accompaniment of some laughter: 'The Old Bailey is my great place, I would much rather be there than here!'

'After he came out of prison, did Wilde lead the same life as before?'

'He did certainly. But don't try to put that on me!'

'Did he get any discouragement from you?'

'Certainly he did. I disapproved of the life he was leading during the last part. He was killing himself with excesses and drinking.'

'You left him in 1897 under pressure from your mother?'

'Yes, that is right.'

'Then did you start writing letters to him from Paris?'

'Yes. Those letters were stolen when Wilde was lying dead.'

Questioned about the letter in which the plaintiff expressed annoyance at being in Paris with insufficient money 'to live the life one would like to live', counsel asked, 'What sort of life is that?'

'To have a good time,' the plaintiff answered.

'You also say, "the facilities of Naples are so enormously superior" – superior to what?'

'I suppose it refers to immorality.'

'You go on, "Here I have not the energy to go to the trouble of doing that sort of thing" – what sort of thing?'

'I do not deny that I was living an immoral life,' the witness replied, 'but I do deny that it had anything to do with boys. I do not say it with any pride, but during the last three years of Wilde's life in Paris I was practically living with a girl. I was merely writing rubbish about things that I thought would amuse Wilde.'

'Wilde died at the end of 1900,' Hogg went on. 'May I take it that the letters you were writing, of which I have read some samples, were letters which may fairly be called letters which showed symptoms of degeneracy?'

'I think they showed symptoms of wickedness, I don't know about degeneracy,' the witness replied. 'I was a man who was leading a healthy life. I owned my own horses, I won the mile and two-mile races at my college sports. I am a horseman, a good shot, a manly man, able to hold my own with other people.'

Asked whether he thought the letters showed signs of moral degeneracy, the plaintiff replied: 'Moral degeneracy perhaps. Degeneracy means lapse from a higher standard. It does not follow that I may not have risen higher than the average man since. They prove that at that time I was a wicked man, and I certainly was. I have not the slightest desire to conceal it. I was leading a bad life; an immoral, wicked man. I have regretted bitterly, and I have suffered from it all my life.'

In further cross-examination the witness was asked about his prosecution for criminal libel by Colonel Custance in 1913. 'The trial took place because you wrote a series of letters and postcards to Colonel Custance and his friends making violent attacks upon him?'

'I accused him of swindling his daughter, of being a dishonourable and dishonest man, and I stick to that now. I think it is perfectly true, every word of it.'

' "A scoundrel and a thief"?'

'Quite so. So he was, and so he is.'

Admitting that he wrote to a number of people about Colonel Custance, the plaintiff said he had a letter from the King thanking him for his letter and saying that 'it would receive attention.'

'The King is accustomed to receive letters from eccentric persons?' defence counsel went on.

'There is nothing eccentric about that in my case,' the plaintiff answered blandly. 'I knew that the King was in the habit of meeting Colonel Custance when shooting at Sandringham, and I wanted him to know the kind of people he was associated with.' This reply raised a loud laugh from the onlookers.

Hogg then read a leter from the plaintiff to the Earl of Clonmell, calling him 'You damned Irish pig doctor.'* Asked to comment upon it, the plaintiff said that in his opinion it was disgraceful that counsel should read the letter, which was a private and intimate communication from him to Lord Clonmell. The matter had long since been made up. But he had thought it was a mistake, he said, that his wife should go to a boxing-glove fight with Lord Clonmell. 'What the hell right,' he added, 'had he to go about with my wife to prize fights? I would call him or anyone else the same thing tomorrow if he did it.'

Questioned about the Chancery Court proceedings, the plaintiff admitted that he had committed contempt of court by removing his son to Scotland. Afterwards, he said, he had written a poem about it called 'Eve and the Serpent.' Hogg thereupon produced it and described it as 'a disgraceful and scurrilous attack on one of the Chancery judges'. He read a few lines, at which the plaintiff raised a laugh by commenting, 'That is a quotation from Shakespeare. Prince Hal says it to Falstaff!' It was unfair to read a few lines only, the witness added. Hogg then handed up the poem to the bench where the judge proceeded to read it with evident relish. 'It was not exactly meant for Mr Justice Eve,' said the witness, hoping to soften its effect. 'It was just a punning skit on the Chancery Courts, based on the fact that one of the judges is called Eve.'

'Come, come, Lord Alfred,' said the judge. 'Do yourself justice. You know you meant it for Mr Justice Eve.'

'Well, I suppose I did – to a certain extent,' the plaintiff admitted, nothing loth.

Questioned further by Hogg on this subject, the witness said that, in July, 1921, when he was editor of *Plain English*, there was an article headed 'Balmy Eve.' It was an attack on certain aspects of the law courts, and he brought Mr Justice Eve into it.

'Was there not also a paragraph about the Lord Chancellor, Lord Birkenhead?' Hogg went on.

'F.E. Smith you mean.' This answer raised another laugh. 'That is the name by which he is best known.'

'Your name for the Lord Chancellor is "Shameless Smith"?'

'He said he had no shame at all with reference to going back upon Ulster.'

'You still think you will not be remembered for being violently eccentric?

'I do not think I shall. I shall also be remembered for quite a lot of

*Rupert Charles Scott 7th Earl of Clonmell (1877–1928) was an Irish peer, whose family seat was Bishopscourt, Straffan, Co. Kildare. Bosie suspected him of having an affair with Olive.

other things. The scandals and quarrels will be remembered, but not necessarily against me.'

'Many of the Douglas family were violently eccentric?'

'If you had read the history of Scotland, there were some who were exceedingly eccentric, especially from the English point of view!' More laughter followed this remark.

'You don't suggest that these letters which have been read and put to you are not discreditable?' Hogg concluded his cross-examination.

'No,' the plaintiff replied. 'But I have done many creditable things which have not been mentioned.' Defence counsel then sat down without enquiring what they were.

In a brief re-examination, Comyns Carr asked his client about the suggestion that he had ruined the life of Oscar Wilde. 'Was it in consequence of your position with regard to him that he was exposed?'

'Yes,' was the reply. 'It was in consequence of my father's action that Oscar Wilde was exposed.'

'Was there any other sense in which you were responsible for his exposure?'

'No, not at all.'

Before the witness left the box, the judge asked to see a copy of *Oscar Wilde and Myself* which the plaintiff had published after the Ransome trial. He said he understood that it was a denunciation of what the plaintiff had previously defended. Douglas Hogg, who had put in the work as an exhibit, said he understood it was partly so of Oscar Wilde as a literary man and an explaining away of the plaintiff's association with Wilde.

'It seems to me important,' said Mr Justice Horridge, 'that this man as far back as 1914 published a book disassociating himself from Oscar Wilde. It seems that when a newspaper comments as the *Evening News* has done it is important.' At this the jurymen nodded their approval.

The judge, who was now obviously sympathetic to the plaintiff, had the book handed to the witness, telling him to read any passage he liked to the jury. This the plaintiff did in support of his contention that the book was an indictment of Oscar Wilde both from the literary and moral points of view. It will be recalled that Crosland had written most of it, and the jury certainly enjoyed the passages from Crosland's trenchant prose which they heard. 'You put it in, you know,' the judge told the crestfallen-looking defence counsel who realised that what had been read was rebounding on his client in the jury's eyes.

A final question was put by a juryman. How old was Oscar Wilde compared with the plaintiff?

'When I met him,' the plaintiff replied, 'I was twenty and he was thirty-seven or thirty-eight. He was old enough to be my father.'

Mr Justice Horridge began his summing up of the evidence to the jury with these words:

> We have had a good many dates in this case, but there is one date which I should like you to remember, and that is February 4, 1921. That was the date on which the obituary article appeared in this newspaper, the *Evening News*. You have got to consider what the article meant, and whether it was true on the date on which it was published.

Having re-read the obituary to the jury, the judge went on to say that nobody who heard the plaintiff under cross-examination, saw the way he gave his answers, and heard the literary and general knowledge he disclosed, could have any doubt that it was true to state that he was a man of brilliant capacities. But was it a true summary of this man's life to say that if he had died on February 4, 1921 he had done worse than nothing? 'Members of the jury, you may think that perhaps the most pregnant word in the libel is that the plaintiff would "only" be remembered by the scandals and quarrels in which he had involved himself.'

The judge went on to say:

> I should think that a sadder and more horrible life up to 1900 it would be impossible to find. There was this young man, with every promise and every capacity, at Oxford. He, unfortunately, fell under the fascination of this man Oscar Wilde. You may think that Oscar Wilde fell under his fascination; but, at any rate, this connection sprang up between them, which was the most awful thing I should think that ever happened to Lord Alfred Douglas in the course of his life. Those horrible letters – because horrible they were, disgusting and filthy – were written by Oscar Wilde in a sort of sham beauty of poetic expression.

The jury might think, the judge continued, that up till Wilde's death in 1900, short of absolute conviction for crime, the plaintiff's was about as damning a record as a young man could have against him. But from that time they might think that different considerations had to be thought of. In 1902 he was married – a runaway marriage with a lady who, as far as could be seen from this case, had been one of the elements in what the jury might think was the plaintiff's salvation. Between 1902 and the Ransome case the plaintiff was the editor of *The Academy*, in which there were articles of a laudatory character of Oscar Wilde as a literary man, but in no way did they defend Wilde's immoral proclivities. In 1911 the plaintiff joined the Catholic Church. In 1913 he brought an action for libel against Mr Ransome, but this case involved matters which occurred in Oscar Wilde's lifetime. The present case was quite different. The jury's verdict in the Ransome case did not carry matters much further than the plaintiff's own admissions in the present case as to his association with Wilde – that his conduct up to 1900 was detestable. The question they now had to deal with was the plaintiff's life, not up till 1900, but up to February 4, 1921.

Having referred to the plaintiff's prosecution of Ross, the plaintiff's book *Oscar Wilde and Myself*, and his evidence in the Pemberton Billing case, in all of which Lord Alfred Douglas had denounced homosexual immorality, the judge told the jury that if they thought the obituary notice was true in substance and in fact, the defendants were entitled to a verdict, no matter how reprehensible their conduct in the way it was published. But if they thought it was not true, the judge concluded, the plaintiff must have the verdict, in which event they could consider, on the question of damages, the circumstances under which the libel came to be published. They might think that a more shocking exhibition of carelessness and haste could not be imagined, but they should not give damages because they were indignant at the way it was done. Again, they might think that a man who came into court with a character such as Lord Alfred Douglas's was up till 1900 could not expect such damages as a man whose life was entirely clean.

The jury then retired and after an absence of fifteen minutes they returned a verdict for the plaintiff and awarded him £1,000 damages. 'It is the opinion of the jury,' the foreman added, 'that the original Wilde letters should be destroyed.' Judgement was accordingly entered for the plaintiff with costs, and, although Mr Justice Horridge granted a stay of execution pending an appeal on defence counsel's application, the judge made it clear that he was not doing this 'with any view that there is any ground for appeal or that the verdict is in any way wrong.'

Immediately afterwards the successful plaintiff shook hands with his counsel and thanked him for what he had done. 'It was nothing to do with me,' replied Comyns Carr with characteristic modesty. 'You won the case yourself in the witness box.'[55] Of all Bosie's many cases in the courts, it was his most successful and the one in which he shone with with most distinction. Hence its description here at more than the usual length.

'I went through an awful purgatory in the three days,' Bosie wrote to Sorley Brown when the trial was over, thanking him for his telegram of congratulation. 'The only time I felt all right was in the witness box (5½ hours).... I won the fight because it was a spiritual fight, and I had, to help me, the great Spiritual Forces which I have so long believed in and invoked. Excuse scrawl, I am pretty well worn out, and have a hundred letters to write as well as the paper (*Plain Speech*) to bring out.'[56]

To wind up: the appeal was dropped, Bosie got his full £1,000 damages, the defendants had to pay all the costs, which were quite substantial, and the *Evening News* relieved its feelings by sacking Arthur Machen who had written the offending obituary.

VI

Prison and After

We must now return briefly to Bosie's career as a journalist. He owed the fact that he got another paper indirectly to his brother Percy who was staying in Scotland with a rich man named James Conchie and his wife. Conchie, who had also met Bosie, asked Percy one day why 'a clever fellow like your brother does nothing'. 'It's all very fine,' Percy replied. 'What can he do? All the papers boycott him. He can't get an article printed anywhere. His only chance would be a paper of his own.'

'Very well,' said Conchie, to Percy's amazement. 'I'll start a paper for him.'[1] Conchie proved as good as his word, but before describing what followed some further mention should be made of Percy, who had, since his father's death, been tenth Marquess of Queensberry. His first wife Minnie had died in 1917 and in the following year Percy married again, his second wife, Mary Louise Morgan, being the widow of a prosperous fish merchant in Cardiff and well-known in hunting circles. As a wedding present to her husband the new Marchioness decided to give him a horse and revive the Queensberry racing colours – salmon with green sleeves and cap. The idea was to buy a three-year-old and enter him for the Derby. 'What's the use of buying a three-year-old to run in the Derby, when it is quite impossible, even for a great deal more than your wife would be likely to give, to buy one that would have the slightest chance of winning?' Bosie wrote to Percy. 'Why not buy a horse to win a big handicap at the beginning of the year (1919)?' In fact Bosie knew of such a horse called Royal Bucks which belonged to the owner and racing journalist, editor of *The Winning Post*, Robert Sievier, who Bosie thought might be willing to sell since Sievier did not have enough money to back the animal to the extent he wished.

Bob Sievier invited Bosie and the Queensberrys to stay at his house in Newmarket. On their first night at dinner Louise Queensberry bought Royal Bucks for £3,000. But Percy could not wait to see it run, since he went off to America on a property speculation, in which he had no success. On his return he found that Royal Bucks had won two classics, the Lincoln Handicap and the City and Suburban. But he was annoyed that the horse had run in his wife's name and the Queensberry colours had been changed, besides which if he had stayed in England he would have made several thousands by backing it instead of losing his investment in America. This caused a family row in which Sievier was involved, but in the event it was settled amicably.

Early in 1920 Percy went off to South Africa to look for diamonds in the Transvaal and as the result of a successful survey became managing director of a diamond company. At last his luck seemed to have turned, but it came too late and he died suddenly and somewhat mysteriously in Johannesburg on 1 August 1920, by which date Bosie was running the paper which Conchie had started for him. Percy's South African friends subscribed to have his body shipped home, and at the Requiem Mass in Westminster Cathedral which preceded his funeral, there was an enormous turn-out since his generosity was legendary; he used to hand out bank notes to the beggars on the Embankment as if they were coppers – on one occasion he did this to the extent of £1,000. 'Poor old Percy,' in Bosie's words, 'was recklessly generous, confiding and extravagant.' He died literally penniless, although he had inherited nearly three-quarters of a million from his father.[2]

The paper for which Conchie put up the money was a weekly which Bosie called '*Plain English*: with which is incorporated *The Academy*,' since at Bosie's request for the sake of the old association Conchie paid £100 for *The Academy* title, which was still viable. Not much is known about James Conchie apart from the fact that he was rich, he was a Presbyterian while his wife was a Catholic, and he had a London house in Great Cumberland Place and a castle and grouse moor in Perthshire. He gave Bosie a free hand as editor and a salary of £50 a month. 'I must say that as a proprietor to work for, he was a very pleasing contrast to Eddie Tennant in the first days of *The Academy*,' wrote Bosie afterwards. 'Not only did he never dream of interfering with my editorial functions, but he frequently sent me letters and telegrams of congratulations when a particularly good number came out.' The first number sold only about three hundred and fifty copies, but when Bosie gave up the editorship sixteen months later, in October 1921, the circulation was around three thousand and rising every week. Crosland, with whom Bosie had made up his quarrel following on his refusal to give evidence for him in the Ross criminal libel case, was taken on as a contributor, but he insisted on being paid £4 on delivery of every article he wrote, an arrangement to which the obliging Mr Conchie agreed, although many of the other contributors wrote for nothing. The assistant editor was the Irish poet Herbert Moore Pim, whom Bosie had met some years previously through Crosland and stayed with him at his home, Finaghy Cottage, near Belfast, when Pim was running a strongly Nationalist and pro-Sinn Fein journal, *The Irishman*.[3]

Herbert Pim was a Catholic convert of Ulster Protestant stock and the nephew of a Dublin High Court judge Sir Jonathan Pim. He had become a Catholic and an ardent Fenian when Bosie stayed with him at Finaghy. On this occasion, Bosie's only visit to Ireland, Bosie had read John Mitchel's celebrated *Jail Journal* and had become sympathetic with Pim's Irish Nationalist views.[4]

'My views have greatly changed since I have been in Ireland,' Bosie wrote to an English friend at this time. 'In fact I am now a convinced Sinn Feiner. I am completely "fed up" with England. What brought about the breaking point was the damnable cowardice and pusillinamity of the House of Lords and carry on over the Franchise Bill and finally the appointment of Robert Ross by Lloyd George to be manager of the Imperial War Museum. It is plain that England as a whole definitely stands for Ross and what he represents are part of the "official programme" of the country. So I have now definitely decided to have nothing more to do with England and I am able to take this line with a clear conscience as I am a pure Scot on both sides and have scarcely a drop of English blood in my veins. I have joined the Scottish Nationalist Party as represented by Erskine of May in his quarterly *The Scottish Review*.'

But this was only a passing fancy of Bosie's and also of Pim's. In Bosie's words, 'When the Sinn Feiners started murdering people, cutting off the noses of donkeys, and dragging the Catholic Church in the mire for political ends, Pim revolted and left them' and 'ended being as violently "anti" as he had been before pro-Sinn Fein.' When he was still editing *The Irishman*, Pim published Bosie's sonnet 'The Unspeakable Englishman', a fierce attack on Crosland who had written *The Unspeakable Scot*.[5]

> You were a brute and half a knave,
> Your mind was seamed with labyrinthine tracks
> Wherein walked crazy moods bending their backs.
> Under grim loads. You were an open grave
> For gold and love. Always you were the slave

Of crooked thoughts (tortured upon the wrecks)
Of mean mistrust). I made myself as wax
To your fierce seal. I clutched an ebbing wave.

Fool that I was, I loved you: your harsh soul
Was sweet to me: I gave you with both hands
Love, service, honour, loyalty and praise;
I would have died for you! And like a mole
You grubbed and burrowed till the sifting sands
Opened and swallowed up the dream-forged days.

This sonnet was reprinted in Bosie's *Collected Poems*, which appeared under the imprint of Martin Secker in 1919 and was very fairly reviewed in the literary papers, although Bosie used to complain that he was boycotted by the press. (It was simply that he had nothing suitable to offer in the way of articles, as Percy had told Mr Conchie). Bosie accepted Pim's change of view in Irish politics and between them they produced what Bosie called 'a very lively sheet.'[6]

'The paper was a "Diehard" Conservative (indeed I claim to have invented the Diehard party), Catholic – although seventy-five per cent of my readers were non-Catholics – and very anti-Lloyd George-and-Coalition,' Bosie recalled later.

We also put up a strenuous fight (far stronger than that made by any other paper) against the iniquitous surrender to Sinn Fein, and the betrayal of the Irish Loyalists, which will ever remain the darkest blot on the history of the Neo-Georgian period of English history.

It is a fact that the Ulster Defence Council came to us after having been, in vain, to every other paper in London, including *The Morning Post*, and asked us to give details of the Sinn Fein outrages which were going on, unreported in the craven London press, week by week. I saw the President and agreed to print anything they liked to send in, and we went on printing details of outrages every week in spite of the fact that I was threatened with 'reprisals', and warned anonymously that I would be shot. It is rather remarkable that *Plain English*, for which I claim that it was the only secular Catholic paper published in England since the Reformation, should have been the one paper in London to fight the battle of Ulster and the Irish Loyalists.

It was thanks to Pim's extensive knowledge of the whole history of Ireland that I was able to point out that nearly all the Irish revolutionary leaders in the past had been Protestants and not Catholics, and that therefore the attempt that was being made in certain quarters to identify the Catholic Church with Sinn Fein was a perversion of the truth. As a matter of fact, a great deal more than half the Irish men and women who were murdered or reduced to beggary by the Sinn Feiners were Catholics, just as the vast majority of those Irishmen who fought and died for Great Britain in the [Great] War were Catholics.[7]*

On June 22, 1922, Field Marshal Sir Henry Wilson, former Chief of the Imperial General Staff and then an Ulster Unionist MP was assassinated on the steps of his London house by two members of the IRA, who regarded him as an implacable enemy. This terrible act inspired Bosie to write a poem in rhyming verse called *The Devil's Carnival* which was later published as a four-page pamphlet by Sorley Brown's printers in Galashiels. The first three and the last six stanzas read as follows:

> Shame like a pall shrouds this degenerate land
> Where armoured honour once was wont to stand.
> And the mocked sceptre slips from the weak hand.
>
> Greed, Lust, vain Pride, and open Treachery
> Cluster about the Throne. Behold and see
> Asquith and Churchill, Smith and Bottomley.
>
> Jew-bolstered Balfour, turn-coat Chamberlain,
> 'Converted' Curzon, and the lesser train
> That hug with joy the Welsh attorney's chain.
>
> * * *
>
> One man there was enriching a high place
> Who dared to beard dishonour to the face
> And held no truck with salaried disgrace.
>
> And he lies murdered now. Murdered by whom?
> Whose will, conceived in what infernal womb
> Of bloody thought consigned him to his doom?

*Before Catholic Emancipation in 1829 the Irish 'revolutionary' leaders were mostly Protestant, such as those of the 1798 rebellion – Wolfe Tone, Lord Edward Fitzgerald, the Sheares brothers and Robert Emmet. Daniel O'Connell was the first Catholic parliamentary leader after Emancipation. The other two parliamentary principals in the nineteenth century, Isaac Butt and Charles Stewart Parnell, were Protestants. The principal leaders of the Easter Week Rising in 1916 were all Catholics, only a few who played supporting roles, such as Roger Casement and Countess Markievicz, being Protestants. Later leading Nationalists who were Protestants included Erskine Childers, Douglas Hyde (first President of Eire) and W. B. Yeats. Bosie's statement that the vast majority who fought for Great Britain in the Great War were Catholics is inaccurate. Many Catholics did so fight but in fact they were outnumbered by the Protestants, particularly those in the 36th (Ulster Division).

Look you, to whom the profit? Whose the dread
Of Wilson living? Whose uneasy head
Makes softer sleeping now that Wilson's dead?

Who fawned on Collins like a mongrel cur?
Who handed Ireland to a murderer?
Who gave the feeble King dishonour's slur?

We see the shaft, but darkness hides the bow.
Who nursed the spirit that impelled the blow
That laid the Welshman's adversary low?

God Knows, we guess, to what void soul it came
Reeking of hell, co-habitant with shame,
Judas companioned from th' eternal flame.

Although Bosie wrote in his autobiography that the policy of *Plain English* was also strongly 'anti-Semitic', this was not true in the sense that the term is commonly understood today. Its anti-Semitism was of the Belloc-Chesterton variety, and subsequently adopted by the exponent of Social Credit Major C.H. Douglas and the *New Age*, in other words a belief in financial conspiracies, and not a rabidly racial matter as under the Nazis. Thus *Plain English* attacked a 'clique of rich Jews', such as Sir Alfred Mond and Sir Ernest Cassel, whose machinations in the City were allegedly responsible for the faults of international finance which were the cause of unemployment and other contemporary social and economic ills. Perhaps the nearest the paper came to a specific attack was when it published the quatrain later popularised in *The Week-End Book*:

> How odd
> Of God
> To choose
> The Jews.[8]

On 26 April 1922, by which date Bosie was no longer editing *Plain English*, the Conservative daily *Morning Post* printed the following paragraph:

> It must no longer be a paying proposition for men like Mr Crosland and Lord Alfred Douglas to invent vile insults against the Jews.[9]

Encouraged by his success in the *Evening News* case, Bosie, who felt that this statement also impugned his honour, instructed his solicitors to issue a writ for libel against the offending journal. For various reasons, mostly delays by the defendant newspaper in securing the evidence of its two principal witnesses, Mr Churchill and Lord Balfour, the case did not come on for some fifteen months. Meanwhile in October 1921 Bosie had ceased to be the editor of *Plain English*. 'The editorship was taken away from me as the result of an ignoble intrigue, which did very little credit to those who engineered it,' Bosie wrote afterwards. 'These people were apparently fatuous enough to imagine that *Plain English*, which was largely written, as well as closely edited and supervised, by me, could be more successfully carried on with another editor.' Bosie is not at all specific about exactly what happened. He does not mention Mr Conchie, but it appears that Conchie sold the paper for some reason and it was bought by or on behalf of Captain Harold Spencer who became editor. Spencer, it will be recalled, was the former British secret intelligence officer, who had given evidence along with Bosie for the defence in the Pemberton Billing trial, having previously been declared insane. What particularly upset Bosie was Crosland's behaviour at this time. 'The real character of the man,' Bosie afterwards told Crosland's biographer Sorley Brown, 'was shown by the fact that the moment I had been done out of the editorship of *Plain English* (my creation and the apple of my eye), he went straight round to the people who had done me out of it and offered to write for them, and did, in fact, write for them. From that day till his death I never saw him or spoke to him again.' But even Sorley Brown, whose biography on the whole is favourable to Crosland, did not hesitate to write in this work that on this occasion 'Crosland's course of conduct towards his old friend was thoroughly contemptible.'[10]

Captain Harold Spencer did not last long as editor, since he was prosecuted shortly afterwards for publishing a criminal libel in the paper and was sent to prison for six months. That was the end of *Plain English*.*

Meanwhile off his own bat Bosie had started a new paper which he called *Plain Speech*, in which Herbert Pim was assistant editor, and he

*The libel was contained in an article entitled 'Our Foreign Frescoes' which appeared in *Plain English* on 26 November 1921, and attacked the painter Sigismund Goetza for the frescoes he had done for the Foreign Office. ('Our Foreign Office is quite foreign enough in our opinion, without the spacious decorations of a foreign Jew at the expense of the British taxpayer'.) At the trial, Goetza gave evidence that he was born of British parents and baptised in the Christian faith and that the frescoes were done at his own expense. Although Spencer stated that the article appeared a week before he bought the paper and he had nothing to do with it, he was not believed and was convicted. In passing sentence Mr Justice Salter described Spencer's offence as one of the most scurrilous and malicious libels he had ever read on a man who never did any harm: *The Times* 4 February 1922.

also took with him some of the best contributors to *Plain English*. Money came in as the result of his appeal for funds when he got £25 immediately, and a City merchant named Ernest Brown weighed in with £50 weekly which continued until Bosie became seriously ill with influenza after the *Evening News* case and had to close the paper.

After he had recovered, Bosie kept Sorley Brown posted with information about the *Morning Post*, pending the trial of his libel action. On 22 August 1922, he wrote to Brown:

> Lady Bathurst, who owns the *Morning Post*, is the daughter of old Algernon Borthwick, who was created a peer (for various villainies) and took the title of Lord Glenesk. I believe he was a Scotsman and it is just characteristic of Lady Bathurst that she should continuously employ her own paper to curry favour with the English by abusing her father's and her own country.
>
> Although I agree with the politics of the *Morning Post* (and indeed they have stolen all my thunder and got all their ideas from *Plain English* and *Plain Speech*) I look upon it as a most contemptible paper. It is always doing something crooked and at the back of it is George Lewis who manages all its business affairs.[11]

2

The trial of *Douglas v The Morning Post* for libel opened before Mr Justice Salter and a special jury at the Law Courts on 17 July 1923 and lasted for two days. Mr Arthur Comyns Carr led for the plaintiff, and Mr Patrick Hastings, KC, MP, with Mr William Jowitt, KC were for the defendant newspaper.[12] By his pleading the plaintiff alleged that the plain meaning of the words complained of, which have already been quoted, was that the statements made by him, or for which he took responsibility as editor of *Plain English*, were statements which he knew to be untrue and that they were invented for the purpose of making money out of them. In its defence *The Morning Post* pleaded justification, the particulars of which consisted of various extracts from articles in *Plain English*. These purported to show the sinister influence exercised by the Jews in recent world events, notably the death of Lord Kitchener and the Battle of Jutland, to which latter event Lord Balfour and Mr Winston Churchill were accused of being parties.

In his opening speech Mr Comyns Carr said that the information about the Battle of Jutland had been supplied to the assistant editor of *Plain English*, Mr Pim, who got it from an officer in the British Intelligence Service. Lord Alfred Douglas accepted it as the truth, said Mr Comyns Carr, and he reasserted this conviction when he came to be examined by his counsel in the witness box. He had no personal prejudices against Jews and had many friends among them, Bosie explained. It was simply a question of evidence. All the articles were based on information received by him or in his possession, and he believed them to be true. He also expressed the belief that the articles on the Battle of Jutland exposed him to the danger of imprisonment, an opinion which incidentally was to be translated into hard fact after he had repeated the substance of them at a public meeting a few weeks later.

In previous actions, as he have seen, Bosie had proved himself to be a formidable witness, especially under cross-examination. On this occasion he claimed, in his own words, to have 'wiped the floor' with Patrick Hastings. The reality of this boast must remain the determined manner, bordering indeed on the offensive, in which Douglas replied to the leading counsel's opening questions.

'Do you think', asked Hastings, 'that it is the action of a gentleman to make the kind of statements you have made against people like Lord Balfour and Mr Churchill?'

'Of course,' Bosie answered, 'it's the action of a gentleman to tell the truth about people.'

'You think it was a gentlemanly thing to say?'

'I would not take my views as to what a gentleman should do from a Labour Member and a sympathiser with Bolshevists.'

Hastings looked sharply at this impudent witness. But he made no remark about this personal reference to himself, as he put his next question.

'If anyone had brought an action against your newspaper, had it enough assets to pay damages if they had been awarded against it?'

'I suppose it has as much assets as the *Morning Post*, which is "debentured" up to the eyes,' was the impertinent answer.

Hastings then picked up a copy of *Plain English* and proceeded to question Bosie about his alleged story of the false report of the Battle of Jutland, which was supposed to have depressed British stocks on the New York market, thereby enabling certain Jewish financiers to make substantial profits when the true facts of the naval engagement became known.

HASTINGS: In your article on the Battle of Jutland you say that 'during the actual fighting of the Battle of Jutland, Germany was in communication with some powerful individual at the Admiralty' and that the escape of the German Fleet was being devised by these means?

WITNESS: Yes. Absolutely.

HASTINGS: Who was the powerful individual at the Admiralty?

WITNESS: He was in charge of the wireless during the battle. I am not going to tell you his name.

HASTINGS: Do you decline to tell me who it was?

WITNESS: Yes. I will write it down for my Lord.

HASTINGS: Your article says, 'It may also be said that the Cabinet Minister who drew up and issued the false report about the Battle of Jutland which produced this fall in stocks had spent the week-end with one of the most powerful members of the financial group, Sir Ernest Cassel.' Who was the Cabinet Minister referred to there?

WITNESS: Mr Churchill.

HASTINGS: Do you happen to know that Mr Churchill had not been First Lord of the Admiralty for twelve months before the Battle of Jutland?

WITNESS: That has been explained as being a slip of the pen.

HASTINGS: Do you know that Lord Balfour has stated in his evidence taken on commission that the only person who drew up the so-called false report was himself?

WITNESS: I know, but I don't believe it.

HASTINGS: You suggest that he has committed perjury?

WITNESS: He has either committed perjury or his memory has failed.

HASTINGS: Do you suggest now that Mr Churchill drew up that report?

WITNESS: Certainly.

HASTINGS: What information have you on the point now?

WITNESS: The same information as I had then. It was told me by Captain Spencer.

HASTINGS: You say no proceedings were taken against you. Do you realise that there are some people too contemptible to be prosecuted?

WITNESS: You are an impudent scoundrel to speak to me like that.

HASTINGS: Do you think there was a single person in this court, until my learned friend Mr Carr mentioned it, who had ever heard of *Plain English*?

WITNESS: I can point to fifty people in Court who have read every word of it and think it is the finest newspaper on earth. It has a circulation of 3,000 including about eighty Members of both Houses of Parliament and twenty Bishops.

HASTINGS: You say later on in reference to Mr Churchill: 'It is true that by most subtle means and by never allowing him more than a pony ahead, this ambitious and brilliant man, short of money and eager for power, was trapped by the Jews. After the Jutland business his house was furnished for him by Sir Ernest Cassel.' Do you mean to say that Mr Churchill was financially indebted to the Jews?

WITNESS: Yes, certainly.

HASTINGS: Do you want to persist in that now?

WITNESS: Of course I do.

HASTINGS: Who were the Jews in whose clutches he was?

WITNESS: Chiefly Cassel.

HASTINGS: What justification had you in your own mind for making that charge against Mr Churchill?

WITNESS: I had the evidence of what was told me by men at the Admiralty, and Sir Alfred Fripp told me that Cassel had given Mr Churchill £40,000 in one cheque.

HASTINGS: Was it after the Battle of Jutland he got a cheque for £40,000?

WITNESS: Certainly.

HASTINGS: Do you realise that Mr Churchill is coming here and can be asked questions, financial and otherwise, which it is desired to ask him?

WITNESS: Of course I realise it.

HASTINGS: What do you expect to find when he is cross-examined?

WITNESS: You had better wait and see.

Questioned about an alleged statement by Lord Kitchener in one of the articles, 'I regard the blood of the best men in England as too great a price to pay for educating the Jews: can no Christian occupy a position of trust in the War Office?' and the comment, 'That statement signed his death warrant,' Douglas replied: 'That is what appears in the article.'

'Do you mean by that that the Jews caused the death of Lord Kitchener in the *Hampshire*?'

'Certainly.'

'What information had you which enabled you to charge the Jewish race with the death of Lord Kitchener?'

'You will see that I did not go that length at the time, because I had not the whole story: but I had enough in my mind to convince me that Kitchener was murdered to prevent him from reaching Russia, because, if he had arrived there, the revolution would not have taken place and the war would have been shortened by two years.'

While his client was being cross-examined, Mr Comyns Carr realised that the only line open to him with any possible chance of success with the jury was to urge on them that the question they would have to decide was not whether the statements contained in the articles were true, but simply whether Bosie, in making them or accepting responsibility for them, had acted honestly. Consequently as soon as Bosie had left the witness box and his case was concluded, his counsel rose to say that, before Hastings opened the defendants' case it might be useful if he informed the Court that he would not think it necessary to put any questions in cross-examination to any witnesses which the defendants might call as to the facts stated in the articles either about the Battle of Jutland or the death of Lord Kitchener.

Mr Jowitt, for the defendants, then read the evidence of Lord Balfour, which had been taken on commission. Lord Balfour had been First Lord of the Admiralty at the time of the Battle of Jutland in May 1916. According to his testimony, he had drawn up the *communiqué* on the battle in his own handwriting. After trifling alterations were made in Admiral Oliver's room, the document was then released to the Press through the usual official channels on 3 June 1916. Mr Churchill had nothing to do with the drafting, the preparation or the issue of the *communiqué*. But he had called at the Admiralty on the following day and had been shown telegrams received from the Fleet. The first Lord had invited Mr Churchill to issue an appreciation of the situation, which Mr Churchill consented to do, the object being 'to inform neutral Governments of the material and relevant facts, of which they had no knowledge, to counteract the misleading statements issued by the German Admiralty'. Mr Churchill's appreciation was released on 4 June.

When Mr Comyns Carr intimated that he did not propose to read Lord Balfour's cross-examination Bosie jumped up and gave his counsel a furious look. 'If you are not going to read the cross-examination,' he said, 'I shall leave the court.' Bosie thereupon stalked out. It was as well that he did so, since he left the field clear for the next witness to give his evidence unhampered by his interruptions. The next witness was Mr Winston Churchill, and he was examined by the defendant's leading counsel.

Mr Churchill flatly denied that he had ever entered into a plot with the Jews or anyone else in relation to reports of the Jutland engagement or that he had been paid a farthing by Sir Ernest Cassel or anyone else for anything he had done in this connection. 'It is an absolute lie,' he said.

'When you first saw these articles,' Hastings asked the witness, 'did you consider the advisability of prosecuting the man who wrote them?'

'I sent the articles to the Law Officers,' Mr Churchill replied, 'and the Attorney-General (Sir Douglas Hogg) gave a great deal of attention to the matter. He most strongly advised me against instituting a prosecution either personally or through the Director of Public Prosecutions. His view was that the status of the paper was so obscure and contemptible that it would only give it a needless advertisement and notoriety if a State prosecution or an action for libel were started. Lastly, he considered that the character of Lord Alfred Douglas made it unnecessary for me to take any notice at that stage of these very gross and cruel libels, but he assured me that if at any time the question was raised why I had not taken action to clear my honour, he would himself testify to the advice he had given me and the reasons for doing so. That was the reason I abstained from prosecuting.'

'Between the date when you left the Admiralty and the date of the battle – just over a year – did you have any share or part in the direction of the Admiralty?'

'None whatever, except that I was a member of the Cabinet and had an opportunity of discussing Admiralty matters.'

Mr Churchill added that Lord Balfour was in exclusive charge of the Admiralty, and repeated that he himself had nothing whatever to do with the preparation of the *communiqué*. 'I never saw it until I read it in a newspaper.'

As for the appreciation written at Lord Balfour's suggestion, Mr Churchill denied that it was written at the instigation of Sir Ernest Cassel or any Jew.

'Had it anything to do with any manipulation of stocks in any market in the world?'

'Such an idea never entered my mind.'

'Did you make a penny piece of money in any way out of it?'

'No.'

As soon as Mr Churchill had left the witness box, Hastings said he did not propose to call any other witnesses who had been at the Admiralty, since they would not be cross-examined. But he would call Mr W.D. Geddes, who had been business secretary to the late Sir Ernest Cassel. Sir Ernest, said this witness, did not make any investments at the time of the Battle of Jutland and it was quite untrue to say that he had brought off any *coup*. 'He neither bought nor sold stocks for months before or after the battle.'

The question which the jury had to determine, as the plaintiff's counsel had foreseen, was not whether the stories about the Jews were true or not, but whether in publishing them Lord Alfred Douglas had acted in good faith or whether he had 'invented' them – in other words, as the judge told the jury, whether he neither knew nor cared if they were true or false. The jury could not bring themselves to find that the plaintiff had gone the length of 'invention'. Hence they brought in a verdict in his favour, but at the same time they showed what they thought of his conduct by awarding him the contemptuous sum of one farthing damages. In consequence Douglas was deprived of the costs to which he would otherwise have been entitled, the judge saying that he thought the jury's verdict indicated an opinion which he entirely shared and to which he must give effect. Each side therefore was ordered to pay their own costs.

'I won a great victory,' Bosie wrote to Sorley Brown after the trial, 'in spite of the miserable cowardice of my counsel and the gross unfairness of the judge who allowed Balfour's cross-examination to be excluded.' He enclosed a copy of a letter he had written to Hastings, adding that he had sent copies to Lewis & Lewis (the *Morning Post*'s solicitors), Balfour, Churchill, and Salter, the judge who tried the case.[13]

The letter to Hastings was one of Bosie's more vituperative literary efforts:

> 16 Draycott Place,
> SW3
>
> Sir,
>
> #### *Douglas v. The Morning Post*
>
> In the course of the ridiculous and disgusting exhibition of impotent rancour and malice which you provided in your opening speech for the defence in the above named action, you made a reference to the 'place where the plaintiff so properly belongs' by which you were understood to mean prison. You ought to know all about it considering that your father did five years penal servitude for heartless frauds, the victims of which you have never compensated to the extent of a penny out of the enormous income which you get from the silly people who are foolish enough to employ your fifth-rate abilities as counsel.
>
> Your delightful clients and the gang behind them, including 'dear Winston', may make the best of the fact that I was done out of the heavy damages which were my due, because my counsel had not the pluck to use the ample material with which I supplied him for cross-examining Churchill, and because he and you between you succeeded in keeping Balfour's cross-examination out.
>
> But you can tell them with my compliments that this action is only the first round. There is still my action against the *Jewish Guardian* to come. Sooner or later the whole truth will emerge.
>
> *Mon pied dans ta queue*
> Alfred Douglas[14]

Taking the most charitable view of Bosie's behaviour, it was due to his ignorance of the law and his counsel's tactics that he reacted as he did. Comyns Carr was quite justified in not commenting on Balfour's evidence and not cross-examining Churchill or any other of the defendant's witnesses, the reason being that such tactics would not have helped his client's case. There was no point in attempting to prove the truth of Bosie's allegations and using the material regarding Churchill with which Bosie had supplied his counsel. The only question at issue was *not* whether the allegations were true or false but rather whether Bosie regarded them as being true when he made them, although in fact they were not so. Nor could Comyns Carr's use of this material conceivably have increased the contemptuous damages which the jury awarded the plaintiff who should never have brought the case against *The Morning Post* at all. Brilliant as he had shown himself as a witness in earlier cases, this time he had brought his pitcher to the legal well once too often. The result was a warning which he chose to ignore with what were to prove tragic consequences to himself.

3

It was a pity that Bosie did not heed the lesson of the *Morning Post* case and let the matter of Kitchener and the Battle of Jutland drop. Instead he chose to repeat the charges he had made against Winston Churchill at a public meeting in the Memorial Hall, Farringdon Street, London, a few weeks later, on 3 August 1923. The meeting was organised by a committee called 'The Lord Kitchener and Battle of Jutland Publicity Committee'. The committee included General Cyril Prescott-Decie, who had won the DSO in the Great War, and also Bosie's sister Lady Edith Fox-Pitt and his friend the explorer Harry de Windt. It was the first time in his life that Bosie had addressed a public meeting and he did so for over an hour, being loudly cheered by the large audience which had come to hear him, the meeting having been extensively advertised in advance.[15]

In the course of the speech he made the following statement:

> I made a definite charge against Mr Winston Churchill in *Plain English*. I stated that a large sum of money was given to him by Sir Ernest Cassel after he [Winston Churchill] had issued what is admittedly a false account of the Battle of Jutland. ... I have always taken it to be fairly well established that if you bring a serious accusation against a man involving his honour, and if you bring that accusation in the most public manner possible, and if that man ignores your accusation and takes no proceedings against you, you are entitled to believe that your accusation is true.

He went on later in the same speech:

> If the positions were reversed, if Mr Churchill were editing a paper and if he printed in his column one-half, one-quarter, one-fifth of what I printed about him, I would have him round at Bow Street magistrates' court with his nose hanging over the edge of the dock to answer a charge of criminal libel, I promise you. (Loud applause.)

As for Kitchener and the loss of the *Hampshire*, he continued, 'I said plainly in my paper that Lord Kitchener had been murdered by the Jews. I thought so then and I think so now. I never said I could prove it or could prove exactly who were his murderers. As I explained in Court in answer to the questions put to me by Mr Hastings, I did not profess to have the complete story, and for that reason I never did more in my paper than say that I was convinced Kitchener had been murdered. ... His object was to go to Russia to replace the corrupt Bolshevised Jews who were holding all the key positions by loyal men of British birth. If he had got to Russia and succeeded in his mission the Russian Revolution would have been nipped in the bud. Obviously if the Revolution was to come off according to Jewish plans, at all costs Kitchener and all with him must be got rid of. Well, this is what happened.' The *Hampshire*, which was supposed to have struck a mine, he believed had been blown up from inside by time-bombs deliberately put there by a shore-gang under the direction of a Jew called Nathan, since dead, who was head of the Secret Service in Ireland.

Bosie sent a copy of his speech to Sorley Brown who published it verbatim in his paper the *Border Standard*. It was subsequently issued from the same type as a pamphlet entitled *The Murder of Lord Kitchener and the Truth about the Battle of Jutland and the Jews*. 30,000 copies were sent from Scotland to London for distribution, and of these about 6,000 had been sold when the authorities stepped in and on 6 November arrested him on a charge of criminally libelling Mr Winston Churchill. It was an unusual type of case for a public prosecution, but the Attorney-General, Sir Douglas Hogg, felt that Mr Churchill should not be called upon to bear the expense of a private prosecution when the libel was really in connection with his work for the Government. The warrant was specially issued by the Chief Magistrate, a procedure designed to keep Alfred Douglas in the dark as to what was in store for him until the latest possible moment. On being brought before the Chief Magistrate at Bow Street, Bosie intimated that he would plead justification. He was duly committed for trial and allowed bail.

On December 1923, he surrendered to his bail and entered the dock at the Old Bailey. There he pleaded Not Guilty to the charge of 'publishing a malicious and defamatory libel of and concerning Mr Winston Leonard Spencer Churchill' in the form of the pamphlet already mentioned. The Attorney-General, Sir Douglas Hogg, KC, MP, later Lord Hailsham, and the Senior Treasury Counsel, Sir Richard Muir, appeared for the prosecution. The accused was defended by his friend Cecil Hayes, since he no longer trusted Comyns Carr. The case was tried before Mr Justice Avory and a jury, and it last for four days.

Since much of the evidence, such as that of Balfour and Churchill as well as the defendant's testimony, which had been given in the *Morning Post* action, was repeated in the present trial, it is only necessary to describe the proceedings briefly here.

Among other matters, Churchill was cross-examined about a civic luncheon given to Lord Haig in Dundee when he (Churchill) was the local MP and he was asked whether on that occasion he remembered meeting Captain Harold Spencer, who had figured conspicuously in the 'Black Book' case and who had been mentioned in the Press as a prospective candidate for Dundee at the next Election. Churchill replied that he could not remember any such meeting; he also denied that he had had any conversation with Spencer in which he attempted to justify 'that Jutland business'.

Churchill was also questioned by Bosie's counsel, Cecil Hayes, about an article published in *Plain English*, headed 'Publish and Be Damned', and for which his client was responsible. Churchill was asked why he had not prosecuted at the time of its publication. To this the witness replied that he had put the facts before the Law Officers of the Crown, who had advised him not to institute proceedings, as he has already been noted. Churchill said that he wished that he had prosecuted the defendant then. He also denied that one of the reasons why there had not been an earlier prosecution was that he did not wish to be cross-examined.

At this point the judge intervened and raised a laugh. 'You were not labouring under that delusion when you came here and knew that Mr Hayes was defending?'

'Oh, no,' answered Churchill. 'I knew I was going to be cross-examined. Lord Alfred has said on several occasions that he was going to do it himself!' What he complained of, Churchill added, was 'the continued circulation of these foul libels.'

When it came to his turn to go into the witness box, the defendant was asked by his counsel in his examination-in-chief what happened after he gave up the editorship of *Plain English* in October 1921. 'Captain Spencer became editor, and shortly afterwards became the proprietor,' Bosie replied. 'When I left the paper I was very angry. I thought I had been badly treated, and Captain Spencer and I had a violent quarrel.' At the same time the defendant antagonised the judge, and no doubt also the jury, by repeatedly protesting that he had been treated throughout most grossly unfairly. 'Every time I tried to present my case to the jury I have been prevented from doing so,' he said. 'I have never been able to tell the jury why I did it or where I got the information, and everything has been stopped. It is the most abominable unfairness I have ever seen in my life.'

The judge let this pass, but when the defendant repeated this again at the end of his evidence, he received a stern rebuke from the Bench. 'Will you leave the box and not make speeches!' For once the loquacious Bosie remained silent and did as he was told.

The next witness was Harold Spencer who attended the court under sub-poena. In his examination-in-chief Captain Spencer, as he styled himself, swore that 'the conversation he alleged he had with Churchill at Lord Haig's luncheon in Dundee was as put by counsel to Churchill in cross-examination, but which Churchill had denied in every particular. He had told Churchill, the witness maintained, that he was going to turn him out of Dundee at the next election, adding 'Your Jutland report was a bit thick, wasn't it?' To which Churchill was supposed to have replied, according to this witness, 'What do you care? We did it to get the money out of the Yanks.'

Cross-examined by the Attorney-General, Spencer was asked whether he had the right to the title of Captain with which he had come into court. He replied that he had been told that there was an order in the *Gazette* depriving him of it. He also admitted that he had been twice convicted by the civil power, once for libel for which he had been imprisoned for six months and once for insulting behaviour for which he had been fined forty shillings. He asserted that, when he had been certified insane by a medical board, it was a plot to get him out of the army. The witness was reminded of a statement he had made that he had met Churchill before the alleged Dundee incident at Lady Randolph Churchill's flat in St James's Place. 'Do you know that Lady Randolph Churchill never had a flat in London at all, and never lived in St James's Place since 1883?'

'I can only speak of the time I saw her there,' the witness replied, having stated that he was not sure of the exact date but it might have been in 1913.

'How old are you?' the Attorney-General continued.

'I am thirty-three.'

'So that you were not alive in 1883?'

'No.'

The witness was then asked whether he had met Mr Churchill on any other occasion. He paused for a few moments before replying. 'I really did not want to mention it,' he finally said, 'but I remember when living in St James's Place I once met Mr Churchill coming out of Boodle's Club in rather an unfortunate condition!' This statement caused considerable laughter in which Churchill himself joined.

When the defence case closed, the Attorney-General asked the judge if he could recall Mr Churchill to the witness box, and this he was allowed to do.

Replying to Sir Douglas Hogg, Churchill said that his mother never owned a flat in St James's Place. She lived there in his father's lifetime but had left about 1883 or 1884. He further stated that he had never been a member of Boodle's Club and, so far as he could remember, had never been there.

Mr Justice Avory summed up strongly against the defendant, much more so than Mr Justice Salter had done in the *Morning Post* case. He also had some scathing things to say about Harold Spencer. The defendant, when called to the witness box, Avory told the jury, had been unable to give them any material evidence in support of his plea of justification, while the only evidence given by Harold Spencer which could be said in any sense to support the plea was the alleged conversation which he said he had with Mr Churchill in Dundee in 1919, and this Mr Churchill had denied. 'Who is Mr Harold Spencer whose evidence you are asked to accept?' the judge went on.

> He has had to admit that on 17 September 1917, a medical board examined him and certified that he was insane and unfit for further military service, and you have his admission that on 3 February 1922 he was convicted in this Court of publishing a defamatory libel, for which he was sentenced to six months' imprisonment. What is perhaps more to his discredit is that in February of this year he was convicted of disgusting behaviour and fined, and an appeal from that conviction was dismissed. That is the man whose testimony you are asked to accept – a man concerning whom *Plain English* itself has published a statement that he was a person whose word could not be relied upon.

As for the defendant, the judge considered that he was 'absolutely reckless in what he wrote and published,' and if the jury also drew that conclusion, said Avory, it might assist them in deciding whether these alleged libels upon Mr Churchill the defendant was not 'writing and publishing something for which he had no justification.'

It took the jury exactly eight minutes to reach their decision – Guilty.

Mr Justice Avory then addressed the man in the dock:

Alfred Bruce Douglas, it is to be regretted that your undoubted literary abilities should have been degraded to such purposes as these. If I could have taken the view that you have been honestly deceived into believing the truth of these accusations, I should have taken a different and more lenient course. In view of the fact that in the action tried in the High Court against the *Morning Post* you had full notice that these accusations were untrue, and in view of the fact that the only person upon whom you apparently sought to rely in support of this plea of justification was a person like Harold Spencer, whom you yourself had denounced in your own paper as a person unworthy of belief, I must act on the view that you have deliberately persisted in this plea of justification without the slightest excuse, or without the slightest ground for believing that you are now telling the truth in this plea. . . .

In view of your previous experience in this Court it is obvious you must be taught a lesson, and like other persons suffer punishment. The sentence of the Court is that you be imprisoned in the second division for six months, and at the expiration of that period find a surety in £100 to keep the peace and be of good behaviour to all his Majesty's subjects, and particularly to Mr Winston Churchill: and in default of your finding a surety that you be imprisoned for a further six months.

Next day *The Times* came out with a leading article approving the verdict and sentence. 'To those who have watched the career of the man, it will be regarded as a moderate sentence. For years, in newspapers, and in circulars and in pamphlets, he has conducted a campaign of irresponsible calumny regardless of facts and intrepid in defamatory invective. At last he has been laid by the heels in quite a gentle way, but in a way which we hope – not with great confidence – will teach him a lesson.'[16]

4

In those days there were three divisions of imprisonment, which along with hard labour and penal servitude were continued until 1948. While prisoners in the first division could wear their own clothes and enjoyed other privileges, including having their own food sent in, there was little difference between the treatment of those in the second division and the third (those sentenced to 'hard labour') except that those in the second division were unlike those in the third not deprived of their mattresses on their plank beds during the first fortnight of their sentences and they were also allowed to write and receive more letters and visits, one a month in each case. In every other respect their treatment was the same. They occupied the same cells, did the same labour, kept the same hours and got the same food.

Bosie was taken in a Black Maria from the Old Bailey to Wormwood Scrubs prison on 13 December 1923 immediately after he had been sentenced. For the first ten days he was employed sewing mailbags indoors. He was then transferred with fourteen other prisoners in both the second and third divisions to 'the garden', where he was put to shovelling coal into carts and then dragging the carts. 'This "swinging the shovel" is fairly hard work,' he wrote after his release, 'and I did my share of it, although the officer who looked after the gardeners, a charming and kindly fellow, named Belcher, told me that I need not do it if it overtired me. My natural desire was to do the same as everyone else did, and, if I had had enough to eat, my work in the garden, which conferred the privilege of being in the open air for five or six hours a day, without a hat in all weathers (this was in December and January), would have done me no harm at all. But, unfortunately, starved as I was and weak for want of food, it caused internal injuries from which I have never recovered.'[17]

> The worst part about prison, materially speaking, is the food. It is so disgusting that a dog would certainly not eat it unless he were starving. I was quite unable to eat it, and for the first three weeks of my sentence I ate nothing but a few crusts of dry bread, and very nasty bread at that. As a result, of course I lost weight with great rapidity. Curiously enough, however, I did not feel ill at first. I lived fairly comfortably 'on my tissues', my health remained good, and I slept nine hours every night, in spite of a plank bed, and a mattress and pillow as hard as nether millstones. It was only after a month that I began to feel weak and ill as a result of under nourishment. I went on a vegetarian diet after the first three weeks, and I was able to eat slightly more of this diet than the other. But by the middle of the seventh week I had lost more than eighteen pounds and was on the verge of collapse, and I was then sent to the hospital. ...

He was only too glad to go, since by that time he was so weak that the officer who took him there had to put his arm round him to hold him up.

It shows what a state of collapse I was in that I remember being filled with horror and apprehension because, when I got to the hospital, there was a cat standing at the door with a mouse in its mouth. I dislike mice very much, and I had never seen a sign of one in my cell in Hall B (No 69), to my great relief. So when I saw the cat I remembered that someone had told me that there were swarms of mice in the hospital. I said to the officer: 'Will there be mice in my ward?' He said: 'Well, there *might* be, but you needn't mind them, they won't hurt you.' (People never can understand that one's dislike to mice is not connected with any apprehension that they may be liable to bite one!) I was frozen with horror. I thought to myself: 'If the place is going to be full of mice it will just about finish me.' When I was left alone I prayed desperately to St Anthony of Padua to keep mice away from me. It is the extraordinary fact that I never saw one again, or heard the slightest sound of one, the whole time I was in hospital, though other prisoners told me that the place was full of them.

The hospital has two floors. There are wards with beds in them just like ordinary hospital wards, and there are also rows of separate cells. The wards are airy and cheerful, and the cells are much less forbidding than the cells in the ordinary prison. They have much larger windows, which you can look out of without standing on a chair, and the hospital itself is pleasantly situated in the garden of the prison. When I got into a private cell, with its green walls and a little cot (actually with real sheets and a pillow) I began to feel better. The food seemed too delicious to be real. It was just ordinary roast beef or roast mutton, and rice-pudding, but, starving as I was, it seemed like ambrosia. I also got half-a-pint of milk a day and some *real* bread. There was no butter, only margarine, which I never would eat. So I preferred my bread dry.

I was horrified, after I had been in hospital about three weeks, to gather from something the doctor said on one of his visits that when my weight got back to normal, I would have to go back to Hall B. I was so much less wretched in my cell in the hospital that the idea of going back to starvation gave me cold shivers. I again had recourse to St Anthony, and though I was weighed every week, and though I really was 'fed up' and had plenty of good food, I never anywhere near got back my weight, and I stayed in the hospital right to the day of my release.[18]

The Catholic chaplain, Father Musgrave, was particularly kind to Bosie, and when the prisoner who played the organ in the chapel left on completing his sentence, Father Musgrave asked Bosie to take his place which he willingly did, since he was a sufficiently good musician to play it at Mass and Benediction. 'This was a treat since it gave me a little variation from the deadly monotony [of Wormwood Scrubs],' he wrote. Bosie also joined in the 'choir' practices, the 'choir' chiefly consisting of a few Borstal boys and a sprinkling of Sinn Feiners. He was friendly with the Sinn Feiners, since although he was himself anti-Sinn Fein, he felt sorry for them because they were Catholics and political offenders who had been interned. They included the notorious Art O'Brien, and when Bosie went out he smuggled a letter to his sister. He later wrote to Arthur Henderson, then Home Secretary in the Labour Government, with the result that the Sinn Fein prisoners were transferred to Brixton as political offenders and put in the first division. Some weeks later they were all discharged, 'so, even if I had no part in securing their release,' said Bosie, 'I certainly brought them luck.'[19]

Bosie had a friend a few years younger than himself, called Arthur Rose, who probably visited him in Wormwood Scrubs. How or when the two first met is not known, but it may well have been when Bosie was editing *The Academy* in Lincoln's Inn Fields, and Rose, who had an office in the same area, published a medical directory. At all events, while Bosie was still in prison, Rose also wrote to the Labour Home Secretary and persuaded him to let Bosie have writing materials on the ground that the prisoner was a distinguished poet and it was 'outrageous' to deprive him of the means of exercising his art. Accordingly he was given a school exercise book, of the type supplied to Borstal boys, together with a pencil. This was early in February 1924, since he states that on 5 February he began to write what turned out to be a series of sonnets. The first one he wrote with considerable difficulty, and to begin with he had no intention of writing any more. But shortly afterwards he succeeded in writing a second sonnet and then a third. 'Quite accidentally they hung together, and I conceived the idea of writing a long poem all in sonnets. I worked hard at it, invoking St Anthony and St Thomas Aquinas whenever I got "stuck", and produced the seventeen sonnets which make up my poem *In Excelsis*....' It was finished on Good Friday, 18 April.

A week before he was due to be released, something prompted Bosie to repeat the poem to himself every night in bed so as to get it by heart. It was fortunate he did this, since two days before he left Wormwood Scrubs, the Prison Commission, apparently on the instructions of the Home Office, confiscated the exercise book in which Bosie had written the poem. The Commissioners refused to return it to him, although Bosie twice asked them to reconsider their decision. Why they should have acted in this way is inexplicable, bearing in mind that Oscar Wilde was allowed to take the *De Profundis* manuscript with him when he left Reading.

Bosie served five months of his sentence, the remaining month being remitted for good conduct. But up to the last moment he thought he might be kept further in confinement since the Governor had not received word from the Home Office about the acceptance of his surety, as provided for by Mr Justice Avory's sentence. This surety was Bosie's cousin Sholto Douglas. The Governor, whom Bosie could see was worried, advised him to write to the Home Office himself which he did with the result that the acceptance came through in the nick of time, although Bosie was in agonies until the last day.[20]

On his release he went straight to Alfred Rose's office, where he wrote out the whole of *In Excelsis* which he had memorised. 'I consider it is far the best poetical work I have ever done,' he told Sorley Brown a week later. At the same time he wrote to Herbert Pim from his mother's house in Draycott Place where he was staying:

> I can't understand how I did it, as what I wanted to do seemed so difficult as to be impossible. But I pulled it off sonnet by sonnet, each involving a desperate struggle, by the assistance of St Anthony of Padua whose aid I invoked. . . . It is mystic and introspective and owes much to St Thomas of Kempis whose *Imitation* [*of Christ*] I was reading day by day in prison. I read it all through that way 5 times, so many pages each morning.
>
> Rose is placing the poem for me. He is frantically excited about it, and is asking £500 advance royalties for the American rights and ditto for the English. Of course he won't get so much, but I think anyway I shall do very well with it.[21]

The poem was later published less three of the sonnets by John Squire in his well-known monthly magazine *The London Mercury*, also in full by the faithful Sorley Brown in the *Border Standard*, and finally in book form in December 1924 by Martin Secker in an ordinary hardback edition and also in a special signed edition limited to one hundred copies and printed on handmade paper, both editions being dedicated to Alfred Rose.

Bosie, an essentially trusting character, was apt to be taken in by charlatans as we have seen in the case of Harold Spencer. Unfortunately he was to be duped by Alfred Rose, whom he evidently was unaware had been convicted of the theft of some valuable books from a monastic institution twenty-six years previously. On this occasion he was defended by Edward Marshall Hall in one of his last cases as junior barrister before becoming a Queen's Counsel. But not even this silver-tongued advocate's eloquence could save Rose from a verdict of guilty and the subsequent severe sentence passed on him by Mr Justice Grantham of three years penal servitude.[22]

Some time after the publication of *In Excelsis* with its dedication to Rose, Bosie learned that Rose had improperly acquired some of the manuscripts of Bosie's writings and disposed of them to W. & G. Foyle, the well-known booksellers in Charing Cross Road. 'Thanks for your letter,' he wrote to his friend and fellow writer Rupert Croft-Cooke, who had supplied him with some of the particulars of Foyle's purchases.

> I had already heard that Rose had sold some of my mss to Foyle's, but did not know the details. 'The Wilde Myth' I myself sold, but all the rest, except the copy of 'The Devil's Carnival' which I gave to Rose, were stolen or appropriated by this person. I really don't know what to do about it, as of course Foyle bought them in good faith. A friend of mine who knows Foyle personally is going into it for me. Rose is a dangerous and unscrupulous person.[23]

Although strictly speaking in law Bosie could have obtained the return of the manuscripts had he been able to prove that Rose had sold them to Foyle's, it is likely that the fact that Foyle's had bought them in good faith induced Bosie good-naturedly to let the matter drop. At all events there is no evidence that he took any further action in the matter.

5

Pending the advance on account of royalties or serial rights which he expected to receive from *In Excelsis*, Bosie was hard-pressed for money. Sibyl Queensberry was unwell and he did not like to worry her, since her finances had been depleted by the Great War and also the depredations made upon her by her eldest son Percy the tenth Marquess to meet the losses he had incurred in his unfortunate speculations. In those days it was more economical to live in a good hotel on the continent than in England, and for this reason many English continued to 'winter' in the south of France or Italy as they had done before the war. Consequently, Bosie went ahead to Bruges, where he stayed in the Hotel de Londres, which was kept by an Englishman called Blake-Hales, and from there after a few months moved on to Brussels, where his mother joined him and they put up in a similarly modest establishment, Wiltcher's Hotel in the Avenue Louise. Also staying in Brussels were a young English poet, Norman Roe, and his mother, who were friends of Bosie's.

What happened to Roe was described by Bosie in a letter to Herbert Pim:

Wiltcher's Hotel. 15 October 1924. . . . I came here with my mother a few days ago and like it very much, but everything has been darkened by the dreadful tragedy that has befallen poor Norman Roe, of whom I told you. He drowned himself in a canal here and I have had to go through all the horrors of interviewing the police and identifying him at the Morgue and telegraphing to his poor mother who left here on Friday (Roe's body was found on Saturday morning 10 October) and has just returned. He had just finished dictating an article on my poem (which he raved about) and he went out and wandered about the town and was found in the canal. It is too awful for words. I had taken a great affection for him.

It appears (though I had never seen a sign of it) that he had a frightful drink mania which came on from time to time. I saw him last on Thursday when he and I and his mother sat on the *terrasse* of a café after dinner. His mother left for England next morning and I had an appointment to go to his little flat on Saturday morning. When I went he was not there and I left a note for him, but by that time, although I did not know it till the Monday morning he was already dead.

He was a man of the most lovable character and disposition and a real poet. I spent last night awake praying for his soul. His poor mother got back here this morning and is now in this hotel. I have a sort of consolation in the remembrance that when I was in prison I offered my suffering for the souls in purgatory, and that as he was so affected by my poem (although not a Catholic) somehow this may help him. Is this fantastic?

I am sure he didn't commit suicide. Undoubtedly he was drunk. He was found upright in the canal with his hat on and his stick in his hand over his shoulder. I had some difficulty in inducing the civil authorities to delay his burial till his mother's arrival, as they told me at first that he *must* be buried this morning at 8 o'clock. But I persuaded them to wait and his mother is now arranging for his funeral. Say a prayer for him.[24]

'Poor Roe was buried yesterday,' Bosie wrote to Pim on 17 October, 'to the accompaniment of an abbreviated and futile ceremony performed by the Protestant parson, who all the same is a very nice fellow and was very kind and sympathetic. But the whole thing filled me with unutterable sadness. I can't see how he *can* have saved his soul, and I certainly get no light on it as I did when my brother Percy died. But he *was* a Catholic of sorts and had extreme unction.'[25]

Bosie had felt unwell in Bruges which he attributed, probably wrongly, to blood poisoning resulting from his sufferings in Wormwood Scrubs. However he distinctly improved in Brussels. 'I am better since I came here, and have now got a clever doctor who is giving me High Frequency electric treatment,' he wrote to Sorley Brown towards the end of October. 'He says there is nothing seriously wrong with me and that I have the heart of a young man. He measured my heart-beats [i.e. took his blood pressure] with a sort of clock arrangement communicating with a rubber pad pressed tightly round my wrist and said *"Magnifique!"* So I suppose my heart is so good I can't be such a wreck as I sometimes feel.' At the same time, as he added a few days later, 'I am getting horribly tired of being out here. I have no friends here and there is nothing to do, and also I feel it is dull and uncomfortable for my mother. But we shall have to stick it out here till Xmas for financial reasons.'[26] However he was much encouraged by the publication of *In Excelsis* in book form, which Martin Secker brought out in December, due not to the efforts of Alfred Rose, to whom the poem was dedicated, but to those of the literary agent Curtis Brown; he also placed it in America, although the literary agent could only get £30 for the British serial rights from J.C. (later Sir John) Squire in *The London Mercury*, who published it in the October issue. Incidentally Bosie was puzzled as to why Squire should have omitted the poem's first stanza, but it was no doubt on account of the author's anti-Semitic reference.

> Torment of body, torment of mind,
> Pain, hunger, insult, stark ingratitude
> Of those for whom we fought, detraction rude
> But sanctimonious, cruel to be kind,
> (Truly for bread a stone): all these we find
> In this our self-appointed hell whose food
> Is our own flesh. To what imagined good
> Have we thus panted, beaten, bound and blind?
>
> God knows, God knows. And since He knows indeed,
> Why there's the answer: who would stay outside
> When God's in prison? Who would rather choose
> To warm himself with Peter than to bleed
> With Dismas penitent and crucified
> Facing with Christ the fury of the Jews?

In January 1925, while Sibyl Queensberry returned to London to her Kensington house, which had apparently been let, Bosie went down to Bormes, near Hyères on the French Riviera, to stay with his friend, the explorer Harry de Windt, and later a millionaire friend called Steadman, who had a villa in the same neighbourhood. March found him staying at a pension in Nice where, as he wrote to Sorley Brown, Frank Harris, who was living there with his wife, was 'making desperate efforts to get at me.... So far I have declined to have anything to do with him.' What eventually happened Bosie recounted in a later letter to Brown:

> Finally he [Harris] sent a man I knew [Mr Wade Chance] to say that he had discovered quite by chance that his *Life and Confessions of Oscar Wilde* contained a mass of lies and misrepresentations about me, all of which had been dictated to him by Robert Ross or by Wilde himself, and he begged me to meet him so that he might put right the bitter injustice he had done me. Therefore I consented to meet him, and in the end I stayed for 3 weeks at his flat and went through the whole book with him.
>
> In the result he has written a new preface (about 50 pages) in which he admits that practically everything he says about me in his book is untrue and that *De Profundis* is a 'malevolent and lying caricature of the facts.' He is now arranging for the publication of the preface and a revised edition of his book in England.[27]

Douglas's first meeting with Harris was as the luncheon guests of Wade Chance, a well-to-do American socialite, who owed his position to an older wife of considerable means, a great-niece of Washington Irving. Wade Chance, whom the present writer knew in his later years, liked to move in 'Society' which he did, since he had been presented at Court in the reign of Edward VII, and although he was considerably impoverished by his wife's death he continued to be a guest in many great houses both in England, America and the Riviera. On this occasion, however, he was the host, and the meeting led to the result described by Bosie in his letter to Sorley Brown quoted above.

According to Harris, Bosie began by admitting at Chance's lunch that he had been misled into attacking him. 'But you showed venomous dislike to me in your book on Oscar Wilde,' Bosie went on. Harris asked for instances, and, to quote him, 'he soon convinced me that I had misrepresented him again and again through believing Wilde and Ross. The end of it was that he came to stay with me with documents in hand and threw a new light on many occurrences that I had not presented fairly. I found that I had been misled by Oscar Wilde, first, and afterwards by Robert Ross, and in both cases with forethought and deliberate malice.'

Immediately after the lunch with Wade Chance, Bosie wrote the letter from which extracts have been quoted above, in which he described for the first time the precise nature of his sexual relations with Wilde. He concluded by assuring Harris that he was at liberty to make any use he liked of this letter and that he had no objection to its being published, a rash assurance of which, as will be seen, Harris was to take full advantage when it suited him.[28]

Meanwhile Harris wrote in the preface:

> It may be asked, if I wish to repair the wrong I have done Douglas, why not rewrite the book, *The Life and Confessions of Oscar Wilde*. Simply because it is Lord Alfred's opinion as well as mine, indeed first suggested to me by him, to leave Wilde's misstatements and Bosie's untruths, and contradict them both, allowing, in Milton's phrase, truth to wrestle with falsehood.
>
> Now, when I review the whole case, I have to admit that in many essentials I misjudged Lord Alfred Douglas again and again, and did him grave injustice. My excuse is that I trusted Oscar Wilde's word in the main, especially when it was supported by Robert Ross, who, as I first learned from Douglas in 1925, had annexed after Wilde's death all Douglas's letters to Wilde and used them against him in suit after suit relentlessly.[29]

The original idea was that the Preface should be a joint venture, at least to the extent that Harris would embody in it the letter that Bosie had written correcting Harris's more blatant errors and misstatements. On this understanding Bosie returned to England where he stayed with his mother in Horn's Lodge, Tonbridge, a house which she had taken from her relative Lord Eglinton. No sooner was Bosie established there than Harris wrote to say that he would prefer to write the whole Preface himself. To this Bosie good-naturedly agreed: indeed he thought it would be better if Harris did so. But when he received Harris's revised version, he was bound to criticise it:

> The two blemishes in your preface as it stands are that (1) while still leaving my attack on my father's character, you have cut out all my justification for the attack; (2) you have omitted all my reply to *De Profundis* and have not said a word about its falsity on your own account.
>
> I have tried to remedy the first blemish by altering (only as suggestions of course) your text in the matter about my father. If you put it as I have altered it, it may serve fairly well.
>
> As regards *De Profundis* please try and get in a few words embodying my answer to Oscar's wild accusations. I answered them in my letter to you in the first Preface. You might especially repudiate his accusation that I got money from him. If I had ever got any money from him (leaving out the give and take of a fiver here and there), it would have appeared in my pass book, whereas in his pass book there is only one cheque to me of £15 (repayment of

a loan made in Algiers), while in my pass book, produced at the Ransome trial, there appears £390 given to him in one year (as well as £360 paid for his law costs). You might also point out the lying nature of his accusation that he never did good work when I was with him which is of course the exact opposite to the truth. Having convicted him of flagrant lying on these two points, the rest of his diatribe can be left to the judgement of impartial readers.[30]

Bosie added that Harris's book could not be published in England as it stood, even with the original Preface, unless it were rewritten in the sense of the corrections which Bosie had made to the text when they went through it together. The other objectors to whom he had shown it included the publishers Martin Secker and Grant Richards, R.D. Blumenfeld, editor of the *Daily Express*, as well as Bosie's solicitors and his nephew Francis Queensberry. In the event Harris refused.

'My dear Frank', Bosie replied, 'I am sorry that, if you will not re-write your book on Wilde, we are at a dead lock. Even if I wished, I could not consent to its coming out in England in its present form. I find that the feeling among my friends and family is too strong on this point. It is impossible that, for example, your utterly untrue and frightful account of my first meeting with Wilde should stand, and there are dozens of other passages all of which at your request I marked and made marginal notes on. Unless it is completely altered in all these particulars I cannot allow it to appear in England. As it stands it is full of lies as you have yourself admitted. . . . So if you won't alter the book, it will perhaps be best to leave things as they are. Or bring it out if you like and let me prosecute [the English publisher]. That would suit me just as well, except that I should not like to be forced into a fight with you. Because when all is said, in spite of the frightful injury you have done me (the extent of which you still don't seem to realise), I like you and want to remain friendly with you.'[31]

Harris's response was to threaten to publish the candid and compromising letter Bosie had written to him about his sexual relations with Wilde. This infuriated Bosie, who had by this time moved back with his mother from Horn's Lodge to her house in Kensington. He now sat down and told Frank Harris what he thought of him and his conduct:

> 16 Draycott Place,
> SW3
> 16 September 1925

Dear Harris,
  I have been re-reading and thinking over your last letter with

its blackmailing threat about the letter I gave you concerning my relations with Wilde during the three years before his conviction. I wrote that letter, as you know, as an act of the very highest moral courage to serve as a basis for you as the more or less official biographer of Wilde, so that you privately might know the exact truth (bad enough I admit but a great deal less bad than you in your black malice and vindictive spite has made it out to be). To write such a letter and give it to a man of your character was, of course, from a worldly point of view, the height of folly on my part. Nevertheless as my actions are not, and never have been, dictated by considerations of worldly wisdom, I don't regret it. I would rather put myself right by telling the truth, even to a heartless enemy, than pose as the possessor of virtue I did not pretend to have all those years ago. The immorality I was guilty of took place more than thirty years ago. I have long since bitterly repented it, you have gone on living like a hog all your life and glorying in it and making money by it. You talk about the effect of my letter to you about my relations with Wilde would produce before a jury. Well, I know a great deal more about juries than you do, and I can tell you that if you produced my letter in a law court and put it to me in cross-examination, I would turn it into a two-edged sword for my own justification and your utter damnation. It would just about add six months to your sentence.

And what about the effect of reading a few passages from your filthy book *My Life and Loves*? What would a jury think of that? Also how would you like it if I were to start and do [to] you what you have done to me, namely write and publish all I know about your private life, while strictly confining myself, as you have *not* done, to the truth? I know, for example, the details of some of the things you did at Eze (I am not referring to your getting two thousand pounds out of me in my youth in exchange for 'dud' shares in your restaurant and casino with an alleged, but really non-existent, gambling concession attached to it). I am referring to other things.

When you have the infernal impudence to write to me as you do and complain about the expense you have been put to in making the corrections of your self-admitted lies from material supplied by me at your own urgent request, you ignore the fact that you have already made thousands of pounds by selling your disgusting book with its filthy and deliberate lies about me.

Go to, Frank Harris; you are a clumsy fool as well as a rogue. I wash my hands of you. I tried the effect of generosity and kindness on you, but it was simply 'casting pearls to hogs'. I shall take care to let my friends at Nice know the line you have taken up and the way you turned on me with blackmailing menace directly you found you were not going to have things all your own way. Meanwhile you can do what you please about your preface.

I have the original with your own autograph corrections and signature and I also have your letter admitting that practically everything about me in your book is false and humbly apologizing. I want nothing more.

Yours et cet,
ALFRED DOUGLAS

P.S. I am keeping a copy of this letter.[32]

In the result Bosie got the Fortune Press, a small firm in London, to publish Harris's original Preface with his own letter under the title *New Preface to 'The Life and Confessions of Oscar Wilde'* as being 'by Frank Harris and Lord Alfred Douglas'. It was meagrely noticed in the English press because the publishers did not send out more than a few review copies, but Bosie was mistaken in thinking that it was deliberately boycotted. Harris was living largely from the royalties from his pornographic autobiography *My Life and Loves*. Hoping to supplement his dwindling income and increasing debts due to poor health and the medical care he needed, he got an American publisher, Covici Friede, to reprint his Wilde biography with Shaw's 'Memories of Oscar Wilde' and Bosie's letter on the subject of his physical relations with Wilde. Bosie subsequently complained to Shaw that Harris had 'added (or forged) a permission to publish the letter which was not contained in it.' Bosie was wrong, since in fact he had given Harris permission as evidenced by the original of the relevant letter which is still in existence. ('You are at liberty to make any use you like of this letter. I have no objection to it being published.')[33]

Meanwhile Bosie continued to prosecute any retail bookseller who sold Harris's book, one offender again being Harrods from whom he obtained £200 damages. However, Harris's death in 1931 left his wife very badly off, and in an endeavour to help her Bernard Shaw asked Douglas if he would allow its publication in England and America with a preface by himself on the understanding (at least by Bosie) that Harris's errors and misstatements should be corrected. This was largely done in Shaw's fifty-two-page preface, Shaw having arranged with his own publishers Constable in London and Dodd, Mead in New York for simultaneous publication. 'This will involve their [Dodd, Mead] buying out Covici and buying up their reprint, which could hardly be worse from your point of view,' Shaw told Bosie. 'When it is got rid of (pulped) the smugglers can get nothing but my edition, which will be equally available in Constable's edition, so that there will be no point in smuggling it.'[34]

The work was published in one volume on 18 July 1938 as *Oscar Wilde*, without Harris's sub-title: *His Life and Confessions*. 'I think this Newgate Calendar sub-title should be dropped,' Shaw wrote on the proof of the title page. 'It was one of Frank's less reputable tricks.' Nearly a hundred pages, which had appeared in the original two-volume edition, were omitted, including some of the suppressed portions of *De Profundis*. Also Bosie's poems 'Two Loves' and 'In Praise of Shame', Robert Ross's 'Criticisms' and Shaw's 'Memories of Oscar Wilde', together euphemistically described by Shaw as 'a few emendations which are now needed to prevent its misleading readers to whom the subject is new.' Otherwise Harris's text remained unchanged, except for the omission of some of Wilde's vitriolic denunciations of Bosie and the charge that it was Bosie who had introduced him to the male prostitution of London.[35]

In his preface, with the aid of Sherard's biography which sticks to the facts, Shaw differentiated between fact and fantasy, particularly in regard to Wilde's alleged conversations with Harris on homosexuality and other matters, which, though imaginary in their wording, Shaw accepted as being true in substance. At the same time Shaw stuck to his original view that Harris's book was 'the best life of Wilde, whose memory will have to stand or fall by it.'

Bosie complained that Shaw had not referred among other things to Harris's accusation when he met Bosie at Chantilly that Bosie had 'run down' *The Ballad of Reading Gaol*. 'It is of no importance in comparison with the main drift of the edition, which clears you for the first time of your father's innuendo,' Shaw replied, 'and of the reproach for having left Wilde penniless, besides giving you your proper prominence in the tragedy. Be content with that.... It is your cure to back this edition up for all you are worth. At least it does not ignore you.

'Besides critically (you have some reputation as a critic to lose) Harris's book has very considerable literary merit in its Plutarchian way; and its effect is, on the whole, true as corrected as far as you are concerned. It was always true of Wilde.'[36]

6

'I am so far from regretting my imprisonment or from having any ill feelings against those who are responsible for it, that I can truly say that I regard it as the best thing that ever happened to me,' Bosie wrote in his preface to *In Excelsis*. 'That is not to say that I did not suffer a great deal. I did suffer, more especially in a spiritual way, to an extent that I would not have believed to be possible, consistently with remaining alive: but what I think about this is better expressed in the poem than I could explain it in a hundred pages of prose.'

At the same time he became aware of the change in attitude of 'Society' towards him, particularly after he had returned to England from what was to prove his abortive meeting with Frank Harris over the Wilde biography.

> All of a sudden everyone I met, wherever I went, began to be kind and amiable. This was entirely due to the sympathy which my imprisonment and sufferings aroused. The English are like that. They have very little imagination, and they will go on behaving in a perfectly brutal way for years to a man, not out of ill-nature, for really they are the most good-hearted and kindly people *au fond*, but simply, as I say, from want of imagination and because they have never taken the trouble to find out the facts about the man in question for themselves, but have been hypnotized by parrot cries and mass suggestion. Then one day insensibly the scale tips in the other direction, probably as the result of a long process whose details are hidden in obscurity.[37]

As Bosie's biographer Rupert Croft-Cooke has pointed out, this was a very characteristic way of saying that Bosie himself had become more amenable and was no longer involved in the litigious strife which bored most of his friends and frightened others. If 'the English' felt anything about it at all, it was the admiration they always have for a good loser. Instead of coming out of prison spitting venom and swearing revenge, he spoke of his ordeal with amusement and also wrote of it as he did in the preface to *In Excelsis* and also in his second autobiographical work *Without Apology* (1938) where he gives a more detailed account of his experiences in Wormwood Scrubs than he does in the first. Here he makes one particularly interesting point, fortunately no longer valid. Although it was not etiquette in prison to ask another prisoner what he was 'in for', a great number of Bosie's fellow inmates, in spite of the ban on talking, confided in him the nature of their misdemeanours. 'Bigamy was the fashionable offence. About half the men in my Hall were in for bigamy, which is the poor man's substitute for divorce. If they had been rich or well-to-do, these prisoners would have got divorces, but being poor they resorted to bigamy.'[38]

When he got back to his mother's house from Nice in May 1925, Bosie found a letter from his son Raymond whom he had not seen for nearly ten years asking for his forgiveness, 'which of course I gave him,' Bosie told Sorley Brown. 'I have now seen him and spent a great part of two days with him. He is very nice, poor boy, and he now realises that he was fed with lies and calumnies about me and his eyes have at last been opened to all the villainies of which we have both been the victims. This reconciliation is a great comfort to me.'[39] Three months later he wrote to Frank Harris from Horns Lodge, the house which Sibyl Queensberry had taken near Tonbridge:

> I have had my son Raymond here for the past week and he is coming back here again tomorrow. He is a nice, dear boy and has now found out how wickedly he was deceived about me by his grandfather and others. He was in the Scots Guards for a few months and though now he has left he still remains on the Reserve of Officers and is entitled to be considered in the Guards and belongs to the Guards Club. It has been a great consolation to me to be friends with him again after all these years.[40]

Raymond's premature retirement from the Scots Guards was due to medical reasons, since he was apparently considered not mentally fit enough to continue on the active list, a condition which was unfortunately to increase.

In January 1926 Bosie took his son to Nice for a short holiday and when he was there Raymond met a twenty-three year old English girl named Gladys Lacey. Her father, who was now dead, had kept a grocer's shop in Oswestry, Shropshire, and her mother, who had been left almost penniless, managed a small pub in the same town. Raymond fell in love with her and wished to marry her. Such an inappropriate alliance was strongly opposed by both Raymond's parents and also by his grandmother, the Dowager Lady Queensberry. In the result Raymond was prevented from marrying Gladys Lacey and the incident may have contributed to the deterioration in his mental condition. In August 1927 he was admitted to St Andrew's Hospital, Northampton, the best-known private mental institution of its kind at that time, suffering from schizophrenia, for which he was treated by electro-convulsive therapy and narcosis. When he was well, he was allowed to go about in Northampton, where he was said to be well-liked and 'full of jokes', and also by train to London and elsewhere to see his parents and grandmother. He would, too, go to race meetings with his father whose interest in horses and betting he shared. But his condition remained unstable, and although he was twice de-certified for short periods, he was eventually to return to St Andrew's in November 1944 and to spend the remaining twenty years of his life there.[41] St Andrew's was a fee-paying institution, but the charges in Raymond's case, which were defrayed by the Custance family, were certainly not exorbitant, those when he first entered in

1927 being six guineas a week, including accommodation, food and medical treatment, and when he again became a patient in 1946, the charges despite the Second World War had only increased to ten guineas weekly.[42]

One particular friend which Bosie made at this time was the twenty-six-year-old eccentric Albert James Alroy Symons, founder of the First Edition Club, an authority on the characters and literature of the eighteen nineties, and the author of *Frederick Baron Corvo*, which developed into his fascinating biography *The Quest for Corvo*, with which he made his name in the contemporary literary world. His acquaintance with Bosie began with a letter from him to Bosie on the bibliography of the nineties and quickly ripened into friendship, stimulated by the fact that Bosie was a compulsive letter writer. He was generally known as 'A.J.' but Bosie preferred to call him 'Ajaccio'. They took to each other immediately, particularly when Symons told Bosie that he hoped to follow up his life of the pseudonymous Baron Corvo with a biography of Wilde. Unfortunately this project, on which he obtained much help from Bosie, was never completed, the only part of it being several short chapters which appeared in the magazine *Horizon*, under the editorship of Cyril Connolly. He was also a moving spirit in the foundation of the Wine and Food Society, which appealed to Bosie who was always a gourmet. For his part Ajaccio greatly admired Bosie's verse. He once entertained Bosie and two other guests for dinner in a famous London club of which he had recently become a member. In the result he was called before the Committee and admonished for bringing into the club a man who had been in prison. 'If I cannot dine here with a major living British poet,' he replied, 'I shall resign.' And he did so. He later joined the Savile, where the Committee was not so particular. Bosie stayed with Ajaccio on occasion at his house in Finchingfield in Essex, where he had a magnificent collection of musical boxes, mostly Victorian.[43]

The year 1926 also saw the publication of Bosie's *Collected Satires* under the imprint of The Fortune Press which had also published his *New Preface to 'The Life and Confessions of Oscar Wilde.'* This small publishing firm had recently been founded in Buckingham Palace Road by Reginald Caton, a strange shadowy figure, who ran it virtually single-handed for forty-five years. Among other authors, he published Cecil Day Lewis, Kingsley Amis, Cecil Roberts, Dylan Thomas, and Montague Summers, besides several works which contravened the obscenity laws, out of which he did not fare badly since he left £130,000 at his death, having published some six hundred books.[44] Bosie's *Collected Satires* was a handsome production on handmade paper, printed by Maurice Darantière in France, who had also printed the original edition of James Joyce's *Ulysses*. Bosie was very pleased with the way in which the satires had been produced, but he complained that the book was not reviewed. This was because only one review copy had been sent out, to *The Times Literary Supplement* where in fact it was reviewed, albeit somewhat belatedly, although some of the satires were plainly defamatory, such as 'The Rhyme of F Double E' (Lord Birkenhead) and 'To a Certain Judge', the judge being clearly recognisable as Mr Justice Avory who had sent Bosie to prison for six months for libelling Winston Churchill. In the sonnet 'All's Well with England', which he wrote in 1916 and included in the satires, there were offensive references to the Asquiths, 'merry Margot' being 'crowned with Lesbian fillets', while her husband 'Old Squiffy', then Prime Minister, 'hands the purse to Robert Ross', both sitting at home when 'out there in Flanders the trampled ground is red with English blood.'

The following year witnessed some further publicity from Bosie. He had heard that a large collection of letters and other manuscripts relating to Oscar Wilde were to be offered for sale by Messrs Dulau & Co, then a firm of bookdealers in Bond Street, and that they contained references to himself. The collection, which comprised 342 items, consisted for the greater part of Wilde's letters to Robert Ross from Reading prison but also a considerable quantity of manuscript poems, plays and letters formerly in the possession of Robert Ross and Christopher Millard (Stuart Mason) which had been left to Wilde's younger surviving son, Vyvyan Holland, who decided to sell them. Dulau's could not print the extracts from this extremely important material particularly the letters that they wished without first obtaining Bosie's permission for fear of being sued for libel. This permission Bosie gave after he had examined the manuscripts 'in view of their historical and self-revealing interest', Dulau's stated in their catalogue, adding that Lord Alfred Douglas considered that his consent was 'sufficiently indicative of the attitude he takes up towards the references to himself which they contain.' This was the first occasion on which Bosie saw the letter from Wilde to Ross of 1 April 1897 from Reading, the only letter known to exist in which Wilde gave explicit instructions about the *De Profundis* manuscript. ('The copy done and verified from the manuscript, the original should be despatched to A.D. by More [Adey].')[45]

When he had read this letter, Bosie considered that, quite apart from the copyright position, he was entitled to possession of the *De Profundis* letter, since it was addressed to him, particularly in view of Wilde's written instructions. Robert Ross, on the other hand, as we have seen, felt that he had no right to it since he had never obtained possession of it. Alas, as it will be recalled, Ross, in presenting the MS to the British Museum, definitely stated that when Wilde handed it to him on the day after his release from prison, he requested Ross to keep it for possible publication after his death, and that he was to have two typewritten copies made, one of which should be sent to Bosie. Wilde may conceivably have changed his written instructions orally when Ross was staying with him at Berneval, about the time Ross states that he sent the typed copy to Douglas, but if the instructions were changed it was certainly not at the time Wilde handed the MS to Ross when he arrived in Dieppe, as is shown by Wilde's reference to it in letters which he subsequently wrote to Ross.[46]

On 27 January 1927, the *Daily Express* ran a story on its front page headed:

OSCAR WILDE MANUSCRIPT
LORD ALFRED DOUGLAS CLAIMS POSSESSION

'I am sure the Museum authorities will see the justice of my claim,' Bosie stated optimistically in an interview. 'I don't anticipate any difficulty and my request will be made in the friendliest possible way.'

The request was so made on a number of occasions. But the Museum authorities felt that in the circumstances of its acceptance they had no right to hand it over, although Lord Hailsham, the father of the present peer, who had been one of the ex-officio Trustees of the Museum when he was Lord Chancellor, thought he had a good claim to it. In the result Bosie never got it. Nor did his literary executor, Mr Edward Colman, fare any better, although he tried hard and was prepared to leave the manuscript in the custody of the Museum (now the British Library) if the authorities would concede the Douglas estate's right to its ownership. But this they have always declined to do. However, as far as the public is concerned, the manuscript has been available for general examination since 1 January 1960.[47]

VII

The Final Phase

1

By this time Bosie's mother had sold the lease of her house in Draycott Place and, after a brief spell in Limpsfield, Surrey, they moved to Hove, eventually settling in 35 Fourth Avenue, which was to remain Bosie's home until shortly before the Dowager Lady Queensberry's death in 1935. Meanwhile Bosie had begun to write his autobiography, a project facilitated by two friends lending him a large quiet room in their house in Brunswick Square. Here he completed the autobiography which was published by Martin Secker in March 1929 in a handsome production of 340 small quarto pages, illustrated by nine family portraits, six of which are of Bosie by himself and one with Oscar Wilde at Oxford. It was a sincere and passionately written work, and although it began conventionally enough with a chronological account of his boyhood and youth, when he came to his relations with Wilde, he spoiled the effect to some extent by his prejudices particularly against Robert Ross and Frank Harris. Consequently anyone who relies on it for a faithful account of Bosie's life is apt to be misled by his distortions of the facts. Nevertheless it was published in America, Germany and France (where it had an extra chapter about his literary associations there) as well as in England, where it went into a second edition after 10,000 copies had been sold, and from the commercial point of view it was no doubt his most successful publication. It is obvious that he tried to be truthful and sincere; certainly he made no attempt to conceal the true nature of his physical relations with Wilde and he regretted the denials he had felt obliged for the sake of his family to make in his earlier *Oscar Wilde and Myself.*

'I have been very nervous about my book, because no such ruthless candour has been exhibited in a book before,' he wrote to Sorley

Brown to whom it was dedicated.

> I think if one writes an autobiography, it ought to be *really* true, otherwise it is better not to write it at all. If I have said that I was good-looking in my youth, I have only done it because it is true, and because it is absolutely essential to the story. It is not vanity. But I can't expect the average journalist and reviewer (of whose work I enclose a sample) to understand my motives.
>
> I am trying to break down certain barriers. I want to make it easier for those who come after to tell the truth even when it is (as often in my case) dreadfully against themselves. I would rather everyone knew the truth now about me (good and bad) than that it should all be bottled up till the day of judgment. I hope my story will save and help thousands of young people. I also hope it will throw light on the dark places of English schools and colleges where to keep virtuous is made utterly impossible.[1]

On the whole *The Autobiography of Lord Alfred Douglas*, to give the work its full title, had a good press and the majority of the reviews were favourable. There were of course some exceptions. Although the one in *The Times* damned it with faint praise, that in the same paper's *Literary Supplement* was flattering. What particularly irked the author was Desmond MacCarthy's 'peculiarly offensive' notice in the *New Statesman*, in which the reviewer described him as a 'minor poet', adding that no critic placed him higher than that. 'Of course he [MacCarthy] is a mere little shit and has no qualifications at all,' Bosie remarked to Sorley Brown. 'He has made his way by toadying and log-rolling.'[2] However that may be, Desmond MacCarthy seems to have disapproved of other poets, some better-known and more popular than Bosie, such as the great Lord Tennyson, an anthology of whose poetic works he was later to decry in an equally disparaging review in *The Sunday Times*.

The advances on account of royalties on his autobiography were supplemented by a legacy of £1,000 from his friend Mr Griffiths-Masters, who had lent him the room in his house in Brunswick Square where the book was largely written and who died at this time. He also had a few hundreds a year from Olive. Thus for the first time for many years Bosie was relatively 'flush'. His poems were also republished in Paris at this time in a translation by Francis D'Avilla (Mme Fabienne Hillyard). In the additional chapter to the French edition (*Mes Fréquentations Littéraires A Paris*) Bosie recalled his associations with such writers as Stephane Mallarmé, the founder of the so-called Symbolist Movement in French literature, and other literary figures, some of whom he had met with Wilde, such as Paul Verlaine, J.K.

Huysmans, Pierre Louÿs, Marcel Schwob, Eugene Tardieu (the editor of *Echo de Paris*) who translated the first French edition of his poems published in *Mercure de France* in 1896, André Gide, Ernest La Jeunesse, and Sarah Bernhardt. Mallarmé had written him an enthusiastic letter when the poems first appeared ('One of the rare occasions on which I was happy to understand English was the day your Poems reached me.'). Unfortunately Mallarmé's letter was in a brief-case which was stolen while Bosie was travelling in a train between Monte Carlo and Antibes in 1905. Gide he remembered particularly because Wilde had described him as 'an egoist without an *ego*' who had reproached him for his moral, or rather immoral, conduct. 'He is a French Protestant,' Wilde had added. 'The worst type of Protestant except apparently the Irish.' Bosie recalled too how the last time he and La Jeunesse met, in 1903, La Jeunesse had said to him in an allusion to the prolongation of his youthful beauty: 'You are beginning to look like the picture of Dorian Gray!' On the same subject, Bosie resented how, when he met Sarah Bernhardt with Wilde, the great actress called him '*mon cher enfant*' and gave him a box of chocolates and told him to sit in a corner of the room, while she talked to Oscar. The latter was highly amused by this incident, but Bosie thought it was a painful slight on his '*amour-propre.*'

While he was arranging for the French version of his autobiography, Bosie had his attention drawn to a book by a certain Mme Lucie Delarue-Mardrus which had just appeared in Paris under the imprint of Flammarion entitled *Les Amours d'Oscar Wilde*. In it the authoress repeated many of the passages in Frank Harris' biography of Wilde to which Bosie had objected. Bosie's reaction he described in the additional chapter. He dashed over to Paris, saw the erring authoress in her house on the Quai Voltaire, and gave her copies of the English version of his autobiography as well as Frank Harris's *New Preface* to his own book. He described the result of his visit in the additional chapter in the French edition and also in a letter to Sorley Brown:

> After I had threatened legal proceedings the affair was settled in a friendly way. Flammarion withdrew the book from circulation and Madame Mardrus sat up all night correcting all the libels. Simultaneously with the appearance of this new edition of her book there are to appear in *Le Journal* (the paper with the largest circulation in Paris) a letter I wrote to Madame Delarue-Mardrus and her reply in which she admits her errors, apologises, and promises reparation.[3]

Unfortunately the authoress's description of Bosie as 'a ferocious young beast who would not let go of his prey' appeared in the corrected version of her book. When Bosie again complained, the lady replied that she would have been glad to change this reference, but that Bosie had not objected to it when he read the original text and the fact that she had retained it was his own fault. In these circumstances all that Bosie could do was to point out in the additional chapter that far from Wilde being his 'prey', it was rather the reverse, as writers like Tardieu had pointed out in articles at the time.

It was about this time in April 1930 that I received a letter from Bosie who had heard from the editor of *The New Age*, a London weekly to which I contributed and with which Bosie had some dealings, that I was occupying the same rooms in Magdalen College, Oxford, which Wilde had done fifty years before and which had subsequently been tenanted by Bosie's friend Encombe. I had told the editor that I should be glad to entertain Bosie in these rooms, should he feel inclined to come and meet me there. 'I should like to see them and Magdalen again before I die!', he consequently wrote to me. 'I have not been there for more than twenty years. I was asked a few months ago to make a speech or read a paper by the "Oxford University Poetry Society" and I more or less accepted but afterwards funked it and excused myself. Perhaps one day next month I might come down for the day if you would give me lunch?'

I have just got back from Paris where I have fixed up with *La Nouvelle Revue Francaise* to do the French translation of my autobiography. It will be out in the autumn with a *chapitre inedit* called '*Mes Fréquentations Littéraires à Paris*.' Also two facsimile letters of O.W.'s written to me from Berneval. *La Nouvelle Revue Francaise*, who are easily the best publishers in Paris, have also agreed to do a French edition of my poems. English text and French verse translation. I am rather pleased about this as I do not think any other living English poet has a French edition.[4]

In a subsequent letter written a few days later Bosie told me that he had backed out of the Oxford Poetry Society's invitation because he had been asked to speak on the poetry of the nineties and he did not think he had 'any particular message' in this context. He went on:

I do not consider that I belong to the 'nineties' movement at all. I always disliked and despised *The Yellow Book*, and except Lionel Johnson, who was a great friend of mine, I did not admire very much any of the writers of that period. However, since then I have promised to read some of my poems for the 'Catholic Poetry Society' of which I am a Vice-President. I hate reading my poems and in fact I have never done it. But I couldn't refuse when I was asked several times. I have now put it off to the autumn, making all sorts of insincere excuses! I expect if once I get started I shall go on.

I only made one speech in my life when I spoke about the Battle of Jutland and Winston Churchill for two hours in the Memorial Hall in Farringdon Street. The result was that I got 6 months imprisonment! But I discovered that I was a very good speaker which I didn't know before. I hope you have read my *Autobiography*?[5]

Indeed I had read his autobiography, and, if I remember right, I replied congratulating him on its having gone into a second edition. However, in the event Bosie never did come to Oxford in my time, since he went back to Paris to see his French publishers and while he was there he became ill and had to go into a nursing home for an operation. 'Please understand that this is quite a secret,' he wrote to Rupert Croft-Cooke from the home. 'My mother does not know anything about it![6] I had told him that it was my last term and he wrote that he was 'really distressed' to have to write that it was impossible for him to get to Oxford that term. 'If by any chance you will still be at Magdalen next term perhaps you will let me know,' he added. 'Anyhow I hope we may meet elsewhere,'[7] In fact, we did, at his house in Hove the following year, as is described below.

While I went abroad for some months on coming down, Bosie went to Galashiels to recuperate with his friend Sorley Brown. Although they had been corresponding since 1912, this was their first meeting. It was a happy one, mostly spent trout fishing. 'Lord Alfred is almost as proficient at dry-fly fishing as he is at writing sonnets,' his friend wrote afterwards in *The Scottish Field*. 'Many a fine basket we have caught from the Tweed....' Sorley Brown also took Bosie to Abbotsford, where Sir Walter Maxwell Scott showed them the Waverley treasures. 'In the evening, warm and still,' Bosie recalled, 'we had dinner in the dining room overlooking the river, and at a late hour were ferried across to the opposite bank, where a car was waiting to take us to Galashiels.'[8]

Now, as the evening of his life approached, Bosie became temperamentally calmer and much less quarrelsome and inclined to litigation than he had been. Frank Harris he could never bring himself to forgive, but he made it up with Sherard, with whom he became very friendly. Most of his other enemies had passed on, and Frank Harris was to do so in 1931. Meanwhile Bosie could afford to look back on his past battles with a sense of nostalgia and forgiveness. 'I see tonight that Birkenhead is dead,' he wrote on 30 September 1930, a few days before his sixtieth birthday. (Birkenhead was only fifty-eight when he died of pneumonia.) 'Poor man he must have suffered a lot in these last few months. He was almost the last of the gang that Crosland and I fought and beat in 1914. Ross, George Lewis, F.E. Smith, Millard, all dead, and More Adey in a lunatic asylum.'[9]

On 24 November, he wrote to Rupert Croft-Cooke:

> I gave an 'address' and a recital of my poems to the Catholic Poetry Society last Tuesday. I had quite an ovation and very nice speeches about me by Padraic Gregory and Shane Leslie. They both called me 'the greatest living poet.' I was really quite overwhelmed, being more used to abuse than praise!

This was some consolation for John Squire's slighting reference to him as a minor poet. 'I was entranced by his nostalgic sonnet about Oscar Wilde – one of the most moving sonnets in English,' Shane Leslie wrote of the occasion. 'It was not only because we were sorry for him but because his poetry rang true that we were glad to give him an ovation.'[10]

In the same letter to Croft-Cooke, Bosie said that he was probably going over to Paris as the French translation of his autobiography was coming out there in the following week. 'I shall be rather thrilled to see it spread about all over the Boulevards.'

Croft-Cooke's subsequent comment on this admission from a man of sixty, so long after he had met 'Florifer' on those same boulevards, was that he found it a touching one, as well he might.

2

My postponed meeting with Bosie took place on 19 May 1931 in the house at 34 Fourth Avenue in Hove, where he was then living with his mother. 'I have a young Oxonian coming to lunch on Tuesday,' Bosie had written to his friend A.J.A. Symons. 'His name is Montgomery Hyde (late of Magdalen) and I have not yet met him. He wrote a good article about O.W. in the *New Age* the other day, at the head of which he quoted my sonnet.' The sonnet was 'The Dead Poet', which Bosie had written in the year after Wilde's death. The article was a review of the first popular edition of Wilde's collected works in a single volume of some 1,200 pages, price half-a-guinea, which in spite of a few omissions, such as *The Soul of Man Under Socialism* and *De Profundis*, I felt justified in describing as 'a triumph of modern publishing', working out as it did at rather more than ten pages a penny.[11]

'I thought it very well done,' he kindly wrote to me about the review. 'I am glad you quoted my sonnet. I think the false and malicious story that I "deserted" Wilde or "ruined" him or treated him badly in any way which was invented by Ross and carried on by the "faithless blood hound" (otherwise Frank Harris) has at last been more or less exploded. The real truth is of course that the boot was very much on the other leg.'

Part of a Letter from Douglas to the author written 11 May 1931.

I travelled down from London on the Brighton Belle, a comfortable and spacious Pullman train quickly abolished by British Rail when it took over Britain's railways. I arrived about one o'clock and we had lunch almost immediately after a preliminary glass of sherry, and an excellent meal it was – smoked salmon, chicken, meringues, a bottle of wine apiece, liqueurs and coffee, accompanied by incessant talk, chiefly about Bosie himself. His mother did not appear as he told me that 'she did not come down to lunch'. After the meal, there were cigarettes, more coffee and talk. At the same time my host showed me some of Wilde's letters to him which he had kept, also letters he had had from my Magdalen contemporary, John Betjeman, the future Poet Laureate, who had begun to correspond with him when he was a boy at Marlborough school, but had to desist, Bosie said, when Betjeman's parents discovered Bosie's identity and promptly stopped the correspondence.

He spoke at length about Wilde and *De Profundis*, Robert Ross, Asquith, Frank Harris and others, as already related in this book, so that it is unnecessary to repeat it, except to emphasise his assertion that he stuck to Wilde when everyone among his so-called friends had deserted him. 'The true facts of the case are at last coming to be recognised,' he said. Much of our conversation took place when we walked into Brighton in the afternoon and sat on the pier until the wind drove us away and so back to Hove for tea. I thought he looked 'remarkably boyish' – in fact considerably younger than I had expected. 'To get on with him at all,' I noted at the time, 'you must be a good listener and sufficiently "up" in his affairs to appreciate all the points in the Wilde business. He is a good talker and there is something about him which compels attention. He has indeed suffered, and with his air of nervous excitability he gives one the impression that he still labours under many injuries.' I was particularly struck by his charm, good manners, and affability as a host. He told me that he still liked to bet on horse races, although to nothing like the extent that he once did. He proudly added that, a few days previously, he had won £37 10s on a two shilling double.

Before I left he mentioned that he had recently sued Harrods for selling a copy of Frank Harris's biography in which Bosie was grossly libelled, and he had been awarded £100 damages, as mentioned above, and he managed to obtain possession of the offending copy, which a friend of Bosie's had bought. This Bosie gave me as a souvenir of my visit. He also gave me nicely inscribed copies of his *Collected Poems* and the French edition of his autobiography with the additional chapter in which he said he had dealt with André Gide, who had also libelled him in his book *Si le Grain ne meurt*. When I asked him what he thought of this author, Bosie replied: 'Gide is a shit! Like a person who has an abcess on his bottom and continuously displays it to the world.'

Finally he showed me a letter which he had received a few weeks previously from Bernard Shaw, to whom he had written complaining that Shaw's contribution to Frank Harris's biography of Wilde in the form of a letter containing his recollections of Wilde conveyed the impression that Shaw was 'endorsing and countersigning Harris's malicious lies and misrepresentations?' At the same time Bosie sent Shaw a photograph of himself at the time of their Café Royal meeting. In his reply to Bosie, Shaw stated that he had deleted all his references to him in the letter which appeared as an appendix in Harris's book in case he should republish it. 'They were not unjust as statements of what we felt at the time,' Shaw added. 'Your hatred of your father may have been very natural, and richly deserved; but you were very young then; and if you had been older and unblinded by that passion, you would have made Oscar ignore the card left at the club as the act of a notorious lunatic lord, and clear out before the police could be moved to proceed. Consequently we were all rather down on you at the time. Harris's advice was sound.'

In the same letter, Shaw, who wrote from the Grand Hotel in Venice, said he thought it was a pity that Wilde still tempted men to write lives of him. He went on:

> It is inevitable that you should appear in these biographies as a sort of *âme damnée* beside him, not in the least because you were a beautiful youth who seduced him into homosexuality (how enormously better for him if you had: you might have saved him from his wretched debaucheries and guttersnipes!) but because you were a lord and he was a snob. Judging from the suppressed part of *De Profundis* (Carlos Blacker lent me his copy) I should say that you did one another far more harm socially than you could possibly have wrought by any extremity of sexual affection. You had much better have been at the street-corner, preaching Socialism.
>
> However, you need not worry. Your autobiography and your book anticipating the publication of *De Profundis* in full* (I have read both of them attentively) have made your position quite clear; and you need not fear that any biographer will be powerful enough to write you down. . . .
>
> Your picture has not been sent on to me. I shall find it in London on my return presently. I wonder, is there any man alive who would take such a step as defence against a diagnosis of narcissism![12]

Bosie next asked Shaw to write a preface to the new and cheaper edition of his autobiography, which Martin Secker was shortly bringing out, as it would help with the American publication. 'What! YOU among the preface hunters!' Shaw replied crushingly. 'Have you *no* self-respect?' However, Shaw added, 'you are quite welcome to print my letter, but not as a preface, nor in any way that would enable an American publisher to announce me as a contributor, or to play on me the trick you accuse Harris of playing. . . .'[13] And this is precisely what Bosie's publishers did both in London and New York.

Some time before this Douglas heard that a young writer named Patrick Braybrooke had written a short study of Wilde as a man of letters. Braybrooke's publisher warned him to be very careful about any references to Bosie he might make for fear of libel. In fact there were no references to Bosie in what he had written. Nevertheless Braybrooke sent the manuscript to Bosie who approved it and promptly invited its author to lunch. Their meeting was very much like my own, with a blustery walk along the sea front, except that

---

*Oscar Wilde and Myself (1914).

Braybrooke told Bosie that he would now like to write a book about him. To this Bosie, who found Braybrooke 'a very nice chap, gentle and unassuming', agreed with some reluctance. Braybrooke's book appeared in the autumn of 1931 under the imprint of Cecil Palmer, who had published Sorley Brown's biography of Crosland.

'I did not want Braybrooke to write my life at all,' Bosie said at the time of its publication. (He always wanted Sorley Brown to do it.) 'But I did not like to refuse permission as he is a poor man and depends entirely on his pen. I said I had no objection but could give him no more information than is already contained in my autobiography. He has merely re-hashed my autobiography.'[14] In fact, there was nothing new in it apart from a hitherto unpublished private letter about the Winston Churchill case from Bosie's counsel Cecil Hayes. In this Hayes referred to his description in his defence of 'a professional politician' like Churchill as 'an animal with the blood of a chameleon, the hide of a rhinoceros, a short memory, and the cheek of the devil.' This had been headlined in a prominent evening paper on the same day as his speech as 'Remarkable Oratory at the Old Bailey' but two days later, after the verdict, his speech had been described as 'scurrilous' and 'vitriolic' by the editor, who had evidently repented of his earlier opinion, possibly at the prompting of the paper's proprietor. Braybrooke's book also contained a friendly critique of its subject's poems which gave the faithful Sorley Brown the pretext for again lauding the poet's 'genius' in reviewing the book for the *Border Standard*.

Frank Harris died at his home in Nice in August 1931. When he heard the news, Bosie wrote to Symons on 3 September: 'Frank Harris's death removes the last of my enemies from this world.... I have had a Mass said for Harris.... I attended the Mass and prayed for his soul.'

Among his friends whom Bosie had recently got to know well was Lord Hailsham's step-son Edward Marjoribanks, the thirty-two-year-old barrister and MP for Eastbourne. Marjoribanks, who had had a brilliant career at Eton, where he was captain of the school, and at Oxford, where he got a 'double first' and was President of the Union, had written a successful life of the advocate Sir Edward Marshall Hall and in addition to his work at the Bar was now working on a life of Edward (Lord) Carson, of which the first volume had just been completed. This dealt with Carson's defence of Queensberry in the first of the three Wilde trials, and Marjoribanks, who had already appeared for Bosie in the courts, naturally consulted him on the subject. Unhappily Marjoribanks committed suicide in April 1932, the result, it was said at the time, of his having been jilted in a love affair. The news came as a great shock to Bosie. 'He was a friend of mine and junior counsel for me in my case against Harrods Stores when I got damages for Harris's book', Bosie wrote afterwards. 'I was dining at his home in Victoria Square only a month or two ago. He was going to try to get the MS of *De Profundis* for me and said, "I can almost promise that you shall have it." He was a most brilliant and charming fellow. It is dreadful.'[15]

In the following month Bosie eventually went up to Oxford again, his 'come-back', as he called the weekend he spent there after such a long absence. 'I am cheered by the thought that actually I am still an undergraduate as I never took my degree!'

> I stayed with young Richard Rumbold at Christ Church. He had a party for the 'leading undergraduates', from the literary point of view, to meet me, the editors of the university papers, the *Isis* and *Cherwell*, secretary of the Oxford University Dramatic Society (the OUDS), et cet: et cet, about 20 of them. They were all awfully nice to me and Rumbold tells me I made a great hit with them. I also met a lot more later at another party. I went to tea with Father D'Arcy, the leading Catholic at Oxford, at Campion Hall, the Jesuit House. I enjoyed it all immensely. I have written a sonnet about it which is to appear in this week's *Cherwell*.[16]

Richard Rumbold was a rich young Irish undergraduate; he was a nephew of the diplomatist Sir Horace Rumbold, whom Bosie had met in Cairo in 1893 while staying with the Cromers at the British Residency and Horace Rumbold was an attaché. Richard, who had been brought up as a Catholic, was something of an aesthete – he had his rooms in college wrecked by the 'hearties' and his furniture smashed and was also thrown in to the college fountain. But he liked Bosie and remained a faithful friend to him. At this time Richard began to keep a diary, from which it appears that in the summer of that year when he first met Bosie he was staying with his aunt May at Stacumny, her house in County Kildare. 'Today a letter came from Alfred Douglas saying that he was broke and homeless,' Richard noted on 6 August 1932. 'Very tragic. I offered to raise a public subscription for him, and asked May if she would put him up at my expense for a short time. She refused. What futile, shocking intolerance!'[17]

Bosie often grumbled about his poverty, and this was a typical example of his grumbling. In fact, he was neither 'broke' nor homeless at this time, and although his mother may have closed the house in Hove for a fortnight or so to give the servants a holiday, while she went to an hotel, the house was his home and he was to continue to live there for the next three years, after which he was to move to a nearby flat, for which his nephew Francis Queensberry paid the rent. Young Rumbold no doubt mistook Bosie's complaints as a direct appeal for money. 'There was a great deal of the child in him,' Richard Rumbold wrote in his own autobiography: 'his mood and the expression of his features would change from blank despair and depression to merriment.'

> There was also about him a kind of charming whimsical naivety – the whimsy of the ballads and the *Pongo Papers* – combined with a childish belief in angels, daily occurring miracles, and all the simpler aspects of Catholicism. As I was then violently anti-Catholic, this was the only topic on which we ever disputed. I did not mind his violent hatred of the Left, or even of all modern poetry, which he believed to be empty and formless, but about religion I felt as deeply as he, and I rarely renounced my point until I perceived him trembling with agony and rage. I must also confess that later on I grew embarrassed by his improvidence and his pathetic appeals for money.[18]

At Oxford, Richard Rumbold revived the English Club, which had lapsed. For the inaugural meeting, which took place in the Randolph Hotel on 26 October 1932, he invited Bosie as the first guest speaker. 'Despite the immense opposition the meeting was a howling success,' Rumbold noted in his diary, 'the hall being chock full, and the Press giving us many and favourable notices'. About four hundred people were present. Besides Bosie, Rumbold's guests at the dinner, which preceded the meeting, included among others the historian Philip Guedalla, the poet Edmund Blunden, and the economist Roy Harrod. 'Altogether a very enjoyable, profitable and successful evening,' was Rumbold's comment as chairman.[19]

3

At this time Bosie was working on a book, really a long essay, on Shakespeare's sonnets, and no doubt he mentioned the subject in his speech to the English Club in Oxford. The book was published by Martin Secker in the spring of 1933 under the title *The True History of Shakespeare's Sonnets* and it was dedicated to Olive. In it Bosie adopted and expanded the theory first put forward by the eighteenth-century Shakespearean critics Tyrwhitt and Malone and repeated with some fictitious embellishments by Wilde in his work *The Portrait of Mr W.H.* that the Master W.H., described by Shakespeare's publisher Thomas

Thorpe as the 'onlie begetter of these insuing sonnets' (first published by Thorpe in quarto in 1609, and so dedicated) was a young boy actor named Will Hughes or Hewes, as the name was alternatively spelled. The youth was supposed to have played the parts of some of the heroines in the plays, since in Shakespeare's time female parts were always taken by males, usually boys, and never by women who were debarred at this time from performing on the stage.

Bosie strongly rejected the charge advanced by Samuel Butler, Frank Harris and Arnold Bennett among others, that Shakespeare was homosexual, and he asserted that the bard's relations with Master W.H. were perfectly innocent, although Shakespeare expressed his admiration of the youth in what may be regarded by some as extravagant language.

> The truth is, in spite of Frank Harris and Arnold Bennett and all the other frantic worshippers at the shrine of what they are pleased to call 'the plain facts of life', that Shakespeare was a good deal of a puritan. He was almost certainly brought up a Catholic, and though he undoubtedly succumbed to the pressure of the times in which he lived and outwardly abandoned his religion, he never lost the Catholic view about purity and impurity. Doubtless he had mistresses, we know at any rate he had one, 'the dark woman' (why call her lady?) of the Sonnets, but he had no romantic feelings about her or about any other woman of easy virtue. All his heroines, with the solitary exception of Cleopatra, were chaste and pure and lovely, and he could not take a 'charitable view' even about Cressida in these regards.
>
> On the other hand he openly adored Mr W.H. and celebrated his adoration in the most perfect poetry. *Honi soit qui mal y pense.*[20]

Bosie's work was not, and did not claim to be, a work of scholarship. All he claimed to do, as he observed, was to piece together the story in plain English, rescuing it on the one hand from commentators like Samuel Butler and on the other from would-be moralists like Hallam, who found it 'impossible not to wish that Shakespeare had never written the Sonnets.' It was reviewed favourably on the whole, Desmond MacCarthy on this occasion giving it two whole columns in *The Sunday Times* in a notice in which the worst he remarked about its author was that 'being a poet he has read Shakespeare from a poet's point of view, and without the preoccupations of a literary scholar.'[21]

The only new discovery on the subject which Bosie made was after his book had appeared. It was a reference in the archives of Canterbury Cathedral to a 'Master Will Hewes formerly apprentice to John Marlowe,' the shoemaker father of the playwright Christopher. Will Hewes was not described as an actor, but Bosie surmised that Christopher Marlowe took him to London and put him on the stage to act girl's parts and in this way he met Shakespeare. 'I always intended to write a new chapter about this in a new edition of my book,' Bosie later told Hesketh Pearson, 'but various things have so far prevented the publication of a new edition.' As Bosie died a few months afterwards, the desired new edition never appeared.[22]

Later in the same year as Bosie's book was published, the second Lord Birkenhead wrote the first volume of his life of his father, to which Winston Churchill contributed a glowing Foreword. The volume contained accounts of the subject's principal cases as a barrister, among which was the Ross-Crosland trial which the author incorrectly described as 'the Ross Libel Case,' whereas it will be recalled that it was a prosecution of Crosland and Bosie for conspiracy to bring a false charge against Ross. Secondly, the author stated that Ross obtained an injunction in the interest of Wilde's family to prevent Bosie from writing his book *Oscar Wilde and Myself*, whereas the injunction was to stop Bosie from quoting from *De Profundis* in his published book. Finally, young Birkenhead had included an account of a meeting between his father and Wilde in Oxford which was not particularly flattering to Wilde. In the letter of protest he wrote to Birkenhead Bosie characterised this story as 'utterly untrue from beginning to end', adding that 'your father never met Wilde at Oxford, nor was he a friend of mine there as he tried to make out.' Bosie also accused Birkenhead of completely misrepresenting the part he played in his fight with Ross of which the role of the boy Garratt was only one incident, and he declared that his autobiography and poem 'The Rhyme of F Double E' in his *Collected Satires* would long outlive young Birkenhead's 'absurd and dishonest book.'

Bosie wished to take libel proceedings against Birkenhead and his publisher Thornton Butterworth. However, Bosie's solicitor Edward Bell wanted £150 down before he started any such action. Bosie did not have this sum available, and a long correspondence ensued, in which Butterworth joined in. Butterworth knew Bosie personally, since he had been a member of John Long's publishing house when it brought out *Oscar Wilde and Myself*. The upshot was that Butterworth admitted that he had not read Birkenhead's biography before publication and having taken counsel's opinion he offered to withdraw the book and make the corrections which Bosie demanded. He also paid Bosie £250 in full settlement of his claim. Thus ended with one exception the last attempt at litigation which Bosie was to make in his lengthy ligitious career.* The only person left with a grievance was the unfortunate author. 'I was extremely annoyed at the time,' wrote Birkenhead afterwards, 'as there was nothing whatever injurious in what I said.'

What really angered Bosie was the story about the first Lord Birkenhead's meeting with Wilde at Oxford, which the author got from Edward Marjoribanks who had repeated it in his life of Carson. It was to the effect that F.E. Smith, as he then was, was invited to an undergraduate lunch at which he met Wilde who held forth not particularly well, telling his sycophantic listeners among other things, in reply to a request that he should tell them a fairy story, about a little snowdrop he had met in a wood and how he had spoken to it. As Smith rose to leave after the lunch he thanked Wilde for his talk, adding – 'but before I go, Master, could you not tell me something about yourself?' In the one-volume revised edition of his biography, published in 1959, the second Lord Birkenhead referred to what he called the violent onslaught made on the authenticity of this story by Bosie. 'I personally do not believe a word of it,' he added. Indeed there seems no doubt that it was wholly fictitious, and Bosie was quite right to question it.

'I barely knew F.E. Smith [at Oxford]; in fact I only spoke to him once or twice on the running ground,' Bosie wrote to Robert Sherard at this time.

> *He was never inside my rooms*, and *never* met Oscar there.... He told my nephew Queensberry at the Carlton Club that he used to be a friend of mine at Oxford. This is quite untrue. When my nephew first told me, I denied that I had ever spoken to him at Oxford, but afterwards it occurred to me that I might have spoken to him on the running ground, because I knew he used to go there and I at one time used to do a bit of 'training' there myself. Consequently if he says he knew me I would not like to contradict it. Very likely I spoke to him without knowing who he was or what was his name. Naturally I would speak to anyone who spoke to me first.[23]

Bosie had always been a compulsive letter writer – over the years, for instance, three hundred letters to his publisher Martin Secker and to his friend Sorley Brown, besides smaller numbers to friends and enemies alike such as Frank Harris, Hugh Walpole, St John Ervine,

*The exception was *Oscar Wilde and the Yellow Nineties* by Frances Winwar, which libelled Bosie. It was published in New York in 1940. Some copies appeared in England as a result of which Bosie was awarded £150 and costs. Bosie wrote the Foreword to the second edition of her book in 1941, correcting her errors based on Frank Harris's biography and quoting from his *New Preface*.

Britten Austin, John Galsworthy, and, of course, Bernard Shaw, whom he called 'St Christopher', while Shaw reciprocated by addressing Bosie as 'Childe Alfred.' He was, too, very hospitable, although it is only right to point out that the luncheons and dinners to his friends were largely at the expense of his mother and his wife as well as others who gave him money from time to time, such as Richard Rumbold and Henry ('Chips') Channon. On one occasion Shaw also guaranteed his bank overdraft.

One individual with whom Bosie failed to establish any satisfactory communication was Wilde's surviving son Vyvyan Holland. Bosie wrote to him about a life of Frank Harris which was being written by an American author named Gertz, who had invited Holland's opinion on the veracity of Harris's biography of his father. Holland, according to his own account, replied that he knew nothing whatever about it apart from having heard Robert Ross say that, although it was a thoroughly bad book, written with the sole object of glorifying Harris himself, it did, on the whole, contain some elements of truth. 'I think Robert Ross meant that Harris had put Alfred Douglas into his proper perspective,' Holland wrote in his *Son of Oscar Wilde*, adding that six months later he had received 'an infuriated letter' from Bosie, who had received a copy of extracts from the letter which Holland had sent Gertz. However, apart from pointing out that Harris admitted that his story about him was 'untrue in almost every particular,' and that Gertz's quotations from Holland's letter to him conveyed the impression that Holland was supporting Harris against Bosie, it is difficult, if not impossible, to see what was infuriating about Bosie's letter, which was quite friendly in tone; while appreciating Holland's feelings of loyalty towards Ross, at the same time he expressed his failure to understand why Holland should show similar loyalty to 'a blackguard like Harris who robbed your father of his play *Mr and Mrs Daventry* and who was to a great extent the cause of his death, which was hastened, if not actually caused, by his rage against Harris.'

> I feel very sorry that you should persist in carrying on a feud against me [Bosie continued]. I was your father's greatest friend and I was also a great friend of your mother's. I knew you as a child. The legend that you have imbibed about me in relation to your father is almost entirely false. It is true that I attacked him in my book *Oscar Wilde and Myself*, but I did it under frightful provocation, and I have now repudiated the book. Could you not manage to get out of your mind the ill-feeling which you appear to cherish? I have only good feelings towards you.

Vyvyan Holland replied that he did not think that a meeting

between them, which Bosie had also suggested, would serve any useful purpose on the ground that 'your own declarations upon several occasions has made it impossible for any friend of Ross's to be a friend of yours.' In spite of a further plea from Bosie that he could not admit that he had 'ever done anything which ought properly to prevent your being friendly with me,' Vyvyan Holland was unmoved and persisted in his refusal to see Bosie. Yet they did meet accidentally some years later. The occasion was the coming-out ball of Lady Jane Douglas, Francis Queensberry's daughter by his second wife, the artist Cathleen Mann. Vyvyan, who had become friendly with Queensberry, who was to dedicate his *Oscar Wilde and the Black Douglas* to him, was invited to the ball, as also was Bosie, since he was the debutante's great-uncle. There they met. 'We chatted on general subjects for about five minutes and then parted,' Vyvyan wrote afterwards. 'I never saw him again.'[24]

Bosie resumed his association with John Betjeman after Betjeman had married Field Marshal Lord Chetwode's daughter Penelope, and used to drive over from Brighton to the Betjeman house in Berkshire with a mutual friend, Sir Frederick O'Connor, who had been an adventurous envoy in Tibet and Nepal. In return Betjeman used to dine with Bosie and Olive in the various flats she inhabited, and he subsequently recalled these meetings:

> They got on very well and he was very fond of her and was always pleased to come and see her. She was a most amusing person – quite as witty as Bosie. I remember her telling us about how she walked outside Cromer with her father Colonel Custance who was an enormous man and had sold some of his land to a speculator who had erected bungalows on it. The Colonel, who seemed bigger than the bungalows, leaned down and peered into one of them and said to his daughter – 'Do you mean to say people *live* in these things?'
>
> Olive lived at Bembridge in the late twenties, then moved to Westbourne Terrace [London] where I used to lunch with her in the early thirties.... She was round-faced, plumpish, with enormous brown eyes and was extremely vivacious and funny. She must have been very beautiful in a curly-headed way, rather like a Hilda Cowan watercolour of a schoolgirl. She was devoted to the poetry of Byron and could quote him at length.[25]

Rupert Croft-Cooke surmised, probably rightly, that her devotion to Byron was to more than his poetry. 'Perhaps she saw in him a forerunner of her own idealised "Prince", for it is easy to find parallels between the two. If so, it was, in the later years, with humour and common sense. There was nothing in the least mawkish about her.'[26]

The Dowager Lady Queensberry now suffered from a diminished income as well as a decline in health. This probably resulted in the sale of her house early in 1935 when she was obliged to go into a nursing home. Bosie moved into a ground floor flat in a modern block in St Anne's Court, Nizells Avenue, in Hove. 'My nephew Queensberry has made me a present of this charming flat (sitting room, dining room, 2 bedrooms, bathroom and kitchen, electric fires and cooker and electric boiler),' Bosie wrote to Sorley Brown from his new abode on 9 April 1935. 'That is to say, he pays the rent (£130 a year). So here I am very comfortable and with a lot of nice furniture. My mother and sister have got another flat, No 13, in the same building. My mother, who is better, was moved in from the Nursing Home yesterday.'[27]

Apparently Sibyl Queensberry was suffering from cancer. She died in her Hove flat on 30 October 1935 in her ninety-first year, after a lengthy and painful illness. She had become a Catholic like her son and was fortified by the rites of the Church at the end. Although he had been expecting this for some weeks, Bosie was shattered by the event, as his letters at the time reveal. For instance, he wrote in one of them:

> The pain of losing my darling mother has been simply unbearable, but I feel better now that she is buried in the Franciscan Friary at Crawley. After the burial Father Walstan, who performed the final rites, said to me: 'We have just buried a little saint.' He scarcely knew my mother and had not seen her more than twice for a minute or two more than a year ago. But he is a man of marvellous spiritual perception.... Indeed no other word describes her.
>
> After she died (about an hour later) all her wonderful beauty of face, hands and arms returned to her as if by magic. I never saw anything more beautiful than she looked. All the distortions and disfigurements caused by her long cruel illness, pains and sufferings, disappeared, and she looked about thirty – not a wrinkle in her lovely face which had a faint pink tinge like the face of a girl. Her arms and hands were of surpassing beauty, white as snowdrops. She went on looking like that just as though she was only asleep for 24 hours, and then the colour faded from her cheeks, but otherwise she remained unchanged to the last....
>
> She gave me, all her life, the most wonderful and perfect love that every mother gave to her son. I feel at present as if I don't know how I shall go on living without her.[28]

4

In the autumn of 1935, shortly before his mother's death, Bosie found new publishers, Rich & Cowan, who agreed to bring out his poems in two separate volumes, *Sonnets* and *Lyrics*, which duly appeared. They included all the poems which had originally been published in the Mercure de France edition in 1896 such as 'Two Loves' and 'In Praise of Shame' but which he had subsequently declined to republish in *The City of the Soul* (1899) and in the two editions of his *Collected Poems* (1919 and 1928), brought out by Martin Secker. The reason, which he repeated in his preface to the *Lyrics*, was that 'although there is no actual harm in them, they lend themselves to evil interpretations' and had been used against him in the law courts 'by the very persons who most applauded them at the time they were written.' The only omissions in the Rich & Cowan volumes were the satires and the light verse such as *The Pongo Papers*.

Bosie complained, as was his wont, that he was being boycotted by all the reviewers, on this occasion because in the preface to the *Sonnets* he had ventured to disapprove of 'the deadly and dismal heresies of T.S. Eliot and company.' On 29 December he wrote to Sorley Brown: 'Did you ever hear anything like it? Not only do these people destroy poetry, but they have a conspiracy of silence against anyone who defends it. The *Sunday Times* and the *Observer* both today publish long articles on the "poetical publications of 1935". Not a word about my books in either of them, though they both have huge advertisements from Rich & Cowan, and though both papers have hitherto praised my poetry in the highest terms … the only reviews I have had have been in Scotland except one in the *Daily Telegraph*, quite short, by Harold Nicolson. Even he is afraid to praise me much!'

Bosie may have written to Nicolson thanking him for the review. At all events they had some acquaintance, since Bosie lunched with Nicolson in May 1936 at Nicolson's chambers in the Temple (4 King Bench's Walk). Nicolson afterwards wrote in his diary:

> *26 May 1936.* Alfred Douglas comes for luncheon. There is little trace of his good looks left. His nose has assumed a curious beaklike shape, his mouth has twisted into shapes of nervous irritability. He makes nervous and twitching movements with freckled and claw-like hands. He stoops slightly and drags a leg. Yet behind this appearance of a little, cross, old gentleman, flits the shape of a young man of the 'nineties, with little pathetic sunshine-flashes of the 1893 boyishness and gaiety. I had fully expected the self-pity, suspicion and implied irritability, but I had not foreseen that there would be any remnant of merriment and boyishness. Obviously the great tragedy of his life has scarred him deeply. He talked very frankly about his marriage and his son, who is in a home in Northampton.[29]

Among those who came to see Bosie at Hove were three fellow writers, Hugh Kingsmill, who had written a biography of Frank Harris, Hesketh Pearson, who was to write an equally good one of Wilde, and Malcolm Muggeridge who was to collaborate with Pearson on a book about Kingsmill. Kingsmill afterwards described his first visit to Pearson. Bosie came out into the hall as he entered and they began talking about Robert Ross, of whom Kingsmill expressed a profound distrust. 'Our talk, or rather his, for he talks incessantly was interrupted by lunch,' where the talk was rather restricted owing to the presence of Bosie's sister Edith Fox-Pitt, 'each subject that occurred to me seeming on a moments reflection to be left till later.' After the meal they repaired to Bosie's study where they talked about Bosie's sonnets, Harris, Sherard, Gide and other subjects. Afterwards Kingsmill told Pearson:

> Douglas struck me as rather simple and unsophisticated, and I am not surprised that Ross made rings round him. He is very self-centred, but there is something touching and likeable about him. Being so irritable and conceited, and not having much natural force or vitality, but wanting to live up to the deal of a reckless aristocrat, he inevitably got into the most frightful muddle. I should say that all the troubles of his life were due to his never having grown beyond a juvenile idea of what a combined poet-aristocrat ought to be like, and having tried to realise this idea in spite of being a timid and unworldly-wise person.
>
> Though far from a humorist, he had surprising outbursts of laughter, and I can understand him being an amusing companion to Wilde when things were going smoothly. We had some laughs over Sherard, whose habit of treating anyone he is defending as a Galahad had obviously maddened Douglas of late. Douglas told me that Wilde and Sherard quarrelled because Sherard would insist to Wilde that the charges against him were a tissue of foul lies. Douglas is now suffering in the same way. 'He will keep on trying to make out,' he said, 'that nothing ever occurred at Biskra.... It's very irritating.... And his proofs of anything he is arguing are so unconvincing....'
>
> The thing that appealed most to my imagination during the afternoon was our walk along the front. A bitter east wind; Douglas wizzened and bowed; his nose jutting out from beneath his soft hat. If anyone had been told by God (he would not have accepted it from lesser authority) that one of these two men had been the handsomest man in England in his youth, he must have picked me out. We struggled along, left the promenade and made for a bun shop to get some cakes for tea. I thought of the world-wide hurricane that had raged over Douglas, and here he was lamenting in the most ordinary tones that Wilde 'never could get any work

done after he left Naples.... You know he really did all his best work with me, all his comedies. Why even *De Profundis* was written to me. By Jove, that never occurred to me before,' he laughed. 'When he wasn't with me he couldn't work except in the form of a letter to me.'

Best touch of all, which much endeared me to him, was as we neared the bun shop. I said something about Harris having made out that Wilde was heartless. 'He was the kindest chap', said Douglas, 'the kindest chap.'[30]

Pearson described the second visit, when he was accompanied by Kingsmill and Muggeridge, in characteristic vein:

Tea was ready when we arrived, but it was more like a meal for lads of fourteen or fifteen than for men, two of whom were nearer fifty than forty. We sat up to the table, just as we had done in our teens and faced a spread of buttered toast, scones, cream cakes, jam puffs, tarts and all that class of confectionary which we had viewed with satisfaction as school-boys; so that we could only guess that the usual gatherings at Douglas's flat were juvenile, especially as we were grouped round one end of a long table with the housemaster sitting at the other. The conversation, between mouthfuls, was agreeable but uninspiring, and we were relieved when, no longer in front of the pastry, we sat by the fire and discussed poetry.

Douglas was amiable and urbane, though he showed irritation when a theory he had put forward about Shakespeare's Sonnets provoked Kingsmill's disagreement. He talked chiefly about him-self and his poetry, as indeed we wished him to do, though he made a few friendly references to Shaw and some less friendly ones to Robert Ross and Frank Harris. I did not think it opportune to remind him that he had once written me a violent and menacing letter because I had described Ross in print as a pleasant little man.[31]

Meanwhile the publishers Rich & Cowan asked Bosie to write another work for them, in the shape of a book of memoirs or reminiscences to supplement his autobiography. Bosie agreed and worked on the book throughout the latter part of 1936 and the earlier part of 1937, while continuing his ever-widening correspondence with Bernard Shaw, Sorley Brown, Robert Sherard, A.J.A. Symons and a host of others who wrote to him. Bosie called his new book *Without Apology*; it was largely autobiographical and anecdotal and to some extent it repeated earlier writings, lambasting Harris as well as several living authors like Yeats, H.G. Wells and St John Ervine.

When Bosie sent the manuscript to Rich and Cowan, their solicitors read it for libel and passed it as 'perfectly safe', whereupon the publishers advanced the author £150 on account of royalties. The manuscript was then sent to the printers who set it up in type and afterwards showed the proofs to their solicitors, who said it was 'dangerous'. They 'reside in Bungay and are evidently the village idiots of that place,' Bosie told Shaw in Janaury 1938. 'I carefully refrained from making it dangerous and it is really mild and genial. . . . It does not really much matter to me except for the irritating delay, as if Rich & Cowan won't publish it (it is already printed and could have come out last October) I have another publisher who is panting to get it.'[32] The other publisher was Martin Secker, and, Rich and Cowan having refused to go on with the publication, Martin Secker brought it out in April, 1938.

Rich and Cowan's reaction was predictable, as Bosie told Sorley Brown:

> . . .those crooks Rich & Cowan, having done their utmost to squash my book are now threatening me with an action *to recover the advance they made* (I refuse to return it as they broke their contract) and *the printers' bill* (the printers having refused to print the book!!) and *damages for the loss they sustained by not publishing the book* (which they declined to publish!!!)
>
> I had no money to fight them and my nephew let me down badly. I told Shaw this in the course of correspondence; whereupon, by return of post, he offered to guarantee £100 overdraft! Can you beat it? He now calls me 'Childe Alfred' and is re-writing his Preface to Harris's book in the light of *Without Apology.* . . . He sent me the proof of his Preface, written before he had read *Without Apology.* It is quite brilliant and 'puts me right' for ever in the Wilde business. He is now adding to it.[33]

When Rich and Cowan heard that Shaw would back any legal action against them by Bosie, they dropped the matter, but revised it a year later when their solicitors wrote to Bosie's suggesting that he should write a book for them for nothing. 'They really seem to be out of their minds,' Bosie told Shaw. 'However I shall not do anything about it and just wait and see what happens.' In the event, nothing did, and as Bosie anticipated that was the end of the matter. But it was a pity for Bosie financially that they shied off his book. '*Without Apology* I fear is already as good as dead,' he wrote to Shaw in August 1938. 'Secker is a charming fellow but he has no business instincts (and precious little money), whereas if Rich and Cowan had published the book they would certainly have sold at least five thousand copies. Secker has sold about a thousand.... They [Rich and Cowan] have a tremendous organisation and an army of canvassers, and producers and publicity agents, in contrast to Secker whose business is distinctly "one-horse". Rich told me they were "sitting on top of the book trade" and could place any book they published with the booksellers all over the country.'[34] (However that may have been, Rich & Cowan were eventually to be taken over by the powerful Hutchinson Publishing Group.)

Another publishing house, Duckworth, now asked Bosie for a short book on Wilde of 30,000 words for their 'Great Lives' series. Bosie accepted this commission, and was paid a small advance – £30, he told Sherard. In July 1939 he wrote 22,000 words in a week, as he told Shaw, and went off to stay with A.J.A. Symons and to finish it in his house in Finchingfield. 'I still feel nervous about it,' he wrote to Shaw. 'For one thing I don't know whether Duckworth and the public will stand for my chapters about homosexuality. Of course I do not defend it, but my argument is that it is a moral offence (a sin) and not a crime and that therefore the law ought not to take cognizance of it (as is the case with the Code Napoleon in France).'[35]

When Bosie had finished the book he had it typed and sent the script to Duckworth '... who,' as Bosie wrote at the time, 'liked it so much that they have "promoted" it out of their "Great Lives Series" at two shillings and made it a five shilling book with four illustrations.' At the same time he sent a copy to Bernard Shaw for his opinion. 'I hope you will not think it too bad,' he told Shaw, 'and I hope you will approve of the first three chapters where I have dealt with the whole question of homosexuality.... After going through frightful agonies during which I was on the point of writing to Duckworth and telling them I couldn't do the book and returning the advance, I wrote the whole thing in about three weeks.'

Shaw did not like it, particularly the form in which it was written, and he sent Bosie his suggested chapter headings which he elaborated in a letter:

> You must arrange that idiotic book as follows. You must begin with Wilde's birth and follow his history to his grave as matter-of-factly as the *Dictionary of National Biography*. Then, when the reader is in full possession of all that Wilde was and exactly what happened to him, you can moralise about him to your heart's content; for not until then will your alarums and excursions be intelligible.
>
> You must explain why the new biography is needed in spite of the admirable work by Harris, revised by yourself and, considering its date, a model of what a biography should be (just as your manuscript is a model of what it shouldn't be).

You must explain that Harris and Sherard were hampered by the fact that in their time it was generally believed that homosexuality involved the most horrible depravity of character, and was unnatural and unmentionable. Since then the work done in England by Havelock Ellis and Edward Carpenter and abroad by Freud and the psychoanalysts has completely changed all that. Not only have sexual subjects become mentionable and discussable (compare Thackeray's novels with D.H. Lawrence's) but it is now known that a reversal of the sex instinct occurs naturally, and that the victim of it is greatly to be pitied and may be a person of the noblest character. Wilde's life therefore must be taken out of the old atmosphere in which Harris and Sherard wrote, and retold with a healthy objectivity which was impossible before the war.

In doing this you must clear your mind of Sodom and Gomorrah and the Catholic categories of sin-as-distinguished-from-crime and all the rest of it. You will have to explain that Wilde was prosecuted not for sodomy but for offences under the Criminal Law Amendment Act for the protection of boys, as to which he was guilty. It is not necessary to pester the reader with assurances that you are bound as a Catholic to proclaim Pickwickian opinions and values that are now obsolete, irrelevant and ridiculous.

You must cut out the sentimental rubbish about Mrs Wilde, which is just like Sherard.... As for its being her duty to stick to Wilde, did your mother think it *your* duty to stick to Wilde? You forget that Constance had two sons to bring up, much younger than the one son your mother felt responsible for. To combine your pious condemnation of Mrs Wilde with your disclosure of [Vyvyan] Holland's parentage is unspeakable....

P.S. As you have rashly sent the book to Duckworth without waiting for my instructions you had better send him my 'reader's report' also and ask him whether he agrees. You will thus get an independent opinion. Of course he will agree with every syllable.

You are an exceedingly troublesome Childe.[36]

Among other matters about Oscar Wilde's early life, which he got from Sherard's books, Bosie stated that Oscar always had an exaggerated idea of his mother's social standing. But Shaw contradicted him: 'He did not exaggerate his mother's social importance *in Dublin*. You don't understand Ireland and Irishmen. Ireland is *all* plantation. Macaulay's notion that the planted Irishman is English is as absurd as the idea that the planted Englishman is a Norman Frenchman.'[37]

Although Bosie only made minor changes in response to Shaw's criticisms, his book remains his best and most detached writing on Wilde. He saw Wilde as neither a superman nor a gross sensualist, as neither 'a martyr to progress' whose place was 'at the very summit of

English literature', as he described him to his mother, nor 'the greatest force for evil in Europe during the past three hundred and fifty years', as he described him in the Pemberton Billing trial, but as a dear friend and artist of considerable merit. He wrote of Wilde with affection and admiration for his finer qualities and achievements, praising his qualities as a dramatist and as a poet in *The Ballad of Reading Gaol*.

'By the time I got to know Oscar he had outlived his posing period,' Bosie wrote:

> I can only speak to him in this respect from my personal knowledge of him during the time when I knew him, that is to say during the last nine years of his life, two of which he spent in prison; and I can testify that I never saw, nor expect to see, a distinguished and celebrated man who posed less than Oscar. On the contrary, one of his greatest charms was that he was entirely natural, and said, utterly without fear or 'respect of persons', exactly what he thought or meant to express on any given occasion. He was gifted also with a superb sense of humour which never deserted him right through his appearances in the criminal courts and even on his death-bed....
>
> Oscar Wilde's last days in Paris were by no means all dismal and gloomy. He had, as Shaw truly says, an unconquerable gaiety of soul which ever sustained him, and, while he had lost the facility of writing, he retained to the last his inimitable supremacy as a talker. I retain glowing memories of dinners at *cafés* and subsequent amazing 'talks' when he held his audience spell-bound as he discoursed in his exquisite voice of all things in heaven and earth, now making his hearers rock with laughter and now bringing tears into their eyes. Such talk as Oscar's now no longer exists. I have never known anyone to come anywhere near him.[38]

'I am glad I've written this,' Bosie told his friend Rupert Croft-Cooke, about *Oscar Wilde: A Summing Up*. 'It will set things right for ever.' On the subject of Oscar and himself, Bosie always liked to think he was writing for posterity, and in the circumstances of course he was.

5

The strangest friendship which Bosie made during his last years, and a most unexpected one, was with a woman. None other than Marie Stopes, the high priestess of birth control, as Bernard Shaw called her. It began with a letter from her out of the blue asking Bosie for his opinion of some of her verses, examples of which she enclosed in the letter. She signed it 'Marie Carmichael', the latter being her middle name. Her main reason for approaching him was that she wished for an opinion from one she regarded as 'a great poet', but she deliberately concealed her identity since she felt that, if Bosie was aware of it, he would ignore her request. Bosie thought that she was a widow or divorcée with one or two sons, since she did not mention her husband, and as he always replied to strangers, particularly when they referred to him as 'a poet', so he responded in kind. 'Dear Mrs Carmichael,' he wrote. 'Of course if you *are* a real poet, nothing on earth will stop you from writing poetry. So go ahead with my blessing! I may tell you that your poem "Out of the Noise" is a fine piece of work.' He added that he would gladly have published it when he was editing *The Academy* and printed a poem every week, 'almost invariably by someone unknown to fame,' such as Flecker, Rupert Brooke, Siegfried Sassoon, 'and a lot more, all of whom at that time were utterly unknown.'

The correspondence continued, and when Bosie went down with a bad attack of bronchitis towards the end of November, she expressed her regret and sent him a present, probably of money. He replied that he supposed he 'ought to refuse it *with hauteur*' but on the contrary accepted it with the greatest gratitude and was deeply touched. 'I owe you an apology about your poem,' he went on, 'But I have been so ill (near death) with a first-class imitation of pneumonia that I have been incapable of thinking or doing anything. My illness is now in its fourth week and I really came to the conclusion that my "number was up". My wife, who is much better off than I am, is ill in London, and we are separated for Xmas for the first time in many years. Neither of us can move out of the house.'

> As it happens I am just now desperately hard up. My nephew Queensberry told me the other day that he could not go on paying the rent of my flat. Although I have been so ill, I have not had a doctor as I can't afford it, and I know if he came he would simply tell me to get a nurse and remain in bed all the time, or go to the South of France, all of which is wildly impossible. I really think however that I have staved off pneumonia and that I will now gradually get back to health. . . . So your kindness has cheered me in my loneliness.

Marie Stopes responded by sending him 'a bottle of the very best tonic for regaining health', although she did not say what it contained. Her maternal instinct was aroused so that she wrote: 'About the flat's rent it is too distressing that you should be so worried by Lord

Queensberry. Would you honour me by telling me how much the rent is and also whether you would allow me to write to the Royal Literary Fund about it.... There are so few on Parnassus, you must graciously allow me to do the little I can. Believe me, always your sincere and honoured pupil, Marie Carmichael.'

Bosie replied:

> It is sweet of you to be so concerned about me. I will start taking that medicine as soon as I have really got rid of that cough.
>
> As for the Royal Literary Fund it is *quite out of the question*. I know all about it and have on several occasions got grants from it for other people. But in my case I really am not eligible. I have £400 a year (and of course that does not include earnings from books) and my nephew Q has so far paid the rent of this flat, £130 a year. At the time of the war scare crisis [Munich] he wrote and told me he was nearly ruinèd and was closing down his house and establishment. He now says he will go on till next March.
>
> Poor Francis Q came into nothing. My father and my brother (the late Q) got rid of £700,000 between them and there was nothing left. So Francis made all his own money. He is a stockbroker. Up till two years ago he was making thirty thousand a year, but he has been frightfully hit by the slump. I am hoping my niece (or rather ex-niece) Irene Dunn, who was Francis's first wife and afterwards married Sir James Dunn, will ask me to her lovely villa at Cap Ferrat. I was there last year for a month....[39]

In the event Bosie was not asked to the Dunns' villa, since the Dunns were drifting apart and were soon to be divorced. But, as will be seen, he was to stay twice in 1939 at Norbury Park, Marie Stopes's Surrey home near Dorking, by way of consolation for missing the Riviera. Meanwhile Marie told him to take hypophosphates and iodine to relieve his cough, also hot water sea baths as well as drinking sea water. She also sent him a collection of her 'love songs' to read if he was well enough. In reply he wrote to her on 7 January 1939:

> All your poetry is about physical passion. The best poetry is not about it. When Shakespeare wrote about love he sublimated it and spiritualised it, and the same applies to all the best poets. All this does not prevent your poetry from being unusually good. But if I were to tell you all I really think, you would only be amazed and you would not be convinced.
>
> I can't do better than I've done already and I refuse to do worse. In *In Excelsis* I believe to be my highest point, and I admit that it's frightfully difficult and metaphysical and has not the lyric grace and charm of my earlier work.

Do come and see me one day. I can give you tea any day. I have a charming little flat here.

It was not until five weeks later, in the middle of February, that Marie disclosed her identity in a letter with her surname added to her signature. Bosie was 'astounded', as well he might be. 'I had not the remotest idea that you were Marie Stopes,' he replied.

It is really very extraordinary because (as you perhaps know) I have in the past criticised you rather strongly. Naturally as a Catholic I disagree with your views about birth control. But now that you have written one so many kind letters and shown so much interest in me and my poetry and my health, and my worldly condition, I feel remorseful to think that I have ever had unkind thoughts about you.

Marie suggested coming to see him three weeks later, by which time her son would have gone back to school. This suited Bosie and they got on so well together that she invited Bosie to spend a weekend at Norbury Park. Bosie gladly accepted and arrived there on 18 March. The weekend went off well despite a violent argument between one of the guests, a Mrs Munro, and Bosie about the merits and demerits of T.S. Eliot as a poet. Marie Stopes took an early opportunity of telling Bosie laughingly that her husband was 'very illiterate and laughed at poetry' and that her son despised it. 'He responded charmingly,' she noted afterwards, 'and developed an amusing geniality and wide interest, talking about hunting and shooting ... and was full of humorous anecdotes and very much the man of the world, appreciating good food and wine and making altogether very entertaining company. Talk naturally tended to a monologue as everyone was only too interested to listen to him. He told me he often stayed with hunting people and was accustomed to an environment which despised poetry.'

At dinner on the first night, where the guests included Mr Knox, the editor of *Punch* and his wife, Bosie related how the original acting copy of *The Importance of Being Earnest* made Earnest ten years older than Wilde intended him to be, because George Alexander was so pleased with himself in the part that he made it to suit himself. Bosie went on to say that he had talked to John Gielgud at his recent reproduction, in which Gielgud played the part for the age of twenty-nine, the age Wilde had really intended. After the verbal fracas between Bosie and Mrs Munro, the hostess cleverly steered the conversation back to Wilde when Bosie 'became extremely interesting and reminiscent.'

He told us that he was personally with Wilde, staying with him and in and out of his study all the time he was writing *The Importance of Being Earnest*; that they talked and laughed about it and a number of the jokes were the repartee Lord Alfred had made himself to Wilde and which were worked up and incorporated in the play.

He told us that they were staying in rooms with a balcony at Worthing. The house was then called, I think, 'The Haven' and Lord Alfred had recently been down and found it, though the name of the street and the house have both been changed. He found an old fisherman who remembered it under its old name.

The beautiful large room he and Wilde had, had been spoiled by partitioning, but otherwise the house was unchanged.

On the Monday morning, after the others had gone, Bosie and Marie talked in front of the fire, when Marie read him one of her published poems and urged him to write some more poetry. 'I cannot,' he said, almost crying, as he turned his head into the back of the armchair in which he was sitting. 'I wish I were dead. There is nothing for me to do but die. I should like to die. My life is done.' Marie told him that with his wisdom he must not feel like that but give the mellow results of his experience to younger people. He then started talking of Tennyson. 'Look what rubbish Tennyson wrote in his last years,' he said. 'You would not have me do the same? And then Tennyson did that one lovely thing, "Crossing the Bar", but he did that on his deathbed. I could only do another good thing now on my deathbed, and I could not do anything less than I felt to be my best.'[40]

A few weeks after his return to Hove, he wrote to Marie Stopes that he was 'full of worries and anxieties' about the rent of his flat and that it had occurred to him that there might possibly be a chance of his getting a civil list pension for 'services to literature.'

I don't know how these things are arranged, but I imagine it is a question of pulling a certain number of strings. I could, I know, count on the backing of Bernard Shaw, and also I feel quite certain of Harold Nicolson, who is the sort of man who would have influence in the right direction. I am, as it happens, I think I may say, 'in the good books' of Mr Chamberlain, the Prime Minister, although I am not personally acquainted with him. I could think of many more names of people who have a very high opinion of me as a poet and who would probably think I am entitled to a pension ... £200 a year, or even £150, would make it possible for me, with what I have already, to go on living in this flat, and save me from having to clear out and store my furniture.

Marie Stopes immediately reacted, saying she would get up a petition to the Prime Minister. Bosie then wrote to Bernard Shaw and John Betjeman. Shaw was not encouraging, since he considered Bosie's £400 a year he was getting from his wife would not be considered to amount to 'straitened circumstances'. Bosie told Betjeman about the petition being got up by 'a very kind friend of mine, a lady', but he did not mention her name.

'I know the lady's name is MARIE STOPES,' Betjeman replied. 'There's nothing I don't know.' He went on:

> The people I would approach are Lord Dufferin, Hugh Walpole, Cecil Roberts, Beverly Nichols, Evelyn Waugh, Edmund Blunden, Sir Jack Collings Squire, T.S. Eliot, Rose Macaulay, Grahame Greene, Lord Clonmore, Lord Camrose, Elizabeth Bowen. I have sounded none of these people and there are probably others.

Bosie sent on Betjeman's letter to Marie Stopes, explaining that Betjeman had signed himself 'Moth' because that was the name Bosie had bestowed on him when he was a boy at Marlborough, after Armado's page in *Love's Labour's Lost*, a 'well educated infant.' He added that he had scratched out two of the names on Betjeman's list, Beverly Nichols and T.S. Eliot. 'Jack Squire is a great friend of mine and he would certainly sign. I am also friendly with Hugh Walpole.... But I would rather leave the names to you.'[41]

A few people whom Marie Stopes approached refused to sign the petition. They included Bernard Shaw and John Masefield. But the final list, which Marie Stopes forwarded with the application to No 10 Downing Street on 21 June 1939 was quite impressive – James Agate, Edmund Blunden, Lord Clonmore, Sir Arthur Quiller Couch, St John Irvine, John Gielgud, Christopher Hassall, Harold Nicolson, Sir John Squire, Sir Hugh Walpole, Evelyn Waugh, Humbert Woolfe, Virginia Woolf and Marie Stopes. In reply Marie received a letter from the Prime Minister's office to the effect that civil list pensions were considered in March and that in Bosie's case he would have to wait until June 1940. Meanwhile Walpole did his best to keep the ball rolling. 'I talked to the Prime Minister two days ago at great length,' he told Marie Stopes, 'and he was satisfactorily impressed.'[42]

The petition, which was drawn up by Marie Stopes, stated that Bosie had no income except small and spasmodic returns from his poetry and writings and a voluntary allowance from his wife which was 'quite precarious'; nor had he any expectations of any inheritance. Shortly before the petition was due to be considered Marie again wrote to Mr Chamberlain reminding him of Bosie's claim and expressing the hope that the Prime Minister might be able to grant the pension. 'Lord Alfred is frail and old,' she added, 'and we have not his equal as a writer of sonnets.'

Although they had corresponded for some years, Bosie had never met Walpole. The opportunity to do so occurred shortly after the outbreak of the Second World War when they met at a weekend party at Norbury Park. Bosie formed a suitable subject for a slightly malicious entry in Walpole's journal:

> How astonished was I when this rather bent, crook-bodied, hideous old man came into the room. How could he ever have been beautiful, for he has a nose as ugly as Cyrano's, with a dead-white bulbous end?
>
> He talks ceaselessly on a shrill almost broken note, agitated, trembling. He is so obviously a gentleman, full of little courtesies, delicacies, that, as gentlemen are now as rare as dodos, he seems remarkable. He loves to talk of his ancestors fighting in border raids, of Oscar whom he now always defends. When someone he hates like Wells is mentioned, he gets so angry that all his crooked features light up....
>
> He *is* a real poet – witness 'the ribs of Time', one of the finest lines in all English poetry – but he has a streak of craziness running through his charm and talent. When I went to bed on Sunday evening not very well, he came in to see me with most tender solicitude.
>
> He and Marie make a strange pair in this ugly eighteenth century house, dark and wall peeling.

Among the other guests was a young man called Keith Briant, who was to write Marie Stopes's biography, and with whom Bosie became embroiled in an argument about Tsarist Russia. 'Young man', said Bosie to him, 'you may have edited *The Isis* at Oxford, but I edited *The Spirit Lamp* and you are talking utter nonsense. You know nothing about Russia.' Marie's future biographer had the grace to admit that Bosie was 'probably right'.[43]

'I hope the war is not depressing you,' Bosie wrote to Sorley Brown about this time, 'I feel pretty cheerful about it on the whole. I think, in a way, the foul invasion of Finland by the Bolsheviks is providential. Nothing less than such a villanous act would have cured the besotted half-wits in this country who for the last 20 years have been grovelling before their Soviet idol, who was behind the Reds in Spain.'[44]

'What a pleasant fellow Hugh Walpole is,' Bosie wrote in his thank-you letter to Marie, 'though I cannot see many signs of him being really interested in the great issues of either life or literature.' This was a shrewd and perceptive judgment of the man whom Bosie thought (wrongly) 'double-crossed' him over the pension, which was turned down in a letter from the Prime Minister's secretary, Anthony Bevir, on 12 March 1940. This stated briefly that, 'while Mr Chamberlain has great sympathy with him in his difficulties, he regrets that he has not felt able to submit his name to the King for the award of a pension.'[45]

The truth of the matter was conveyed by Bosie to Marie in a letter he wrote a few weeks later:

> Richard Rumbold who came here for 2 nights seems to know all about the pension. He says that there was a lunch party at No 10 and that Chamberlain was *entirely* in favour of it and said, 'He is a fine poet and ought to have it.' Then someone (Richard either didn't know or would not tell me who it was) raised objections (based on the Wilde scandal!) and Chamberlain reluctantly gave in.
>
> Richard is a great friend of Harold Nicolson. He (that is Richard) says that Walpole did support me as much as he could. It is all rather mysterious but I think Richard Rumbold is well informed. He is a nephew of Sir Horace Rumbold, the ambassador. His father is Captain Rumbold who belongs to the Royal Yacht Squadron.[46]

Bosie was considerably shaken over the collapse of the pension, as he wrote to Marie. 'It is not so much the loss of the money, though God knows I need it badly (as I have lost another £50 a year since the war started) as well as losing my nephew's contribution of £130 a year for my rent, as the wounded feeling that I have so many enemies, and also my instinct that warns me of treachery. I have been badly treated all my life (though I don't deny that it is partly my own fault) but I began to think that the hostility and unfairness had died down. Now I find it is still there....' The £50 which he lost was due to Olive reducing his allowance to £350 (it was later reduced by another £50 to £300). In this he thought he had been treated 'very shabbily', as he confided to Marie, since his wife had £2,500 a year from Custance trust funds.

Marie Stopes continued to struggle on Bosie's behalf. She introduced him to Lady Diana Cooper who thought him 'delightful' and told Marie that she would do anything she could to secure him the pension and did not think it would be difficult to get more names if the application were renewed. But, as St John Ervine told Marie, it would be useless to petition again if Bosie were getting an allowance, 'especially now when there are authors who are destitute.'

My recollection is that Lord Alfred thought the allowance would be stopped [Ervine wrote to Marie Stopes]. If it has been, then a pension should be easy to obtain for him. His distinction as a poet is indisputable, and he requires no certificate from anybody: his work is his certificate. But until this question is settled, it is pure waste of time to try to organise an appeal, and you will do Lord Alfred himself more harm than good. I will most gladly sign an application, but only when I hear what the financial position is.[48]

Among those whom Diana Cooper appproached was Evan Morgan, then Lord Tredegar. 'I have been seeing a good deal of Bosie lately and he has spoken to me of his financial worries,' Tredegar replied, 'and I quite agree with what you and Marie Stopes say. . . . If you can assure me that no appealing to Winston will have the slightest effect, then the only thing to do would be for a few of us to get together . . . and each contribute so much per year for seven years, which would relieve Bosie of immediate anxiety.' Lady Diana forwarded Tredegar's letter to Marie who led the way with a seven-year covenant. Tredegar followed in kind and in addition managed to secure Bosie a grant of £100 from the Royal Literary Fund.[49] Among others who helped financially were two Members of Parliament, Henry ('Chips') Channon and Alan Lennox-Boyd, who were married to Guinness sisters, daughters of the millionaire brewer Lord Iveagh.

On 10 December 1942, Chips Channon and Lennox-Boyd, then a junior minister in the Churchill government, who had been in Newhaven on political business, came on to Brighton and went to see Bosie whom neither had met before. Afterwards Chips described the meeting with Bosie in his diary – rather different from Hugh Walpole's impression at Norbury Park:

> He now lives in a tiny semi-basement flat at 1 Anne's Court, Hove, and opened the door to us himself, and was generally gracious and friendly. He ushered us into his small sitting room where there were books and a few rather pathetic bibelots, relics of his youth. He is 72, looks much younger, and is lithe, lean and smiling, and has pleasant eyes. But he no longer listens to what one says, and scarcely took in our conversation. He just rattled on himself. We had resolved not to mention Oscar Wilde, prison, Winston, Robbie Ross or Frank Harris, but we were soon well embarked on all five subjects, though not at once. He told us much of Wilde, and after some sherry, said that although the Wilde story had ruined his life, he did not regret him. . . .
>
> He made no secret of being Wilde's catamite, and he showed us the photograph of a drawing of himself taken about that time. It was Dorian Gray himself . . . a young man of almost unbelievable

good looks, staggeringly handsome. He went on to tell us that both Ross and Harris had behaved like scoundrels, and that he himself had served six months in Wormwood Scrubs, in the second division, for having libelled Winston Churchill, to whom he had recently (and with the Prime Minister's permission) written and dedicated an ode.

He was very pathetic ... alone, poor, almost friendless, and married to a woman whom he rarely sees – but who does live in another flat in Brighton. Alan and I melted towards him, especially when he told us that he can no longer afford to keep his flat, for which Francis Queensberry pays the rent. I do not know what will become of him. I think I shall give him a small allowance, and then perhaps someone will be kind to me in my advanced age.[50]

Channon was as good as his word, and both he and Lennox-Boyd henceforward regularly gave him money, as did Tredegar, Marie Stopes and others.

6

During the war and immediate pre-war years, Bosie continued to write, though somewhat spasmodically. Besides *Oscar Wilde: A Summing Up*, already mentioned, he contributed introductions to two books by others, Robert Sherard's *Bernard Shaw, Frank Harris and Oscar Wilde* (1937) and the artist John Piper's *Aquatints of Brighton* (1939); in addition he wrote a trenchant pamphlet, *Ireland and the War Against Hitler* (1940), also four sonnets, including one to Winston Churchill praising his conduct of the war, and finally he gave a lecture in September 1943 on the principles of poetry to the Royal Literary Society, in which, while praising Chaucer, Shakespeare, Marvell, Milton and Keats, he attacked 'modern versifiers' such as Ezra Pound, T.S. Eliot and W.H. Auden. In addition he wrote an introduction to a volume of poems by his friend Marie Stopes, *Wartime Harvest* (1944), his last published prose.

'There was a time when Mr Sherard and I disagreed rather acrimoniously over Wilde,' Bosie wrote in the foreword to Sherard's book, 'and it has taken years of slow-grinding mills, and buckets of mud slung by, among others, Frank Harris, to bring us together again, united in our devotion to the memory of a great genius and cruelly-treated and injured man.' Sherard's work, not the most happy of his literary efforts, consists for the most part of a violent diatribe against Harris. However, there is one noteworthy story in it about Bosie and Oscar in Worthing when Oscar was writing *The Importance of Being Earnest* in the summer of 1894. Bosie, who no doubt told Sherard of the incident, noticed an unopened letter which had been lying for several days on the mantelpiece of the room where Wilde was working.

'Why don't you open this letter?' Bosie asked his friend.

'Leave that letter alone,' said Oscar, flaring up. 'If you touch it I'll never speak to you again. I wrote several days ago to George Alexander telling him I needed £300 and asking him to advance it to me. Of course that letter is from him and contains a refusal. I'm not going to open it!'

Disregarding Oscar's threat, Bosie seized the letter and tore it open. It was indeed from Alexander, and out of it there fell a cheque for £300.[51]

John Piper's interest in aquatints had been inspired by John Betjeman who had taken him over to Dublin, where eighteenth-century topographical guide books illustrated by aquatints could be bought for a few pounds. As a result Piper took lessons in the engraving department of the Royal College of Art in London and produced *Brighton Aquatints* under the Duckworth imprint in the summer of 1939. There were twelve aquatints in all, each depicting a different aspect of the town and reflecting what the artist described as its 'seaside nursery gaiety'. *Brighton Aquatints* was published in two editions, one of which was limited to fifty copies, each coloured by hand. The work certainly put John Piper 'on the map' as an artist.

Incidentally it was John Betjeman who suggested that Bosie should contribute the Introduction and it was Betjeman who conducted the negotiations between the two men and the publisher. Bosie agreed to meet Piper in London, but stipulated that the rendezvous should be as near as possible to Victoria railway station. Consequently they met for lunch at Overton's restaurant opposite the station, where Bosie, being the gourmet that he was, no doubt appreciated the excellent fare customarily provided by this establishment, renowned for its sea-food. It was the only occasion on which the poet and the artist met. However, the result enhanced the artist's work by adding to its interest.

'Looking with admiration, not unmingled with emotion, at these charming aquatints of Mr Piper's', Bosie wrote in his Introduction, 'it is surprisingly borne in on me that there is still a good deal left of the old Brighton which I knew in my youth.' He went on:

> I have lived in Brighton (or, to be more strictly accurate Hove) for the last ten years, but somehow it has never hitherto seemed to me to be the same place as it was when between the ages of twelve and

sixteen I used to come for a week or two's stay with my father in lodgings kept by a retired butler and his wife in Oriental Place, between the Bedford and the Metropole.

As a rule, children don't go for a week or two to 'stay' with their father, but in my case this was the process, simply because my father, equally famous as the author of the 'Queensberry Rules' and the vindicator of late Victorian morality, did not reside at home with his wife and children. In fact we very seldom saw him, and though I was in my childhood devoted to him and regarded him as a marvellous and heroic figure, who, according to the firm belief of my brothers and myself, was capable of wrestling single-handed with a bull or 'taking on' seven men in single combat (with or without boxing gloves), my devotion to him was largely, if not mainly due to the circumstance that I never saw him. . . .

At the time when my father used to sit nightly with me in the 'lounge' (horrible, but now firmly established word) of the newly-built Metropole Hotel, and when goat-carriages still abounded on the front, it was a place given over to the most profound decorum and placid respectability. It was also intensely 'fashionable'.

When I was staying with my father, generally also accompanied by my sister, four years younger than myself, I seemed (looking back at it all now from the distance of about fifty years, more or less) to spend a large part of my time on the Pier . . . and when I was not on the Pier I was generally to be found gazing at the fish or the seals in the Aquarium. . . .

I had almost forgotten all this till I saw Mr Piper's aquatints and discovered that the Brighton of my youth is still in existence, and that nearly all the old landmarks remain exactly as they were. . . . I notice that in the long run nearly everyone ends by coming to live (and die) in Brighton. When I say 'everyone' I mean, of course, just what the papers mean when they announce that 'everyone now agrees' that so-and-so is the case. I mean that I could give at least a hundred cases of people I know, among what the Paris newspapers used to call *les High-lifers*, turning up late in life and announcing that they now live in Brighton. Refreshing myself with another glance through Mr Piper's aquatints, and looking back with my mind's eye to Oriental Place, I arrive at the conclusion that they might easily do worse.

On 2 February 1940 the following letter from Bosie was printed in the *Catholic Herald*:

Sir, I shall not attempt to enter into a 'slanging match' with your numerous Irish or pro-Irish correspondents who are so ready to accuse me of ignorance. I wish merely to ask you to allow me to repeat my strictly accurate statement that de Valera was a member of the Irish Republican Brotherhood, a secret society condemned by the Pope. He continued to be a member of this society, thereby *de facto* incurring excommunication, right up to the time when Lloyd George finally 'double-crossed' the Irish loyalists, just at the moment when Sinn Fein was beaten to the ground.

It is difficult to discuss anything seriously with people who think that they advance their cause by substituting the ridiculous word 'Eire' for the historic name of their own country and by applying the word 'Partition' to the honourable refusal of the British Government to hand over the North against its wish to its enemies.

The fact that I am a Catholic and that I am by no means enamoured of Ulster Protestantism cannot force me to condone injustice.

Ireland was originally invaded and conquered by Henry the Second of England on the order and instructions of Pope Adrian IV, who declared that the state of Ireland, its immorality and its savage, bloodthirsty feuds, was a scandal to Christendom. That was the first 'plantation'. That the Irish were subsequently badly treated by the English, I do not deny. All Catholics were badly treated after the 'Reformation'.

I am not an Englishman, and my own country, Scotland, was often brutally wronged by England. But the Scots do not go on howling and wailing through the centuries over their wrongs. They accepted the situation and made the best of it. Why cannot the Irish do the same? Most of us in this country are sick and tired of their endless whining and self-pity.

The people of Ireland live under the protection of the British Empire and the British Navy. Deprived of this protection they would inevitably fall a prey to Germany or some other predatory country. Would Germany or any other country treat them as well and as fairly as England does?

It came as a surprise to Bosie that the editor should have published this letter, and he put it down to the fact that at the same time he had written a personal letter to the editor pointing out that as he had previously printed columns of abuse about him in his paper he could hardly as an honourable man refuse him the space to make a reply. Further abusive letters from the *Catholic Herald* readers followed, and when Bosie sent the editor 'a very short reply', in which he explained that he did not propose to spend the rest of his life arguing about the 'Irish question', and accordingly that he had only to say that nothing which his excited correspondents had written would alter the plain historical facts which he had cited, the editor simply suppressed his letter altogether. 'From his own point of view and that of his heated correspondents this was probably the best thing he could have done,' Bosie subsequently wrote in *Ireland and the War against Hitler*, which he composed during the Battle of Britain in the summer of 1940. 'There would be no point in giving publicity to this rather distressing exposure of editorial or journalistic ethics if the whole Irish question were not now once more *sur le tapis* and if that question did not happen to be, as it is now, fraught with the most deadly peril for this country.' He continued:

> Mr de Valera and his Government are determined to preserve 'neutrality' in the war against Hitler and they professed to be outraged and amazed because Lord Craigavon [the Prime Minister of Northern Ireland], representing the unanimous views of the Loyalists of Ulster, has definitely declined to seize this moment of peril to end what Mr de Valera is pleased to call Partition and to embrace 'neutrality' which would entail Ulster's acquiescence in the keeping in Dublin of a German Ambassador and an ambassadorial staff and in the removal of all British troops from Ireland, North and South.[52]

Bosie's 37-page pamphlet was published by Martin Secker's The Richards Press in October 1940. It concluded with the following advice to the Churchill government:

> Our Government should politely request Mr de Valera's permission to take over the Irish ports which Ireland cannot defend, and he should be told that if he refuses our polite request the ports will be taken over whether he consents or not. Two months ago I wrote a letter to *The Times* which, characteristically, that paper would not print, saying that unless we took over the Irish ports, with or without the consent of Mr de Valera, we deserved to lose the war against Germany. Since I wrote that letter many of our ships have been torpedoed in waters contiguous to the Irish ports and the situation has steadily deteriorated.
>
> Foolishly, idiotically one might say, we tried, twenty years ago, to propitiate our implacable Irish enemy by kindness and generosity. The experiment has been a complete failure both from the Irish and the English point of view. We abandoned our friends in Ireland in the vain hope of propitiating our enemies; and the result has been what it always has been and always will be in similar conditions.
>
> Now is the time to act. If we wait till Germany has actually landed an army in Ireland (which is liable to happen any day) it may be, it probably will be, too late. It is for the armed forces of the Crown to act because the present crisis is not a political but a strategic one. Fortunately we now have a Prime Minister whose courage is unassailable and indomitable.[53]

In fact, although Bosie was unaware of it, this was precisely what Chamberlain had proposed in the War Cabinet, of which he was still a member though no longer Prime Minister, but he had coupled this with the suggestion that in return Britain should declare its support for 'the establishment of a United Ireland.' This was not acceptable to Churchill, who replied that the Government must avoid putting 'undue pressure' on the loyal province of Ulster and that he 'was not convinced' that the military threat to Eire was as serious as it had been represented, and that if the Germans did in fact land in Eire, 'our forces should be ready to pounce on them'. The Prime Minister repeated this when he wrote to President Roosevelt at the time Bosie's pamphlet appeared: 'His Majesty's Government would of course take the most effective measures to protect Ireland if Irish action exposed it to German attack. It is not possible for us to compel the people of Northern Ireland against their will to leave the United Kingdom and join Southern Ireland.'[54]

On 12 December 1940, Bosie wrote to Sorley Brown: 'The last I heard from Admiral Beamish, MP for Lewes, was a letter which had a postscript saying "*I think the PM is at last preparing for a swoop on Eire*".... I got his letter more than a week ago and nothing has happened, which is very disappointing. I cannot understand Winston's failure to come up to scratch. I always credited him with an unbounded courage and daring. He has got to choose between offending that skunk de Valera and letting this country be starved out.'[55] Here again Bosie wrote without full knowledge of the facts. There was no question of Britain being starved out, particularly after the passing of the Land-Lease Bill by the US Congress, which was the result of the letter Churchhill wrote to Roosevelt, from which a short extract has been quoted above.

7

The first of the four sonnets which Bosie wrote during the war years and the first poem of any kind he had written for the past seven years was dedicated to the Prime Minister. Entitled *Winston Churchill* it was originally published in the *Daily Mail* on 4 July 1941 and figured prominently on the paper's leader page.

> Not that of old I loved you over-much
> Or followed your quick changes with great glee,
> While through rough paths or harsh hostility
> You fought your way, using a sword or crutch

To serve occasion. Yours it was to clutch
And lose again. Lacking the charity
Which looks behind the mask, I did not see
The imminent shadow of 'the Winston touch'.

Axe for embedded evil's cancerous roots,
When all the world was one vast funeral pyre,
Like genie smoke you rose, a giant form
Clothed with the Addisonian attributes
Of God-directed Angel. Like your sire
You rode the whirlwind and outstormed the storm.

It was not one of Bosie's best sonnets, but his nephew Queensberry, who sent Churchill an advance copy before publication was glad he wrote it. 'Thank you very much for the sonnet you sent me which I shall keep and value,' the Prime Minister replied. 'Tell him from me that "Time Ends All Things".'[56]

For this sonnet Bosie received ten guineas from the *Daily Mail* ('I rather expected more!'). However, he got twenty guineas for his second sonnet, *The Old Soldier*, from the *Evening Standard* which published it on 21 July, barely three weeks after the Churchill sonnet. It too had a war-time theme, since Bosie personified himself as 'Colonel Blimp', the fussy and mossbound imaginary British officer who was the butt of the newspaper and magazine cartoonists of the time.

I say my prayers and wear an old school tie,
I was for France in the Spanish war.
I cherish peace but never took the floor
In favour of disarmament. I try
Not to forget that self-sufficiency
Was England's motto in the days before
The idiot 'League'. But doubtless I'm a bore
And sheer anathema to Bloomsbury.

I never would have crawled before Sinn Fein,
Or licked the boots of 'Dev'; I thought with Foch
About Versailles. I rate hell's murkiest imp
Above a pacifist. I'd say again
All that I said about the unchanging 'Bosche'.
But then, of course, I'm only Colonel Blimp.

'I had a letter about it from Captain Margesson, the Minister of War, and he says: "It is full of sadness and truth",' Bosie wrote to Rupert Croft-Cooke who was then training in Combined Operations.

'But as it's almost all in defence of "Colonel Blimp" most people took it for a mere joke. The Minister of War had the acumen to see that it is quite serious poetry.'[57]

The third sonnet, which was addressed 'TO ONE who thinks or pretends to think that we are fighting this war "to uphold the principles of the French Revolution",' was also accepted and published by the *Evening Standard*, (14 April 1943) which Bosie had not expected since it was 'a kick in the pants for democracy'. It was later included in the pocket edition of *The Sonnets of Lord Alfred Douglas* published by The Richards Press (Martin Secker) in 1943.*

The fourth and last sonnet which Bosie wrote, dated January 1944 and called *Class War*, was inspired by Bosie's dislike of Ernest Bevin, the dictatorial Socialist Minister of Labour, particularly for his action in directing inexperienced youngsters to work in the mines, the so-called 'Bevin boys', after he had withdrawn experienced miners from the pits to serve in the armed forces.

> Puffed up with not too brief authority
> Dropping his aitches and exuding spite,
> Reincarnated Cade distils his blight
> On 'rose-cheeked Youth'. Infatuate England! see
> To what abortive shapes 'Democracy'
> Has spawned her litter. Is there none to smite
> This blatant mouth? Or do we now invite
> A second Cromwell's fouler tyranny?
>
> Where is the charter that can make us slaves
> To this rank upstart? Shall his mines devour
> Our proscript children, while with hate he reads
> The unvenomed ukase, 'mid the applause of knaves
> And fustian 'patriots' who time their hour
> To 'strike' (for Hitler) while their country bleeds?

Bosie told Donald Sinden, then a young actor, who admired him and to whom he gave a manuscript of the sonnet, that it would be published in the next edition of *The Sonnets* by The Richards Press.[58] But it was not included in the next edition which appeared two years after Bosie's death, since this was really a reprint of the original edition, although the sonnet had been published by the *Evening Standard*.

In 1943 Bosie was invited by the Royal Society of Literature to

---

*The anonymous addressee of this sonnet was believed to be Frank Owen, former Liberal MP and editor of the *Evening Standard*. He later served in the Royal Armoured Corps.

deliver an address on any subject of his choosing. He chose *The Principles of Poetry* and delivered it on 2 September, when his friend Lord Tredegar acted as chairman. Martin Secker agreed to publish it afterwards as a paper which he did to the amount of 1,000 copies.[59]

Bosie started mildly enough by claiming that 'as recently as thirty years ago there was a fairly general agreement among educated people as to what was poetry and what was not, leaving out any consideration of its comparative merit... It was universally accepted that poetry must be metrical, and all through the history of English Literature, from the time of Chaucer down to thirty years ago, there could scarcely have arisen a difference of opinion as to whether any given piece of writing was in fact verse or not. This uniformity of opinion on the necessary and essential characteristics of verse as opposed to prose no longer exists.' He then proceeded to criticise his *bête noire*, T.S. Eliot, as the leader of the new school of self-styled poetry which used bald prose written out in lines and seriously claimed it was poetry.

As an example of what he meant Bosie took a sentence from a leading article in the *Daily Telegraph*, which he cut up into the following lines:

> We are clearly in the presence of something
> Very different from what the allies
> And the enemy alike used to try
> In the way of strategic bombing.

With this he contrasted three lines of a 'poem' by T.S. Eliot:

> Miss Helen Slingsby was my maiden Aunt
> And lived in a small house near a fashionable square,
> Cared for by the servants to the number of four.

Bosie went on to claim that there was nothing in Eliot's lines to differentiate them from prose, like the passage from the *Daily Telegraph*. 'It is a frightful reflection on the miserable and abject state to which criticism has sunk in England,' he told his audience, 'that this pitiable stuff has for years been accepted without protest as poetry. Mr Eliot is the supreme example of the contempt of form. Far less blatant is the case of the late Mr Yeats concerning whom about twenty-five years ago in a Note to an edition of my *Collected Poems* I said that he was "tainted with the anti-formal heresy". Unlike Mr Eliot he *did* write poetry, sometimes fine poetry in correct form: but he also very often wrote incorrect lines which cannot be made to scan'.

The heretical modern poets, in Bosie's view, professed two heresies.

The first was the 'anti-formal heresy' of which T.S. Eliot was the leading exponent. This heresy claimed that 'strict forms and rules in poetry may and should be broken whenever it suits the "poet" to break them.' The second heresy was the 'Art for Art's sake heresy which the speaker considered was 'nothing like so deadly as the anti-formal heresy which for many years now I have recognised as the truly diabolical enemy and destroyer of poetry.'

> The 'Art for Art's sake' heresy by itself will not prevent a poet from writing good stuff. A man might be tainted with it and yet write very skilful and pleasing verses. Oscar Wilde summed up the heresy, even if he did not invent it, by saying that 'in all Art style is of more importance than sincerity', which is both untrue and pernicious. It is precisely this lack of sincerity in Wilde's poetry which, on the whole keeps him a mere minor poet, although he was an accomplished expert in the art of versifying. It is only fair to him to say that in the end, being essentially an artist, he produced one great and really sincere poem, *The Ballad of Reading Gaol*, which is an answer to, and an implicit repudiation of, his own heresy. So, I repeat, a man may be more or less infected with the 'Art for Art's sake' heresy and yet remain a poet; whereas any man who is thoroughly imbued with the anti-formal heresy cannot be a poet at all except by fits and starts.

'I am so glad you liked my lecture,' he wrote to Marie Stopes. 'I was much pleased and gratified to find my attack on T.S. Eliot so well received. I quite expected that some people would object, but apparently the feeling of the audience was unanimous. The secretary told me (confirming what you say in your letter) that she had never seen another meeting of the Society like it before.'[60] The secretary also gave him £25, pointing out at the same time that this fee included the Society's exlusive right to publish it in its annual *Essays by Divers Hands*. 'This is all poppycock!' Shaw wrote on a postcard to Bosie when he heard about this. 'The R.S.L. volume appears only once a year; and distribution to the members is not a real publication. You are, I should say, quite free in the matter.' Shaw added that he had meant to come and see him in Hove but mistook the day. 'I am always making these senile blunders.'[61]

Bosie sent Shaw's card to the secretary of the Society which climbed down completely and withdrew their objection, but added that they would not print it in *Essays by Divers Hands*. 'I think sufficiently well of my lecture (which they professed to admire enormously) to think that the loss is theirs and not mine,' he wrote back to Shaw. 'I really couldn't see why they should get a ten-thousand-word essay for nothing, which is what it amounted to, and then claim that I was debarred from publishing it elsewhere.'

'I shouldn't bother about the Royal Society of Literature,' Shaw rejoined. 'When the time comes to publish their annual budget of lectures they will think better of omitting yours. If not, it will make no difference to you, and get them into trouble with the members who don't attend the meetings. Englishmen must have their quarrels, preferably about nothing.'*[62]

So the lecture duly appeared under the imprint of The Richards Press. In its review *The Times Literary Supplement* called it 'a gallant defence of the principles of poetry' but feared that it had come too late to upset so many established reputations. Nevertheless for Bosie it was a worthy literary swansong.[63]

Bosie's last published prose was the short introduction he wrote for a volume of poems, *Wartime Harvest*, by Marie Stopes, in which he observed that fine poets sometimes wrote bad verse, such as Wordsworth who, though he wrote 'about half a dozen superlatively fine poems', produced about 220 sonnets, of which a large number were 'simply very bad'.[64]

'Did you see Agate's idiotic remarks about your poems in my preface?' he wrote to Marie on 7 December 1944. 'I wrote a "stinker" in reply but of course they did not print it.'[65]

8

In August 1942 Bosie made the acquaintance of a twenty-year-old Wykehamist named Adrian Earle, as the result of an advertisement in *The Times* expressing a wish to buy some of Bosie's manuscripts. Earle was then living in Tite Street, Chelsea, as a paying guest of the Hedley Hope-Nicholsons (Hedley's father Adrian Hope had been the guardian of Oscar Wilde's two children). He hoped to go up to Oxford and aspired to be a poet. Bosie was greatly taken by his ingratiating ways, particularly after Earle proposed to become a Catholic in 1942. ('Congratulations, dear boy!') In fact Bosie fell so much under Adrian Earle's influence, writing to him nearly every day, that nine months after their first meeting, Bosie made a new will leaving everything he had to Earle, including his copyrights and appointing him his literary executor. It was an infatuation of which Earle took unscrupulous advantage. 'I miss you very much, my dear little Adrian, and hope to see you again soon', Bosie wrote after one of Earle's frequent visits, which included a dinner at the Bedford Hotel where they quaffed

*The lecture was not published in *Essays by Divers Hands*.

'ruby wine' to celebrate Earle's twenty-first birthday, a celebration for which Earle apparently allowed Bosie to pay, though he must have known that Bosie was extremely hard up and 'living in terror' of learning from Olive that she could not go on paying his 'pittance which is already reduced so much.'[66]

Meanwhile the war took its toll of human life among Bosie's friends and neighbours. A.J.A. Symons (Ajaccio), with whom he corresponded to the last, died in 1941, followed by his staunch supporter William Sorley Brown a year later. 'I have lost my most faithful and constant friend whose sympathy and support in all my troubles were an unfailing source of comfort to me,' he wrote to Brown's widow in August 1942. Then on 1 February 1943, Bosie wrote to Mrs Sherard:

> I have just heard the sad news about dear Robert on the wireless and I write to send you my most profound sympathy and condolences. I would have liked to go to the dear old chap's funeral but, alas, I am laid up with a bad chill which has turned to bronchitis and it is impossible for me to go out yet. I have been laid up for nearly 3 weeks. I get these attacks every year about this time. I am having a Mass said for dear Robert and shall always pray for him as I have done for years.[67]

A month later Brighton and Hove were bombed by the Germans. Four people were killed during the air raid in Nizells Avenue and two houses were destroyed.

Bosie's young Oxford friend Richard Rumbold had spent most of the early years of the war in the Royal Air Force where he became a qualified pilot but was discharged on medical grounds in the spring of 1943. He recuperated partly in a sanatorium and partly with friends of his, Sheila and Edward Colman, who lived at Old Monk's Farm, Lancing, which was quite close to Hove. He wrote inviting Bosie to lunch with him on Easter Monday in Brighton to meet the Colmans, whom Bosie described on this occasion as 'very nice people'. After lunch they all went back to their farmhouse, where, as Bosie wrote to Adrian Earle, Mr Colman 'produced most hospitably some excellent port (Cockburn 1909 I think it was) and also some first rate absolutely pre-war Havana cigars!'

Bosie suggested to Adrian that he should stay with the Colmans as a paying guest, since Edward Colman 'supplies eggs, bacon and vegetables et cet to the Naval Base here so you would live like a fighting cock. Colman has a lot of books, including, amazingly, a copy of my autobiography!'[68] In the event the Colmans told Bosie that they would be pleased to put Adrian up but only for a week since they did not take paying guests as a rule. It was at this time, in May

1943 that Bosie made a new will leaving his copyrights to Adrian and appointing him his literary executor.

After a month's rest in the Cotswold Sanatorium in Gloucester, Richard Rumbold returned to Brighton. On 21 July he noted in his diary: 'Spent a day with the Colmans at Lancing with Alfred Douglas and his young friend Adrian Earle. He is 21 and writing a life of Lionel Johnson, whose MSS he showed me.'[69]

Bosie was still devoted to his wife and continued to see her regularly, although her health, both physical and mental, steadily deteriorated. At first she lived in a flat, 9 Viceroy Lodge, on the sea front in Hove and then moved into a house in London of which she speedily tired. Marie Stopes once asked Bosie why, since his circumstances were difficult, he did not again join forces with Olive and live in the same house with her. He replied, with a whimsical laugh, 'Poets are difficult to live with, and I am a specially difficult poet!'[70]

'Olive lunched with me here yesterday Xmas Day on the usual Turkey and Plum Pudding,' he wrote from St Anne's Court on 26 December 1939. 'She brought champagne (a very excellent unusual brand from Hedges & Butler) with her, also Bristol Cream and excellent Cherry Brandy ... "a memorable meal" supposed to be rounded off by an admirable *pâté de foie gras* from Fortnum & Mason's, but by the time we had got to that stage neither of us felt able to cope with it. So it remains intact for another day.'[71]

When Bosie saw her on 11 June 1943, he thought she was very ill and noted that she had lost three or four stones in the past year. He saw her again on 30 September when he remarked that she could hardly move or speak. 'She told me she deeply regretted leaving the Church. First time she had ever admitted her fault. If I can get her back to Hove, I will get a priest to go to her.'[72]

On 24 October Bosie remarked that she had moved back to Viceroy Lodge but showed no signs of returning to the Church. 'Just lies in bed and moans. Frets if I do not see her every day. But I can do nothing for her.' Two days later he wrote that he thought she was going to stop his allowance. 'Yesterday she suddenly said she knew I didn't love her. I said it was very unkind and unfair to say such things to me. She replied by saying "I am only kind if I give you money, but I can take it away."' Bosie thought she had a persecution mania. 'Says her maid Eileen mistreats her which I am quite sure is untrue. Till yesterday Olive said I was her only comfort, and that my visits were the only thing that did her any "good". Then she turned on me. She abuses Eileen and accuses her of all sorts of things.'[73]

'My darling little Olive died this morning,' Bosie wrote on 12

February 1944 to Adrian Earle from Lancing where he was staying with the Colmans. 'I am too upset to write more.' A week later she was cremated; 'dismal business', Bosie noted. 'I couldn't have a Requiem Mass as she had left the Church.'[74] Raymond and Francis Queensberry were both present at the service. 'As you ask me if I was with Olive when she died,' Bosie later wrote to Bernard Shaw, 'I may tell you that I spent several hours holding her hand on the afternoon and evening before she died, though I don't think she was conscious at the time. I had to go back by the 7 o'clock train to Lancing, where I was staying, and I heard of her death from her maid on the telephone at nine-thirty next morning.' Shaw's wife, Charlotte, had also died recently, and when tidying up her effects Shaw came on a bundle of letters which turned out to be those Bosie had sent her husband. 'I dare not destroy them,' Shaw wrote to Bosie at the time: 'I leave them to you.' As a result of this fortunate accident Bosie had both sides of their interesting correspondence, which as Bosie told Marie Stopes 'is now something worth having'.[75]

In her will, which was dated 4 August 1943, Olive left Bosie her opal necklace and all movable chattels and effects, including the money in her bank account, an annual allowance of £500 and the residue of her estate. But all this was claimed by the Official Receiver, since Bosie had never obtained his discharge from bankruptcy, and mostly took effect, although Bosie was allowed to keep the furniture and for the time being to occupy Olive's flat in Viceroy Lodge where he was looked after by her maid Eileen, 'the Irish giantess', as Evan Tredegar called her, since she was 'truly enormous'.

Among Bosie's visitors when he was in Viceroy Lodge was the Rev Richard Blake Brown, the chaplain of HMS *Vernon*, the torpedo establishment which had taken over Roedean girls' school. The Chaplain, who went there at least twice, has left the following description of it and its new occupant:

> A charming flat with white glass-doored cupboards, with glass and china; blue was the predominate colour of cushions and curtains but it seemed to be all painted or papered with white which gave it a light and cheerful air in which Lord Alfred was completely at home. He spoke most affectionately of Olive and seemed thoroughly to enjoy living in the flat she had occupied. He talked vivaciously and happily, never growing angry over his memories. His face seemed sharper, the nose almost ugly....
>
> On the last time I had tea with him Lord Alfred was particularly charming and showed me his wife's Byron books, while a big fat Irish servant who had been I fancy with his wife bustled about, red-faced, merry and with sparse black hair. She no doubt looked after

him magnificently, even dotingly. His talk was as fascinating as ever.[76]

Evan Tredegar, sometimes accompanied by his second wife Olga, the former Russian Princess Dolgorouki, habitually stayed in one of the sea-front Brighton hotels, where they would entertain Bosie and other friends. One of these was the writer Hector Bolitho, who has recalled being there when on leave from the Royal Air Force. He subsequently recorded his recollection of the occasion:

> I remember a big sitting room with grey shadows outside, and the miserable winter tide beyond the sea wall; Alfred Douglas walking in, slowly, with a sad face but quick, lively eyes. Then some naval cadets from *H.M.S. Alfred* joined us and our hostess, Olga Tredegar, tried to manage a rather confused conversation; the boys on one side talking of war; on the other Alfred Douglas talking of poetry. There was a tough little midshipman who had never heard of Alfred Douglas. He no doubt felt that his place was with the erudite, so he piped up: 'Oh, I know a poem right through. I learned it at school, Milton!'
>
> Instead of frowning at the interruption, Lord Alfred Douglas said 'I love Milton. Which poem was it?'
>
> The boy began, but his memory failed. Alfred Douglas prompted him, line by line, so that the midshipman navigated his way to the end of the sonnet. After this Alfred Douglas turned the conversation to the Navy, so that the boy would feel that he was in home waters. It was a charming gesture, from an old, distinguished poet to an eager boy.[77]

Before moving out of St Anne's Court, Bosie sent most of his possessions, including pictures and furniture, to Sotheby's to be auctioned. At the same time he threw out a large quantity of letters and other papers as 'rubbish'. 'The only things I have kept,' he wrote to Adrian Earle on 24 May, 'are Bernard Shaw's letters and the manuscript of my poems and books. I am in a state of dull and dazed despair.' When Edward Colman heard about the papers he tried to retrieve them from the pulping machines, but although the local refuse department were as helpful as they could be, it was too late, since the authorities at that stage of the war were constantly ready to pulp every scrap of paper they could. Another blow was the poor price the other Douglas possessions realised at Sotheby's, where the sale was poorly attended owing to the prevailing flying bombs scare. All they fetched was £298 – 'bloody sickening' Bosie called it.

The doctors at St Andrews Hospital in Northampton now considered that Raymond was well enough to go and live in his mother's flat in Viceroy Lodge. They accordingly decertified him and he duly appeared in Hove, when he told his father that, once probate of Olive's will had been granted, he would give him an allowance of £300 a year, since he had inherited all the property of which his mother was life tenant. This coupled with what Bosie was getting from Marie Stopes and other covenanters now relieved Bosie of the financial anxiety under which he had laboured for years. Unfortunately Raymond was unable to occupy the flat for long. After about a week he had a brain storm with which the resourceful Eileen was fortunately able to cope effectively, and poor Raymond was taken back to St Andrews which he never left until his death twenty years later.

When Bosie left Viceroy Lodge, which he had to do, Evan Tredegar arranged for him to move to London, where a mutual friend, Poppoea Vanda, the ballet agent, offered him board and lodging in her Hampstead house for £150 a year. Miss Vanda, an ardent admirer of Bosie's poetry, had originally written to him in 1942 for copies of Bosie's *Sonnets* and *Lyrics* which she had been unable to find in the London bookshops. In the result they became friends and met regularly either in London or Hove.

Bosie's clothes were actually sent to Poppoea Vanda's house, but eventually Bosie decided not to go, possibly on the advice of his sister Edith who thought he should stay in Hove. Eventually, thanks to a young friend, W.A. Gordon, who was a schoolmaster, and also collected manuscripts like Adrian Earle, he was found a satisfactory lodging with a Mrs Turle at 16 Silverdale Avenue, which was not far from St Anne's Court and where he settled in July 1944. 'A nice little house with a small garden,' Bosie called it. Mrs Turle proved an obliging landlady, accommodating Bosie with two rooms and a kitchen on the ground floor, and a bathroom and two bedrooms on the first, in one of which Bosie slept and in the other the gorgon-like Eileen, who had come on from Viceroy Lodge to 'do' for him. Mrs Turle also supplied him with all meals, the total cost of which with the accommodation was four guineas a week.[78]

He managed quite well during the summer. One of his first visitors was Donald Sinden, then a young actor of 21, who was making his way in Brighton repertory. Sinden had been lent a biography of Oscar Wilde in which Bosie figured prominently, and when he heard that 'the Lord Alfred Douglas' was living in Hove he was determined to meet him. So one morning he called at the house in Silverdale Avenue. Eileen opened the door and Sinden enquired somewhat nervously 'I-I-I- would it be possible to speak to Lord Alfred Douglas?' Eileen asked him his name, and he managed to stammer it out, whereupon he heard a frail voice in the darkness of the hall: 'Can I help? Good morning.' As Eileen retreated to the kitchen, Bosie said to the visitor, 'Please come in.' He did so and was taken into the back room which overlooked the small garden.

By sheer luck, as he later recalled, Donald Sinden opened by talking about Bosie's poetry, 'having done my homework and borrowed and read his sonnets.' Bosie, who was probably flattered that a young actor was brave enough to call on him, responded charmingly and invited him to tea the following week. So began a series of visits, during which Bosie would talk of his life and times, finally getting round to Wilde of whom he spoke with great affection, tears sometimes coming into his eyes. One day Donald Sinden produced a book which he had bought for half-a-crown in a second-hand bookshop in Brighton. 'I've just been reading this,' he told his host. It was *Oscar Wilde and Myself.* Suddenly Bosie leaped to his feet, his whole body twitching. 'Where did you get it,' he screamed. 'Where did you get it?'[79]

As Donald tried to explain, Bosie seized the book and Donald thought he was going to put it on the fire. Then he calmed down, and throwing the offensive volume on the table, took a pen and wrote on the fly-leaf:

> This book (nearly all of which was written by T.W.H. Crosland) has long since been repudiated by me. It does not represent my real views about Wilde as I have explained in numerous places. I much regret that it was ever published.
>
> > Alfred
> > Douglas
> > Sep. 1944[80]

However, they continued to meet and to correspond after Donald Sinden left Sussex for Hampshire later in the year. At one of their meetings in Silverdale Avenue, Hove, Donald asked Bosie about the famous love poem about 'those red rose-leaf lips of yours' which figured conspicuously in the Wilde and other trials; and the young actor found it extraordinary that Bosie should have been so careless as to have left the letter in a suit of clothes he gave away. 'My dear darling,' Bosie replied, 'you must realise that this letter was by comparison with others insignificant. I had received scores of letters from Oscar far more beautiful, far more personal than this one. I kept them locked away, but I burned them after the Ransome case.'

On two occasions Donald Sinden, who was as impoverished as Bosie, if not more so, scraped up enough money to invite him to lunch at the Pavilion Hotel in Brighton, a haven of his theatrical company.

He prayed that Bosie would not stray from the 3s 6d table d'hôte, but offered him a drink. 'No, thank you,' Bosie replied. 'The wages of gin is breath, as Oscar would have said.'[81]

After he had moved to Hampshire Donald Sinden again incurred Bosie's displeasure when he saw a copy of the original American edition of Frank Harris's biography in a bookshop in Petersfield and told Bosie he was thinking of buying it. Bosie's reaction was in character:

> With regard to Harris's book I definitely refuse to give any authorisation for you or anyone else to purchase a copy of it. It is a disgusting book full of lies and calumnies not only about me but also about O.W. and others. The bookseller at Petersfield is liable to *criminal* proceedings for selling a copy and has no right to have it in his possession. Only a few months ago I obtained £100 damages (and an abject apology never to lend the book again) from the British Museum for having lent a copy of it to a holder of one of their reader's tickets.
>
> What possible reason can you have for wanting to possess such a book? No one but a dealer in filthy books for profit could possibly wish to have anything to do with it. If I catch any bookseller selling it, I go for him at once, and have collected hundreds of pounds from various dealers for selling it, including Hatchard's and Harrod's about 15 years ago.

Presumably Donald Sinden desisted from his intention to buy Harris's book. At all events Bosie bore him no ill will and sent him a manuscript copy of his last sonnet *Class War*, which Sinden wished to have.[82]

During the autumn Bosie had a heart attack, brought on, he thought, by a letter from the Custance family solicitor to the effect that the £500 annuity which Olive had left him had been reduced by taxation to £163. 'Imagine the cruelty of not making it tax free,' he protested to Shaw.[83] But this made no difference since the capital sum represented by the annuity, as well as Olive's other bequests to him, were seized by the Official Receiver. 'I am really ill and my heart is in a shocking state with a leaky valve,' he wrote to Marie Stopes on 24 September 1944. 'I am liable to drop dead at any time. I am going into a nursing home on Tuesday ... the sale of my furniture provided me with the necessary funds.' He spent four weeks in the nursing home in Hove, but he felt no better when he went back to his lodgings. 'I rather gather my number is up,' he wrote to Marie on 24 November. 'I don't mind at all and am quite happy because I have complete faith and trust in my darling Jesus, and after all, I have lived seventy-four years which, considering the frightful strains and wear and tear which my heart has subjected me to on and off all my life, is really remarkable. I never expected to be so old. I expect I shall hang on for a few months but don't see how I can expect to recover. I don't go out at all, just sit in a chair and read and drowse.'

Three days later he wrote again to Marie:

> This just to tell you that I had an amazing recovery yesterday (Sunday), for having been given Extreme Unction (that is anointing eyes, lips, nose, ears, hand and feet by a priest) I was so bad I could hardly speak and the ghastly feeling of suffocation which I had for weeks had become almost unbearable. The priest for some reason came a day sooner than he promised to come. He was to come today, but he came yesterday. On Sunday at 4.30 he rang up to say he was coming. Extreme Unction is given to Catholics only when they are in immediate danger of death.
>
> I have often been told that dying people sometimes make a recovery in a miraculous way after being annointed, but I was so little expecting or hoping for anything of the kind that I was quite resigned to death and only hoping for relief from the suffocation. The whole thing only lasts for about five minutes during that time but I was overcome by terrific emotion and the tears rained down my cheeks. To my amazement when it was finished, the suffocation was completely gone and I was breathing normally (I was panting like a dog when it began). I simply couldn't realise or believe it, and thought to myself I suppose it will all start again in a few minutes. So I didn't tell the priest I felt better.
>
> But nothing happened and except for extreme weakness, now much relieved, I felt perfectly well. I had a boiled egg and a glass of sherry for supper, went to bed and slept without a drug for six hours for the first time for weeks. The priest came this morning and gave me Holy Communion at nine. Today I feel nearly well and am writing to Q[ueensberry] and my sister [Lady Edith Fox-Pitt] who were both coming to be at my deathbed! Colman wants to cart me off to Lancing to give me good food and wine but I don't suppose I shall leave till Friday. I haven't dressed for three weeks and have just sat in a chair in a dressing-gown....
>
> P.S. A lot of people called and others rang up as I was prayed for in Church yesterday. I didn't know I had so many friends.[84]

9

Bosie was fetched by his friends Edward and Sheila Colman from his lodgings in Hove on 1 December 1944, expecting to stay with them at their farmhouse in Lancing until Christmas. But, apart from visits to the local Catholic church to hear Mass, he was never to leave Old Monk's Farm except in his coffin. The Colmans gave him a cheerful room with a bath on the ground floor and supplied him with newspapers and books, besides seeing that he was regularly attended by their kind Irish doctor Brendan Betty, as well as the local Catholic priest Father Corley, also Irish. His first visitor was his nephew, Francis Queensberry, whom he had asked to send him a bottle of old brandy, since a bottle for which he had paid five guineas was quite undrinkable. 'He also told me,' Queensberry remarked at the time, 'that he hated brandy, which showed a remarkable change in his tastes.'[85] Besides his sister Edith and his other nephew Cecil, Bosie's visitors included Evan Tredegar, Marie Stopes, Hesketh Pearson and several young admirers, including Donald Sinden, but apparently not his prospective heir Adrian Earle. Bosie's last recorded letter to Earle was written the previous September when he told him that his heart was 'very bad' and that he was going into a nursing home. 'My affairs are now, I hope, satisfactorily arranged,' he added, 'thanks to Raymond.'[86]

What caused the breach between them which followed should be mentioned here. Like Alfred Rose, Adrian Earle was not absolutely honest and like Rose he was later to be convicted of fraud. It appears that Bosie caught him out after he returned to Silverdale Avenue from the nursing home. Adrian Earle had written an article on Shakespeare's sonnets and the identity of Master W.H., from which he borrowed extensively from Bosie's book on the subject, without apparently any acknowledgement. They were both at the Colmans' farmhouse in Lancing when Adrian showed Bosie the text of the article. Bosie flared up at his young friend's flagrant plagiarism of his own work, and they had a somewhat acrimonious altercation.

Bosie was also annoyed with Earle for habitually referring to him as his godfather when talking to Marie Stopes. 'Adrian Earle is *not* my godson,' he wrote to Marie, when he was in the nursing home in Hove, in answer to her enquiry on the subject.

> When I first met him as the result of an advertisment in *The Times* expressing a wish to buy some of my MSS – he bought one (not the original of *In Excelsis*) he told me he was on the point of being received into the Catholic Church. A little later, after I had got to know him and like him, he asked if I would be his godfather and attend the reception ceremony in St James's, Spanish Place, when it took place. I agreed, but he never was received and he told me later in reply to my enquiries that he had 'put it off'. He has never said anything more about it. So I presume it is all off.[87]

The result of all this was that Bosie made a new will on 4 December 1944 in which Adrian Earle was not mentioned. In this will he left his money in his current account at his two banks to his sister Edith, with the exception of £50 to his former housekeeper Mrs Humphry and £25 to Olive's maid Eileen. To Poppoea Vanda he left Olive's opal necklace (which after his death could not be found), and to Edward Colman he bequeathed his books, manuscripts and copyrights, while at the same time appointing Colman his literary executor.

'My miraculous cure on being anointed has, I'm sorry to say, not persisted, and I'm almost as bad as before I had Extreme Unction,' he wrote to Bernard Shaw on 6 December. 'I am staying at Lancing with my farmer friend and his girl wife, so at least I get good pre-war food which farmers alone now have. Also they are exceedingly kind to me and do their best to coddle me. I don't mind dying but I would rather it were not such a long-drawn-out and painful business.' Shaw replied by asking if he had been overhauled by an osteopath. ('It is possible that it is not your heart that is the root cause of the trouble.')

'My miraculous recovery after Extreme Unction was, I fear, only a dying flicker, as I'm worse than ever now,' Bosie wrote again to Shaw a few days later, thanking him for a medical pamphlet he had sent him in reply to his previous letter. 'I don't require converting to nature cure and osteopathy because I have always believed in them. I also have great faith in homeopathy but there doesn't seem to be a homeopath in Brighton. I am trying to hear of one in Worthing. . . . I'm afraid I'm too far gone for care now, and I don't expect to recover. I'm not afraid of death and have many consolations, but the long *process* of dying is painful and miserable. I wish it were over.'

'Dear Childe Alfred,' Shaw rejoined, 'In jumping to a conclusion be careful not to jump too far. The Unction cured you. Only for a day; but it did cure you for that day, proving you are not incurable. The problem is to cure you for many days and not too many years, but enough. I have nothing to contribute but my strong wish that the problem will be solved, which is my form of prayer, and as good, I hope, as anybody's. . . . From your letters I should say you have a lot of life left in you yet.' (In fact he had a little more than three months.) This was Shaw's last letter in a long correspondence which began in 1908 and continued regularly from 1931.[88] Yet despite their lengthy exchange of letters over the years they only met once, at the celebrated Café Royal encounter in February 1895 at which Oscar Wilde and Frank Harris were also present.

On 3 February 1945, Bosie wrote a long letter to Marie Stopes, who visited him twice during his illness. It was his last, hitherto unpublished, letter to her and was written in pencil.

... I am at last a little better. It is really almost a miracle as I was *twice* supposed to be dying and I did not expect to live, in fact I got to the stage of hoping to die to end my sufferings which were (Wordsworth's word) unimaginable. . . .

Evan Tredegar is coming on Sunday and he is trying to get me a pension.* He hopes to get Lord Crewe to support me, and wrote me a charming letter about the lecture [The Principles of Poetry]. Evan tells me they (the Royal Literary Fund) got Mrs Thomas Hardy £180 a year. I have signed the papers and Evan has them. However *please* say nothing about it yet. Anything I get will all be ultimately traceable to your kindness and generosity.

Excuse scrawl. I am still frightfully weak and wobbly and am still in bed nearly all day. The Dr has given me opium, and it does actually work without (literally) poisoning me as all the other stuff he gave me did. Incidentally it benefits my heart in a remarkable way and quite unexpectedly. De Quincy always said it was in itself a beneficent drug! There is not much fear of my becoming an opium addict. It nearly always makes me sick every time I take it when all else fails for sleep.

The cold too was awful for me. I could *not* get warm even in bed with 2 bottles, and the change of weather is a godsend to me. I also had yesterday (Feast of the Purification of our Lady) a sort of spiritual revelation which changed everything in a flash and lifted me out of a pit of dereliction and wretchedness which was worse than anyone can imagine. It looks as if I am not to die just yet after all. Not that I fear Death, and I was quite resigned to God's wish.

I suppose you saw all the dust I raised up with my letter to Winston and his reply about Poland? Or didn't you? On the whole it was tremendously successful. I've had dozens of letters of gratitude from Poles including the Polish ambassador.

With love, ever affectionately, from Bosie

P.S. The Colmans send their best regards. They have been *angelic* to me, dear people.[89]

When he felt well enough during the early days of his stay at Old Monk's Farm, Bosie would go upstairs and play the piano, particularly Chopin, Mozart and Bach, and he would also sing Bach's 'Jesu joy of man's desiring.' Besides this he would like to cook and made omelettes, toffee and the Colmans' Christmas pudding. Sheila

---

*On the subject of Lord Tredegar, Edward Colman has written: 'He was indeed a good friend to Bosie and came frequently to see him with succulent titbits such as oysters and champagne to tempt his failing appetite, and often brought with him a somewhat strange entourage of youthful admirers whom Bosie enjoyed immensely.' Others whom Tredegar brought with him included Lord Annaly, the playwright Terence Rattigan, and Hedley Hope-Nicholson, whose father Adrian Hope had been the guardian of the Wilde children, Cyril and Vyvyan Holland.

Colman recalls that he was generous and whenever he received a royalty cheque or had a betting win he would take her and her husband out to lunch.

At this time Hesketh Pearson was writing his life of Wilde and he sent Bosie the two chapters which covered the period of Wilde's trial and imprisonment. 'I read the chapters you sent this morning,' Bosie replied. 'They are admirable and moving (in fact I found it exceedingly painful to read once more the dreadful story of hypocrisy and humbug). Your book will be by far the best written on the subject.' He continued:

> I can't write at length. I am far too ill, but hope you will come and see me *any afternoon* between 3 and 4. My hosts, the Colmans, quite charming, will give you tea after we have had our talk.
>
> I really have no criticisms to make except that the last few pages about the *De Profundis* letter are less than fair to me. You do not sufficiently make clear how monstrous and ridiculous O.W.'s charges against me were. 'Refusing' to give him lemonade when he was ill! Is it really a serious charge! He was in his own house and only had to order what he wanted. His statements about money are fantastically untrue. I gave him far more money than he gave me, including the many hundreds I gave him in Paris after he left Naples when I myself was by no means wealthy. However perhaps you will put this right when you come to that part of the book.[90]

Needless to say, Hesketh Pearson did put it right when his book appeared in 1946, although Bosie was not alive to read the revised version which is both fair and true. Pearson also accepted Bosie's invitation and came down from London to see him at Old Monk's Farm.

Bosie's last visitor, if not one of his last, was Donald Sinden, who turned up from Hampshire expressly to see him. By this time Bosie was permanently confined to bed and he had a nurse, who with the Colmans watched him day and night. 'I sat beside him for some time,' Donald Sinden has recalled, 'but he was very weak and conversation was difficult. He signed a photograph for me – the last thing he ever wrote.'[91]

His mind was quite alert to the last. The Saturday before he died was St Patrick's Day and he was able to give Sheila Colman a long explanation of why the Irish Catholics take their saints' days more seriously than the English, because in Ireland there was no real break in the continuity of Catholicism, as there was in England with the Reformation and the establishment of the Church of England by King Henry VIII.

On the Saturday morning he also rallied sufficiently to ask Mrs Colman to place a bet for him with his bookmaker: 'Mixed bark doubles – Nicholson's mounts'. If these were his last articulate words, they were characteristic, as he loved a wager on a horse, 'the other side of his nature', as he called his racing and sporting activities.[92]

In the early hours of Tuesday 20 March the night nurse called the Colmans to his room since she sensed from his breathing that the end was near. They held his hand in turn but it is doubtful if he was aware of any human presence in the room and he died peacefully at about 4 am.

The funeral took place three days later, 23 March, at the Franciscan Friary in Crawley, Sussex. Father F. Herbert celebrated the Requiem Mass and after the burial service Bosie's remains were interred beside his mother in the same grave in the Friary cemetery as he wished.[93] It so happened that I was home on leave from the army and so was able to travel down to Crawley from my London home along with Evan Tredegar and other mourners. Tredegar brought a large wreath with him, the only one to do so. The members of Bosie's family who were present were his sister, Lady Edith Fox-Pitt, his nephew Francis Queensberry and the latter's second wife, the artist Cathleen Mann, his nephew Lord Cecil Douglas, his great-niece Lady Jane Douglas, and his cousin Lord Leconfield. Others among the thirty or so present whom I particularly remember were Edward and Sheila Colman, Father F. Corley, (the Irish priest from Lancing), Donald Sinden, Adrian Earle and Mrs Fabienne Hillyard, who as Francis d'Avilla had translated Bosie's poems into French. Afterwards most of us lunched together in The George, the pub in High Street, Crawley, as guests of the Colmans. There we spoke of our recollections of the poet and man of letters for whom, in spite of his faults and the troubles which spoiled much of his career, we had a sustained admiration and affection.

The remainder of Bosie's family story may be briefly told. Olive, who was cremated after her death in the previous year, had expressed the wish that her ashes should be scattered at sea. For some inexplicable reason there was a delay of six years in carrying out her wish, and this ceremony did not take place until 1950, when her ashes were strewn over the waters off the Brighton sea front. Bosie's elder nephew Francis Queensberry died in 1954, aged fifty-eight, and was succeeded by the present Marquess, David, who is Professor of Ceramics at the Royal College of Art in London. Bosie's only sister, Lady Edith Fox-Pitt, his junior by four years, lived until 1963, dying in her ninetieth year, while his younger nephew, Lord Cecil Douglas, died in 1981 aged 82. Finally, Raymond Douglas, Bosie's and Olive's only son, died in St Andrews Hospital, Northampton, on 10 October 1964, never having recovered his mental health. Had he lived another few weeks, he would have been 62. He is buried in Brookmount cemetery, Northampton, and perhaps he may be fairly regarded as the last of the 'mad bad line' in Wilde's phrase in *De Profundis*.

As for Bosie, if he was not mad, he was certainly bad in his early homosexual years before his marriage. His reformation was undoubtedly due in great measure first to his marriage, and secondly to his conversion to the Roman Catholic faith, which gave his life a stability and a spiritual substance which it had previously lacked. Nor can there be any question that he was a poet of much more than ordinary merit, as *The Times* described him in his obituary. The Wilde tragedy was to a great extent his own and he added to it by his action in never letting the world forget it. However, it is now beyond dispute that he neither ruined his friend nor deserted him, as his enemies so often alleged. To those of a younger generation, like the present writer, he was an essentially kindly man.

As a poet he excelled as a writer of sonnets in the strictly formal style of Petrarch. He also wrote some fine lyrics and amusing 'nonsense' rhymes, as well as trenchant satires, three autobiographies (although he later repudiated the first) and a study of Shakespeare's sonnets, not to mention 'introductions' to the works of others of such mutually differing personality as Robert Sherard, John Piper and Marie Stopes. That his poems should have commanded the admiration of Sir Arthur Quiller Couch, for many years Professor of Poetry at Cambridge, gave him considerable pleasure, and he was justifiably proud of the fact that they should have found a place in the Professor's anthologies of contemporary verse.

As a young man of twenty-seven, after he had been reunited for a few months with Oscar Wilde in Naples, Alfred Douglas thus expressed his aim and object as a poet in the 'Sonnet on the Sonnet' which was published shortly afterwards in *The City of the Soul*:

> To fight with form, to wrestle and to rage,
> Till at the last upon the conquered page
> The shadows of created Beauty fall.

The attainment of this objective must be accounted his outstanding personal achievement in the literary field. One likes to think that it will still be held in high regard long after the follies of his association with Wilde and the quarrels with Robert Ross and Frank Harris and others which marred his tempestuous career have been forgotten.

Sources

The following abbreviations are used:

Berg	The Berg Collection, New York Public Library, New York.
BL	Department of Manuscripts, British Library, London.
Bodleian	The Bodleian Library, Oxford.
Clark	The William Andrews Clark Memorial Library, University of California, Los Angeles.
Hyde Collection	Manuscripts and printed books in the collection of Mrs Mary Hyde, Somerville, New Jersey.
NLS	The National Library of Scotland, Edinburgh
Texas	Humanities Research Center, University of Texas, Austin.
QUB	Queen's University, Belfast, Northern Ireland.

I *Family and Youth*

1 Oscar Wilde. *Letters*. Ed Rupert Hart-Davis (1962), 435.
2 Brian Roberts. *The Mad Bad Line* (1981), 142ff.
3 H. Montgomery Hyde. *Oscar Wilde* (1975), 171.
4 Sir Herbert Maxwell. *History of the House of Douglas*. (1902) II, 284.
5 Because of this Marquessate which was overlooked, the Queensberry titles were later renumbered correctly by Burke and Debrett in their *Peerages*. But they are inaccurate in the *Dictionary of National Biography* where, for example, Alfred's father John Sholto appears as the eighth marquess whereas he was really the ninth.

6   Queensberry and Percy Colson. *Oscar Wilde and the Black Douglas* (1949), 11–12.
7   W.M. Thackeray. *The Four Georges*, 65.
8   *Dictionary of National Biography*, Roberts, *passim*.
9   The frayed rope is preserved in the museum at Zermatt.
10 Alfred Douglas. *Autobiography* (1929), 5.
11 Roberts, 44ff.
12 *Id*, 27.
13 Their seat was known as The Hall, and they seem to have been connected with the Montgomerys of Moville, Co Donegal, ancestors of Viscount Montgomery of Alamein, since their crest and motto are the same: an arm of armour with the hand grasping a tilting spear above the words '*Gardez bien.*' See on the Montgomerys, baronets of The Hall, B.G. de Montgomery. *Origin and History of the Montgomerys* (1948), 135.
14 Alfred Douglas. *Without Apology* (1938), 233–4.
15 Roberts, 50. Alfred Montgomery died 5 April 1896, aged 82.
16 Register of Wills, Somerset House. Her will was dated 13 September 1887. She died 27 January 1893, aged 72.
17 Roberts, 51.
18 *Id*, 55.
19 *Id*, 64–5.
20 Register of births, Church of St Peter, Powick. Hereford and Worcester County Record Office: X850 Powick BA 8444/2b (i) Vol 11. Lord Robert Bruce (1851–93), whose elder brother was Earl of Elgin, disapproved of Queenberry's subsequent treatment of his wife Sibyl and son Alfred. As a result for the remainder of his life he cold-shouldered Queensberry and was not on speaking terms with him.
21 Douglas. *Autobiography*, 2, 7.
22 Roberts, 116–118.
23 Douglas. *Autobiography*, 16.
24 *Id*, 8.
25 *Id*, 17.
26 Douglas. *Without Apology*, 316.
27 Douglas. *Autobiography*, 26–27.
28 Stapleton-Cotton was killed at Ladysmith in the Boer War.
29 Elizabeth Longford. *A Passionate Pilgrimage* (1979), 246.
30 Douglas. *Autobiography*, 48–9.
31 Douglas. *Without Apology*, 174.
32 Harris. *Oscar Wilde: His Life and Confessions* (1918), I, 148.
33 Mary Hyde (ed). *Bernard Shaw and Alfred Douglas* (1982), 4.
34 Douglas. *Without Apology*, 176–8.
35 Douglas. *Complete Poems* (1928), 5.
36 Douglas. *Autobiography*, 52.
37 Warren's official biography by Laurie Magnus (1932) is a flattering panegyric which contains no mention of either Wilde or Douglas, although many others of the college's distinguished *alumni* figure in it.

II *The Fatal Friendship*

1 Wilde. *Letters*. 254 and note.
2 Douglas. *Autobiography*, 56–58.
3 *Id*, 59.
4 Mason. *Bibliography of Oscar Wilde*, 341ff; personal knowledge.
5 Rupert Croft-Cooke. *Bosie*, 65.
6 *The Court and Society Review 13* December 1887 (*Un Amant de Nos Jours*). *The Spirit Lamp* 6 December 1891. Douglas told Marie Stopes in 1942 that he subsequently discovered that Wilde had written this sonnet before he met Douglas: Marie Stopes. *Lord Alfred Douglas* (1949), 51.
7 Douglas. *Autobiography*, 76.
8 Wilde. *Letters*, 440.
9 Queensberry and Percy Colson. *op cit* 55.
10 Douglas to Harris 20 March 1925: Douglas MSS: Texas.
11 Wilde. *Letters*, 314.
12 Stuart Mason. *Bibliography of Oscar Wilde*, 374.
13 Max Beerbohm. *Letters to Reggie Turner* (1964), 23.
14 Wilde. *Letters*, 316. E.P.S. Pigott was examiner of plays for the Lord Chamberlain from 1875 to 1895. After his death Bernard Shaw described him as 'a walking compendium of vulgar insular prejudice.'
15 Clark. Victoria Alexandrina Marchioness of Lothian, who lived at Blickling, was the eldest daughter of Bosie's kinsman, the 5th Duke of Buccleuch.
16 Douglas. *Autobiography*, 59–60.
17 Wilde. *Letters*, 327.
18 *The Trials of Oscar Wilde*, ed Montgomery Hyde (1948), 112. Wilde. *Letters*, 326. The sonnet was definitely 'In Sarum Close' and not, as Sir Rupert Hart-Davis suggests, possibly 'In Praise of Shame'. The third line of the sonnet reads 'In this calm twilight of gray (*sic*) Gothic things.' Many years later Bosie described this sonnet as 'an example of what I call "art for art's sake" heresy. It lacks sincerity and is therefore merely an exercise in Verse': Douglas. *Sonnets* (1935) 19n.
19 Wilde. *Letters*, 867–8.
20 *Id*, 333.
21 *Morning Post*, 7 March 1912.
22 Wilde. *Letters*, 431.
23 *Id*, 336, 457.
24 Queensberry and Colson, 32.
25 Wilde. *Letters*, 337.
26 Hyde. *Oscar Wilde*, 156–7. *Trials* (1973), 66–9.
27 Beerbohm. *Letters to Reggie Turner*, 37.
28 *Id*, 39–42.
29 Wilde. *Letters*, 340.
30 Hyde. *Oscar Wilde*, 162.
31 Douglas. *Without Apology*, 181.
32 Hyde, *Trials* (1948), 152–3.

33 Wilde. *Letters*, 341.
34 Beerbohm. *Letters to Reggie Turner*, 53.
35 Frank Harris. *Oscar Wilde: His Life and Confessions* (1918), I, 178.
36 Wilde. *Letters*, 431–2.
37 *Id*, 344.
38 Queensberry and Colson, 32. *The Artist* Vol. XIV (1893), 99.
39 Douglas TS: Texas.
40 *The Artist* Vol XIV. Reprinted as 'In an Aegean Port' in *Poems* (1896).
41 Douglas TS: Texas.
42 Wilde. *Letters*, 432–3.
43 Douglas TS: Texas. *Autobiography* (2nd ed 1931), 160 footnote.
44 Margery Ross (ed). *Robert Ross Friend of Friends* (1952), 28.
45 For details see H. Montgomery Hyde. *The Cleveland Street Scandal* (1976).
46 Mary H. Lago and Karl Beckson (ed). *Max and Will* (1975), 24 note 1.
47 Wilde. *Letters*, 346.
48 *Id*, 347.
49 *Id*, 426.
50 Douglas TS: Texas.
51 Croft-Cooke. *Bosie*, 89.
52 Robert Hichens. *Yesterday* (1947), 60ff.
53 Croft-Cooke, *Bosie*, 92–5.
54 Wilde. *Letters*, 443.
55 Beerbohm. *Letters to Reggie Turner*, 80–92.
56 Douglas TS: Texas.
57 Wilde. *Letters*, 435.
58 Hyde. *Trials* (1948), 153.
59 Douglas TS: Texas. Wilde. *Letters*, 354. The first volume of *The Yellow Book* was published on 16 April 1894. On *The Yellow Book*, see particularly *The Artists of the Yellow Book and the Circle of Oscar Wilde* (1983) with introduction by the present writer.
60 Wilde. *Letters*, 355.
61 *Id*, 360.
62 Hyde. *Trials* (1948), 24–6, 154–5.
63 *Id*, 161–2.
64 Roberts. *The Mad Bad Line*, 200.
65 Beerbohm. *Letters to Reggie Turner*, 95.
66 Wilde. *Letters*, 363.
67 Beerbohm. *Letters to Reggie Turner*, 97.
68 Wilde. *Letters*, 369, 436ff.
69 *Id*, 373 and note 1.
70 Introduction by Robert Hichens to 1949 edition of *The Green Carnation*, xiii.
71 Wilde. *Letters*, 375, 440.
72 *Id*, 376.
73 Personal knowledge.
74 Stuart Mason. *Bibliography of Oscar Wilde*, 14ff. John Francis Bloxham (1873–1928) was later ordained a minister in the Church of England,

becoming Chaplain to the Forces in the First World War when he was awarded the Military Cross and Bar; he was subsequently Vicar of St Saviour, Hoxton. *The Chameleon* was reprinted by the Eighteen-Nineties Society in 1978 with an Introduction by the present writer and an Essay by Timothy d'Arch Smith.

75   *To-Day*, 29 December 1894.
76   Wilde. *Letters*, 441.
77   Communicated by Sir Rupert Hart-Davis.
78   André Gide. *Oscar Wilde* (1951), 74. Translated from Gide's *Si le Grain ne meurt* (1926).
79   Personal knowledge.
80   Wilde. *Letters*, 383.
81   *Id*, 384. For a photocopy of the original of the whole letter, which is in the Clark Library in the University of California, Los Angeles, see Hyde. *Trials*, 33.

III *The Exile*

1   Hyde. *Oscar Wilde*. 197ff.
2   Wilde. *Letters*, 430.
3   Harris. *Oscar Wilde* (1918), I, 198; II, 24. (Shaw's 'Memories of Wilde'). Harris and Douglas. *New Preface to 'The Life and Confessions of Oscar Wilde'* (1925), 30. Hyde. *Trials*, (1948), 349. Queensberry's plea of justification is printed in Appendix A to Hyde, *op cit*.
4   Wilde. *Letters*, 386.
5   Douglas. *Without Apology*, 310–12. A.J. Balfour, later Prime Minister and Earl Balfour, was at this time Conservative leader in the House of Commons. Lord Houghton (later Earl of Crewe), a Liberal, was Viceroy of Ireland. It should be noted with regard to the first paragraph of Wyndham's letter that none of Wilde's homosexual associates who gave evidence against him at his trials had been 'ruined' by him. They were already practising homosexuals, mostly prostitutes.
6   Douglas TS: Texas.
7   Ross TS: Clark. Written on the subject of his relations with Douglas for his solicitor Sir George Lewis about 1913–14.
8   Wilde. *Letters*, 389–90.
9   *Id*, 391.
10   Douglas. *Autobiography*, 108. Wilde. *Letters*, 392.
11   Douglas. *Autobiography*, 110. Taylor's solicitor was Arthur Newton. On Newton, who was subsequently imprisoned for fraud, see Hyde. *The Cleveland Street Scandal*, *passim*.
12   Douglas. *Autobiography*, 112.
13   Douglas MS: Clark. Wilde. *Letters*, 396 note 2.
14   Hyde. *Trials*, 78–9.
15   Queensberry and Colson. *Oscar Wilde and the Black Douglas*. 66–9.

16 Hyde. *Trials*, 346–7.

17 Croft-Cooke. *Bosie*, 133.

18 Home Office Papers. Cited in Hyde *Oscar Wilde: The Aftermath*, Appendix B. The Home Secretary was Sir Matthew Ridley.

19 Douglas to Adey 20 November; Bowden to Adey 9, 11 June; Douglas to Adey 1 August, 25 August 1895: Douglas MSS: Clark. Douglas to Gide 22 September 1895 *Revue de Littérature Comparée* 484. All Douglas's letters to Gide are in French, except one in English.

20 *Daily Chronicle* 28 September 1895. Wilde. *Letters* 453–4.

21 Douglas to Adey 30 November 1895: Douglas MS: Clark. Adey to Douglas 3 December 1895: Douglas. *Oscar Wilde and Myself* (1914), 177–8.

22 Croft-Cooke, 139. Wilde, *Letters*, 399. Douglas. *Without Apology*, 269–71. Douglas sent the sonnet to Stuart Merrill. 'It explains itself,' he wrote in the accompanying letter. 'So I need add no more than express to you my deeply-felt thanks for your generous efforts on behalf of one who is dearer to me than any thing or person in the world': Douglas to Merrill 17 February 1896. Douglas MSS: Texas. On Stuart Merrill generally, see H. Montgomery Hyde. 'Some Unpublished Recollections by Stuart Merrill' in *Adam International Review*. Nos 241–3 (1954), ed Miron Grindea.

23 *Revue Blanche* 1 June 1896. Hyde. *Trials*, 362–5. There is another translation of the *Revue Blanche* article in the Clark Library.

24 Wilde. *Letters*, 400.

25 Sibyl Queensberry to Adey, 13 February, 16 May, 27 February 1896: Douglas MSS: Clark.

26 Hyde. *Oscar Wilde: The Aftermath*, 24. Personal knowledge.

27 Douglas MSS: Clark.

28 Douglas to Adey 8 February 1897: Douglas MSS; Clark.

29 Hyde. *Oscar Wilde: The Aftermath*, 134–5. Wilde. *Letters*, 588–91.

30 Wilde. *Letters*. 591–2.

31 *Id*, 610, 613.

32 Ross to Douglas 23 June 1897. Douglas MSS: Clark.

33 Douglas to Adey 4 July 1897: Douglas MSS; Clark. Wilde to Ross 20 July 1897: Wilde. *Letters*, 624.

34 Sibyl Queensberry to Adey 26 July 1897: Douglas MSS: Clark.

35 Wilde MSS: Clark. I have been unable to identify silk.

36 Wilde. *Letters*, 635. Douglas. *Autobiography*, 151–2.

37 Wilde. *Letters*, 637.

38 *Id*, 638–9.

39 Vincent O'Sullivan. *Aspects of Wilde* (1938), 195–7.

40 Douglas. *Autobiography*, 152.

41 Wilde. *Letters*, 644–5.

42 *Id*, 649, 657 and note.

43 *Id*, 664.

44 *Id*, 659, 661. Douglas to Adey 20 November 1897: Douglas MSS: Clark.

45 *Id*, 685. Douglas. *Without Apology*, 302–5.

46 *Id*, 709–10.
47 Sibyl Queensberry to Douglas 6 January 1930: Hyde Collection. Wilde. *Letters*, 739.
48 Douglas. *Autobiography*. For an account of *Mr and Mrs Daventry* see the present writer's Introduction to his edition of the play, the first time it was published (1956).
49 Wilde. *Letters*, 705. Hyde. *Trials*, 372–3. Wilde. *Letters*, 738.
50 *Id*, 732, 752.
51 *Id*, 753, 754, 759.
52 Douglas MSS: Clark.
53 Wilde. *Letters*, 761, 763, 767. Shaw to Douglas 31 August 1940: Mary Hyde (ed). *Bernard Shaw and Alfred Douglas A Correspondence* (1982), 132.
54 Wilde. *Letters*, 746, 801 and note 3. Douglas. *Collected Poems* (1919), 125–6.
55 Croft-Cooke, 175–6.
56 Wilde. *Letters*, 816. Croft-Cooke, 179–80.
57 Wilde. *Letters*, 828, 831.
58 Croft-Cooke, 185. Douglas. *Autobiography*, 323.
59 Douglas. *Autobiography*, 182–3.
60 Douglas MSS: Clark.

IV *Racing, Marriage and Journalism*

1 Douglas. *Autobiography*, 168ff.
2 *Id*, 180.
3 Douglas MSS: Texas.
4 Pearson. *Modern Men and Mummers* (1921), 168–9.
5 Karl Beckson. *Henry Harland* (1978), 90. On Olive Custance, see generally Brocard Sewell. *Olive Custance Her Life and Work* (1975).
6 Douglas to Olive Custance 24 January 1901. Custance MSS: Berg.
7 Douglas. *Autobiography*, 204ff. George Wickes. *The Amazon of Letters: The Life and Loves of Natalie Barney* (1977), 58ff.
8 *Id*, 208.
9 20 August 1901. Custance MSS: Berg.
10 Douglas to Harris 19 October 1901. Douglas MSS: Texas.
11 Douglas to Olive Custance 2 December 1901. Custance MSS: Berg. Douglas. *Autobiography*, 190–2.
12 'The Traitor' was later published in *Sonnets* (1909) and reprinted in all subsequent editions of Douglas's poems. The Taylor incident was communicated by Sir Sacheverell Sitwell.
13 Douglas to Olive Custance. nd 1901–2: Custance MSS: Berg. Douglas. *Autobiography*, 196.
14 Douglas. *Autobiography*, 198–9.
15 Sibyl Queensberry to Douglas 4, 11 March 1902: Hyde Collection.
16 Croft-Cooke, 204.

17 Olive Douglas to Douglas 1944: Hyde Collection. Douglas to Olive Douglas 28 August 1902. Douglas MSS: Berg.
18 Douglas. *Autobiography*, 215–6.
19 *Id*, 218ff.
20 Douglas to Olive Douglas 22 January 1906. Douglas MSS: Berg. W. Sorley Brown. *The Life and Genius of T.W.H. Crosland* (1928) 182, 192.
21 *Motorist and Traveller* 1 March 1905. Reprinted in Hyde. *Oscar Wilde: The Aftermath*, Appendix D.
22 Compton Mackenzie. *My Life and Times* (1964), III, 225.
23 Douglas to Olive Douglas 28 July 1905; 21 September 1906. Douglas MSS: Berg. Ross TS: Clark.
24 Sorley Brown, 208–9.
25 Croft-Cooke, 212.
26 Douglas to Olive Douglas 29 October 1908. Douglas MSS: Berg. Douglas to Ada Leverson, nd 1908. Douglas MSS: NLC.
27 Douglas to Michael Field. British Library: Add MSS 54851 f.218.
28 Douglas to Lane 14 December 1908. Lane Papers: Westfield College, University of London.
29 J. Lewis May. *John Lane and the Nineties* (1936), 196.
30 Mary Hyde (ed). *Bernard Shaw and Lord Alfred Douglas* (1982), 207–10.
31 Ross TS: Clark.
32 *Id.*
33 *Id.*
34 Douglas. *Autobiography*, 221. J.A. Spender and Cyril Asquith. *Life of Lord Oxford and Asquith* (1932), I, 236.
35 Douglas. *Id* 223.
36 *Id* 232. Sorley Brown, 239.
37 Douglas. *Autobiography*, 232–3.
38 William Freeman. *Lord Alfred Douglas* (1948), 205ff.
39 W.S. Blunt. Diary. 23 August 1909: Fitzwilliam Museum Cambridge (9/75). Elizabeth Longford. *A Passionate Pilgrimage* (1979), 382.
40 Freeman, *loc cit.*
41 Sorley Brown, 240–1.
42 Freeman, 215ff.
43 Douglas. *Autobiography*, 224. Sorley Brown, 244.
44 Douglas to Olive 21 October 1909. 27 January 1910, 27 November 1911. Douglas MSS: Berg.
45 Douglas to Lane 13 March 1912. Lane Papers: Westfield College.
46 Douglas to Olive 14 October 1911: Douglas MSS: Berg.
47 Douglas. *Autobiography*, 245–7.
48 W.S. Blunt Diary, 1911. Fitzwilliam Museum (9/1975).
49 Douglas to Olive 3 June 1911. Douglas MSS: Berg. Freeman. *Lord Alfred Douglas*. 227–9.
50 Douglas. *Autobiography*, 254–7.
51 Shaw to Frank Harris 4 September 1916: Harris. *Oscar Wilde* II, 32.

V *The Litigant*

1 Douglas. *Oscar Wilde and Myself* (1914), 163–4.
2 Ross TS: Clark.
3 Ross holograph on verso of title page of *The Suppressed Portion of 'De Profundis'*, published by Paul R. Reynolds, New York, 1913: Clark.
4 Kenyon to Ross 29 October 1909. *Oscar Wilde De Profundis* Departmental file. British Library: Add. MSS 50141.
5 Ross to Kenyon 5 November 1909: *id.*
6 Kenyon to F.S. Salaman (Douglas's trustee in bankruptcy) 19 June 1913: *id.* 'The MS of *De Profundis* was presented to the Trustees [of the British Museum] by the literary executor of Mr Oscar Wilde. Although in the form of a letter addressed to Lord Alfred Douglas, there is nothing to show that it was ever sent to him, and it appears to have remained in Mr Wilde's possession until his death, and then to have been treated by his literary executor as the manuscript of an unpublished work.'
7 Rose TS: Clark.
8 Arthur Ransome. *Autobiography*, ed Rupert Hart-Davis (1976), 143. Ransome. *Oscar Wilde A Critical Study* (1912), 157.
9 Ross TS: Clark.
10 For a full account of this trial see *The Times*, 18, 19, 22, 23 April 1913. There is an abbreviated account in Montgomery Hyde. *Cases that Changed the Law* (1951) 164–76. Until Ross explained to the British Museum trustees the relevance of the *De Profundis* MS at the trial, there was some reluctance on their part to produce it. See Kenyon to Lewis & Lewis, 27 February 1913: British Library Add MSS 50141.
11 Douglas to Adey 23 April 1913: Clark. The last twelve words of the third paragraph of this letter and the postscript are omitted in the text as given by Sorley Brown in his life of Crosland, 319.
12 Douglas, *Autobiography*, 256.
13 *Id*, 259–60.
14 Douglas to Olive 3 June 1913. Douglas MSS: Berg.
15 *Daily Telegraph* 13 June 1913.
16 Douglas. *Autobiography*, 255–6.
17 Olive Douglas to Sibyl Queensberry 14 January 1913: Brocard Sewell, 25.
18 Douglas to Olive 15, 17, 19 September 1913: Douglas MSS; Berg.
19 Douglas to Harris 31 December 1906. Douglas MSS: Texas.
20 Douglas to Harris 2 November 1913. Douglas MSS: Texas. Annotation by Douglas in copy of *The Collected Poems of Lord Alfred Douglas* (1913): Hyde Collection. This copy was originally given by Douglas to Alfred Rose who sold it to Rupert Croft-Cooke.
21 Douglas to Olive 18 December 1914. Douglas MSS: Berg.
22 *Id*, 14 August 1915: Douglas MSS: Berg.
23 Douglas to Sorley Brown 22 August 1915. Brown MSS: NLS.
24 Douglas. *Autobiography*, 263–4.
25 Douglas to Lewis 28 October 1913. Ross TS: Clark.

26 Sorley Brown, 309–10.
27 *Id*, 311.
28 *Id*, 312 and note.
29 Birkenhead. *Frederick Edwin Earl of Birkenhead* (1933), I, 250ff.
30 Sorley Brown, 322, 329.
31 Douglas to William Morris 4 March 1916. Catalogue 286 item 263. *Literary Manuscripts*. George S. Macmanus Co Philadelphia.
32 Douglas. *Collected Satires* (1926) 14–15.
33 Douglas. *Autobiography*, 285–6.
34 *Id*, 286–8.
35 Douglas to Olive 5, 13 November. Douglas MSS: Berg.
36 Douglas. *Autobiography*, 289–90. Freeman, 245–8. Sorley Brown, 333ff.
37 Douglas to Olive 30 November 1914. Douglas MSS: Berg.
38 *Id*, 11 December 1914, Douglas MSS: Berg.
39 Douglas to Sorley Brown 3, 7 December 1914. Brown MSS: NLS. Sorley Brown, 334–7.
40 Sorley Brown, 338. Douglas *Collected Satires*, 22.
41 Douglas to Asquith 22 January 1915. Asquith Papers: Bodleian (MS Asquith 26).
42 Simon to Sir Charles Mathews (DPP) 31 January 1915. Asquith Papers: Bodleian. In his letter Simon stated that he could not have granted the application for a *nolle prosequi* without the joint application of both prosecution and accused. Douglas's solicitors had originally objected to the grant of a *nolle prosequi* but subsequently withdrew their objection. Simon added that he 'was left in complete ignorance of any of the alleged terms of the compromise.'
43 Douglas to Churchill 21 May 1915. Asquith Papers: Bodleian.
44 *Morning Post* 29 March 1915.
45 Douglas. *Collected Satires*, 23.
46 *Id*, 35.
47 Mary Hyde (ed). *Bernard Shaw and Lord Alfred Douglas*, 4.
48 Douglas to Sorley Brown. Brown MSS: NLS. There is a copy of *The Wilde Myth* in the Clark Library. The original is in Texas.
49 Douglas to Olive 19 June 1917. Douglas MSS: Berg. *Autobiography*, 291.
50 Douglas to Olive 3 January 1917, 9 October, 1 November 1918. Douglas MSS: Berg. Brocard Sewell, 27.
51 *Verbatim Report of the Trial of Noel Pemberton Billing MP* (1918). Douglas's evidence. 277ff. See also Michael Kettle. *Salome's Last Veil* (1917) and Douglas. *Autobiography*, 193–4.
52 *The Spirit Lamp*. Vol IV No 1. May 1893.
53 *Daily Telegraph* 25, 26, 29 Nov 1921.
54 Douglas. *Autobiography*, 306.
55 *Id*, 309.
56 Douglas to Sorley Brown 29 November 1921. Brown MSS: NLS.

VI *Prison and After*

1   Douglas. *Autobiography*, 300.
2   *Id*, 186–7.
3   *Id*, 292, 301.
4   *Id*, 292.
5   Sorley Brown, 391.
6   Douglas. *Autobiography*, 329.
7   *Id*, 329–30.
8   Douglas. *Collected Satires*, 55. Croft-Cooke, 294.
9   Hyde. *Sir Patrick Hastings* (1960), 110.
10 Sorley Brown, 391–2. Douglas to R.H. Edleston 22 January 1918. Edleston Papers: Durham County Record Office.
11 Douglas to Sorley Brown 22 August 1922. Brown MSS: NLS.
12 Hyde. *Sir Patrick Hastings*, 111–7. Douglas. *Autobiography*, 302–3.
13 Douglas to Sorley Brown 19 July 1923. Brown MSS: NLS.
14 *Id*. Douglas's contemplated action against the *Jewish Guardian* was dropped.
15 Hyde. *Their Good Names*. (1970), 215–46. ('Winston Churchill and the Battle of Jutland.')
16 *The Times* 14 December 1923.
17 Douglas. *Autobiography*, 310.
18 Douglas. *In Excelsis* (1924), Preface, 8–9. *Autobiography*, 311–13.
19 Douglas. *Autobiography*, 313.
20 *Id*, 314–16.
21 Douglas to Sorley Brown 12 May 1924. Brown MSS: NLS. Douglas to Pim 8 May 1924. Pim MSS: QUB.
22 Edward Marjoribanks. *The Life of Sir Edward Marshall Hall* (1929), 110–13.
23 Douglas to Croft-Cooke 14 October 1927. Douglas MSS: Texas. Croft-Cooke, 318.
24 Douglas to Pim 15 October 1924. Pim MSS: QUB.
25 *Id*, 17 October 1924. Pim MSS: QUB.
26 Douglas to Sorley Brown 17 October 1924. Brown MSS: NLS.
27 Croft-Cooke, 401. Douglas to Sorley Brown 17 October 1924, 18 May 1925. Brown MSS. NLS.
28 Harris and Douglas. *New Preface to 'The Life and Confessions of Oscar Wilde'* (1925), 17–18.
29 *Id*, 52, 53.
30 Douglas to Harris 26 August 1925. Douglas MSS: Texas.
31 *Id*. 4 September 1925. Douglas MSS: Texas.
32 *Id*. 16 September 1925. Douglas MSS: Texas.
33 Mary Hyde (ed). *Bernard Shaw and Alfred Douglas*, 10. The letter, which appeared in the Covici Friede edition of Harris's biography (1930), contained the addition which was not added or forged as Douglas suggested. For the text of the letter, dated 20 March 1925, see above p.27–8.

34 *Id*, 63.
35 Shaw wrote 52 pages by way of preface.
36 Mary Hyde. *op cit*, 67–8.
37 Douglas. *Autobiography*, 306.
38 Croft-Cooke, 319. Douglas. *Without Apology*, 187.
39 Douglas to Sorley Brown 15 August 1925. Brown MSS: NLS.
40 Douglas to Harris. August 1925. Douglas MSS: Texas.
41 Mary Hyde. *op cit*, 218–9.
42 Communicated by St Andrews Hospital, Northampton.
43 Julian Symons. *A.J.A. Symons* (1950), 55.
44 Timothy d'Arch Smith. *R.A. Caton and The Fortune Press* (1983) 32, 49, 58.
45 Dulau Catalogue. *A Collection of Original Manuscripts Letters and Books of Oscar Wilde.* (1927), vii, 22. Items 1 to 64, as well as the volumes of press cuttings, were purchased by the late Mr William Andrews Clark and are now in the Clark Memorial Library, University of California, Los Angeles.
46 Wilde, *Letters*, 609, 624.
47 Croft-Cooke, 332. The present writer was the first member of the general public to examine the original, which he was allowed by the Museum authorities to do on 1 January 1960. See H. Montgomery Hyde. *Sunday Times* 3 January 1960: also '*The Riddle of De Profundis. Who Owns the Manuscript?*' in *The Antigonish Review* No 54 (1983), 106–27.

VII *The Final Phase*

1   Douglas to Sorley Brown. 25 March 1929. Brown MSS: NLS.
2   *Id.* 4 September 1929. Brown MSS: NLS. Croft-Cooke, 403.
3   *Id.* 26 January 1930. Brown MSS: NLS.
4   Douglas to Montgomery Hyde. 28 April 1930. Hyde Collection.
5   *Id.* 2 May 1930. Hyde Collection.
6   Douglas to Croft-Cooke. May 1930. Douglas MSS: Texas.
7   Douglas to Montgomery Hyde. 6 June 1930. Hyde Collection.
8   Croft-Cooke, 336.
9   *Id*, 403. William More Adey (1858–1942) was a close friend of Robert Ross with whom he ran the Carfax gallery. Adey's later years were clouded by mental illness, on which see Siegfried Sassoon. *Siegfried's Journey* (1945), 55–6.
10 *Id*, 335.
11 Douglas to A.J.A. Symons 18 May 1931. Douglas MSS: Clark. *New Age* 9 April 1931. The review article appeared above the pseudonym 'Eric Montgomery', so that Douglas did not realise the author's identity until I told him.
12 Mary Hyde, *op cit*, 3.
13 *Id.*

14 Croft-Cooke, 403.
15 Douglas to Sorley Brown 2 April 1932. Croft-Cooke, 403.
16 *Id*, 25 May 1932. Brown MSS: NLS.
17 Richard Rumbold. *A Message in Code* (1964), 28.
18 Rumbold. *My Father's Son*, cited Croft-Cooke, 346.
19 Rumbold. *A Message in Code.* (1964), 29.
20 Douglas. *The True History of Shakespeare's Sonnets* (1933), 28–9.
21 *Sunday Times* April 1933.
22 Croft-Cooke, 337.
23 Birkenhead. *The Life of F.E. Smith First Earl of Birkenhead* (1959), 67–8. Douglas to Sherard 2 May 1933. Hyde Collection.
24 Vyvyan Holland. *Son of Oscar Wilde* (1954), 193, 265–7. The biography of Frank Harris was written by Elmer Gerty and A.I. Tobin and published in Chicago in 1931.
25 Croft-Cooke, 345.
26 *Id.*
27 Douglas to Sorley Brown 9 April 1935. Brown MSS: NLS.
28 Croft-Cooke, 338.
29 Harold Nicolson. *Diaries and Letters* (1966), I, 261.
30 Hesketh Pearson and Malcolm Muggeridge. *About Kingsmill* (1951), 138–9.
31 Cited Croft-Cooke, 341–2.
32 Douglas to Shaw 29 January 1938. Mary Hyde. *op cit*, 28.
33 Douglas to Sorley Brown 10 May 1938. Brown MSS: NLS.
34 Douglas to Shaw 11 August 1938. Mary Hyde. *op cit*, 86–7.
35 *Id.* 27 July 1939. Mary Hyde. *op cit*, 116.
36 *Id.* 11 August 1939. Shaw to Douglas 16 August 1939. Mary Hyde. *op cit* 120–1.
37 Shaw to Douglas 9 August 1939. Mary Hyde, *op cit*, 117.
38 Douglas. *Oscar Wilde A Summing Up* (1940), 138. Croft-Cooke, 352.
39 The Douglas-Stopes correspondence is in the Stopes Papers in the British Library Add. MSS 58494, 58495. Douglas's letters are originals and Marie Stopes's copies which she kept. The correspondence has been used by Keith Briant in his biography of Marie Stopes (1962), 195–232.
40 Briant. *Marie Stopes*, 204–5.
41 Mary Hyde, *op cit*, 106–8. Betjeman to Douglas 21 May 1938: Briant, 207. British Library Add. MSS 58494.
42 Briant, 210.
43 *Id.* 218. Rupert Hart-Davis. *Hugh Walpole* (1952), 413.
44 Douglas to Sorley Brown 23 December 1939. Brown MSS: NLS.
45 Douglas to Stopes 2 October 1939. Stopes Papers: BL. Briant, 219.
46 *Id.* 22 April 1940. Stopes Papers: BL.
47 Briant, 219.
48 *Id.* 225.
49 *Id*, 226. Douglas to Stopes 26 April 1943. Stopes Papers: BL.
50 Channon. *Chips The Diaries of Sir Henry Channon.* Ed R. Rhodes James (1967), 338.

51 Sherard. *Bernard Shaw amd Frank Harris and Oscar Wilde*, 14, 169–70.
52 Douglas. *Ireland and the War against Hitler* (1940) 5–6.
53 *Id*, 36–7.
54 Winston S. Churchill. *The Second World War* (1949), II, 498.
55 Douglas to Sorley Brown 12 December 1940. Brown MSS: NLS.
56 Queensberry and Colson, 143.
57 Croft-Cooke, 368.
58 Douglas to Sinden, 23, 30 November 1944. Communicated by Mr Donald Sinden.
59 The text of the lecture ran to 26 pages and was published in November 1943.
60 Briant, 228.
61 Shaw to Douglas 17 September 1953. Mary Hyde, 156–7.
62 Mary Hyde, 157–8.
63 Briant, 228.
64 *Wartime Harvest*, which was published in 1944 (2nd ed 1945), also contained a Note by Shaw. Mary Hyde, 189.
65 Briant, 232. Briant states incorrectly that this was Douglas's last letter to Marie Stopes. His last letter was written on 3 February 1945: see below.
66 Douglas to Earle 23 November 1942; 22, 27, 30 May, 1943. Clark.
67 Douglas to Muriel Sherard 1 February 1943. Sherard MSS: Reading University.
68 Douglas to Earle 30 March; 25 April, 14 May 1943: Clark.
69 Rumbold. *A Message in Code*, 75.
70 Marie Stopes. *Lord Alfred Douglas* (1949), 22.
71 Douglas to Symons 26 December 1939: Clark.
72 Douglas to Earle 30 September 1943. Clark.
73 *Id*, 26 October 1943. Clark.
74 *Id*, 12, 19 February 1944: Clark.
75 Mary Hyde, 158, 177, 180.
76 Croft-Cooke, 373.
77 Hector Bolitho, cited Freeman, 308.
78 Douglas to Earle, 24 May, 10 July, 1944: Clark. Croft-Cooke, 374. Mary Hyde, 183.
79 Donald Sinden. *A Touch of the Memoirs* (1982), 47–8.
80 *Id*, 50.
81 *Id*, 49.
82 Communicated by Mr Donald Sinden.
83 Mary Hyde, 184.
84 Douglas to Stopes 24 September, 24 November 1944. BL: Add MSS 54895. Briant, 230–1.
85 Queensberry and Colson, 187.
86 Douglas to Earle 14, 21 September 1944: Clark.
87 Douglas to Stopes 7 October 1944. BL: Add MSS 58495.
88 Mary Hyde, 193, 195, 197.
89 Douglas to Stopes 3 February 1945. BL: Add MSS 58495 (Not in Briant). According to Bosie's biographer William Freeman, during one

of these visits Bosie handed Tredegar a bundle of letters which he kept under his pillow and which turned out to be from his mother: *Lord Alfred Douglas*, p.311. But this has been denied by Rupert Croft-Cooke in his biography: p.377 note. However there are a number of letters from Sibyl Lady Queensberry to Bosie which are in the Hyde collection, so that Freeman's story cannot be entirely discounted.

90   Croft-Cooke, 377–8.
91   Sinden, 49–50.
92   Croft-Cooke. 378. 'Mixed bark' was the bookmaker's code words for an accumulator, in this instance in all the races in which Nicholson was a jockey.
93   *The Times* 24 March 1945.

Select Bibliography

I *Manuscripts and Typescripts*

The work of which Lord Alfred Douglas was prouder than any other consisted of the seventeen sonnets which he wrote in the hospital of Wormwood Scrubs prison in 1924 and entitled *In Excelsis* in contrast to Oscar Wilde's *De Profundis*. But, unlike Wilde, he was not allowed to take the MS with him when he was released and, in spite of repeated requests from him, the Home Office refused to let him have it. However, he had taken the precaution of memorising all the sonnets and he immediately had them typed as soon as he was at liberty. The typescript with the author's autograph corrections and annotations is now in the William Andrews Clark Memorial Library in the University of California in Los Angeles. There are MSS of other poems in the Clark Library, including the famous sonnet on Wilde 'The Dead Poet', which he transcribed for Frank Harris in 1917.

The Humanities Research Center in the University of Texas in Austin has the original typescript of Douglas's *Autobiography*, the typescript and page proofs of his unpublished prose work *The Wilde Myth*; also autograph MSS of poems and sonnets including *The Duke of Berwick*, *The Rossiad*, 'All's Well with England', 'Forgetfulness' 'The Old Soldier', 'Winston Churchill' and 'Class War'.

Douglas was a compulsive letter writer and there are several thousands of his letters in existence at a conservative estimate, both in public and private collections. There are at least 500 in Texas and nearly as many in the Clark Library. Apart from his mother and for a short period Wilde, his most intimate correspondent was William Sorley Brown ('my faithful and constant friend whose sympathy and support in all my troubles were an source of comfort to me'), editor and proprietor of *The Border Standard*, a Scots journal which afforded Douglas a useful medium for anything he wished published. 237 of his letters to Brown (well summarised with apposite quotations by Rupert Croft-Cooke in the appendix to *Bosie*, his biography of Douglas) are in Texas, while a further seventy-two letters, entirely unpublished, on which I have largely drawn, are in the National Library of Scotland: MS 9925. Those in Texas include his interesting letters to Frank Harris.

Other important letters from Douglas in the Clark Library are to Charles Kains-Jackson, editor of *The Artist*, More Adey, director of the Carfax Gallery and joint editor of the *Burlington Magazine*, A.J.A. Symons, founder of the First Edition Club, and Adrian Earle whom Douglas thought of making his heir. Those to Rupert Croft-Cooke are divided between the Clark Library and the University of Texas. Similarly with Douglas's letters to Robert and Muriel Sherard; half are in the University of Reading, and the remainder, which the present writer bought from Mrs Sherard, are now in the Mary Hyde Collection in New Jersey. Most of the late Francis Marquess of Queensberry's papers are also in the Hyde Collection, as well as many of Sibyl Lady Queensberry's letters to her son Alfred. Also Douglas's letters to the present writer and his correspondence with Bernard Shaw.

Douglas's letters to his wife are in the Berg Collection in the New York Public Library. His correspondence with his publisher, John Lane, is in Westfield College, University of London. There is also a considerable amount of relevant material in the Asquith Papers and the Hugh Walpole Papers in the Bodleian Library, Oxford.

The letters to Herbert Pim, the Irish poet, are in the Queen's University, Belfast. Those of Marie Stopes with her replies are in the Stopes Papers in the British Library. Add MSS 58494, 58495. A few to Robert Holmes Edleston, the antiquarian, of Gainford, near Darlington, are in the Durham County Record Office: D/Ed/12/5.

Douglas destroyed considerable quantities of letters received by him, including 150 from Wilde. Only 27 original letters from Wilde to him have survived, of which all but one are in the Clark Library. The remaining one, written on the evening of Wilde's arrest, formerly belonged to the present writer and is now in the Hyde Collection. There are only three letters from Douglas to Wilde known to exist: these are also in the Clark Library.

There is an important typescript of a statement prepared by Robert Ross about 1913 for his solicitor Sir George Lewis (62pp), including copies of correspondence with Douglas, in the Clark Library. This is referred to in the source notes below as Ross TS. Some of it deals with *De Profundis*.

The departmental papers concerning *De Profundis* and Ross's gift of the MS to the British Museum in 1909 are in the British Library: Add MSS 50141.

II *Printed Books*

Douglas produced three volumnes of autobiography, *Oscar Wilde and Myself* (1914), *The Autobiography of Lord Alfred Douglas* (1929, 2nd ed 1931), and *Without Apology* (1938). All must be treated with caution, particularly *Oscar Wilde and Myself*, which was largely written by T.W.H. Crosland and which Douglas later repudiated. Biographies of Douglas have been written by Patrick Braybrooke (1931), William Freeman (1948) and Rupert Croft-Cooke, *Bosie* (1963). Only Croft-Cooke had access to copyright and previously unpublished material. Also biographically relevant are *The Life and Genius of T.W.H. Crosland* (1928) by W. Sorley Brown, *The Sporting Queensberrys* (1942) by the Marquess of Queensberry, *Oscar Wilde and the Black Douglas* (1949) by the Marquess of Queensberry and Percy Colson, and *The Mad Bad Line* (1981) by Brian Roberts. The article in the *Dictionary of National Biography* 1941–1950 by William Freeman is inadequate and inaccurate. Appreciations of Douglas's verse have been written by W. Sorley Brown, *The Genius of Lord Alfred Douglas* (1913), and by Marie Stopes, *Lord Alfred Douglas: His Poetry and His Personality* (1949).

There are naturally numerous references to Douglas in the mass of literature concerning Oscar Wilde. In this context I would respectfully refer the readers to the sources and bibliographies in my own writings, *The Trials of Oscar Wilde* (1948, revised eds 1962 and 1973), *Oscar Wilde: The Aftermath* (1963), *Oscar Wilde: A Biography* (1975), and *The Annotated Oscar Wilde* (1982). Of particular interest are the references to Douglas in *The Letters of Oscar Wilde* (1962) and *Selected Letters of Oscar Wilde*; both brilliantly edited by Sir Rupert Hart-Davis, they include the complete text of *De Profundis*, Wilde's work in the form of a letter to Douglas written from Reading prison in 1897.

Fourteen of Douglas's letters to André Gide between 1895 and 1929, all except the last written in French, have been published in the *Revue de Littérature Comparée*, No 3 July-September 1975. Vol XLIX, pp 493–502. Edited by Francois J.-L. Mouret. Libraire Marcel Didier, Paris.

Douglas's correspondence with Bernard Shaw, *Bernard Shaw and Alfred Douglas* (1982), has been impeccably edited by Mary Hyde.

Besides his published contributions to newspapers and periodicals, Lord Alfred Douglas wrote and published the following:

1896   *Poems*. With French prose translation. Mercure de France, Paris.
1898   *Tails with a Twist*. Verse by A Belgian Hare. Drawings by E.T. Reid. Edward Arnold, London.
1899   *The City of the Soul*. Grant Richards, London. Illustrated by Anthony Ludovici.
1899   *The Duke of Berwick* Leonard Smithers, London.
1906   *The Placid Pug*. Gerald Duckworth, London.
1907   *The Pongo Papers and the Duke of Berwick*. Illustrations by David Whitelaw. Greening, London.
1909   *Sonnets*. With a note by T.W.H. Crosland. The Academy Publishing Co London.
1911   *The City of the Soul*. 3rd ed. John Lane, London.
1914   *Oscar Wilde and Myself*. John Long, London.
1919   *The Collected Poems of Lord Alfred Douglas*. Martin Secker, London.
1924   *In Excelsis*. Martin Secker, London.
1925   *The Duke of Berwick and Other Rhymes*. Martin Secker, London.
1925   Foreword to *A New Preface to 'The Life and Confessions of Oscar Wilde' by Frank Harris*. The Fortune Press, London.
1926   *The Collected Satires of Lord Alfred Douglas*. Printed by M. Darantière, Dijon, France. The Fortune Press, London.
1926   *Nine Poems*. Privately printed for A.J.A. Symons, London.

1926   *Selected Poems.* Martin Secker (The New Adelphi Library), London.

1928   *The Complete Poems of Lord Alfred Douglas.* Martin Secker, London.

1928   Introduction to *Songs of Cell* by Horatio Bottomley. Southern, London.

1929   *The Autobiography of Lord Alfred Douglas.* Martin Secker, London.

1931   *The Autobiography of Lord Alfred Douglas.* 2nd ed. Martin Secker, London.

1933   *The True History of Shakespeare's Sonnets.* Martin Secker, London.

1933   Introduction to *The Pantomime Man* by Richard Middleton. Rich & Cowan, London.

1935   *Sonnets.* Rich & Cowan, London.

1935   *Lyrics.* Rich & Cowan, London.

1937   Preface to *Bernard Shaw, Frank Harris and Oscar Wilde* by Robert Harborough Sherard. T. Werner Laurie, London.

1939   Introduction to *Brighton Aquatints* by John Piper. Duckworth, London.

1940   *Oscar Wilde: A Summing Up.* Duckworth, London.

1940   *Ireland and the War against Hitler.* The Richards Press, London.

1943   *The Principles of Poetry.* An Address delivered by Lord Alfred Douglas before the Royal Society of Literature on September 2nd, 1943. The Richards Press, London.

1943   *The Sonnets of Lord Alfred Douglas.* The Richards Press, London.

1944   Preface to *Wartime Harvest* by Marie Carmichael Stopes. A. Moring, London.

Index